Leeds Trinity University

LIBRARY

This book is due for return on or before the last date stamped below

Withdrawn from Library Stock Leeds Trinity

D0235109

Get Me a Murder a Day!

A History of Media and Communication in Britain

Second Edition

KEVIN WILLIAMS

BLOOMSBURY ACADEMIC

302.23 WIL
3368354

Withdrawn from Library Stock
Leeds Trinity

LEEDS TRINITY UNIVERSITY

First published by Hodder Education in 1997

This edition published in 2010 by:

Bloomsbury Academic

An imprint of Bloomsbury Publishing Plc
36 Soho Square, London W1D 3QY, UK
and
175 Fifth Avenue, New York, NY 10010, USA

Copyright © Kevin Williams 2010

All rights reserved. No part of this publication may be reproduced, stored in a retrieval system, or transmitted by any means, electronic, mechanical, photocopying or otherwise, without the prior written permission of the publisher.

No responsibility for loss caused to any individual or organization acting on or refraining from action as a result of the material in this publication can be accepted by Bloomsbury Academic or the author.

CIP records for this book are available from the British Library and the Library of Congress.

ISBN 978-0-3409-8325-6
e-ISBN 978-1-8496-6011-2

This book is produced using paper that is made from wood grown in managed, sustainable forests. It is natural, renewable and recyclable. The logging and manufacturing processes conform to the environmental regulations of the country of origin.

www.bloomsburyacademic.com

Contents

History of mass communication in Britain – timeline

1450s Gutenberg invents printing press.
1476 Caxton begins printing at Westminster.
1557 Stationers' Company awarded Royal Charter.
1621 First coranto is assumed to have appeared in London.
1621 *Weekely Newes* launched.
1625 Ben Jonson's play, *The Staple of Newes*, criticizing the newsmongers is performed.
1642 *Perfect Diurnall* established.
1644 John Milton's *Areopagitica* published.
1661 Parliament prohibits publication of its proceedings.
1662 Printing Act passed.
1663 Sir Roger L'Estrange appointed Surveyor of the Press.
1695 Parliament allows Licensing Act to lapse.
1702 *Daily Courant* established as first regular daily newspaper.
1711 *The Spectator* published by Joseph Addison and Richard Steele.
1712 Stamp Act introduces press taxation.
1757 Increase in taxes on newspapers (further increased in 1776, 1780, 1789, 1797 and 1815).
1763 John Wilkes publishes the 45th number of *The North Briton*.
1771 Press wins right to report Parliamentary debates.
1779 First Sunday newspaper, the *British Gazette and Sunday Monitor* appears
1785 *Daily Universal Register* – later known as *The Times* – started.
1791 *The Observer* founded.
1792 Free distribution of newspapers by Post Office begins.
1792 Fox's Libel Act introduced.
1802 William Cobbett's *Weekly Political Register* is published.
1814 Koenig steam presses introduced by *The Times*.
1817 Thomas Barnes appointed editor of *The Times*.
1837 The launch of the *Northern Star*.
1840s Introduction of electric telegraph.
1842 *Lloyds Weekly News* begins.
1843 Launch of the *News of the World*.
1848 Rotary presses first used.
1851 *Reynolds News* launched.
1851 Reuter opens office in London.
1853 William Howard Russell appointed by *The Times* as war correspondent to report Crimean War.
1855 Launch of the *Daily Telegraph*.
1855 Stamp duty abolished.
1881 George Newnes starts *Titbits*.
1883 The Parliamentary Lobby begins.
1885 W.T. Stead, editor of the *Pall Mall Gazette*, imprisoned for his expose of child prostitution in London.
1888 Alfred Harmsworth (later Lord Northcliffe) starts *Answers to Correspondents*.
1889 First Official Secrets Act.
1895 New lightweight camera invented by Birt Acres.
1896 Marconi comes to London of wireless telegraphy to exploit his invention.
1896 First screenings of moving image in London by Lumière Brothers and Robert Paul.
1896 *Daily Mail* launched by Lord Northcliffe.
1896 *Lloyds Weekly Newspaper* reaches a circulation of one million.
1897 The Wireless Telegraph and Signal Company is registered.
1900 Pearson starts the *Daily Express*.
1903 *Daily Mirror* founded as first women's daily newspaper.
1904 First narrative British film, C.P. Hepworth's *Rescued by Rover* screened.
1912 *Daily Herald* begins life as strike newspaper.
1913 British Board of Film Censors (BBFC) begins work.
1920 The first advertised public broadcast, a song recital by Dame Nellie Melba from the Marconi works in Chelmsford.
1922 The British Broadcasting Company (BBC) is formed by Marconi and five other companies.
1922 John Reith appointed General Manager of the BBC.
1922 First broadcast made from Writtle near Chelmsford by Peter Eckersley.
1922 Broadcast Receiving Licence started and BBC given monopoly of public radio transmission.
1922 Labour Party and the TUC take over the *Daily Herald*.
1924 Scot John Logie Baird begins experiments in broadcasting sound and vision.
1926 British Broadcasting Corporation formed and Reith appointed first Director General.
1927 Cinematograph Films Act introduces quotas for British films.
1928 Ban on broadcasting controversial matters lifted.
1930 Start of BBC regional service.
1932 First Christmas Day message from the monarch broadcast.
1933 Radio Luxembourg starts transmissions.
1933 Alexander Korda's film, *The Private Life of Henry VIII*, achieves box office success.
1933 J. Arthur Rank becomes involved in the British film industry.
1936 BBC launches television service.
1936 BBC Listener Research section started.
1936 Moyne Committee recommends the continuation of the quota system to support British films.
1938 Lord Reith resigns.

1938 Gracie Fields, the Lancashire Lass, become Britain's highest paid film star.
1939 Rank takes control of Britain's main film distributor and consolidates his hold over British studios.
1939 Television is closed down.
1940 Newsprint rationing introduced.
1941 *Daily Worker* suppressed.
1941 First broadcast of *The Brains Trust*.
1946 Television broadcasting resumes.
1946 Highest ever annual attendance at British cinemas.
1947 First Royal Commission on the Press.
1950 National Film Finance Corporation set up and Eady levy introduced.
1953 The coronation of Elizabeth II shown live on television; nearly half a million TV sets are sold just prior to the coronation and for the first time more people watch event on TV than listen to it on the radio.
1953 Press Council established.
1955 ITV begins broadcasting and first advertisement is shown for Gibbs SR toothpaste.
1955 Newsprint rationing ends.
1956 'Free Cinema' programmes shown at the National Film Theatre for the first time.
1958 The first demonstration of an early video-recording machine (using magnetic tape).
1959 *Room at the Top* kicks off the social realism, kitchen sink dramas that characterize 1960s British cinema.
1960 Start of *Coronation Street*.
1960 Several national newspapers including *News Chronicle, Sunday Graphic, Evening Star and Empire News* close.
1961 Second Royal Commission on the Press.
1962 First satellite transmission with British viewers seeing live pictures from the USA via Telstar.
1962 The Pilkington Report.
1964 BBC 2 starts.
1966 *Cathy Come Home* screened.
1967 Transmission of colour television and launch of BBC Radio 1.
1969 Rupert Murdoch purchases the *News of the World* and the *Sun*.
1972 First domestic VCRs on sale.
1973 Independent local radio commences.
1974 Launch of Teletext: Ceefax on BBC and Oracle on ITV.
1974 Third Royal Commission on the Press.
1981 British Broadcasting Complaints Commission established.
1981 Richard Attenborough's *Chariots of Fire* wins several Oscars, including Best Picture.
1981 Murdoch buys *The Times* and *The Sunday Times*.
1982 Start of Channel 4, which is required to take programmes from independent producers.
1982 Introduction of separate Welsh Language television channel, Sianel Pedwar Cymru (S4C).
1983 First breakfast TV.
1984 Robert Maxwell buys *Mirror* newspapers.
1984 Lowest ever attendances at British cinema.
1986 The Peacock Report into the financing of broadcasting.
1986 Murdoch newspapers move to Wapping.
1988 Daytime television arrives.
1989 Start of satellite and cable television with Sky.
1989 Official Secrets Act reformed.
1991 The Broadcasting Act is introduced, with the 15 regional ITV franchises put up for auction and BBC and ITV forced to commission at least 25 per cent of programmes from independent producers.
1992 Calcutt Commission recommends introduction of privacy laws.
1994 Emergence of the World Wide Web.
1997 Channel 5 begins.
1998 BBC and Channel 4 digital terrestrial channels launched, and Sky Digital is launched.
1998 Irish entrepreneur Tony O'Reilly acquires the *Independent* newspapers.
2000 Channel 4 launches *Big Brother*.
2002 Launch of Freeview.
2003 Communications Act sets up new communications 'super-regulator' Ofcom.
2003 *MySpace* established.
2004 Social networking website Facebook launched.
2005 *MySpace* purchased by Murdoch's News Corporation.
2005 Freedom of Information Act implemented.

Preface to Second Edition

Considerable change has taken place in mass communication in Britain since the publication of *Get Me a Murder a Day!* more than a decade ago. Much of this change is the result of rapid advances in media technology. The arrival of the digital age has not only speeded up the rate of convergence between media but has also increased the amount of information and entertainment available to the ordinary consumer. Media content is now packaged in a variety of forms as multi-platform programming is becoming a common feature of the new environment. The development of new forms of media technology has been accompanied by an expansion of the old technologies; more television to watch, more print to read and more radio to listen to. The window on the world is wider than it has ever been. The media are central to a process of globalization which is enabling viewers, listeners, readers, bloggers, surfers and twitters in all corners of our planet to know more about one another, more quickly than ever before. The rate and nature of the change represent a fundamental shift in the media and the process of mass communication.

There is also more history of the media and mass communication as scholars have attempted to redress the dearth of media history referred to in the first edition of this book. Reclaiming the histories of journalism, mass media forms and the nature of media representation has been a feature of the past decade. New journals on media history have been launched; more conferences on the media's past have taken place and fresh attempts have been made to establish associations or organizations of researchers interested in media history. Even research councils are beginning to fund historical research in this area. Understanding where the media come from, how their past shapes their present performance and how our knowledge of historical events is influenced by the representation by the media has been accorded more attention. However, there is a still a long way to go. Media studies as an academic discipline is still seduced by the here and now, more willing to take up the agenda of the media industries, with their emphasis on the potential benefits of new technology, than delve into the past. History in the media is an increasingly fashionable subject – according to a headline in the *Guardian* newspaper in 2001, 'History has never been hotter'. The history of the media is less sexy; grainy black and white images, crackling sounds and songs or dry and dusty faded paper struggle to compete with the fast-paced, interactive world of digital broadcasting and the internet. However, in the midst of the changes the study of media history highlights that many of the concerns and opportunities of new media have been part of the way in which people have talked about the industry for hundreds of years. Nicholas Garnham notes at the outset of his book *Emancipation, the Media and Modernity* that 'behind the major questions about the media . . . that are debated today lie some very old problems'.

Continuity is as much part of history as change. This applies to the mass media as any other part of the past. The tendency to forget this is magnified by the shiny new world that is represented by and in the mass media. *Get Me a Murder a Day!* drew attention to one aspect of the history of mass communication, the fear of the increased presence of ordinary men and women, the masses of society, that the rise of the media has facilitated. The mass media increasingly make these people visible and this visibility evokes anxieties in the body politic and society at large. The digital world raises these fears as much as the age of print, radio and television. Fear of the internet is manifest in concerns about paedophiles stalking the superhighways of information and terrorists pumping out their hate propaganda to seduce fragile minds. The anxieties of those in positions of authority are accentuated by the perceived problems of controlling the unfettered flow of information unleashed by digital technology. The increased volume and rate at which information circulates, as well as the enhanced immediacy and unpredictability of its content, promises to overwhelm the efforts of those who seek to manage and manipulate information. The rise of the 'spin doctor' and the increasing sophistication and expense of the efforts to mobilise public opinion are a response to the new media environment created by digital technology.

This revised edition of *Get Me a Murder a Day!* attempts to capture the flavour of the contemporary state of mass communication in Britain by updating the chapters on the recent developments in television, radio and film as well as adding a new chapter on the new media technologies and the world they promise to usher in. It also takes the opportunity to correct some of the factual and typographical errors that crept into the first edition. These include some brought about by new technology as the auto-correct programme decided to change some words which radically altered the meaning of a sentence or two, impressing on the author the need to read through one's work even more carefully today.

The author would like to thank several individuals who have made this new edition possible. The commitment of Bianca Knights at Hodder Education was a crucial factor in bringing this about. Thanks to Liz Wilson and Susan Dunsmore for their patience, fortitude and skills under stop–go circumstances, particularly over the Christmas holidays! Special thanks to Emily Salz and Lee Ann Tutton at Bloomsbury for rescuing the book and turning the manuscript around so quickly. Clare Hudson, who in between time shifting *Dr Who*, beamed in at vital times to provide invaluable support. The commitment of Tom O'Malley and Sian Nicholas at Aberystwyth University to media history has been a source of enthusiasm and enjoyment for me in the midst of my managerial trials and tribulations in higher education. Thanks also to colleagues at Swansea, especially Debbie Rideout and Eleanor Parker, who helped share the burden. Finally I owe a debt of gratitude to the late Geoff Mungham who convinced me I should write *Get Me a Murder a Day!* in the first place and whose untimely death left a huge gap in university teaching which can never be replaced; and also to Lesley Riddle at Hodder who always saw the potential of the project and provided unwavering support. The usual suspects again should also be thanked: thanks Ed, Marge, Fran, Alan, Pam, Barry, Griff and Ie who, in spite of a move into an open plan office at the BBC, still survives. Any mistakes in the text are the fault of the author, and him alone.

Preface to First Edition

This is a small book about a big subject – the historical development of mass communication in the British Isles. Many will point out that it is an impossibly large undertaking to outline the main features of the growth of the mass media since the introduction of the printing press at the end of the fifteenth century. And it is. Thus this book can be no more than a snapshot of the main developments of some of the mass media in the nations called the British Isles. However, the book is an attempt to redress a neglect of history in the study of the mass media. The historical development of the mass media, and how media forms and representations have changed over time, have been traditionally of less interest in the growing amount of research, writing and musing on the mass media and modern society and culture. While media studies students have a sound grasp of current debates and issues in media representation and media policy, they have less knowledge about where media came from and how they have evolved. The reluctance to treat media as historical objects has been attributed to a number of factors. There is the nature of the mass media themselves. Hans Fredrik Dahl[1] points out that 'they seem to resist historical exploration by their sheer and monotonous insistence of dealing with mainly contemporary moments – *today*'s news, the situation *now*'. This insistence is reproduced in the disciplines of media and cultural studies. When history is drawn on it can appear as a selective looting of the past to justify the concern of the present. Media researchers have taken their cue from those institutions they seek to understand.

Historians, on the other hand, have been described as 'professionally a conservative lot[2] who depend heavily on print and written sources as their basic data. There is a reluctance to use film, photography, radio and television as historical sources. When such sources are used the focus is on factual sources such as newsreels, documentaries and news reports rather than fictional media forms such as film and drama, despite the centrality of the latter in people's media consumption and leisure activity. Historians by and large have neglected the media in their study of the past. Standard historical texts often ignore the means of communication that are prevalent in the period of the study. How a society came to know and make sense of the events of the time is often secondary to the recording and interpreting of historical facts. And how the process of communication shaped these events themselves is often beyond the scope of traditional histories. The fact that different groups and forces have attempted to set the historical agenda – as well as shape understanding of the events – is under-emphasised. The study of the history of the mass media and the communication process is part of the study of knowledge, of the ways by which society comes to know and understand itself. However, the contribution of the development of the mass media to the origin and development of knowledge is beyond the scope of this book. Its task is simply to provide a basic introduction to the history of mass communication in Britain. The value of such history is to stress the changing nature and role of the mass media in British society as well as the continuous debates and concerns which have accompanied their growth. While it is important to understand the growth of different media in the social, economic and political context of their time, it is also important to be aware of the common threads that run through the development of the various mass media in this country over hundreds of years. Not only will an examination of the historical formation of different mass media enable us to understand their present and future uses but it will also make us more aware of the centrality of the mass media in the development of our society.

The focus of the book is on the emergence, growth and consolidation of the print, broadcasting and film media. As a result the development of other media, such as popular music, publishing, the popular novel, comics, and advertising, which have played their part in the growth of mass communication in Britain are excluded. These other media are only discussed as they have impacted on the growth of the mass media examined in this book. This is a product of a lack of space which permits only the examination of those media which are usually regarded as the most important means of mass communication. The book is organised in a chronological order. This helps to provide a coherence to the narrative as well as indicate how media have changed over time. In this sense it is no different from basic historical texts. However, within the chronology some attempt has been made to acknowledge some absences in media histories. First, comparisons are made between the different media of mass communication. While media histories of the specific characteristics of different mass media exist, less attention is paid to the interaction between media. Second, an attempt will be made to produce a genuine history of the *British* media. Most histories of the British media have been from a London-centric, metropolitan perspective. Regional and national differences within the British Isles have been neglected as the centralisation of mass communication in Britain in the twentieth century has been seen as a self-evident and natural phenomenon. The perspectives of different localities, including the distinct media outlooks of the other nations of Britain, shaped as they have been by issues of language and cultural identity, will be included.

In writing the book it is important to acknowledge the contribution of others. Over the years a number of people have shared their ideas, thoughts, views, commitment and enthusiasm with me. They include Geoff Mungham, John Eldridge, Clare Hudson, David Miller, Chas Critcher, Martin Jordan, Jenny Kitzinger, Greg Philo, Hugh Mackay, Tony Powell, Viv Davies, John Underwood, the late Sir Tom Hopkinson, Ray Boston, Chris Pawling, Granville Williams, Brian Winston and Steve Evans. As a book like this depends considerably on the painstaking research of others, I would also like to thank all those who have lovingly laboured over histories of this newspaper or that programme. There are a number of excellent books in the field of media history awaiting their due attention from the reader. I would also like to thank Lesley Riddle of Arnold for all her support and encouragement. Thanks also to Liz Gooster, Elena Seymenliyska and Sandra Tebbett for their skill, patience and assistance. I would also like to thank Kate Regan, Carole Bulman, Fran Goodwin, Kathleen Davidson, David Dawson, Liz Palser and Elaine Ward who over the years have assisted me to maintain my sanity as workloads have increased in British universities. Finally I would like to thank the least appreciated group in higher education today – the students, who over the years have enabled me to maintain my enthusiasm for the subject of media history and provided me with more than a number of insights and questions about the development of the British mass media. In particular, I would like to thank all those students who were willing and committed enough to attend my lectures on the Part One course, *The Historical Development of the Mass Media in Britain,* at Cardiff University and on *The History of Media Industries* module at Sheffield Hallam University. Thanks also to Edmund, Margaret, Alan, Frances, Pam and Barry and Griff. Of course none of these people are responsible for any of the mistakes and/or errors in this work. They unfortunately are all down to me.

[1]Dahl, Hans Fredrik (1994) 'The Pursuit of Media History' Media, Culture & Society 16, 551–63.

[2]Schlesinger, Arthur quoted in Richards, Jeffrey and Aldgate, Anthony (1983) The Best of British: British Cinema and Society 1930–70. Oxford: Blackwell. Chapter 1.

Acknowledgements

The author and the publisher would like to thank the following for permission to use copyright material: Guardian News Service Limited for Neal Ascherson, 'Crossing the picket line at Wapping', from the *Observer,* 2 February 1986; and Mike Ellison, 'But for TV support industry would be gone with the wind', from the *Guardian,* 19 February 1994; HMSO for 'Letter to Ministry of Information from a member of the public, 1940', from Marion Yass, *This is Your War: home front propaganda in the Second World War,* p. 22 (1981). Crown copyright is reproduced with the permission of the Controller of Her Majesty's Stationery Office; Mirror Syndication International for '20 things you didn't know about the *Sun*', from the *Daily Mirror,* June 1985; The Open University for Tony Aldgate, 'Mainstream cinema and unemployment in the 1930s', from *The British Cinema in the 1930s,* Block 2, Unit 7, of the Open University Popular Culture Course (1981); Routledge Ltd for James Robertson, 'BBFC grounds for censorship, 1926', from *The British Board of Film Censors: Film Censorship in Britain 1896–1950,* Appendix 1, pp. 180–182 (Croom Helm, 1985); Felix de Wolfe for Gwyn Thomas, 'Visiting the local cinema', from *A Frost on My Frolic*, pp. 135–44 (Victor Gollancz, 1953). Every effort has been made to trace copyright holders of material. Any rights not acknowledged here will be acknowledged in subsequent printings if notice is given to the publisher.

Readers, rioters and rick burners: an introduction to the history of mass communication in Britain

People in Britain today spend a considerable amount of their time consuming a range of media products – books, newspapers, radio, television, films, videos, records, tapes, CDs, gameboys, iPods, computers and the range of new interactive technologies tied to the internet – which provide a continuous flow of information and entertainment. The centrality of the mass media in everyday life has led people to blame the media for a range of social ills. Whether it is increased violence in society, the growth of juvenile delinquency, football hooliganism, inner-city riots, terrorism, permissive behaviour, the decline of religiosity, falling educational standards, political apathy or any other social problem, we are ready to attribute 'fabulous powers' to the mass media. Complaints about the influence of the mass media are often underpinned by the assumption that this is something new. However, history shows that the emergence of every new medium of mass communication or popular amusement has been accompanied by great claims about the impact of the medium on the behaviour of men, women and children as well as on the values and mores of society.

The long tradition of complaint against the influence of popular media and entertainment forms in Britain has been documented by Geoff Pearson.[1] In the 1950s, concern was expressed about the corrupting and depraving influence of American comic book magazines and rock and roll music. In the 1930s, the worries were over the cinema which, according to cultural critic, F. R. Leavis, involved the 'surrender, under conditions of hypnotic receptivity, to the cheapest emotional appeals'. One psychiatrist could assert in 1938 that '70% of all crimes were first conceived in the cinema'. At the turn of the twentieth century, the music halls were seen as encouraging lawlessness with their glorification of violence and immorality. The middle of the nineteenth century witnessed the 'penny gaff theatres' and 'two penny hop' dancing saloons criticized for peddling immoral and criminal behaviour among the young. An editorial in the *Edinburgh Review* in 1851 stated:

> **one powerful agent for the depraving of the boyish classes of our towns and cities is to be found in the cheap shows and theatres, which are so specially opened and arranged for the attraction and ensnaring of the young. When for 3d a boy can procure some hours of vivid enjoyment from exciting scenery, music and acting . . . it is not to be wondered that [he] . . . then becomes rapidly corrupted and demoralised, and seeks to be the doer of infamies which have interested him as a spectator.**[2]

At the end of the eighteenth century people talked of the harmful impact of newspapers with the depiction and discussion of villainy and depravity in their columns. The emergence of the first newsbook or 'corantos' at the beginning of the seventeenth century was greeted with charges that they demeaned the role of the writer. The concern can be traced as far back as the Middle Ages when the popular songs of wandering minstrels were accused of sowing dissent and spreading disaffection.

Fear of the mass media

The tradition of complaint is associated with the fear of the masses which has accompanied the growth of mass communication. The history of mass communication is in one sense a history of the fear of the masses. The masses – or those 'dirty people of no name' as the historian Claredon called them[3] – become increasingly visible with the growth of the media and communication industries. Sorlin[4] points out that 'mass' is a pejorative term. When added to other words it provides a deprecatory nuance. Thus mass circulation newspapers are full of trivia and gossip; mass art is cheap and lacking refinement and mass culture is aimed at satisfying the lowest common denominator. Intellectuals, moral guardians, politicians and those in positions of power have always been deeply suspicious of the people, the masses of society. This suspicion underlies their criticisms of the media. The growth of the mass media for intellectuals has been accompanied by cultural debasement; for moral guardians, it is the root cause of moral and spiritual decline and for politicians, it has sullied the conduct of politics by making them respond to what the people want rather than what is best for the nation.

However, the term 'mass' only came into usage in the late nineteenth and twentieth centuries, coinciding with the rapid expansion of the means of communication. The last decade of the nineteenth century witnessed the advent of silent films, the birth of the first mass circulation daily newspaper, the *Daily Mail,* and the development of wireless telegraphy which was to lead to the rise of sound broadcasting in the early twentieth century. These developments marked the beginning of what has been called the 'age of mass communication'. The reach of the broadcast, and subsequently the electronic media, particularly television, expanded enormously in the wake of the economic and technological changes of the early twentieth century. The new capacity to reach a large, heterogeneous and geographically widely dispersed audience is seen as crucial to distinguishing a medium of *mass* communication. Thus only in the 1930s, when daily newspapers began to sell in their millions, annual cinema attendances reached 903 million and the number of households with wireless sets had risen to over 11 million, is it possible to talk of means of communication which truly reached the masses in Britain. The development of each new media, however, has extended the reach of the communication process. The terms 'mass communication' and 'mass media' are often used interchangeably. The use of 'mass communication' in the sub-title of this book is meant to indicate an interest in the media as part of the broader communication process in society. The media can be seen as particular institutions and structures with particular histories, well defined and narrowly delineated. But they are more than this – they are central to the nature and development of society at any given time.

The age of mass communication did not replace previous forms of communication. Communication is as old as society itself. In fact, without communication it is impossible to speak of society. The nature of communication has gone through many changes. Annabelle Sreberny-Mohammadi[5] divides the historical development of communication into three epochs: the earliest period when oral communication was dominant, the print epoch and the electronic media. She argues that each form is important for the *way* in which it influenced *what* was communicated, *how* it was communicated, *who* was involved in the process of communication and in *whose* interests the process took place. The face-to-face nature of oral communication in which speaker and audience were both present was both 'very space bound' and 'highly time bound'. The emergence of a written culture changed the nature of communication by allowing the 'separation of the message from the producer and the producer from the audience' which meant that the writer, in contrast to the speaker, had much less power over how audiences would understand and interpret his or her message. The electronic media, particularly television, reconstituted facets of oral and written communication: face-to-face communication combined with a dislocation between communicator and audience. Sreberny-Mohammadi emphasizes that different forms of communication have not only changed notions of political leadership and social authority but also the way in which society comes to know, understand and evaluate itself. History shows that one communication medium does not simply replace another; it is added on and comes to pre-eminence as older forms change their function.[6] Thus in order to understand mass communication, it is essential to know about the previous stages of communication.

The roots of the present epoch of mass communication are deeply entrenched in the evolution of the print industry at the end of the fifteenth century. Some would argue that they go back even beyond this period to the medieval era when the rituals of the Catholic Church, the mass and other religious ceremonies, acted as a form of mass communication.[7] However, the 'Gutenberg Revolution', which marked the arrival of print culture in Europe, is seen as a crucial advance in communication. Marshall McLuhan[8] sees the arrival of print as the key to modern consciousness. It freed scholars from the time-consuming activity of copying out manuscripts by hand which was the essence of cultural production in the medieval period. The printing press allowed them more time to think and to question the world around them and, above all, share their ideas with a wider audience. The virtues of 'public communication' came to be extolled in opposition to the narrow self-interest of established authority, such as Church and State, that placed limitations on what could and could not be said or written. From the end of the fifteenth century, the growth of communication has in part been about the enlargement of the public space, the freedom of expression and action for individuals and groups. This role in the expansion and dissemination of knowledge brought the print media into conflict with established authority with its fear of the people and public opinion. Such fears, whether real or imaginary, resulted in attempts to control and regulate the development of mass communication.

Freedom and control

Traditional interpretations of the history of mass communication emphasize the role of the media in the struggle for freedom and democracy in Britain. The press is regarded as having gained its freedom from the British State and political interests in the middle of the nineteenth century with the repeal of the 'taxes on knowledge' (taxes on newspapers and periodicals which raised their price to put them beyond the reach of the vast majority of the British people). Following their repeal the press is seen as becoming a check on government – the 'fourth estate' – and by providing information and a platform for the discussion of public affairs newspapers furthered the growth of democracy in Britain.[9] New media are seen as further developing the ways in which the media and communication industries contribute to the extension of democracy and freedom of expression and representation. The birth of the cinema and the wireless in the first half of the twentieth century and the emergence of television and the internet are all seen as expanding and deepening democracy and the democratic process.

This view of the development of the mass media as a steady and inexorable march toward more freedom has been challenged by those who see the communication process in terms of changing forms of control. They see the media as agents of social control in the hands of the 'establishment' or the 'powers that be' or a 'dominant class', which use them to manage and manipulate the growth of mass opinion and mass democracy to serve their ends. This analysis sees the middle of the nineteenth century not as securing the freedom of the press but rather as a change from State to market control of mass communication. James Curran[10] in his account of the struggle for the repeal of the taxes on knowledge argues that this was the main objective of many of those involved in the campaign against the press taxes. The stress was on the role the press could play in the engineering of social consent. The birth of the wireless was accompanied by similar concerns about the impact of the new medium on the mass of people. The government was wary of the power of the new medium to act as an instrument of propaganda and argued strongly against organizing broadcasting on the basis of allowing any private individual with sufficient funds to broadcast. It preferred that the new medium should be placed in trusted hands. The General Strike in 1926 proved that in 'the hands of experts and under firm political control, radio could give the government . . . a most powerful weapon'.[11] The fear of the masses led those in positions of power to see the media in terms of the role they could play in social control.

The conceptualization of the role of the mass media as being *either* the 'fourth estate' *or* 'an agency of social control' is an oversimplification. History shows that the role of the mass media at any time is shaped by a number of factors particular to the period under consideration as well as the medium under study. More detailed examination means that their role becomes more complex and qualified. However, central to the history of mass communication is an understanding of the countervailing pulls on the mass media as the representatives of the public, public opinion and the masses *and* as the agents of control exercised by the State and other powerful institutions in society.

Forms of censorship

The State and other powerful social institutions have intervened in a number of ways to shape what we see, hear and read. In the early days of print, the State exercised direct control over the medium. The Tudors introduced a system of pre-publication censorship and the licensing of printers which proved effective for much of the sixteenth and seventeenth centuries. The exceptions were the English Civil War which, with the collapse of political authority throughout the land, witnessed a vast outpouring of popular political literature, and the early years of the Interregnum when the State allowed considerable popular discussion, which was ended by Oliver Cromwell's dictatorship. Official censorship collapsed in 1695 but this did not see the complete disappearance of direct State intervention in the operation of the media. For example, the British Board of Film Censors (BBFC) exercised rigid control over the content of what was shown in British cinemas in the 1930s and the Broadcasting Ban limited what the British public heard on television screens about the 'Troubles' in Northern Ireland in the late 1980s and early 1990s.

Direct censorship was replaced by economic controls on the press and printed material which were introduced in 1712. Press taxation – or 'taxes on knowledge' – restricted the dissemination of news to those who could pay, the so-called 'respectable' elements of British society. However, these measures failed to crush the sales of radical papers and led the government to look for other means to combat the 'malignant influence' of the radical press which peddled 'doctrines injurious to the middle and upper classes'. The approach of traditionalists, who sought more repressive measures, was overcome by those who saw the press and printed material as a means to secure the good opinion of working people. As one reformer stated in 1851: 'readers are not rioters: readers are not rick burners'.[12] From the 1830s, there was a mobilization of resources to capture the hearts and minds of working people. For example, the Society for the Diffusion of Useful Knowledge (SDUK) published journals to 'train up the lower classes in the habits of industry and piety'.[13] To assist these publications to compete more effectively with the radical press, the government had to free them from the shackles of press taxation which was phased out by the 1860s. The free market did what economic regulation could not. Within 20 years radical newspapers had virtually disappeared from this country. The new forces of competition increased the costs of newspaper production, and made the press more dependent on advertising. The change in the economic structure of the newspaper industry forced radical newspapers either to close down or become less political or turn themselves into specialist political journals selling to dedicated small audiences.

Less direct means to manipulate mass communication have also been used. The law has been regularly resorted to as a means of influencing the media. Criminal and seditious libel and blasphemy laws were used in the nineteenth century to muzzle newspapers. As late as 1925, leaders of the British Communist Party were prosecuted for remarks in their official newspaper, the *Daily Worker,* on the grounds that their 'language tended to subvert the government and the laws of the Empire'.[14] The libel laws and the threat of libel have also been used by prominent individuals, notably Robert Maxwell, to deter investigation of their activities. Throughout the twentieth century, the State devoted more resources and developed new techniques to manipulate the information environment in which the media operated. While the big stick was always part of the government's armoury in dealing with the press, as well as other media, in the twentieth century more indirect means were increasingly used to manage the flow of information, including the introduction of secrecy laws and the expansion of the government public relations and propaganda apparatus to 'sell' information. The State has also exercised influence through the power of appointment. The Board of Governors of the British Broadcasting Corporation (BBC) were always appointed by the relevant government department, as were the members of the regulatory bodies which have overseen the running of commercial television. The State's influence over the BBC is furthered by the fact that the finances of the organization are drawn from the licence fee which is set and collected by the government. The appointment of the secretary of the BBFC, established as a non-official body, was also subject to government approval. However, it is not always the case that the State's influence over the mass media is malign. British broadcasting developed the concept of public service which, as Paddy Scannell[15] argues, has 'unobtrusively contributed to the democratisation of everyday life, in public and private contexts, from its beginning through to today'. The State played a crucial part in the establishment of public service broadcasting: under its auspices, the BBC developed as a public service institution. It is also the case that the mass media have been, and still are, the site of political and cultural struggle between different factions within the British State. Throughout the history of mass communication, State involvement in the development of the mass media has taken a variety of forms.

Issues of control and censorship in the history of mass communication do not appear only as matters of State. The mass media often have not shown the same commitment to disclosure as the State has to restricting the flow of information. Within media organizations there has been conflict between owners and controllers and media practitioners. This is most acutely expressed in the history of the press where owners have interfered in the operation of their newspapers. The concept of editorial freedom has been advocated from the nineteenth century onwards to protect the newspaper editors and their staff from such interference but the struggle to enact the sovereign right of the editor to determine the content of the paper has had to be fought for.[16] Self-censorship is also a theme of mass communication history. Journalists have always told the public only a small proportion of what they know. This is not simply as a result of the imposition of pressure from outside. Often fearful of offending powerful interests, journalists have censored themselves. Humbert Wolfe captured this inclination in a small ditty written during the inter-war years:

You cannot hope to bribe and twist
Thank God, the British journalist
But seeing what the man will do
Unbribed, there's no occasion to.[17]

Self-censorship was also an aspect of the British film industry. The BBFC was not imposed on the industry by the government – it was established by the industry itself. The history of mass communication is a history of changing forms of censorship, self-censorship and regulation. The growth of the media has to be seen in the light of the struggle between those who seek to extend popular access to leisure, information and entertainment and those who seek to control and regulate such access. The concerns and activities of powerful elites, news and information managers and moral campaigners, as well as the changing parameters of public taste and political acceptability, are an integral part of the history of mass media in Britain. However, censorship is only one factor that has shaped the evolution of mass communication in Britain.

Technology, commerce and audiences

Peter Golding[18] describes the development of the mass media as the outcome of the growth of an industry and the evolution of an audience. They interact through what he describes as the 'supply and demand for two basic social communities: leisure facilities and information'. The study of the history of mass communication must concentrate on the development of media industries and audiences, and their interaction. On the supply side, technology and economic organization are necessary for the growth of media industries. Different historical periods are distinguished by their technologies. The growth of the newspaper in the nineteenth century was driven by technical innovations such as the rotary press, which allowed the reproduction of more sheets per hour, and linotype, which enabled pages to be composed on a keyboard rather than by hand. The result was that more newspapers were printed more quickly, encouraging the rise of the mass circulation popular press. However, the relationship between technology and communication is not straightforward. Technology is often represented as having its own internal drive which determines the nature and content of what is communicated. Such a view ignores the social, economic and cultural developments that shape the application of media technology.[19] How media technologies are adopted, adapted and institutionalized and by whom and for what purpose is essential in understanding the development of mass communication.

One important factor in shaping the application of media technologies has been – and continues to be – the economic and industrial organization of the mass media. Entrepreneurs, for example, have played a key role in the development and utilization of media technologies. They have reacted quickly to adapt technological invention to meet the demand for information and entertainment. From the early printing press, the mass media have developed as commercial concerns organized around capitalist methods, primarily motivated by the desire to make profit. McLuhan[20] says that the book was the first commodity manufactured under conditions recognizable as modern mass production. The expansion of newspapers relied on commerce and advertising – the extent of this dependence is illustrated by ads appearing throughout most of the eighteenth and nineteenth centuries on the front page. The economic organization of broadcasting in Britain from the 1920s took a different form in the shape of the philosophy of public service. Based on public subsidy in the form of a licence fee for the ownership of radio sets, the BBC acquired the monopoly of broadcasting, rejecting the free for all that characterized the birth of radio in the United States. The distinction between the 'commercial' and 'public service' model of economic organization has been an important feature of the British media. The history of mass communication is intimately tied up with the growth of the media as industries and businesses. Mass communication involves the production of information and entertainment by industrial agencies operating under commercial or quasi-commercial considerations.

The demand for information and entertainment has propelled the growth of mass communication. Golding[21] identifies several factors crucial to the stimulation of such demand: leisure time, affluence and cultural variation. The increase in leisure time has played an important role in increasing people's consumption of media products. The provision of longer holidays, the decline in the number of hours at work, the improvements in the nature of work brought about by technical change, and the drudgery of the process of industrial production have all provided people with more time, opportunity and incentive for leisure and recreation. The quality of such leisure varies for different sections of society.[22] The ability to make use of the increased free time is a product of affluence. The amount of money individuals and groups have to spend is a crucial determinant of the demand for media products. But the ability of people to make use of the mass media, as well as their attitudes towards them, is shaped by a number of cultural factors. Literacy clearly has had an important role in the development of mass communication. However, it is not an essential pre-requisite for participation in the consumption of mass media. The radical working-class newspapers of the early nineteenth century, for example, were read out aloud to groups of illiterate people. Literacy does not guarantee people will read or find reading a pleasurable activity. The growth of a reading public which played a key role in the early development of communication was the result of education. The better educated tend to read more. The expansion of mass education following the 1870 Education Act acted as a catalyst to the expansion of reading and hence supported the growth of the British press, print and publishing industries.

Mass communication has played a crucial role in the social history of Britain. The growth of print in the sixteenth century fuelled as well as responded to the religious upheavals brought about by the Reformation and the intellectual needs of the Renaissance. In the seventeenth century the political conflict and ideological struggle which culminated in the Civil War in the 1640s created an environment which fed the demand for news and information as well as gave birth to the propaganda tract. The eighteenth century is associated with the growth of industrial capitalism, with its voracious need for business and commercial knowledge and information. The creation of industrial classes also saw communication act as a conduit for the development of class and group consciousness. Newspapers in the nineteenth century were organs of class and community interests. Whereas *The Times* and the other newspapers that constituted the 'respectable press' spoke for and to the rising middle classes, the 'radical' or 'pauper' press sought to articulate, reflect and empower the emerging working classes of Britain. Within the structure of class representation, the newspapers of the nineteenth century were the organs of the political factions that constituted the parliamentary or extra-parliamentary politics of the period. In the twentieth century, mass communication, in particular broadcasting, has been central to the growth of mass democracy, mass consumption and mass culture. But mass communication is also about what people do with the mass media. People throughout history have used the mass media to fulfil their dreams and desires and to provide their pleasures and pastimes. How the mass media have been integrated into daily life and how they have satisfied the needs and wants of their audiences – and helped them to make sense of the world around them – is an important aspect of the growth of mass communication.

One of the features of the development of the mass media from the perspective of their reception is the 'general move away from collective occupation of exterior space towards a family grouping which has withdrawn to interior space'.[23] In other words, as the growth of the mass media has brought about the expansion of public communication, their consumption has increasingly taken place in the private sphere, primarily within the confines of the home. Newspaper reading, which in the eighteenth and early nineteenth centuries took the form of public spectacle, either through reading aloud to groups, in coffee houses, taverns or in the windows of newspaper shops, had by the end of the nineteenth century become an individual private activity at the breakfast table or on the train or tram. Similarly, radio came to be established in the home with the family as the site for listening, despite its origin as a technology that could cater to large crowds. Collective listening groups met regularly in the early 1920s to hear and discuss what was broadcast. Visual culture also developed in this way: cinema took working people off the streets where popular recreation had generally taken place prior to the twentieth century while television confined the mass consumption of the visual image to the domestic environment. The threat of the masses again can be seen as one aspect of this development – combating the 'mob' or 'multitudes' and their drunkenness, violent behaviour and rapacious sexuality are evoked in the domestication of media consumption. Domestic viewing, reading or listening have implications not only for the content of the mass media but also for the nature of public space and how it is constituted.

There is also the question of the 'mass' audience. As Raymond Williams notes, there are no masses but only ways of seeing people as masses. The audience for mass communication is not a homogeneous entity; it is fragmented and has changed over time. In particular, the growth of mass media has been in response to the needs of specialized audiences. Thus the history of mass communication is about the development of media which serve the interests of particular groups or classes in our society – the emergence of women's magazines or the Black press or the working-class press of the last century. Finally, there is a tension in the history of mass communication between the provision of 'information' and 'entertainment'. This is manifest with the roles of the mass media in acting as businesses and in serving the needs of the community. The balance between treating members of the audience as citizens, who must be provided with the information and education necessary for them to play a full and constructive role in the political and social process, and as consumers, who need to be entertained and encouraged to participate in the consumption of products which are made available through mass advertising, is central to tracing the growth of the mass media. For some commentators the cultural impact of the growth of mass media is of paramount concern. Mass entertainment has been accused of threatening to 'cretinize taste', blunting the 'discriminating powers of the mind' and being 'anti-life'. In this sense, mass communication has changed the ways in which people interact on a daily basis, how they make sense of the world around them and, as a result, how they come to terms with what is happening around them.

This book traces the development of mass communication from the social and cultural revolution brought about by the invention of printing to the present communications revolution, which promises – or threatens, depending on your perspective – to bring about as profound a change in our society and culture as print did in the sixteenth century. It outlines the expansion of the audiences, industries and technologies that have provided the basis for the development of mass communication. It explores the fears that have shaped the emergence of the mass media, examines the desires and needs of people that have been served by the expansion of mass communication and discusses how the mass media has represented and reflected the lives of ordinary men and women. In the beginning was the printed word.

Part 1

The age of print

1

The 'naughty and lewd word': the birth of mass communication in Britain

The roots of modern mass communication can be found in the invention and utilization of the printing press in the late fifteenth century. The printing press, using movable type, is attributed to Johann Gutenberg, who first printed the Bible in Mainz in 1453, a breakthrough which was the culmination of a number of technical innovations made in the late Middle Ages.[1] The 'Gutenberg Revolution' not only changed the way in which books and printed material were made but also the whole basis on which knowledge was stored and disseminated in European society. Before the birth of printing, the production of the written word was dominated by the Catholic Church. The process involved monks copying out works in long hand. It is estimated that the average yearly output of one copyist was two books.[2] Only a small number of works were produced and they were costly, which restricted their purchase to people of considerable means. Most of the copied material was kept by the Church which exerted considerable control over what was communicated, known and believed throughout medieval Europe.

The printing press significantly increased the production of books, which in England grew by 400 per cent in the first half of the sixteenth century. This huge increase led to a dramatic reduction in the price of books which meant, for example, it was possible for the works of Martin Luther to be obtained by a craftsman for the equivalent of one day's wages. By making such material available to a larger number of people, printing broadened access to book culture and consequently weakened the Church's hold over knowledge. The technology of the hand printing press was necessary for the wider dissemination of printed material in the late fifteenth and early sixteenth centuries. Necessary but not sufficient. The rise of publishing was also a response to the changes taking place in Europe at that time. The social, political and economic convulsions brought about by the Reformation increased demand for printed material. Printing became an instrument in the cause of the Protestant revolt against the authority of the Church.

The new technology was used to preach the Protestant message. Copies of Luther's attack on the Church in 1517 were sold all over Europe, leading him to say that 'print is the best of God's inventions!'[3] The printing of the Bible in the vernacular as opposed to Latin, the language of the Catholic Church, was an attempt to bypass the priest and challenge the Church's interpretation of the Bible and religious doctrine. The desire of Protestant reformers to spread the word of the Bible led to the growth of a more literate society. As the historian Lawrence Stone states: 'Christianity is a religion of the book, and once this book ceased to be a closely guarded secret fit only to be read by priests, it generated pressure for the creation of a literate society.'[4] The religious struggles of the early sixteenth century led to the emergence of a general reading public which was to sustain the growth of mass communication throughout Europe over the next three centuries.

Printing and culture

The growth of printed material and the development of a reading public had an impact on both the process of communication and the social and cultural development of Western Europe. According to Elizabeth Eisenstein 'the advent of printing was, quite literally, an epoch making event. The shift from script to print revolutionised western culture.'[5] It represented the transformation from the primarily oral and image-based culture of the medieval world to the literate culture of the modern world. In the medieval world, discussion of current affairs usually occurred as a result of face-to-face interaction. Before the invention of printing, book learning was not regarded as a necessary skill of government. Throughout the sixteenth century, however, such knowledge came to be expected of those in positions of power. The last 'cabinet minister' unable to read and write was William Herbert, the Earl of Pembroke, who died in 1570.[6]

Print literacy also promoted the development of vernacular languages. Publishing in pre-print society was in Latin. Most people, however, spoke only in their own language. Printing brought about the output of works in the vernacular languages and assisted the development of these languages through the invention and refinement of alphabets and grammars. For example, the publication of William Tyndale's translation of the Bible into English in 1521 was both an important contribution to the Protestant cause against the Church and to the development of the English language. As more was written and printed, differences of opinion on subjects emerged and individuals were able to make judgements on what they were being told. Print literacy provided the basis for the development of the view that an individual had the right to express his or her own opinion or thoughts in public – a revolutionary concept in an age where most things were the prerogative of the Church and the authorities.

The growth of printing cannot be separated from the development of the modern nation-state. Publishing works in vernacular languages helped to increase the sense of national identity throughout Europe and the growth of nationalism. Printing was, however, harnessed to the interests of those in positions of social power rather than used to democratize knowledge. At first, the new medium was seen by the State as a 'harmless novelty'.[7] But it was not long before the authorities recognized the threat posed by the printing press. Official intervention in the development of printing was seen as necessary to prevent the spread of dissident or dissenting opinions. This intervention took a number of forms, for example, the establishment of pre-publication censorship, the licensing of printers and the regulation of what could be published. But the State also saw the importance of printing as a propaganda instrument and used it to develop, expand and legitimize its power. Print, according to Sreberny-Mohammadi,[8] 'strengthened the power of states, which could now more easily inform their populaces of new laws, gather taxes, print stamps with royal faces, and require written oaths of loyalty'. Henry VIII, for example, used the printing press in his struggle against Rome as well as to issue proclamations and statements to 'instruct the nation in its duty and scotch wild rumours'.[9]

Thus the print revolution at the end of the fifteenth century consisted of technological and social transformations which provided the basis for the growth of mass communication. The rise of the printing press, the collapse of the Church's control over written communication, the advent of the nation-state, the extension of public access to printed material, the growth of a reading public, the development of vernacular or national languages and the emergence of the idea that the individual had the right to express his or her opinion in public were all significant factors in shaping the development of mass communication.

The growth of printing in Britain

The first 150 years up to the English Civil War witnessed a gradual development of the print industry. The number of printers grew slowly throughout the sixteenth century. At the beginning of the century there were only two or three printers; by 1558, this had risen to 13, then to 34 in 1563, 40 in 1577, and as many as 97 at the end of the century.[10] They produced a variety of titles from two sheet pamphlets to folio books. Book production increased from only a handful of titles in the 1470s and 1480s to more than 500 editions by 1520s and reaching 1000 in the 1550s. More than 200 books were published in the year 1550.[11] Much of the material published concerned religious matters. Printers depended for their business on the printing of editions of the Bible, psalters and other religious tracts. For example, over 150 editions of the Bible were printed between 1603 and 1640.[12] They also produced a large amount of material for educational purposes; 40 per cent of the output of one printer, Wynkyn de Worde, at the beginning of the sixteenth century was devoted to grammar school textbooks.[13]

Not all printed material concerned things religious or educational. Many books were concerned with practical guidance and information.[14] Reading was associated with self-improvement and as the old feudal order collapsed, many people sought instruction and knowledge from books on what was considered good behaviour and character in the wake of the social changes brought about by the Reformation. Other kinds of knowledge were also sought. Traders were exhorted to read 'forasmuch as it behoveth every good discreet merchant to have knowledge and cunning in reading and writing'.[15] Popular literature in the forms of the chapbook, the jest book, the ballad and the broadsheet also developed in the sixteenth century.[16] From a very early date, stories on the exploits of notorious villains were popular. In 1566, Thomas Harman's pamphlet on the criminal world in London became a 'best seller'.[17] Traditional ballads found their way into print, appearing as single sheets sold by peddlers as well as by booksellers. The law and medicine also provided great opportunities for the early publishing and printing industry. Almanacs and prognostications made up another profitable area for booksellers. Single sheet predictions of the future had been common before the invention of printing. The first printed prognostication in England was in 1502 and by the middle of the century such publications had taken on a more substantial form, including not only predictions but weather forecasts, farming advice, medical and veterinary matters and other general interest material. Almanacs began to combine political comment with practical advice thereby incurring the opprobrium of the authorities. By 1640, over half of the number of new titles published concerned religious matters.[18]

The growth of printed material is closely connected with the level of literacy. Between 1560 and 1640, the reading public remained relatively small. It is estimated that by 1640 adult male literacy was only 30–40 per cent of the general population.[19] However, the ability to read and write did not develop evenly throughout Britain. Literacy grew more quickly in urban areas, particularly in London and south-east England. In Scotland, the reading habit was democratized faster than south of the border as a result of the strength of the Calvinist tradition of Bible study and the Scottish schooling system. Rates of literacy and book reading in Scotland were higher than in England for most of the eighteenth century and the development of the circulating library north of the border was to have a significant impact on the spread of reading in Britain. Wales was to lag behind the rest of the British Isles. It was not until 1585 that the first book – *Y Drych Gristianogawl*, an essay on loving God – was printed in Wales.[20] There were also class and gender differences. Few labourers and journeymen could read or write while literacy developed more slowly among women. What ability there was to read and write among ordinary people was due to Puritan ministers who used Bible reading classes to promote their religious message. But even among the propertied classes of the period, literacy was limited – only 1 in 10 families before 1700 owned a book.[21] It was among the growing merchant class, where commercial considerations determined the need to read and write, that literacy was most fully established. By the eighteenth century it is estimated that 60 per cent of men and 40 per cent of women were able to read. This growth was the result not so much of educational advances or out of economic necessity but a reflection of the fact that the need to read and write had started to permeate most areas of people's daily life.[22] However, the process of mass communication between 1470 and the beginning of the Civil War in 1641 was limited by the number of people who could read and write. It was also limited by a number of restrictions placed on the publications of books and other printed material.

The Tudor system of censorship

The development of the print media during this period was shaped and influenced by the intervention of official bodies. Tudor Britain saw the establishment of a highly effective and successful system of State control of the media. To contain the 'disruptive potential of print'[23] the system of pre-publication censorship, first introduced into Britain in 1408 to prevent the spread of Lollard literature, was extended. The Church had the right to vet all books dealing with religious matters. The Tudors exerted considerable effort to stamp out all dissenting opinion or what they called 'lewd and naughty matters'.[24] Henry VII issued an edict against 'forged tydings and tales' as early as 1486 but it was not until the 1520s in the effort to control the flow of Protestant literature into Britain that censorship was more rigorously implemented. Henry VIII in his first guise as 'defender of the faith' issued a proclamation in 1529 containing a list of prohibited books, extended in 1530 to include any English translation of the New Testament. Heretical works including Tyndale's translation of the Bible were burned, sometimes alongside those caught selling them. With Henry's break from Rome over his divorce from Catherine of Aragon, there was a complete volte-face and the Bible was printed in English and distributed throughout the land for the first time in 1535. For one modern image consultant, Henry VIII was responsible for the 'first mass communications campaign of modern times'.[25]

The break with the Church increased the role of the secular authorities in regulating printed material. The State's involvement in censorship and regulation was extended in 1538 with the introduction of a licensing system for all books under the charge of the Privy Council. This system was consolidated by Elizabeth I who sought to restrict the number of printers, the content of all printed material and the number of copies printed. To control the number of printers the Tudors granted a royal charter to the Stationers' Company in 1557. Members of the Company, which included printers, publishers and booksellers, were granted privileges to publish particular books in return for complying with royal censorship. Later patents were awarded for the monopoly over the printing of certain kinds of books. The Stationers' Company helped to police what was printed, published and sold; in other words a system of self-regulation was established by the printers. In 1586, the Star Chamber issued a decree aimed at further restricting the number of printing presses in operation, setting out a detailed list of regulations governing the right to print.[26] The number of printing presses were limited to 22, together with the Queen's printer and the two university presses at Oxford and Cambridge.[27] No new presses could be established until a vacancy occurred among existing printers and then were to be granted only to those known for their 'skill, ability and good behaviour'.[28]

In addition to controlling the number of printers, the 1586 decree limited print runs. The number of any one title was restricted to 1250–1500 copies with the exception of 'grammars, accidences, prymers and Catechisms' which were allowed four editions per annum of between 2500 and 3000 copies each.[29] The Archbishop of Canterbury and the Bishop of London were appointed licensers and no material could be published without the approval of one or both of them.[30] The Stationers' Company was charged with searching for illegal presses and seizing

unlawful books. Severe penalties were drawn up for infringements of the law in the hope these penalties would be heavy enough to prevent any more 'Luthers of the book trade'.[31] These measures by and large ensured that dissenting opinion was successfully controlled throughout the Tudor period.

Censorship in the sixteenth century was largely concerned with the 'religious challenge to the state'.[32] The government was almost indifferent to the printing of material dealing with other kinds of news or opinion. Sex and violence were as popular with the general public in Tudor times as they are today. Crimes with particularly bloody and gory details were assured of wide and graphic coverage as was news concerning miracles, prodigies and wonders.[33] There was also a surfeit of royal stories – the comings and goings of the monarch in the sixteenth century received as much attention as they now do. Readers were regularly regaled with descriptions of royal pageantry such as the *Passage of the most dred Soveraigne Lady Quene Elyzabeth to Westminster the daye before her Coronacion* in 1558. Ballads were also popular. However, most printers kept to publishing digests of facts, gossip and rumours, news about events overseas, often reprinting information from publications abroad.

The extent to which printers and publishers refrained from political and religious matters was a testament to the success of Tudor censorship. Despite the panoply of control and regulation and the considerable efforts made to enforce them, it was the high degree of popular compliance to the censorship that marked the success of the Tudors. There were a number of reasons for this success. First, the desire among the ruling elite of the period for peace after the chaos and anarchy of the War of the Roses. Second, the Tudors' ability to identify with the emergent feelings of nationalism. With the decline of medieval institutions, in particular, the Church, the outlook and ambitions of the nation were harnessed to the Tudor crown. This was reflected in the high degree of legitimacy Elizabeth I was accorded during her reign. Finally, the lack of political consciousness of the majority of the population. Literacy was confined to the upper echelons of society and concern about printing restrictions did not extend to the general public. However, this was to change.

The Civil War and the emergence of modern journalism

For Wickham Steed, a noted editor of the inter-war years, 'regular English journalism began with the Civil War and the political strife that led up to it'.[34] Many of the important features we associate with the modern newspaper emerged in the early seventeenth century. It is difficult to identify newspapers as a separate print form from the huge quantity of indeterminate publications that appeared prior to this period. However, it is generally agreed that the first newsbooks or 'corantos' appeared in the 1620s. The first titled newsbook was published in London in 1621 by Nicholas Bourne, a London printer, and Nathaniel Butter, a London bookseller and called *The Weekely Newes*. They took the form of semi-pamphlets, hence the term 'books' of news and were made up of between 8 and 24 pages. Their most distinctive feature was the 'total avoidance of any news having to do with England (*sic*)'.[35] Because of a proclamation issued in that year against 'the great liberty of discourse concerning matters of state', the newsbooks of the time printed only foreign news. Publication of these newsbooks was often erratic and they were usually sold with other forms of street literature outside theatres or at other public gatherings.

The emergence of newsbooks met with hostility from members of the educated classes. For writers such as Ben Jonson, the growth of the news industry was a 'dereliction, a degradation of the proper function of a writer'.[36] References to the 'contemptible trade' were common in Jacobean drama. Jonson himself wrote a play, *The Staple of Newes*, in 1625, a direct attack on Butter and his fellow 'newsmongers'. For Jonson, the writer was a teacher. Through his moral fictions he educated society, whereas Butter and his 'dishonest swindlers' betrayed that function by paying little attention to the truth in order to supply readers with sensational news. Jonson set the tone for a familiar refrain about the role of the press which has rung out over the ages. But, as David Gerard notes, behind Jonson's concern was a threat – the 'new art of journalism' threatened the popularity of what was then the dominant form of mass communication, the theatre. In a culture that was still predominantly oral and visual, despite a century of printing, the stage and the pulpit exerted considerable influence over the ordinary citizen. By 1642, with theatres closed as a result of the Civil War, the function of the dramatist was usurped by the journalist.

By 1644, there were a dozen weekly newsbooks with eight pages or more available in London.[37] The growth of newsbooks had risen steadily in the years before the Civil War. Despite government restrictions, domestic reports of Parliamentary proceedings started to appear in 1628. News workers and pamphleteers became bolder in the face of censorship as the struggle between the King and Parliament developed. With the collapse of all censorship on the eve of the Civil War, newsbooks began to flourish. Newsbooks appeared on both sides; plagiarism was common and titles changed almost on a weekly basis. The circulation of newsbooks increased considerably; *Mercurius Aulicus*, which supported the Royalist cause throughout the war, printed an edition of 1500 copies compared with the 250 copies of most pre-war newsbooks. It is estimated that over 20,000 different titles including sermons, speeches, pamphlets and newspapers were published between 1640 and 1660 – some individual pamphlets attained a print run of 10,000 copies.[38] Most newsbooks during the period of the Interregnum were directed at Londoners as it was only there that enough people were concentrated to make printing a newspaper profitable. However, Scotland's first newsbook, the *Mercurius Scoticus*, was published in Leith in 1651, building on Edinburgh's reputation as a major centre of printing. Printing had flourished in the city since the beginning of the sixteenth century and books, pamphlets and sermons were printed there for readers throughout Britain and Europe in the sixteenth and seventeenth centuries. By contrast, print culture took a much longer time to establish itself in Wales; between 1546 and 1670, only 116 Welsh books were published.[39]

Newsbooks of the Civil War period made several important contributions to the development of the print media. First, they witnessed the reporting of domestic news on a regular basis. The first newspaper to concentrate on covering domestic events is thought to have been printed in November 1641.[40] Second, they started to print comment. Prior to the Civil War, newsbooks had generally avoided comment. Butter and Bourne's attempts to publish controversial material in the 1630s had led to the loss of the right granted to them by the Crown to publish newsbooks. Third, many of the important features associated with the modern newspaper appeared in these papers, including leading articles, advertisements and even illustrations and an agony column. One editor of a Royalist newspaper complained about the employment of women reporters by his Puritan rivals whose 'daughters write shorthand . . . to furnish out the rayling Conventicle (with reports) hot from the pulpit'.[41] Fourth, born in the midst of the Civil War, 'war propaganda' made up much of the content of these newsbooks. Both sides were adept at using the print media to put their case. According to Joseph Frank, many of the techniques of modern political journalism, such as the planted item, the inadequately denied rumour and the inside story were developed.[42] It was not just political stories that filled the Royalist and Parliamentary newsbooks. Invective, personal attacks and innuendo also found their place.

Perhaps the most important contribution made to mass communication in this period was the development of the ideal of freedom of expression and the press. In 1644, John Milton published his pamphlet *Areopagitica* in defence of the liberty of unlicensed printing. 'Give me the liberty to know, to utter and to argue freely according to conscience, above all liberties,' wrote Milton. However, as a statement of the principles of a free press, *Areopagitica* was highly limited. The freedom of discussion that Milton defended was that between 'serious minded men who held honest, though differing opinions'.[43] It did not extend to Catholic literature or ephemeral journalism, that is to 'men of lesser standing with less serious purpose'. More significant was the contribution made by the Levellers. Not only did the Levellers articulate the ideal of a free press, they also demonstrated for it and in 1649 petitioned Parliament to remove all restrictions against free printing. According to one historian of the press, 'nowhere in the literature of liberty can be found a more comprehensive or more logical statement of the argument for the liberty of the press'.[44] The authorities' response was clear and unequivocal – the imposition of strict censorship under Oliver Cromwell's military dictatorship.

The rise and collapse of direct censorship

The years following the execution of Charles I were chaotic and confused. As Parliament tried to establish its authority throughout the country, regulations governing the control of the print media changed by the moment; from being more despotic than anything devised by the Tudors to a near total absence of any discernible regulation. This reflected the ebb and flow of the struggle between the different factions within Parliament. In July 1649, the Treason Act made it a capital offence to print anything critical of Parliament but the means of enforcing the legislation were unworkable (or they just didn't bother) and the growth of both the Royalist and Presbyterian press continued unabated. However, in 1655, Cromwell himself took complete control and banned all newsbooks and rigorously enforced the order using the Army. Within a month of the order, all newsbooks were suppressed and for the remaining years of the Commonwealth no new books were published except those officially sanctioned by Cromwell.

Despite Cromwell's success in controlling the print media, the Civil War had seen a demand for news and information. After the suppression of the newsbooks, there was a growth in hand-written newsletters to satisfy this demand. Written newsletters had been a private source of communication between the rich and powerful for many years.[45] But the control on newsbooks and improvements in the postal services led them to attain greater prominence. Newsletters were, however, used by authority to gather information and intelligence. With the Restoration, Henry Muddiman, the 'King's Journalist', was appointed editor of the *London Gazette*, an official news publication. Developed from the papers set up by Cromwell in the last years of the Commonwealth, the *Gazette* was to dominate the press for the next few decades. In return for free postage, Muddiman made use of his newsletter to set up a system of correspondents throughout the country who, in return for receiving the newsletter, would send in reports. This was to all intents and purposes the first newsgathering service. It was highly dependent on its sources; the recipients were primarily local officials and dignitaries of one form or another. Such a system reflected the view of many in authority at the time that news should be limited to the 'right kind of people'.

The Restoration of the monarchy in 1660 brought no radical change in the system of control set up by Cromwell. The Printing Act of 1662 saw the press placed under tight control and to enforce the provisions of the Act an official Surveyor of the Press, who had unrestricted powers to search and seize printed material, was appointed. The first holder of the office, Sir Roger L'Estrange, clearly disapproved of the wide dissemination of news. He found that it 'makes the multitude too familiar with the actions and counsels of their superiors, too pragmatical and censorious, and gives them not only an itch but a kind of colourable right and licence to be meddling with the government'.[46] The new system soon began to creak under the weight of the political changes of the time. The declining popularity of the new King weakened compliance with the regulations. And Parliament, now formally charged with the control of the press, despite Charles II's attempts to wrest back these powers, began to have doubts about the tight control exerted over newspapers. In 1679, the Printing Act was allowed to lapse, resulting in an increase in the number of publications. Attempts were made to exert alternative controls and, in 1685, the Printing Act was reintroduced – but the growth of the press continued unabated. The reintroduction of licensing was short-lived. The settlement of 1688, the so-called 'Glorious Revolution', which enshrined for the first time some basic rights in the British constitution, led to a growing lack of sympathy in Parliament for censorship and State regulation of the press. The system, however, ultimately collapsed in 1695 because it was unable to cope with the huge increase in the amount of printed material.

The newspaper boom

The end of direct state censorship was a turning point in the development of the British press. In the first two decades of the eighteenth century there was a mushrooming of the number of newspapers throughout Britain. It was only three days after the collapse of the Licensing Act on 3 May 1695 that the *Flying Post* appeared, followed a month later by the *Post Boy* and then in October, the *Post Man*. These tri-weekly papers were to dominate the press for many years and by 1704 their combined circulation is estimated to have been 44,000 copies. More than 20 newspapers of two or four pages soon appeared in London. Most were published weekly, some twice or three times a week, but for the first time a daily newspaper emerged, the *Daily Courant*, which was first published in March 1702.[47] The *Courant* was a single-page newspaper, the first issue having only ten paragraphs, in total amounting to 104 lines. There was no home news with most of the material being translations from French and Dutch publications.[48] The *Courant* was expanded to four pages and survived for over 6000 issues. The eighteenth century saw the sustained growth of the London press; by 1760, there were 89 newspapers published in the capital city. Weekly newspapers also began to emerge for the first time in the English provinces. Between 1714 and 1725, 22 provincial newspapers were born; by 1760, this had risen to 35 and to 50 in 1782. Scotland had a further nine newspapers by the end of the century. Wales had to wait until the beginning of the nineteenth century before producing a home-grown newspaper. Annual consumption of newspapers rose from 7.3 million in 1750 to 12.6 million in 1775.[49] This was the birth of the newspaper industry as we know it today.

Britain developed a newspaper industry earlier than most European nations. France, for example, had to wait until the end of the eighteenth century for its first daily newspaper. This is partly explained by the fact that England and Scotland – though not Wales – underwent a markedly faster rate of urban growth than elsewhere in Europe. The early newspaper developed in the eighteenth century had many of the characteristics we associate with the press today. Newspapers began to appear regularly. As early as the 1620s, Butter and Bourne used a serial number for the *Weekly Newes* to indicate continuity of publication and ended issues by tempting the reader to come back to the next publication with phrases such as 'what they doe there on both sides you shall know by our next newes'.[50] Newspapers began to operate on a commercial basis in that they were openly for sale. At the start of the century the newspapers were primarily distributed to the nation by mail – hence the inclusion of the word 'post' in many of their titles. Printers also attempted to establish a stable demand for their newspapers by encouraging subscriptions. Newspapers were often delivered by couriers to individuals and coffee houses and other places where people passed their time. The newspaper could also be purchased at booksellers and coffee houses and in many towns newspaper shops were opened for the sale of dailies and weeklies. Those unable to buy could look at the papers put up in the shop window. However, many of those charged with delivering newspapers began to sell them openly on the streets. Failure to deliver became a common problem as the 'hawkers' simply bought the newspapers from the printers and sold them on wherever they could. By the end of the century a system of news agents had been set up throughout the country who distributed the newspapers to hawkers who sold them directly to the public.

The eighteenth century is littered with newspapers, journals and periodicals appealing to different slices of life – for example, Samuel Johnson gave vent to the social side of journalism in his publications the *Rambler*, which started in 1750, and the *Idler*, a weekly that was first published in 1758. In the early half of the century specialist publications mushroomed with titles such as the *Lover, Noctural News*, the *Weekly Pacquet*, the *Spectator* and the *Tatler*, ranging from trade papers to political periodicals, literary journals to publications centring on gossip, scandals and manners and moral instruction. In 1693, a broadsheet called the *Ladies Mercury* was published which could claim to be the first publication directed specifically at female readers – it stated in its first edition that it aimed to answer all 'the nice and curious questions concerning love, marriage, behaviour, dress and humour of the female sex, whether virgins, wives or widows'. It contained advice on a variety of topics from the best ways to whiten your teeth to the moral dilemma of a young lady of quality who had suffered the misfortune of having been seduced by a 'lewd and infamous rifler' before her marriage to a rich and worthy man. Should she tell her husband? The *Mercury*'s answer was clear: 'No.'[51] Women played an important role in the early development of the industry. The owners of the first daily and Sunday newspapers in Britain were women. The *Daily Courant* was initially owned by Mrs Elizabeth Mallet while its second editor was Mary de la Riviere Manley who also wrote plays and books and succeeded Swift as editor of the *Examiner* in 1711. In 1780, the first Sunday paper, the *British Gazette and Sunday Monitor*, was started by Elizabeth Johnson. As newspapers grew in size, they were confronted by the problem of filling the space and by the end of the century they could be used for news and information, records, advertising, entertainment, gossip and comment. More than two hundred years after the invention of printing, the newspaper could be distinguished from handbills, pamphlets, tracts and the newsbooks as a recognizable and distinct cultural form.

These decades also saw the appearance of newspapers in the English provinces.[52] The *Norwich Post* and the *Bristol Post Boy* emerged as the first newspapers to be established outside London and by 1719 one newspaper, the *St. James Weekly Journal*, could complain that 'at present both city, town and country are over-flow'd every day with an inundation of news-papers'.[53] Demand from a growing reading public made newspapers a profitable business; competition was intense in this period and many publications were short-lived as printers tried to cash in on the newspaper boom. The content of provincial newspapers was made up mainly of items from other newspapers. The world of journalism during this period was highly enclosed and newspapers would simply reprint stories or items from their competitors with or without acknowledgement. For the London press the most important sources of news were foreign newspapers and the official government newspaper, the *Gazette*, and the provincial and Scottish press was largely made up of accounts taken from the London newspapers. Provincial newspapers used to boast of their efficiency in doing this – the newspapers outside of London aimed to provide 'a faithfull abstract of all the newspapers of note'. Accurate copying was the basis of competition between these newspapers and the *Northampton Mercury* once had to ask its readers not to condemn it for the 'many falsities that have of late been inserted therein, as we took them all out of the London Printed Papers, and those too the most creditable'.[54] This situation reflected the absence of an organized system of gathering news. As there were no reporters, printers had to 'rely on highly unreliable sources: coffee houses, tavern rumour, private tips and eye witness reports from soldiers or sailors returning from the war'.[55] Often accounts could not be checked and many newspapers added to the problem of obtaining reliable accounts by simply making up the news.

During the early decades of the eighteenth century the newspapers began to print news about commerce. Much of what appeared as 'home news' was information about 'the prices of stocks, the course of exchange and the names and descriptions of people becoming bankrupt'.[56] The number of advertisements in newspapers at the beginning of the eighteenth century was small but soon advertisements attained a position of prominence. The importance of advertisements was reflected in an increasing number of newspapers incorporating the word 'advertiser' in their title or sub-title. In 1731, the *Daily Advertiser* was established and its front page with filled with advertisements thereby initiating a trend which was to become a feature of the nineteenth-century press.[57] The increased attention paid to money and markets was in response to social changes beginning to occur in Britain in the mid-eighteenth century. The emergence of capitalism witnessed the rise of the commercial middle class. The potential threat posed to the established social order by the rise of this new class was responsible for the authorities introducing new mechanisms to control the press which was giving expression to the views and aspirations of the new class.

Introduction of the taxes on knowledge

The State's response to the massive expansion of the press in the first half of the eighteenth century was to establish a new system of regulation. In 1712, the government introduced the first Stamp Act comprising taxes on newspapers and the advertisements they printed. Between 1712 and 1815, press taxes were increased sevenfold which meant that sales taxes on newspapers had increased by 800 per cent over this period.[58] The aim of press taxation was to restrict access to those who could pay. Press taxation and legal sanctions such as seditious libel laws were the main weapons the State used against the press. In 1704, Lord Chief Justice Holt made clear the purpose of the government: 'If persons should not be called to account for possessing the people of an ill opinion of the government, no government can subsist; for it is very necessary for all governments that the people should have a good opinion of it'.[59] Press taxes had a profound impact on the development of newspapers – and often not in ways the government had foreseen.

The government failed in its aim to put newspapers out of business, but some newspapers closed and sales did fall. Over time, the growth of the press was slowed down by these tax increases. But what could not be quenched was the demand for news – the 'furious itch of novelty' as contemporaries called it.[60] Unstamped papers began to appear and some of the established papers found ingenious ways around the taxes. However, the policy did help to restrict newspaper reading to the middle and upper classes throughout the eighteenth century. More significant was the impact of taxes on the operation of the press. Taxes changed the delicate balance between profit and loss and pushed newspapers to operate at the financial margins. Most of the money was tied up in getting the newspaper out, with little left over for newsgathering or fighting libel cases that the government might bring. Hence most newspapers came to depend on the official government newspaper, the *Gazette*, for much of their news and avoided politically sensitive topics which might risk prosecutions. Financial vulnerability also made journalists and publishers open to bribery and official payments. Nearly all the leading writers of the period – Daniel Defoe, Richard Steele, and Joseph Addison – were on the government payroll. Some newspapers made bribery a way of life. Scandal sheets became a part of the eighteenth century, accepting money to print 'puffs' or suppress hostile criticism or damaging gossip.[61] Through a combination of bribes, subsidies, the provision of exclusive information and the channelling of official advertising to friendly newspapers, the State was able to exert considerable influence over the content of the eighteenth-century press.

Press taxation also changed the physical appearance of the newspaper. The government put no limit on the size of a sheet to be taxed and as a result throughout the eighteenth-century newspaper owners registered increasingly larger four-page papers as half sheets, hence the birth of the broadsheet.[62] This led to more and more column inches having to be filled. The job of filling these newspapers was not the responsibility of a journalist. The staff of eighteenth-century newspapers was made up of editors whose task it was simply to process the material to be put in the paper, the printer who was legally responsible for the newspaper but was not necessarily the owner, political writers who contributed articles, advertisers and correspondents who sent in material of various kinds. There was no role for a 'professional or occupational group whose task it was to provide an unblemished version of events'.[63] This reflected the fact that the primary role of the press in the eighteenth century was to support and promote the opinions of the different political factions that dominated politics during the period. Hence the most successful voices of the newspaper and periodical world were essayists and pamphleteers whose main concern was to articulate the views and opinions of the political faction supporting their newspaper. The accurate reporting of facts was not an important part of this newspaper world. However, there was one political area in which some degree of accuracy was expected – the reporting of Parliament.

Reporting Parliament: the press and the bourgeois challenge

At the beginning of the eighteenth century, reporting the proceedings of Parliament was restricted. The press fought to obtain the right to record parliamentary debates. However, this struggle was part of a broader conflict which the new media became part of in the second half of the eighteenth century. The new commercial middle class – the bourgeoisie – was denied the chance to play a full and effective role in national politics. The limited franchise meant that power resided in the hands of the aristocracy, the monarchy and the landed elite. The growing economic importance of the bourgeoisie was not translated into political power which was centred on the established oligarchical interests built up around the monarchy. Control of the press was an essential mechanism by which the barriers to increased participation in British political life were maintained. As James Curran states:

> **Legal controls over the press were designed to reinforce normative acceptance of a political system that excluded the mass of the population. Restrictions on parliamentary reporting – including a ban on newspaper reports of Parliamentary debates and unauthorised reports of Parliamentary votes – were justified on the grounds that it would prejudice (i.e. influence) the deliberations of Parliament. Their purpose was the same as the taxes on the press: to restrict political participation that threatened the politics of oligarchy.[64]**

The growth of the press in the face of increasing taxation was in response to the increase in political awareness among the bourgeoisie. At first, there was no focus to this growing political consciousness. However, in the 1750s, the focus was provided by John Wilkes and the struggle over his newspaper, *The North Briton*. The Wilkes affair was a watershed not only in parliamentary politics but also in the development of the British press. James Curran points out that the episode was the first occasion on which the press defined central issues on the British political agenda in opposition to the wishes of the landed elite in Parliament.

The first edition of *The North Briton* proclaimed that 'the liberty of the press is a birthright of a Briton'.[65] Wilkes used his newspaper to criticize Parliament and promote the interests of the rising middle classes. He turned his imprisonment for writing an article critical of the government into a national *cause célèbre* by mobilizing popular discontent. He used his position as a local magistrate to free printers who had published unauthorized accounts of the parliamentary debates and when Parliament barred him from entering the House of Commons after repeatedly winning elections not only did the London mob take to the streets to demonstrate but so did people throughout Britain. Central to Wilkes' struggle was an organized and coherent set of demands for a free press, unencumbered by state controls. The outcome of the agitation was that the ban on parliamentary reporting was lifted in 1771 and general warrants used by the government to gag the press were declared illegal. But in the long run the Wilkes episode initiated the extension of political participation to the bourgeoisie, sustained by a press representing their interests.

By the time of the French Revolution the newspaper had established itself in British society. Its form had been shaped by a series of adjustments in the first few decades of the eighteenth century, the most important of which were in response to the system of press taxation put in place in 1712. For most of the century newspaper content reflected the sleazy world of factional politics within which the press had to operate. But by the end of the century, the press began to act as the 'voice' of the new middle class; advertisements were a response to the commercial needs of this new class while the growth of political comment, instruction in manners and etiquette, discussion of the theatre and literature responded to their social concerns. It was their needs and concerns that secured the position of newspapers in British society.

2

Right against might: the rise and fall of the radical press

The development of print culture prior to the eighteenth century was primarily concerned with the issues of freedom of speech and thought and freedom of worship. Under the Tudors, print developed as part of the struggle for religious freedom while the seventeenth century placed it firmly at the centre of the struggle for political and parliamentary rights. This pitted the emerging print media against the power of the Church and State. Throughout the eighteenth century the print media became an important part of wider social changes. The rise of the newspaper was intimately associated with the growth of commerce and the rise of mercantile capitalism. Competition and the search for profit required knowledge of markets at home and abroad and the newspaper fulfilled this role. The Industrial Revolution had a profound impact on the process of mass communication. Technical changes increased the potential for mass communication: for example, it made it possible for newspapers to reach a larger audience as well as enhance their ability to gather news. Industrial capitalism accentuated the role of mass communication in the economic life of the nation: in fact, an industrial society requires and depends on a developed system of mass communication.

But more important, perhaps, was the impact of the Industrial Revolution on social relations in Britain. The division between capital and labour changed the nature of social interaction. New classes emerged to replace the old feudal order. The rise of the industrial bourgeoisie and the working class led to increased conflict between the emerging classes and with the established aristocratic order. These conflicts manifested themselves in the political arena with the struggle to increase participation in the political system. The growth of mass communication at the end of the eighteenth century and the beginning of the nineteenth century has to be examined not only in terms of the media's relationship with the State but in the context of the 'struggle between competing classes, class alliances and class factions to secure control over mass communications in order to gain or retain dominance in society'.[1]

The Industrial Revolution and class consciousness

The Industrial Revolution did not simply reorganize people's relations in the workplace, it also had a profound impact on their lives. There were changes in family life, sexual relations, the status of women, the relationship between rural and urban communities, the ownership of the land, and so on. People had to make sense of these transformations and the beliefs and values of pre-industrial society were inadequate. The need to articulate the meaning of these transformations furthered the rise of new forms of mass media. The growth of the sense of belonging to a particular class, the emergence of 'class consciousness', was particularly important in shaping the development of mass communication. The print media played a central role to giving a 'voice' to the newly emerging classes. By the beginning of the nineteenth century newspapers such as *The Times*, the *Manchester Guardian* and the *Leeds Mercury* articulated the tastes and interests of the bourgeoisie. They proselytized the ideology of the middle class in their struggle against the aristocracy and inherited wealth – as well as against the working class. The newspapers' exposition of middle-class values was also motivated by straightforward commercial considerations. There were not enough people from the landed gentry to sustain more than a handful of large circulation newspapers. The commercial interests of the press became increasingly tied up with the rapidly expanding, better off and better educated middle classes.[2]

However, the nineteenth century saw the growth of the working class and working-class consciousness. Prior to this time the political voice of the working peoples of Britain had been subsumed in the press that represented the growing challenge to the established aristocratic order. The struggles of the eighteenth century had pitted industrial capitalists and merchant groups, who were excluded or underrepresented in Parliament, against the interests of the King and representatives of the landed interests. The Wilkes affair was crucial in the political development of working class. Radical working-class agitation played an important role in the outcome of the struggle – for example, a massive demonstration in 1768, which involved, among others, 6000 weavers marching through the streets of London forcing every carriage to chalk up the slogan 'Wilkes or Liberty'.[3] This alignment between capitalist and labouring classes was a significant feature of the struggle and the starting point for the organization of working-class demands for reform, of which a free press was a central element. Education was also important in the development of working-class consciousness. Street literature had been a part of working-class life prior to the late eighteenth century. At the start of the nineteenth century there was a more systematic attempt to organize the education of working people. These efforts came from within the ranks of working people; self-education by individual groups or through the Sunday Schools set up by the dissenting churches, such as the Methodists and Baptists.

The last decades of the eighteenth century witnessed a rapid rise of literacy among the peoples of Britain. A bookseller observed in 1791 that 'the sale of books has increased prodigiously within the last twenty years' and even poorer people had begun to have 'entertaining books stuck up on their bacon racks . . . all ranks and degrees now read'.[4] It is estimated that working-class literacy rose 'from around 40% to around 60% in the early nineteenth century'. This assessment is based upon the number of people able to sign their name which by 1839 had risen to nearly two in three people in Britain. School attendance also began to rise with over half of Britain's children having had some period of schooling in 1816; by 1835, 1.45 million out of a possible 1.75 million children had attended school, the average duration of which was a year. The Education Act of 1870 led to literacy becoming universal; all children were to attend school to the age of 12.[5] The nineteenth century witnessed the gradual growth of popular literacy and a mass reading public in Britain as books and printed material came to be accessible to more and more people.

The French Revolution and the rise of radicalism

The rise of literacy at the beginning of the century corresponded with a rise in political interest comparable to the upheaval of the English Civil War. Political tracts, pamphlets and materials of all sorts began to sell in large numbers. In 1776, Dr Richard Price of Llangeinor in Glamorgan published his *Observations on the Nature of Civil Liberty* in the wake of the American Revolution. Price's work sold 60,000 copies within a few months of its publication.[6] It was in response to a sermon by Dr Price welcoming the French Revolution that Edmund Burke wrote his *Reflections on the French Revolution* to warn all 'good thinking people' in Britain about the dangers of the spread of radical ideas to the 'swinish multitude'. In his turn, Tom Paine responded to Burke with his book *The Rights of Man* which was published in March 1791. The book sold 50,000 copies within a short time even though it was published in a three shillings edition. A cheaper edition published the following year sold 30,000 copies within a month and it is estimated that by 1793, 200,000 copies of Paine's work had been purchased by the British public. The success of *The Rights of Man* reflected the major changes that were occurring in British society as a result of the social disruptions brought about by the Industrial Revolution.[7] Paine's philosophy, based on republicanism, democracy, hostility to the aristocracy and commitment to the right of all individuals to speak for themselves, laid down the parameters within which working people initially developed their sense of identity and consciousness. The growing interest in politics and political matters also provided a further impetus to the expansion of the reading public with radical writers leading the way – for example, William Cobbett's pamphlet *Address to Journeymen and Labourers* sold 200,000 copies in two months in 1816. The growth of radical literature was promoted by the development of corresponding societies which were established to further exchanges between those seeking political and parliamentary reform. The London Corresponding Society was formed in 1792 and soon was in touch with similar groups in Sheffield, Manchester and Derby.[8] These societies played an important role in developing popular interest in radical ideas and distributing radical literature to meet the demand.

The dissemination of radical ideas and the mounting political agitation in the wake of the French Revolution led the State to crack down harshly on attempts to extend individual rights. Radical literature was suppressed and in 1793 *The Rights of Man* was banned as seditious libel. Paine fled the country and those found selling radical literature were fined, gaoled and sometimes transported. Legislation was enacted limiting the holding of public meetings and in 1799 the Corresponding

Societies Act was passed which imposed rigid controls on the printing trade. The response of the ruling class was to stamp out through traditional repressive measures subversive literature which it saw as being responsible for popular discontent. Repression was, however, accompanied by attempts to counter the ideology of radicalism. A battle for the public mind was launched by those who saw it as more effective to win over working people. Anti-radical propaganda was first organized by Hannah More when she started to publish her *Cheap Repository Tracts* in 1795. These tracts were issued every month and included a story, an address and a ballad. Political and religious subjects were discussed and *Will Chip the Carpenter* spoke out against the French Revolution.[9] By 1797, it is estimated that 2 million of these tracts had been sold. More and her associates saw education and the new print medium as a means of providing the working classes with 'useful knowledge'. Their view was summed up by Charles Knight, who founded in the 1830s the Society for the Diffusion of Useful Knowledge and published the *Penny Magazine* which at its peak had a circulation of nearly 200,000. He wrote in 1828 that the growth of reading among the lower orders 'could not be stopped although it might be given direction'.[10] This direction, in More's words, took the form of trying to 'train up the lower classes in the habits of industry and piety'.[11] To this end, religious and temperance tracts were published as well as material 'that would divert the mass of working class reading off its natural course by providing escapism and pleasure'.[12] Radical reformers and conservative, religious educators would sometimes be on the same side – for example, in their opposition to the 'taxes on knowledge' or for improved housing or better hygiene – but for very different reasons. The crucial point is that throughout the early nineteenth century, literacy and print culture was a battleground between competing political interests in British society and at the heart of this struggle was the press.

The respectable press

In 1801, the *Anti Jacobin Review* spoke for those opposed to reform when it stated that, 'we have long considered the establishment of newspapers in this country as a misfortune to be regretted; but, since their influence has become predominant by the universality of their circulation, we regard it as a calamity to be deeply deplored'.[13] Following the success of the Wilkes affair, the press had become much more independent of the State and the political factions to which many newspapers had become tied during the eighteenth century. At the start of the nineteenth century, the press was increasingly vocal in its support of the aspirations and demands of the bourgeoisie. The ties between the press and the bourgeoisie were clearly apparent by the increased importance of advertisements in the press. By the middle of the eighteenth century the commercial newspaper was firmly established with advertisements appearing on the front page. The commercial press played an important part in supporting middle-class campaigns for changes in the political system, such as the extension of the vote, the reform of the local government and the civil service, as well as the military, and the repeal of measures that impeded free trade. The commercial press began, as James Curran points out, to provide a positive sense of self-identity to the newly emerging professional middle class. The *Leeds Mercury* trumpeted the virtues of this class when it wrote in 1821 that 'never in any country under the sun was an order of men more estimable and valuable, more praised and praiseworthy than the middle class of society in England'.[14] While the virtues of the middle class were praised by these 'respectable' newspapers, the vices of the other classes were exposed. The aristocracy and the labouring class were equally portrayed as dissolute, idle, feckless, debauched and drunken in contrast to the middle classes who were described by one newspaper as the 'glory of England' and the respectable press argued for the expansion of middle-class values to the whole of British society.

The 'respectable press' was to count among its number *The Times*. Founded as the *Daily Universal Register* in 1785 by John Walter with a loan from the Treasury, *The Times* was to exert considerable influence over the growth of the Victorian newspaper. Walter's grant was an example of the government's use of direct bribes to exert control over the press. Payments were made to newspapers willing to support the government. The government further assisted 'safe' newspapers by placing official advertisements with them. The 'respectable press' operated within the law by taking the stamp and were subject to control through press taxation and bribes and subsidies. The rise of *The Times* to a position of prominence in the British press is seen as representing the growing independence of the press from government and political control. By 1803, it had turned its back on government assistance and in 1834 the newspaper firmly rejected government offers of exclusive information, saying that its news service was better and more reliable. The 'Thunderer' as it became known was able to establish its dominance over rival newspapers as a result of a number of factors. The newspaper was technically superior to most of its rivals.[15] John Walter devoted considerable attention to developments in printing methods. In 1814, he was the first newspaper proprietor to exploit the application of steam power to the printing process when he bought two Koenig steam presses. These machines enabled the newspaper to increase its print runs from 250 per hour in 1814 to 4000 by 1827. Walter, as well as being a shrewd investor in technology, was also an adept businessman. His skills in attracting advertising meant that by 1829 *The Times* was paying twice as much advertising duty as its nearest rival.

But it was in its news and editorial columns that the reputation of the newspaper was built. Editors such as Thomas Barnes and John Delane paid considerable attention to moulding *The Times* into the newspaper that would speak for British public opinion. Under their guidance, *The Times* built up its reputation for a high standard of political reporting and comment. The political influence of the newspaper grew steadily throughout the nineteenth century and was so great that by the Crimean War the Prime Minister of the day could bemoan the 'vile tyranny' of *The Times* over the conduct of public affairs. Barnes and Delane had a clear vision of the role and responsibility of the newspaper – it was to act as an intermediary between government and the governed. A newspaper, in their view, had to be committed to early public disclosure and critical scrutiny of the doings of government. However, *The Times'* commitment to the governed did not extend to mass opinion. Its support for reform was bounded by its ties with the middle class. It campaigned for the 1832 Reform Act which extended the franchise to the middle class but saw no need for reform to go any further. While the newspaper might have opposed the aristocracy and inherited privilege, it had a 'hearty distrust' of extending suffrage to the masses. At the time of Barnes's death in 1841, the newspaper was selling twice as many copies as the combined amount of its three nearest rivals within the ranks of the respectable press. By 1850, this had risen to four times as many.[16] Yet despite its ascendancy among the respectable press, *The Times* was not the best-read newspaper of the early Victorian era – this privilege belonged to newspapers that represented the interests of the working people of Britain.

The early radical press – Carlile and Cobbett

The early phase of the radical press corresponds with the period of political and social turmoil in the immediate wake of the French Revolution. The ideas of these newspapers were strongly influenced by the radical wing of the bourgeoisie which emphasized the philosophy of Tom Paine in shaping their views on the reform of society. In other words, these newspapers were within the tradition of radical dissent, stressing the importance of the individual liberty in the face of political oppression. Ideologically they had much in common with the respectable papers in their commitment to liberalism. Some were more radical as they were influenced more strongly by the revolutionary ideas blown across from the continent. The most famous of the radical newspapers of this period was William Cobbett's *Weekly Political Register*.

William Cobbett founded his paper in 1802 as a pro-government publication with a grant from the Treasury. Its principal aim was to support the war against France but within two years Cobbett had undergone a conversion. On 1 September, the *Political Register* declared that the danger to Britain no longer came from abroad but from 'despotism at home'.[17] Cobbett became more critical of the government as the war with France progressed. In particular, he was outspoken against the way in which the war was financed. He denounced the huge profits bankers were making from war contracts and the widespread distress that the cost of the war was causing among the agricultural workers of Britain. It was the social discontent of the 'journeymen and labourers' that Cobbett increasingly addressed in his newspaper. Cobbett treated the labouring people of Britain as fellow citizens with equal rights and his newspaper provided for the first time a political platform for this previously 'submerged class'. He denounced the state of the press which failed to address the concerns of the people. Through the pages of the *Political Register* he tried to persuade these people that the cause of their distress was political – at the time popular unrest in the form of the Luddites blamed the introduction of new machinery for the problems of working people.

For Cobbett, the enemy of the people was a two-headed monster he referred to as 'The Thing'[18] – one head was 'the accumulated evils of the old system' which included the privileges of the Church and State, as well as their hordes of hangers-on, and a deep-seated hatred for the poor, while the other head was the corruption of the war-making bankers and mercantile classes that was imposing an intolerable burden on the poor. Only through democratic reform of the parliamentary process, Cobbett argued, could the monster be defeated.

The *Political Register*, despite being on the side of the people, was too expensive for most of those it was intended to reach. As a stamped newspaper its cover price was seven and a half pence, which put it beyond what most people could afford. But in 1816, Cobbett identified a loophole in the stamp regulations – if a sheet was not folded up it could not be considered a newspaper and therefore did not need to pay the stamp – which allowed him to publish reprints from the weekly *Political Register* at two pence an issue. The 'Twopenny Trash' pamphlets began with the publication in November that year of the best-selling *Address to Journeymen and Labourers* which stressed that 'the unfortunate journeymen and labourers and their families have a *right*, they have a *just claim* to relief from the purses of the rich. For, there can exist no riches and resources which they, by their labour, have not *assisted to create*.'[19] As an unstamped publication the weekly paper began to reach sales estimated at somewhere between 40,000 and 50,000 copies a week.[20] People would band together to buy radical newspapers such as the *Political Register* as well as Thomas Wooler's *Black Dwarf* and William Sherwin's *Political Register*. There would be collective readings of these newspapers in meetings in taverns which served as the main forum for public discussion in the absence of any trade union or political activity.

William Cobbett on the state of the press

I perceive that you very much want to be enlightened ON THE STATE OF OUR PRESS, which you appear to regard as being FREE, and which, I am going to prove to you, is the most *enslaved* and *vilest* that has ever been heard of in the world under the name of press. I say, that I am going to PROVE this; and proof consists of *undeniable facts*, and not of vague assertions.

Advertising is the great source of *revenue* with our journals, except in very few cases, such as mine, for instance, who have no advertisements. Hence, these journals are an affair of *trade* and not of *literature*; the proprietors think of *the money* that is to be got by them; they hire men to write in them; and these men are *ordered* to write in a way to please the classes who can give most advertisements. The Government itself pays large sums in advertisements, many hundreds a year, to some journals. The aristocracy, the clergy, the magistrates (who are generally *clergy* too) in the several counties, the merchants, the manufacturers, the great shopkeepers: all these *command* the press, because without their advertisements it cannot be carried on *with profit*.

William Cobbett, August, 1830 in the Political Register

Source: **Benn, Tony (ed.) (1984)** *Writings on the Wall*, London: Faber & Faber.

Cobbett's calls to democratic arms made him a popular hero and his writings were read in the households of working people throughout Britain. His success was not just a matter of his political message. Cobbett was able to set up an effective system to distribute his newspapers. Unstamped newspapers could not be sent out by the Royal Mail and Cobbett arranged for shopkeepers in every part of Britain to become his selling agents. Parcels were delivered to them by coach and discounts were available to those who took more than a thousand copies.[21] But it was also Cobbett's writing skills that ensured the large sales. He was able 'to master the art of writing for the working class'[22] which distinguished him from earlier radical writers who often talked above the heads of the people. Cobbett's punchy prose and crude invective struck a chord with ordinary men and women.

The growth of radical publications corresponded with rising unrest in the country. In 1817, the government suspended the Habeas Corpus Act and Cobbett, threatened with arrest, fled to America. His work was continued by, among others, the *Black Dwarf* which upbraided Cobbett for his timidity in deserting the cause. A lively newspaper, the *Black Dwarf* was a bolder and critical voice in the world of radical protest. It specialized in vicious personal attacks on members of the government and proudly announced that it was 'the greatest object of ministerial hatred'.[23] It was joined by newspapers such as *The Republican*, edited by Richard Carlile, who had taken over and renamed Sherwin's *Political Register* in 1819, and *The Gorgon*, edited by John Wade, a former journeyman woolsorter, who devoted considerable space to trade union matters in the newspaper.[24] *The Medusa* – or *Penny Politician* – perhaps best caught the increasingly strident tone of the radical press in the last years of the second decade of the nineteenth century with its banner 'Let's Die like Men and not be Sold like Slaves'.[25] The growth of these newspapers culminated in the Peterloo massacres of March 1819 and the subsequent introduction of the Six Acts, aimed to suppress popular agitation. Two of these Acts were specifically aimed at the radical press – the Blasphemous and Seditious Libels Act and the Publications Act. The former allowed increased power for the authorities to search and seize libellous material while the latter widened the definition of what constituted a newspaper and extended press taxation to views as well as news,[26] Newspapers 'containing only matters of devotion, piety or charity' were exempt from taxation. The result was that sales of radical papers declined and many closed – the first phase of the radical press had come to an end.

Poor men's guardians

The 1820s witnessed disagreement within the ranks of the radical movement over the political organization of working people. Both Carlile and Cobbett, while vociferous in their condemnation of the existing order, believed the growth of clubs, parties and political association in general was an infringement of the rights of the individual. Carlile was strongly committed to the freedom of expression: 'my whole and sole objective, from first to last, from the time of putting off my leather apron to this day has been a Free Press and Free Discussion'.[27] While he expressed republican sentiments, his political analysis did not address the conflict between capital and labour which others were beginning to regard as fundamental to the position of the poor in British society. However, it was through Carlile's efforts that many workers began to see the importance of political organization. He was successful in organizing around him an army of volunteers – General Carlile's Corps – who helped to distribute and sell his publications. In face of rigorous official action Carlile's volunteer army of artisans and labourers were able to keep the voice of radicalism going – in all it is estimated that Carlile's 150 volunteers between them spent 200 years in prison. This example of solidarity and organization was not lost on radicals such as John Wade, who in the pages of *The Gorgon*, began to advocate the need to organize.

The re-emergence of radical newspapers in the late 1820s was associated with the beginning of the trade union movement and the political organization of the working classes. The most famous newspaper of the period, the *Poor Man's Guardian*, founded in 1830, was affiliated to the National Union of the Working Classes and Others, the first attempt to organize working people. The newspaper represented a more radical critique of society than that of Cobbett and Carlile. It argued that poverty and the exploitation of working people were not the result of political oppression or corruption but something inherent in the organization of society which favoured the interests of owners of capital and land at the expense of labour.[28] The editor of the *Poor Man's Guardian*, Henry Hetherington, spelled out in his first editorial the role of his paper in representing the poor classes:

> It is the cause of the rabble we advocate, the poor, the suffering, the industrious, the productive classes . . . we will teach this rabble their power – we will teach them that they are your master, instead of being your slave.[29]

Hetherington stated – as previous radical editors had – that 'knowledge is power' but the knowledge he and his colleagues in the radical press attempted to provide emphasized that working people as a result of their labour were members of the same class. He sought to show that although their experiences were different, the fishermen of Cornwall, the weavers of Lancashire, the miners of Durham and the cabinet makers in London, were all part of a working class as a result of their labour. The sense of belonging to one class was seen as an essential part of the effort to organize and educate working people to play a full role in the political struggle to take their rightful place in society. The radical editor and columnist, Bronterre O'Brien, clearly outlined the kind of knowledge that the radical newspapers of the 1830s sought to impart. He wrote in *The Destructive* in 1836:

> some simpletons talk of knowledge as rendering the working class more obedient, more dutiful . . . but such knowledge is trash; the only knowledge which is of service to working people is that which makes them more dissatisfied and makes them worse slaves. This is the knowledge we shall give them.[30]

The proto-Marxist analysis of radical newspapers such as the *Poor Man's Guardian* placed them firmly against the Great Reform Act which was passed in 1832 and marked the first expansion of the right to vote in this country. The newspaper carried correspondence which declared that the Reform Act would be 'worse' than the old system – as one letter put it, 'to talk of representation, in any shape, being of use to the people is sheer nonsense, unless the people have a House of working men, and represent themselves'.[31] The newspapers like a number of other radical journals strongly featured calls for a general strike to win power. The debate around the Reform Act resulted in a split in radicalism – with the emergence of a radical press under the control for the first time of members of the working class. Newspapers such as the *Poor Man's Guardian, Voice of the West Riding, Working Man's Friend, The Destructive, Slap at the Church, Bonnet Rouge,* Berthold's *Political Handkerchief, Twopenny Dispatch* and *Political Touchwood* represented in an embryonic form the independent voices of the working classes. They thrived between 1830 and 1836 when more than 560 newspapers and periodicals representing a range of opinion and views were launched. They were referred to as the 'Great Unstamped' as they refused to take the stamp, thereby directly challenging the power of the State. The slogan on the masthead of the *Poor Man's Guardian* was 'published in Defiance of the Law, to try the power of Right against Might'. In spite of official attempts to suppress these papers, they quickly attained strong circulations, outselling their 'respectable' rivals. For a number of years the *Poor Man's Guardian* was selling around 12,000 to 15,000 copies a week with a readership of at least 20 times this number – around 300,000 – as the newspapers were circulated in the workplace, taverns and coffee houses. Although the hiring of papers had been made illegal in 1789, people of all walks of life shared the cost of purchasing such newspapers.

The success of the 'Great Unstamped' newspapers was a product of the commitment of radical editors such as Hetherington who was a hardworking political activist, propagandist and organizer as well as a pioneer of modern journalism. Radical publishers developed a number of methods to avoid the stamp. Henry Berthold printed his newspaper on calico and claimed it was exempt from the tax as it contained no paper. Others produced their paper on cotton and called them political handkerchiefs or on plywood and said they were selling political touchwood to light the fires of reform.[32] A system of clandestine distribution was established which saw, among other things, coffins used to send newspapers to the country from London. When circulation started to flag, editors who had gone to considerable efforts to avoid detection by the authorities would submit to a trial. Hawkers sold the newspapers on the streets of the major cities of Britain – many sold them because they were profitable while others laid out their meagre capital to sell newspapers in the name of political reform. Radical editors were also aware of the need to make their newspapers lively and entertaining. With sales falling in 1833, several radical publishers introduced more entertainment material into their papers with Hetherington promising that his *Twopenny Dispatch* would 'abound in Police Intelligence, in Murders, Rapes,

Suicides, Burnings, Maimings, Theatricals, Races, Pugilism and . . . every sort of devilment that will make it sell'.[33] John Cleave's *Weekly Police Gazette* which combined radical political analysis with the inclusion of crime and court reports is estimated to have reached a circulation of 20,000 in the mid-1830s.[34]

For the radical press, their main competition came not from respectable newspapers but from popular ballads, chapbooks, almanacs and broadsides. Murder and execution broadsides were extremely popular in the early nineteenth century – for example, James Catach's broadsides were promoted with bold headlines such as *Horrid Murder* and used illustrations to capture the event or the likeness of the murderer.[35] The Sunday press drew heavily on this tradition. Sunday newspapers first appeared in 1780 with the intention to mix 'instruction with entertainment' and most included a moral essay of some kind.[36] By the 1820s, the Sunday newspapers had established themselves as the most rapidly expanding section of the British press, with leading journals selling somewhere around 10,000 copies. However, useful instruction had been replaced by more emphasis on blood and sex. They now were predominantly popular in their content, combining news with crime, sport and popular amusement and became the subject of disapproval among 'respectable' people who deemed them suitable only for 'shop boys, and millners' apprentices' and unfit for 'decent houses'.[37] A flavour of their approach is captured by the *Observer* which specialized in superior woodcuts of murders and the *Weekly Dispatch*, whose first issue included court reports of 13 people sentenced to death at the Old Bailey, an account of the indecent manner in which people bathed off Ramsgate Beach and a report of the suicide of a man 'who had abandoned his wife and child and lived with a woman of the town in common with another paramour'.[38] In the 1840s, a number of Sunday papers were founded which combined radical opinion with scandal and gossip. *Lloyds Weekly News* (1842), the *News of the World* (1843) and *Reynolds News* (1850) represented attempts to project a radical ideology through entertainment as well as political instruction. The emergence of the Sunday newspapers corresponded to the demise of the 'Great Unstamped' papers in the late 1830s.

Selling the radical press

The following account of conviction which took place at the Courtroom, Stockport, on Thursday, the 27th, October, before Captain Clarke and other magistrates has been transmitted by a friend – JOSEPH SWANN for selling the *Poor Man's Guardian, Hunt's Address*, Unstamped Almanacks, and other publications . . . on Thursday last . . . was asked what he had to say in his defence.

DEFENDANT: Well, Sir, I have been out of employment for some time, neither can I obtain work: my family are all starving; I have applied for relief from the Overseers, but am denied it, and I am glad to sell anything for a living. And for another reason, the weightiest of all, I sell them for the good of my fellow countrymen; to let them see how they are misrepresented in Parliament, and to show them how they may become more fairly represented, for I think it is unjust that men shall be compelled to obey those laws which they have not a voice in framing. It is the *right* of every man to be allowed to sanction every law by which they are led, and I wish to let the people know how they are humbugged.

BENCH: Why do you hawk the unstamped Almanacks?
DEFENDANT: Because I have no voice in stamping them, and no man ought to be governed by laws which he has not previously approved of.

BENCH: Hold your tongue a moment.
DEFENDANT: I shall not! For I wish every man to read those publications (pointing to the *Poor Man's Guardian, Hunt's Address* etc.)

BENCH: You are very insolent, therefore you are committed to three months' imprisonment in Knutsford House of Correction, to hard labour.
DEFENDANT: I've nothing to thank you for; and whenever I come out, I'll hawk them again. And *mind you*, the first that I hawk shall be to your house (looking at Captain Clarke).

BENCH: Stand down.
DEFENDANT: No! I shall not stand down for *you*.

He was then *forcibly* removed from the dock and back to the New Bailey.

It must be borne in mind that J. Swann is the very identical man who suffered four and a half years in Chester Castle for selling *The Republican* (Mr. Carlile's) some few years ago.

Source: *Poor Man's Guardian*, 12 November 1831, in Morris, Max (ed.) (1948) *From Cobbett to the Chartists*, London: Lawrence & Wishart.

The passing of the Great Reform Act was followed by a decline in popular agitation. General disillusionment set in and the National Union of the Working Classes collapsed in 1834. The circulation of the *Poor Man's Guardian* fell to 5000 and in 1835 the newspaper was closed. Intense competition for the working class audience came from middle-class reformers such as Charles Knight who mobilized resources to set up their publications such as the *Penny Magazine* and the *Saturday Magazine* which sold in considerable numbers for short periods in the late 1830s. But political and economic developments in the late 1830s and 1840s began to work against the radical press. These developments eventually were to lead to the disappearance of the radical press but not before the advent of the last great radical newspapers – the Chartist press.

The Chartist press

Chartism was the first political movement of working people. The foundations for the political development of the working class had been laid in the early 1830s but with Chartism these early efforts to organize working people were transformed into a set of political aims and objectives to improve the position of working people in British society. The aims which were outlined in the six points of the People's

Charter included calls for universal suffrage, annual Parliaments, secret ballot, and the removal of property qualifications to be a Member of Parliament.[39] The Chartist movement was a direct response to the failure of the working classes to articulate a set of concrete political proposals around which they could agitate in the debate on the Reform Bill of 1832. Newspapers were seen as having a central role in building of Chartism into a national movement. One of the papers associated with Chartism spelled out the importance of the press in political struggle:

> **Every class, save the labouring class, has its representatives in the newspaper press . . . Why are the working class alone destitute of this mighty auxiliary? The newspaper press, daily and weekly, is the property of capitalists who have embarked on the enterprise upon purely commercial principles, and with the purpose of making it contributory to their own personal and pecuniary interests. It is the course that is profitable and not the course that is just that necessarily secures their preference.**[40]

Newspapers and periodicals were set up all over the country and designated by the National Charter Association to serve as the 'mighty auxiliary' in support of Chartism. They included the *Northern Liberator, True Scotsman, Scottish Patriot, Trumpet of Wales, Advocate, The Charter, Southern Star* and *Merthyr Free News*. But the most important Chartist newspaper was the *Northern Star*. Started in Leeds in 1837, the paper established itself as the champion of Chartism. It played a key role in educating, agitating and organizing its readers by providing information about the actions, theories and tactics of the movement. It was a national platform for debate and discussion, bringing together men and women not only from different trades but different areas of the country. Local activists were made aware through the columns of the paper of their part in the wider class struggle. The newspaper also devoted considerable resources to reporting the struggle of workers' movements abroad. Its role, however, went beyond simply being an information and propaganda sheet: it gave Chartism an identity. The *Northern Star* was 'instrumental in forging and sustaining a specifically working-class solidarity and class consciousness'[41] or in the words of Feargus O'Connor, the Chartist leader, the Chartist press was the 'link that binds the industrious classes together'.[42]

The influence of the *Northern Star* was reflected in its circulation which very soon reached 48,000 per week which made it one of the best-selling newspapers of its era. According to one contemporary observer, 'on the day the newspaper, the *Northern Star*, O'Connor's paper, was due, the people used to line the roadside waiting for its arrival, which was paramount to everything else for the time being'.[43] Reading the *Northern Star* – as with all radical newspapers throughout the first half of the nineteenth century – was a social activity. The newspapers were often read aloud at meetings or to groups at work or in the tavern or to friends at home. They were written to be read aloud and the interaction that came out of such collective reading gave these newspapers a cultural significance and importance much greater than those of modern newspapers.[44] The fate of the Chartist press, and in particular the *Northern Star*, which outlived most of its fellow members of the 'mighty auxiliary', was intimately tied to the fate of Chartism as a political movement. By 1848, the movement had collapsed. The *Northern Star* limped on until 1852 when it was eventually closed with its circulation having shrunk to 1200 – the last of the great radical newspapers had disappeared from Britain, never to return.[45]

The economic structure of the radical press

The development of the unstamped press in the first half of the nineteenth century was assisted by the economic structure of the newspaper industry. The cost of running a radical newspaper was relatively small. Most newspapers were printed on hand presses which were cheap to purchase, at around £10 to £15. Labour costs were low and much of the material that filled the columns of the newspapers was provided by readers either in the form of correspondence or reports of events and meetings from their part of the country. The *Twopenny Dispatch,* founded by Hetherington in 1835, is estimated to have cost only £6 per week to run. The *Northern Star* differed from other radical newspapers in the network of correspondents it employed to provide national coverage; reportedly at a cost of just over £9 per week. But overall the operating costs of most radical papers were small. Distribution costs were kept low by the use of a system of volunteers and, with a high number of readers per copy, print runs could be kept low. A limited amount of capital was needed to establish a radical paper. For example, the *Northern Star* was launched with a capital of £690 raised largely from subscriptions from the public in the main towns of the North of England.[46] The result was that radical newspapers could cover their costs simply on sales alone – the break-even point being relatively low. It is estimated that the *Northern Star* broke even on sales of 6200 copies per week while that of the *Poor Man's Guardian* was as low as 2500.[47] Low capital and running costs had consequences for the ownership of the radical press. They could be owned by working people. Hence the leading publishers, editors and printers were by and large from a working-class background and operated their newspapers in the interests of their class.

The radical papers were also protected from competition from the respectable press by the stamp duty. Radical papers were published without the stamp and this reduced the running costs and made them much cheaper than their mainstream rivals – while the radical papers sold at 1d or 2d, papers such as *The Times* cost 7d or 8d per issue. Advertising was the main means by which respectable newspapers raised revenue. Such finance was not available to the radical press – it is estimated that in 1817 Cobbett's *Political Register* only had three advertisements.[48] However, radical newspapers could be profitable without advertising revenue. Hetherington in 1837 is estimated as making £1000 from his business that year while the *Northern Star* made a profit of £13,000 in 1839 and £6500 in 1840.[49] With no dependence on advertising revenue, the radical press was able to maintain its outspoken criticism of capitalism. The economic circumstances that protected the radical press began to unravel from 1836 when the stamp tax was reduced to 1d and the radical press began to lose its competitive edge. The increasing commercialization of the press and the changing nature of the institutional controls exercised over newspapers in mid-Victorian Britain changed the economic structure that had supported the radical press.

Repeal of the taxes on knowledge

The radical and respectable newspapers were united on at least one thing – the need to repeal press taxation. The struggle for the freedom of the press from regulation returned as a major political issue in the 1830s with the widespread evasion of the stamp duty. Between 1830 and 1836, nearly 800 publishers and vendors of unstamped newspapers were imprisoned for publishing or selling a newspaper without a stamp.[50] The government's campaign to break the radical press had floundered on the unlimited supply of people willing to go to gaol for their rights. In an atmosphere more sympathetic to individual rights, the government found it more difficult to prosecute the press with any degree of success. The system of press control based on taxation began to collapse. Some argued for the introduction of more draconian measures to curtail the growing radical press. Others called for the repeal of the taxation system altogether. They argued that besides being unenforceable, the system restricted trade and the dissemination of knowledge, in particular useful knowledge.

The campaign to abolish press taxation involved a variety of people from different political backgrounds. But the key supporters of the campaign in Parliament were primarily motivated by the desire to remove the threat that radicalism posed to British society. They were not struggling to establish diversity of expression in the press. James Curran[51] has shown that their main objective was to ensure that the press played an effective role in engineering consent from the lower classes for the social order being established by capitalism. To do this, pauper management of the press had to be excluded. For middle-class reformers, a free press, unencumbered by taxation, would be a better instrument of social control than State coercion. It was no longer about whether people should be allowed to read but rather what they should read. 'Instruction rather than the strong arm of the law is the only way to put the unions down', proclaimed one of the leading parliamentary supporters of the campaign. For one of his colleagues, popular unrest among working people was a result of the lack of 'proper instruction . . . caused by the restraints on a free press'.[52] Milner-Gibson, the President of the Association for the Repeal of the Taxes on Knowledge, argued that the removal of press taxes would lead to 'a cheap press in the hands of men of good moral character, of respectability and of capital'.[53] A press 'in the hands of parties who are great capitalists' could be relied on to impart 'sound doctrines' and, as the *Spectator* argued in 1835, help to dispel ignorance and put an end to trade unions, rick burning and machine breaking.[54] As a result of the campaign's success, the duties on newspapers were relaxed.

Advertising duty was reduced in 1833 while stamp duty and the excise duty on paper were cut back in 1836. Advertising duty was eventually abolished in 1853, stamp duty in 1855 and the duty on paper in 1861.

The demise of the radical press

Changes in the economic structure of the newspaper industry and the repeal of the taxes on knowledge were important factors in the demise of radical newspapers from the middle of the nineteenth century. However, there were a number of social and political changes that also contributed to their decline. The struggles of the 1840s and 1850s were successful in ameliorating the conditions of work and wresting better pay for many working people. Average real wages rose by around 40 per cent between 1862 and 1875. Wealthy philanthropists provided housing, schools, orphanages, baths and drinking fountains which improved the lives of working people.[55] The consequence was a decline of working-class militancy from the 1860s onwards. There was also increased acceptance in the ranks of the working classes of 'consensus ideology' that stressed that capital and labour can work together. The mobilization of resources by the middle class to compete with the radical press for the hearts and minds of working people played a role in this process. The mid-Victorian period saw a revival of periodicals devoted to the improvement of the working class. Publications such as *True Briton* sought to educate working people 'not only to morality and Christian principles, to truth and good conduct but also to purely patriotic feelings'.[56] God, King and Country were mobilized. The benevolence of philanthropists as well as the 'fulsome reporting' of royal events was emphasized. Some journals, such as the *British Workman* and *The Cottager and Artisan,* were able to address working people in a less patronizing way. They stressed a 'salt of the earth' approach with heroic depictions of the working man. The nobility of labour was accompanied by the message that by achieving 'respectability', that is cleanliness, temperance, faithfulness and Bible reading, they could better themselves. But new forms of popular entertainment, such as the music halls, were important in propagandizing the values of Empire among working people by which 'domestic "under-classes" could become imperial "over-classes"' and people of all walks of life 'could feel part of a national enterprise on which the majority had been persuaded to agree'.[57] Trade union organizations emerged, such as the National Union of Practical Miners, which preached consensus ideology. In its newspaper, the *Miners and Workman's Advocate,* the union made its position clear: 'We offer no antagonisms to capital. Capital and Labour as far as interests are concerned are identical. Let the union of ALL be cemented and a brighter day will dawn on the poor pitmen of this country.'[58]

Social-economic factors and ideological developments account for the immediate changes in the radical press in the latter part of the nineteenth century. They do not fully explain why periods of political unrest and economic slumps in the early twentieth century did not see the return of such newspapers. Radical papers that were launched in such times, for example, *The Clarion* (1891), the *Daily Citizen* (1911) and the *Daily Herald* (1912), were short-lived.

The fate of the *Daily Herald* is typical of what happened to such newspapers. Begun in 1912 as a strike newspaper, the *Daily Herald* lurched from crisis to crisis with a circulation of 250,000 until the end of the First World War.[59] In 1919, under the editorship of George Lansbury, a future leader of the Labour Party, there was an infusion of capital into the newspaper. Circulation increased but, as George Lansbury stated, 'our success in circulation was our undoing. The more copies we sold, the more we lost.'[60] The rise in sales did not offset the shortfall in advertising and by 1922 the newspaper was only kept going by donations from miners and railwaymen. In that year it was taken over by the Labour Party and the TUC, becoming their official newspaper. However, the financial effort of maintaining the paper proved too much – between 1921 and 1928 the newspaper lost half a million pounds for the TUC. It was sold to the Odhams Group with the stipulation that editorially it remained supportive of the Labour Party. Odhams spent £3 million re-launching the *Herald* and its circulation increased throughout the 1930s with the aid of a variety of free gifts and gimmicks. Many of the new readers were middle class and in attracting these readers the newspaper had toned down the nature of its politics and increased the amount of space devoted to advertising. Despite the increase in circulation and the growth of advertising, the newspaper only obtained a fraction of the advertising revenue per copy of its main rivals, the *Daily Mail* and the *Daily Express*. The newspaper in the 1930s had the largest readership in the western world but still traded at a loss. When the newspaper folded 30 years later, its circulation stood at over 1.25 million, a relatively healthy figure for Fleet Street at the time. However, its share of advertising revenue for the national daily press stood at only 3.5 per cent.[61] The structure of the newspaper market had worked against the *Daily Herald* – the paper was later bought by Rupert Murdoch and renamed the *Sun* in 1969. The economic structure of the newspaper industry which developed in the second part of the nineteenth century, with advertising being central to the profitability of the press, militated against any revival in the radical press. Advertising had become a means to regulate the press – in the words of James Curran, it was a 'new licensing system'.

The increasing reliance of the British press on advertising revenue had profound consequences for radical publications. There were two ways in which this worked against the radical press. First, advertisers were not sympathetic to radical ideas. Second, and more significant, was the perception that advertisers had of the readership of radical papers. In their view, the readers of radical newspapers did not have sufficient purchasing power to make it worthwhile for them to advertise in the pages of such publications. The head of one of the largest advertising agencies in Victorian Britain stated in 1856 that in spite of the large circulations of radical newspapers, 'their readers are not purchasers: and any money thrown on them is so much money thrown away'.[62] The radical press was faced with a number of options in the face of these changes. They either closed down, became more 'respectable' by moving up market, condemned themselves to a political ghetto with small readerships or acquired alternative sources of finance.[63] Karl Marx's *Beehive* was taken over by a Liberal millionaire before its eventual demise while the radical Sunday newspapers such as *Reynolds News* and *Lloyds Weekly News* became less radical. The latter part of the nineteenth century witnessed the rise of a mass-circulation 'popular press' which was different in both content and nature from the radical working-class press of the early nineteenth century.

3

Get me a murder a day: the Northcliffe Revolution and the rise of the popular press

The second half of the nineteenth century saw the emergence of a mass circulation popular press. The radical newspapers of the working classes were replaced by popular newspapers which sold the length and breadth of the British Isles. These newspapers established the press as a medium of mass communication. Newspapers such as the *Daily Mail* and the *Daily Express*, within a relatively short time of their birth, established circulations of approaching a million readers. Not only were they popular with the growing reading audience but they also brought about fundamental changes in the nature, structure and content of the British press. The radical press of Cobbett, Hetherington, Carlile and the Chartists was popular in the sense that it was 'for the people' and placed emphasis on the maintenance of independent political opinion and analysis at the expense of other aspects of popular culture and literature. The economic conditions under which they operated played an important part in their ability to make such a choice. The mass circulation newspapers of the late nineteenth and early twentieth centuries expanded on popular reading material in the areas of crime, scandal, romance and sport at the expense of independent political comment.[1] They changed the format and shape of the newspaper, with the introduction of illustrations and pictures and innovations in the layout and presentation of stories.

They were also 'popular' in commercial terms. The second half of the nineteenth century saw the demise of political radicalism with the extension of the vote and the emergence of new kinds of political parties. The new politics was anchored in fundamental shifts in the nature of British capitalism. The Great Depression of 1875 accelerated the trend to the organization of capital into larger units by increasing competition and forcing small and inefficient capital out of business. The newspaper industry, like many other sectors of the economy, became big business. The industrialization of the press, including the introduction of new technology which expanded the number of copies of papers that could be printed, increased the amount of capital needed to launch and run a newspaper. The changes in the British press in this period have to be seen in the context of developments in the economic organization of British society. Changes in production and distribution in the industry, according to Raymond Williams,[2] changed not only the social relations between newspapers and their readers but also the nature of ownership. The popular newspaper that emerged at the end of the nineteenth century was above all 'a highly capitalized market product for a separated "mass" readership' and controlled by a small number of newspaper conglomerates.

Cheap newspapers for all

The abolition of the 'taxes on knowledge' in the 1860s was followed by the gradual growth of the British press. It is estimated that in 1850 the circulation of the national daily press was around 60,000 while Sunday newspapers sold about 275,000.[3] The development of the Sunday newspaper was more rapid as the Sabbath was the only day on which working men and women had the opportunity and time to read a newspaper. The Sunday papers comprised more fiction, including romance and crime stories, than news and it was a Sunday newspaper, *Lloyds Weekly News*, that in 1896 became the first paper to reach the 1 million circulation mark. The daily popular press emerged more slowly. The *Daily Telegraph* attained a circulation of 300,000 by 1890 but it was not until 1911 that the *Daily Mirror* established itself as the first million-selling daily newspaper in Britain. The total circulation of the national daily press increased to 3.1 million by 1918 and by the eve of the Second World War had mushroomed to 10.6 million.[4] However, it was in the provinces that the expansion of the press happened most rapidly. In the 1850s, only a small number of newspapers were published outside London. Within 15 years of the repeal of the press taxes, 78 new provincial dailies had been founded, 13 of which were evening papers. The growth of evening newspapers was a noticeable feature of the development of the press at this time. By 1880, there were slightly more evening than morning newspapers in the ranks of the English provincial press and by 1914 the disparity had become more marked, with 77 evening compared to 42 morning newspapers published in the English regions.[5] In Scotland and Ireland, the evening press did not have as much impact as in the rest of Britain while in Wales both local daily and evening newspapers emerged much more slowly. By the end of the century most of Britain's major cities had a number of morning and evening newspapers.

The expansion of the British press was facilitated by a number of factors. The demand for newspapers increased with the growth of literacy. The 1870 Education Act brought about a rise in adult literacy and, using the crude measure of the ability to sign one's name, it is estimated that by 1900, 97 per cent of the British people were literate. The consumption of newspapers is not, as we saw with the radical press, simply determined by literacy. Perhaps more important for the growth of the newspaper market was the decline in the number of hours people spent at work and the rise in real wages. Both increased leisure time and purchasing power provided a stimulus to demand. The most significant factor was the improvement in the supply of newspapers. The newspaper industry went through rapid industrialization in the second half of the nineteenth century. In 1868, the rotary press was introduced which made possible larger print runs. The second stage of the industrialization of the press came in 1876 with the introduction of linotype which increased the quality of the product and further increased print runs. Between 1860 and 1900, the electric telegraph, telephone, typewriter and means to reproduce photographs were invented or developed, all of which transformed the practice of news gathering. The telegraph assisted the growth of the provincial press by enabling it to gather news for itself thereby reducing its dependency on London newspapers. The distribution of newspapers was assisted by the growth of the railway system. Distribution was further improved by the arrival of newsvendors and agents, in particular W. H. Smith, which established a monopoly over the distribution of newspapers to agents. The company set up shops for selling newspapers and cheap books, particularly at railway stations. From the 1840s, the London newspapers were disseminated to most parts of the country on their day of publication. This allowed the London dailies to compete with the provincial press and, by the First World War, the London press had increased its reach throughout Britain, with some papers published simultaneously in London, Manchester and Glasgow. Newspaper production became centralized in Fleet Street and the London papers had become a national press.[6]

The 'new journalism'

The growth of the press was accompanied by changes in the nature of journalism. Joel Weiner[7] refers to a 'historic shift' in the British newspaper industry in the period between 1880 and 1914, 'from a press limited by its own traditions and the modest demands of readers to one whose capacity for change was seemingly without end'. The changes were greeted with howls of outrage from the cultural critics of the time. Matthew Arnold labelled what he called the 'new journalism' as 'feather-brained' and the German philosopher, Nietzsche, was dismissive when he said that the 'rabble vomit their bile and call it a newspaper'.[8] For such critics, the 'new journalism' was responsible for the debasement of cultural standards with its emphasis on entertainment and amusement instead of instruction. According to Edward Dicey, a prominent journalist of the period, the newspaper readers 'like to have their mental food in minces and snippets, not in chops or joints'.[9] But to what were these critics taking such exception? There were three kinds of changes in the British press before the First World War: (1) in the content of newspapers; (2) in their layout, design and typography; and (3) in the economic structure of the industry.

The daily press of mid-Victorian Britain was characterized by serious journalism – the content of the newspapers ranged from political polemic to serious consideration and analysis of the pressing issues of the day. This was the 'age of *The Times*'. The newspaper dominated the industry and exercised a 'position of authority never before or since equalled by any other newspaper'.[10] The newspaper spelled out its view of the role of journalism in response to criticisms made by the Prime Minister, Lord Derby, in 1852. Derby regarded the newspaper's criticism of the new French government as irresponsible and an unwarranted intervention into the affairs of state. *The Times* thundered back that 'the first duty of the press is to obtain the earliest and most correct intelligence of the events of the time and instantly, by disclosing them, to make them the common property of the nation'.[11] For *The Times*, the duty of the journalist 'is the same as the historian – to seek out the truth, above all things, and to present to his readers not such things as statecraft would wish them to know but the truth as near as he can attain it'. To this end, *The Times* employed an array of the best shorthand takers to report the proceedings of Parliament and it prided itself on being close to what was going on in the corridors of power, in particular, inside the Cabinet.

From the 1850s, this style of journalism was challenged by a lighter form of reporting. Politics and opinion started to be supplemented, if not replaced, with material of a 'human note', crime, sexual violence and human oddities. These, as we have seen, had always been part of popular literature but from the middle of the century they began to become a feature of the British press. The press had a role to entertain as well as inform its readers. In the face of declining readerships some of the radical press had responded by trying to combine their political analysis with entertainment and popular material. The Sunday newspapers laid the foundations for the content of the popular press, with their emphasis on murders, executions, elopements and a miscellany of small features. The radical Sunday newspapers rapidly attained large circulations in the 1850s, selling well in the areas of the country that had most strongly supported the Chartist press, the textiles areas of Lancashire, Yorkshire and the Midlands and the industrial belts of South Wales and Scotland.[12] Their popularity was based on the sensational reports of murder, robbery and scandal. They carried some serious political news, with, for example, 20 per cent of the news and editorial content of *Reynolds News* before 1880 devoted to such copy, thereby retaining commitment to their roots as radical newspapers.[13] But political analysis was increasingly watered down in favour of more sensational reporting. The importance of such material was apparent from the beginning: the first edition of the *News of the World* in 1843 carried a story entitled 'Extraordinary case of drugging and violation'. By the 1880s, the bulk of the stories concentrated on murder, crime and other thrilling events – which, for example, in 1886, made up over 50 per cent of the news stories in *Lloyds Weekly News*.[14] Sensational reporting was sometimes used as part of the radical propaganda of the Sunday papers with personal revelations and scandals often reinforcing a radical analysis of society. As the Sunday press became an increasingly more profitable venture, commercial gain tended to replace radical politics as the main driving force behind the newspapers.

Fleet Street in the mid-Victorian period

Whenever I talk about Fleet Street sixty years ago, I find that one statement stirs incredible amusement – the statement that in the year of Queen Victoria's Jubilee (1887) journalists all wore top-hats. Not because of the Jubilee. They had worn them for years before that: they went on wearing them for years after. The top-hat was the indispensable hall-mark of the 'gentleman'.

When R.D. Blumenfeld began to frequent the Press Gallery in the House of Commons ten years later, he saw below him 'a pleasing picture of punctiliously mannered middle-aged or old gentlemen in frock coats and expansive collars, white or flowered waistcoats, large watch-chains, flowing hair and much hirsute ornamentation in the way of expansive beards, whiskers and military moustaches. Everyone wore a shiny top-hat'... Lionel James, summoned to *The Times* office to be engaged as war correspondent, felt this to be a 'top-hat affair'; he went out and purchased 'one of the shiniest of its kind'.

They [newspapers] were then regarded as political platforms. They were organs of opinion. They were pretty evenly divided between Conservatives and Liberals. Their contents were in the main political. Leading articles on the matters which divided the two parties occupied a whole page. Reports of speeches ran into four, five, sometimes six columns. They were printed in solid masses of type, unbroken by cross or shoulder heads, hardly paragraphed even. The parliamentary debates took up usually a page, often two. The effect was heavy, portentous, dull. The newspapers wore top-hats as well as those who produced them.

They were stolidly respectable, they clung to tradition, they valued dignity above enterprise. Here is an illustration. One day in that part of London called Brixton, an elephant from a travelling circus broke loose and careered up and down the principal thoroughfare for half an hour. When this piece of news was handed to a sub-editor of *The Times* with the instruction to 'treat it on its merits', the sub-editor read it and frowned. A runaway elephant! Was that dignified enough for *The Times*? He decided that it was not and stuck the 'copy' on the file, the spike which stands at every sub-editor's elbow for the reception of rejected matter. He was known from that day as 'the man who spiked an elephant'. But there was no row about it. The authorities took the view that perhaps he had deserved well of the paper by preserving its dignity. On the other hand, while entertaining news was kept out, almost anything political could get in.

The whole of the press, whether daily, weekly or monthly, was produced for an educated minority wearing top-hats.

Source: Fyfe, Hamilton (1949) *Sixty Years of Fleet Street*, London: W. H. Allen, pp. 7–12.

The *Daily Telegraph* was the first daily newspaper to adopt this style. Launched on 20 June 1855, the day the stamp duty was abolished, the newspaper paved the way for the expansion of a cheap daily press. It was sold at the price of one penny and concentrated on crime and sex with headlines such as 'Furious Assault on Female' (1857) and 'Extraordinary discovery of Man-Woman at Birmingham' (1856).[15] The owners of the *Telegraph* sought to develop a new kind of newspaper which stressed a 'human note' and did not assume that the reader was only interested in politics and current affairs. A number of rival papers soon followed, including the *Morning Star*, established as a penny newspaper in 1856, and the *Daily News* and the *Standard*, which were the *Telegraph*'s main competitors in the latter decades of the nineteenth century. These papers were directed at 'an entirely new public who never saw the weeklies and monthlies' and conceived 'for the man on the knifeboard of the omnibus'.[16]

The late nineteenth century witnessed other trends in the development of journalism. The emergence of socially responsible, campaigning journalism was characterized by the success of the *Pall Mall Gazette*. Launched in the 1880s, the paper under W. T. Stead campaigned on many issues from Turkish atrocities in Bulgaria to conditions in the London slums. His most famous campaign against child prostitution in London ended in a three-month prison sentence.[17] The first of a series of articles on the abuse of young girls appeared on 6 July 1886 under the headline, 'The Maiden Tribute to Modern Babylon', and shocked Victorian society. It was not only the subject matter but the sensational way in which Stead presented the story with the techniques of the 'new journalism' such as the use of interviews and personal testimony as well as bold, sub-headings, such as 'How Girls are Bought and Ruined' and 'Violation of Virgins'. The *Gazette*'s exposé helped the newspaper in the short run to increase circulation but by incurring the wrath of advertisers the newspaper lost revenue.[18] Stead and the *Pall Mall Gazette* furthered the cause of campaigning journalism. His faith in the power of journalism to change society was illustrated in an article, 'Government and Journalism', published in 1886, in which he wrote of the journalist as the 'uncrowned king of an educated democracy' and of the press as 'the voice of democracy', 'the engine of social reform' and 'the apostle of fraternity'.[19]

The 1880s also saw the appearance of illustrated newspapers. One of the first newspapers to use illustrations was the *Northampton Mercury* in 1720 when it carried a number of political cartoons. Inserting block cuts into the frame for printing was unreliable and slowed down the process of production. It was not until the 1830s with advances in print technology that illustrations became more widely available. Pictorial magazines, such as the *Penny Magazine*, used illustrations to make printed material available to many who could not read.[20] The growth of a weekly illustrated press developed from the 1840s with publications such as *Illustrated London News* (1842), *Illustrated Weekly Times* (1843) and *The Graphic* (1869) establishing themselves as important papers. Editors relied on artists for the drawing of events. Actuality was sketched – for example, the *Illustrated London News* sent an artist to accompany Queen Victoria when she toured Scotland in the summer of 1842. However, the rapid supply of pictures was a problem and hence many of the illustrated papers relied on 'long-term "institutional" subjects for which there was no time pressure and on which the artist could work for as long as necessary'.[21] Pictures only began to appear in the daily press in response to the competition provided by silent films at the start of the twentieth century.

Industrialization and technological changes led to a further division of labour within the industry. The advent of the telegraph, telegram and telephone increased the ability of the press to provide on-the-spot reportage. Reporting from more locations became possible as the expansion of transport systems allowed the reporter to go to more places, more quickly. These technological changes introduced the idea that a newspaper's primary function should be to cover the events of the 'day' with discussion, comment and analysis becoming secondary.[22] The importance of the reporter increased. From the middle of the century 'the reporter and his notebook (occasionally even her notebook) bore something of the magic of the new television teams of the 1960s, moving from riot to battlefield, demonstration to sit-in, while being widely accused of causing the scenes which they recorded and reproduced'.[23] The anonymity of the contributors to the British newspaper was slowly replaced by the reporter's by-line and the drawing of a distinction between fact and comment became central to the standards of the profession. The duty of journalism in the first half of the nineteenth century, despite *The Times*'s protestations, was not to discover the truth. The emphasis was on the polemical power of the writer's pen. Opinion and commentary were the essence of good journalism – except in the recording of parliamentary activity where accuracy was considered vital. This was a world of journalism in which the editor was sovereign. By the end of the century technology and commercial need had elevated the importance of accuracy and reliability, as well as the ability to meet the daily news deadlines, to the profession of journalism. The rise of the news agencies, such as the Press Association, Central News and Reuters, which provided domestic and foreign news to the British press, highlights the growth of news as a marketable commodity.[24] The role of the editor began to change. Less interest was expressed in politics or current affairs and more attention paid to the techniques and skills of making newspapers more entertaining and eye-catching in an environment of growing competition. They excelled at improving how a newspaper looked – its layout, style and writing – not what it said or where it stood. As Arthur Christiansen, the editor of the most successful paper of the inter-war years, the *Daily Express*, told the Royal Commission on the Press in 1949: 'I was a journalist, not a political animal. The policies were Lord Beaverbrook's job, the presentation mine.'[25] The enhancement of the power of newspaper owners was another outcome of the changes that occurred in the British newspaper industry in the early twentieth century.

The Northcliffe Revolution

The *Daily Telegraph* never became a mass circulation daily newspaper. This was the achievement of the popular, commercial papers of the early twentieth century, the *Daily Mail* (founded in 1896), the *Daily Express* (1900) and the *Daily Mirror* (1903). It was Alfred Harmsworth's *Daily Mail* that paved the way. Harmsworth entered the publishing world in 1888 when he launched his weekly magazine, *Answers to Correspondents on Every Subject under the Sun*. His publication was copied from the successful weekly magazine, *Titbits*, which had been started by George Newnes in 1881. These weekly magazines were a miscellany of odd facts, curiosities, puzzles, jokes and stories, laid out in short paragraphs of no more than two or three lines. *Answers* was supposed to supply responses to questions sent in by the public; questions such as What does the Queen eat?, Can fish speak?, Why don't Jews ride bicycles?, What is the colour of Gladstone's socks?, Why are no bus conductors bald? Do dogs commit murder?, Why can't clergymen marry themselves? Harmsworth produced scraps of useless information under titles such as How to Cure Freckles, Strange Things Found in Tunnels, and Facts about Fairies. Royal anecdotes appeared in most issues, including information such as 'the Queen never travels at more than 35 miles an hour', as well as jokes such as 'a swallow may not make a summer but a frog makes a spring'. The most significant feature of the publication was its competitions. Every issue invited readers to take part in guessing games – such as estimating how many people crossed London Bridge every day – with prizes that included a winter outfit of clothes, a continental tour, a post in the *Answers* office and a £100 banknote.[26] These magazines were supposed to be harmless, good fun and mildly informative, aimed at developing lower-middle-class readers 'avid for information and subjects fit for family conversation'. Harmsworth made up most of the questions but the venture was a huge commercial and popular success and by 1906 *Answers* sold 800,000 a week. On the basis of this success, Harmsworth started up a variety of magazines, including *Comic Cuts* ('amusing without being vulgar'), woman's magazines such as *Forget-Me-Not* ('a high-class penny journal for ladies') and *Home Chat*, which included articles on careers for women, gossip and free dress patterns, as well as other titles, such as *The Marvel, The Wonder*, and *The Sunday Companion*. The total circulation was nearly 2 million, constituting at the time the largest publishing business in the world.[27] The profits and experience of his publishing empire led Harmsworth to launch the *Daily Mail*.

Four years after its launch, the *Daily Mail* reached a circulation of 989,000 and became Britain's first truly mass circulation daily newspaper. The success of the paper was responsible for a revolution in Fleet Street – often described as the 'Northcliffe Revolution'. Harmsworth – ennobled as Lord Northcliffe – incorporated many of the ideas of *Answers* in the *Daily Mail*. The newspaper's content comprised small features, adventure and human interest stories and readers letters. In particular, he placed great emphasis on crime stories as a staple feature of the paper. Interviews with murderers and the police featured. Northcliffe's motto was 'get me a murder a day'. The first edition of the paper which appeared on 4 May 1896, contained pages on the law courts and police as well as political gossip and a section called 'In Society'. The daily magazine appeared on page 7 and included features and stories which were meant to appeal to women readers. The paper carried lavish sports reports, with cycling, a long-standing interest of Northcliffe, figuring prominently. It is important to stress that Northcliffe's *Mail* was not sensationalist; it did not have much sex or scandal, priding itself on being a respectable family paper. It was a broadsheet newspaper and, in most ways, did not resemble the popular tabloid paper of today. The layout of the *Mail* did not depart from the narrow column format then familiar in Fleet Street. Its content was bright and entertaining not brash and sensational. The success of the *Mail*, and Northcliffe's other paper, the *Evening News*, led others to copy its formula. The focus on entertainment and human interest stories in the *Mail* was not revolutionary. It was simply the continuation of what had been pioneered by the Sunday and illustrated papers and introduced into the daily press by the penny newspapers. Northcliffe simply adapted and built on what had been previously developed.

Northcliffe's publications were aimed at the emerging lower middle classes – clerks, shopkeepers and skilled artisans who, as a result of the 1870 Education Act, the introduction of schooling for all and the growth of economy in the late Victorian period, had established themselves as part of the British social scene. One of the slogans of the *Mail* was 'The Busy Man's daily journal' and Northcliffe told his editors to think of the reader as 'the man who earns £1000 a year'. Men like George Pooter, the hero of George Grossmith's *Diary of a Nobody* (1892), were part of the newly emerging petty bourgeoisie, concerned with bettering themselves. Northcliffe's interest in bringing new readers to the daily press resulted in his launch in 1903 of the *Daily Mirror* as a newspaper for gentlewomen. It employed an all-female staff and was aimed at female readers. However, the paper didn't sell and in 1905 was revamped as an illustrated newspaper. There was not much politics in the early *Daily Mail* – it was not a popular paper in the sense it took up themes and issues that charged the people of the day. The years before First World War were times of political upheaval – in Ireland, the British Army mutinied, Sinn Fein was winning 70 per cent of the vote in Ireland at the elections, suffragettes were campaigning for votes for women, strikes were taking place in most major industries – and some have characterized the country as having been on the verge of revolution.[28] Little of the ferment in the outside world appeared in the newspaper. But as the newspaper grew, it came to speak for the views and values of the new class of readers, articulating popular causes which came to represent suburban, lower-middle-class values – imperialism, jingoism, nationalism.[29]

The more significant aspect of the 'Northcliffe Revolution' was the economic reorganization of the newspaper industry. The industry became intensely capitalized. It is estimated that the capital cost of the *Mail*'s launch was £600,000 which contrasts sharply to the £30 Hetherington needed to start his paper in the 1830s.[30] New technology was expensive and more labour-intensive production practices meant that the running costs of a newspaper increased steeply. However, mass circulation meant that newspapers could be an immensely profitable business. Northcliffe pioneered the use of advertising stunts, such as treasure hunts, free insurance for new readers, competitions where winners received £1 a week for life (declared illegal in 1928) to sell his papers.[31] But, most importantly, Northcliffe used advertising to finance his newspaper business.

Advertising and the popular press

Advertising has always played an important part in the development of the British press. The popular papers of the Northcliffe era were more closely tied to advertising than the newspapers of mid-Victorian Britain. By 1886, nearly 61 per cent of the column space of the *Telegraph*, 49 per cent of *The Times* and just over 40 per cent of the *Scotsman* were devoted to advertising.[32] This expansion was a reflection of the increasing reliance on advertising as a source of revenue. As circulation rose, the costs of newspaper production increased. More pages had to be filled, more reporters hired, and higher distribution costs were incurred trying to circulate the newspapers to all parts of the country. This placed pressure on the cover price of newspapers. Advertising became not only the main source of revenue but the main way of keeping prices down. From the end of the nineteenth century newspapers ceased to be sold at their true costs and the cover price of the newspapers was subsidized by advertising revenue.

Letter of Lord Palmerston to Queen Victoria in 1861

The actual price at which each copy of the newspaper is sold barely pays the expense of paper, printing and establishment: it is indeed said that the price does not repay those expenses. The profit of the newspaper arises from the price paid for advertisements, and the greater the number of advertisements the greater the profit. But advertisements are sent by preference to the newspaper which has the greatest circulation; and that paper gets the widest circulation which is the most amusing, the most interesting and the most instructive. A dull paper is soon left off. The proprietors and managers of *The Times* therefore go to great expense in sending correspondents to all parts of the world where interesting events are taking place, and they employ a great many able and clever men to write articles upon all subjects which from time to time engage public attention; and as mankind takes more pleasure in reading criticism and fault-finding than praise, because it is soothing to individual vanity and conceit to fancy that the reader has become wiser than those about whom he reads, so *The Times* in order to maintain its circulation, criticizes freely everybody and everything; especially events and persons, and Governments abroad, because such strictures are less likely to make enemies at home than violent attacks upon parties and persons in this country.

Source: ***The Royal Commission on the Press*** **(1949), p. 154.**

Northcliffe made a significant contribution to linking newspapers more closely to advertising. Prior to Northcliffe, most of the advertisements in the British press were classified. They fitted into columns and most of the front pages of newspapers were simply columns of classified ads. Attempts to break up columns were strongly resisted by editors who saw it as an infringement of editorial sovereignty. *The Times*, for example, did not change the composition of its front page until 1977. The *Mail* became the first newspaper to accept display advertising. Whole-page advertisements were taken and in 1924 Selfridges became the first department store to advertise in the British press when it took out a full page advertisement with the *Express*. Other new kinds of advertisers were attracted to the press and mail order advertising was developed by the *Mail*. By the late 1930s nearly three-quarters of the income of a national daily was derived from advertising.[33] Northcliffe's most crucial innovation was to introduce audited circulation figures and charge rates for advertising based on the size of circulation. Previously newspaper advertisement rates were tied to space, per column inches. Northcliffe charged advertisers per 1000 readers thereby tying advertising directly to sales. Northcliffe's accountants drew up their estimates of circulation which were published on the front page of the newspaper to attract advertisers. By increasing advertising revenue Northcliffe could cut the cost of his newspapers and compete with the penny press. The *Daily Mail* became the first halfpenny newspaper with the slogan emblazoned on its masthead, 'The penny paper for half penny'. It was this as much as the content of his newspaper that secured the *Mail* the extraordinary sales of its first few years.

The growing importance of advertising increased the need for better and more independent measurement of circulation and readership. The early twentieth century saw the rise of 'middle men' in the newspaper industry, such as media buyers, who were responsible for buying space in newspapers for placing advertisements. These companies began to appear in the years between 1889 and 1910, and, after a period of intense competition, they established themselves in the newspaper industry in the 1920s.[34] One such company was the London Press Exchange. Started up in 1892, it had by 1927 departments which undertook market and consumer research and prepared media data for advertisers. Circulation figures had been carefully guarded secrets by the newspapers who issued their own estimates. Such a system was open to abuse as newspapers talked up their sales. As a result, advertisers campaigned for an independent body to audit newspaper circulations. In 1931, the Audited Bureau of Circulation (ABC) was established. Within five years the Bureau was responsible for monitoring the circulation of 186 publications, estimating that of those who would not participate.[35] By 1946, ABC was accepted by all major publishers and the following year newspaper readership surveys became available on a regular basis.

Started in 1924, these attempted to ascertain not how many but what kinds of people read what newspapers. Between 1866 and 1896 there had been a growth in magazines, from an estimated 557 to 2097, aimed at delivering specialist groups, trade, technical and professional, to advertisers.[36] Advertisers were interested in who read what, in which newspaper. Newspaper readership profiles were crucial in deciding where to place advertisements for particular products. The result was that advertising revenue was central to press finances from the 1920s. The dependency of newspapers on advertising revenue was confirmed during the inter-war years. In 1937, the London daily newspapers made a loss of just over £9.7 million on sales to the public and it was only through advertising that they were able to recoup their losses.[37] If the Northcliffe Revolution was about anything, it was about establishing advertising as the basis of the economic structure of the newspaper industry. This dependency meant that the commercial success or failure of a newspaper was no longer the result of a choice made by the readers.

The increased importance of advertising shaped the content of newspapers. It laid the foundation for the polarization of Fleet Street between mass circulation 'popular' and elite 'quality' newspapers with small sales. Quality newspapers were encouraged to restrict their appeal to readers with high purchasing potential. The economic pressure on quality newspapers to concentrate on specialized readers was illustrated by the history of *The Times* in the 1960s. In the face of mounting financial problems the newspaper, after changing its content and adopting an aggressive marketing campaign, increased circulation by 69 per cent between 1965 and 1969.[38] Profits, however, did not increase. The new readers, mainly lower-middle class, diluted the prestige quality of the paper in the eyes of advertisers and they were unwilling to pay the higher *Times* advertising rate when they could reach such an audience more cheaply through other channels. The newspaper lost money and it was not long before management decided to shed its new readers and emphasize its elitism to attract the advertisers.[39] Popular newspapers, on the other hand, have to maximize their audience appeal to compensate for readers with low purchasing power. This was to lead to increasingly cut-throat competition between popular newspapers during the inter-war years – something which returned to the press in the 1980s.

Dependence on advertising revenue changed the composition of newspapers. The needs of particular readers became crucial in determining what to report, what to fill up pages with and how to lay out stories. The growing recognition of women as consumers, confirmed by market research in the early 1930s, led newspapers to try to tailor their appeal to women readers. From 1934, readership was classed by sex and the growth of items for and about women became a feature of newspapers. The stress on objectivity in news reporting also developed as the role of advertising in press economics grew. The need to reach a wider more heterogeneous, mass audience, cutting across political divides and class divides, reinforced the need for news content which was balanced. The idea of 'neutral news', facts and only facts, was in part a reflection of economic changes in the industry.

Concentration of ownership

By the end of the 1920s other newspapers began to rival the *Mail*'s success. Sales of newspapers more than doubled throughout the inter-war years with three papers, the *Daily Mail*, the *Daily Express* and the *Daily Herald*, accounting for just under half of the total circulation. As the circulation of both the *Herald* and the *Express* soared to beyond the 2 million mark, the *Mail*'s began to fall away and by 1937 its sales had fallen to 1.58 million from a high point of 1.85 million in 1930. The expansion was accompanied by intense circulation wars – gimmicks copied from Northcliffe were used with alacrity by other newspapers to increase their circulation. The huge increase in the staff of newspapers, a rise of 72 per cent between 1924 and 1935, was mainly made up of canvassers, who sold subscriptions at the door, and sales agents.[40] By 1934, nearly 40 per cent of those employed by the national press were canvassers. There was a fundamental realignment in the industry. The growth of the national, Fleet Street newspapers was at expense of provincial press. The 1930s saw the rapid decline of provincial newspapers; in 1921, there were 41 morning and 89 evening provincial newspapers in England which by 1937 had dropped to 28 mornings and 75 provincials.[41] In 1921, of the major 65 towns outside London, 33 had the choice of more than one daily newspaper. By 1947, only 20 of these towns had such a choice. This decline was due to a number of factors including further improvements in transport links which allowed Fleet Street newspapers to extend their tentacles to all parts of Britain and, compared to other European and North American nations, establish a truly national press at the expense of locally or regionally based newspapers. The dominance of the London press in Britain stands in marked contrast to these other press systems.

As the national press was building its pre-eminence in Britain, there was a contraction in the number of national newspaper titles after the First World War. Between 1921 and 1936, 30 national newspapers closed. The rapidly rising circulation was shared by a smaller number of newspaper titles. The ownership of these titles was concentrated in the hands of a smaller and smaller number of men. The Northcliffe Revolution ushered in changes in the nature of ownership of the British press. The first decades of the twentieth century saw the growth of chain ownership. The ownership of the Victorian press was concentrated in the hands of small family concerns. Northcliffe had established a vast press empire by 1921. He controlled *The Times*, the *Daily Mail*, the *Weekly Dispatch* and the London *Evening News*; while his brother Lord Rothermere owned the *Daily Mirror*, the *Sunday Pictorial* as well as the *Daily Record*, *Sunday Mail* and Glasgow's *Evening News* in Scotland. Together they owned the Amalgamated Press, Britain's largest magazine group and their brother, Lester Harmsworth, controlled a chain of local newspapers in the South West of England.[42] The total circulation of these newspapers was just over 6 million. With his death from syphilis in 1922, Northcliffe's family newspapers were divided between his brothers with Lord Rothermere taking control of the *Mail* and associated titles. *The Times* was sold to the Astors, an American family, in 1922.

Northcliffe's main rival was the Canadian, Max Aitken, who became Lord Beaverbrook. He owned fewer titles but his Express Group, which included the *Daily Express*, *Sunday Express* and *Evening Standard*, had a combined circulation of 4.1 million by 1937.[43] At the local level the Berry brothers from Merthyr Tydfil in South Wales, ennobled as Lords Camrose and Kemsley, bought up a considerable number of daily and Sunday newspapers in the provinces of England and Wales. The Berrys built their empire on the basis of two magazines *Advertising World* and *Boxing* and bought into the *Sunday Times*, the *Financial Times* and the *Daily Telegraph*. They went their own ways in the 1930s with

Kemsley taking the provincial titles and the *Sunday Times* and Camrose taking the magazines and the *Telegraph*, which he turned into a passionate supporter of the Conservative Party.[44] Oil millionaire Lord Cowdray took control of *The Financial Times* in the 1930s, having bought into the provincial press to establish the Westminster Press. Lord Southwood, formerly Julias Elias, a self-made millionaire, turned the Odhams Press into the most prosperous printing, publishing and bill-posting business in the world.[45] He had no interest in the content of newspapers or magazines, simply seeing them as things that would keep his presses going. He printed respectable journals, including church publications, as well as Horatio Bottomley's scandal-mongering weekly newspaper, *John Bull*. Southwood first became directly involved in newspaper journalism when he took control of the *People* newspaper which he turned from a small publication into a major-selling Sunday paper with a circulation of over 2 million. The *People*'s success was built on a combination of salesmanship and sensation. The paper pioneered the 'Confession Stories' which were spiced up with sex, passion and exposé. The paper aggressively promoted free gifts, including a free insurance scheme, to sell itself. The success of the *People* led Southwood to look around for a daily newspaper to take up the spare capacity on his printing presses. He became the owner of the *Daily Herald*. Not a Labour supporter and with no interest in the politics of the paper, he acquired the paper as a business venture. He vigorously pursued the objective of building up the circulation of the paper in the 1930s. To attract new readers Southwood placed emphasis on gimmicks and gifts, including offering pens, tea sets, clothes, kitchen equipment and bound sets of Dickens and encyclopaedias. The Odhams publishing group is estimated to have been spending £3 million per year on such gimmicks by the mid-1930s, forcing its rivals to follow suit.[46] It was Southwood's *Daily Herald* that fuelled the newspaper wars of the inter-war years.

The cut-throat competition of the 1930s witnessed the consolidation of the hold of press empires over the British newspaper industry. The five leading companies in the industry by 1937 controlled 43 per cent of all newspaper titles in Britain.[47] The press barons built their empires by takeovers and amalgamations which meant the closure of many newspapers. For a number of observers the coincidence of the emergence of mass circulation newspapers and the concentration of ownership meant that a small number of press barons had acquired a considerable amount of power which directly threatened the development of British democracy.

The press barons

The era of the press barons has shaped our perception of newspaper ownership. The image of a press baron is of megalomania and power, of half-crazed, completely driven, larger than life individuals. Orson Welles's *Citizen Kane* was based on the real-life American press baron, William Randolph Hearst, who refused a photographer's request to return from his assignment in Cuba because the expected conflict had not broken out, with the telegram: 'You supply pictures, I'll supply war.' Northcliffe was referred to as 'Northoleon' by many of his contemporaries. His eccentricities were apparent in the campaigns he ran in his newspapers, including trying to persuade everyone to grow sweet peas and make all men wear a new kind of hat. Beaverbrook is alleged to have hired a Wellington bomber to fly around at night to help him sleep. Such anecdotes reinforce the image of unusual and idiosyncratic individuals. The reality is perhaps a little more mundane. But the press barons were more interventionist than their predecessors. They brought a new style to running newspapers. They exercised more control over the daily operation of their publications. Beaverbrook is reported to have issued 147 instructions in one day to the editor of the *Daily Express*. Every morning at six o'clock he would telephone staff to tell them what he thought of their pieces. Northcliffe's obsession with torture and death led him to intervene directly to insist that his editors incorporated details of murders, including reporting how people died. Failure to comply with what the 'Chief' wanted could mean the sack. Northcliffe once asked one of his employees if he was happy on £5 a week, and on being told yes, Northcliffe sacked him, as he didn't want to employ anyone content with only £5 a week. Newspaper owners before the press barons had intervened in the operation of their titles but the Northcliffe Revolution blurred the division between the editorial and business aspects of the industry. The 'sovereign right' of the editor to run the paper, that had developed under the Walter family at *The Times*, was eroded by the press barons, most of whom intervened in every aspect of the workings of the newspaper. The power of press barons brought commercial interests and values firmly into the day-to-day editorial decision-making process.[48]

This crucial change in how newspapers were run, with increasing power of individual owner to the fore, led to concern about power and political influence of the barons. The press barons saw newspaper ownership as a means by which to impress their views on politicians and political parties as well as shape the pressing issues of the day. Northcliffe was clear that his intent was to achieve political power and influence. He wrote in 1903, 'every extension of the franchise renders more powerful the newspaper and less powerful the politician'.[49] Beaverbrook's purpose for becoming involved in the industry was to 'set up a propaganda paper'.[50] In some ways their motives were no different from newspaper owners and editors in the nineteenth century. Hetherington used his radical newspapers to build a political movement of the working classes while Delane and Barnes of *The Times* sought to influence the conduct of government policy. The press barons differed in their claim to represent the public. They claimed to be 'representative' of their readers in the same way as politicians represented their voters. The owners of mass circulation newspapers competed for the right to speak for British public opinion on an equal footing as politicians. Northcliffe stressed that he represented and spoke for his readers – the '1 104 000 Who Know Daily' – or the 'mobocracy' as one contemporary labelled the readers of the *Daily Mail*.[51] It was the hold the press barons had over public opinion that led contemporary critics, such as Norman Angell, to brand the press barons as 'the worst of all the menaces to modern democracy'.[52] Rather than articulate the voice of the 'masses', Angell, a socialist, saw the cheap, mass circulation newspapers as depriving them of the facts necessary for collective decisions in a democracy. But it was not only critics such as Angell who expressed their concern about the power of the press barons. Tory Prime Minister, Stanley Baldwin, believed that the press lords exercised 'power without responsibility'. Rather than playing a role in building an educated democracy, they used their newspapers for their own personal crusades. He accused them of running their newspapers as 'engines of propaganda for their constantly changing policies, desires, personal wishes, personal likes and dislikes'.[53]

Baldwin spoke for most politicians when he criticized the press barons. Politicians of all persuasions feared the power that newspaper owners had amassed as a result of their hold over public opinion and the masses. The popular press had brought the masses, those 'dirty people with no names' into politics. For the political elite schooled in the oligarchical politics of the nineteenth century, the popular press sullied the conduct of politics by making them respond to what the people wanted rather than what the elites thought was best for the nation. In contrast, the politics of the twentieth century was about mass politics with public opinion being to the fore which, rightly or wrongly, the politicians saw as influenced, if not controlled, by the press. Throughout the development of the British press, politicians and political groups and factions have sought to influence the press directly or indirectly. Much of the nineteenth century saw newspapers owned by or receiving subsidies and loans from parties, political factions and individual political figures. These direct ties continued into the twentieth century – for example, in the 1910s, the *Observer*, the *Globe*, the *Pall Mall Gazette* and the *Standard* all received money from Conservative Central Office. Lloyd George bought the *Daily Chronicle* secretly to promote his interests inside and outside the Liberal Party. The *Herald* was for a number of years subsidized by the TUC and Labour Party.

The close connections between newspapers and politicians also reflected a more practical need. Prior to the 1930s there was no regular flow of information between government and journalists. Press briefings and conferences, press releases, did not exist and in order to do the job, the political reporter had to join the same clubs and wine and dine at the same restaurants to talk to politicians. It was a world of personal connections, between the 'gentlemen of the press' and politicians. It was this close knit, cosy and closed world that the press barons challenged. By and large the press lords were outsiders, self-made men. The rise of a truly commercial press loosened bonds between politicians and newspapers. It allowed press owners to use papers to serve their own agenda rather than the interests of parties or politicians. They tried to use the 'weapon of the press' to break into the world of politics. In the name of representing the public, the press barons sought to coerce government through their newspapers. For Beaverbrook, the press 'when skilfully used, at the right psychological moment, no politician of any party can resist it. It is a flaming sword that will cut through any armour.'[54]

The political power of the press barons

If the press barons sought to influence politics, to what extent were they successful? There is some evidence to show that they had some success, particularly in the early decades of the twentieth century. The First World War was a political high point for the press lords exercising influence on the course of British politics. They are credited with playing a decisive role in the fall of the Asquith government in 1916 and the election of Lloyd George in his place. Beaverbrook and Northcliffe gained political office with their appointments as ministers in the wartime coalition. Their newspapers were used to 'sell' conscription to the British public and changes in army tactics and command were brought about through press campaigns against inefficiency and poor leadership. But it can be argued that it was the special circumstances of the war that gave the press barons their influence. Outside the Great War their political influence seems to have been more limited. Rothermere's *Daily Mail* was regarded as responsible for the Labour Party's failure to win the 1923 General Election when it published an alleged letter from Zinoviev, head of the Communist International, purporting to show Soviet influence in domestic British politics. However, many of the more high-profile interventions by the press barons in British politics ended in overt failure.

Northcliffe failed in his efforts to become a Member of Parliament. Despite buying up all the local newspapers and using them vociferously to support his by-election bid in 1894 for the constituency of Portsmouth, he was defeated at the ballot box. A similar fate befell Rothermere and Beaverbrook when they united to promote a campaign for an Empire Free Trade Zone in the 1930s. Their attempt to mobilize public opinion to try to change government policy failed. They set up the United Empire Party (UEP) to oppose government candidates at by-elections. The full weight of the *Mail* and *Express* groups were put behind the electoral endeavours of the party and two by-election victories were won. But when Baldwin put his personal leadership on line in another by-election, threatening to resign as PM if the UEP defeated the Tory Party candidate, the press barons lost the test of strength. Rothermere's attempts to use his papers to support the British Union of Fascists were also unsuccessful. In January 1934, the *Mirror* ran a story entitled 'Give the Blackshirts a helping hand' while a headline in the *Daily Mail* trumpeted 'Hurrah for the Blackshirts'. The *Evening News* ran a letter competition called 'Why I like the Blackshirts'. In spite of these efforts, the newspapers failed to gain support for BUF and actually lost readers. And even the Zinoviev letter did not actually achieve its intended aim of getting people not to vote Labour – the party's vote actually increased by a million at the 1923 election. Thus the direct influence of the press barons was limited. Often political aspirations had to be considered in the light of commercial needs. When political objectives cut into profits, the press barons backed down. Northcliffe, for example, suspended his campaign against Kitchener's command of the British Army during the First World War when his newspapers started to lose readers. However, as Curran and Seaton point out, to assess the power of the press barons in terms of their ability to persuade people to vote for new parties or candidates or to buy new products or take up new causes is to misunderstand their influence. Rather, this lay in the way in which their newspapers 'provided cumulative support for conservative values and reinforced opposition, particularly among the middle class, to progressive change'.[55] In other words, the power of the press in this sense was to provide support for the status quo and the dominant culture, selecting certain issues for discussion while marginalizing or ignoring others and in particular those voices calling for progressive change. The political influence of the press barons is not to be measured by their direct impact on political events but their indirect influence in helping to shape the whole environment in which politics was conducted. This was the basis of Norman Angell's concern in 1922 that

> **what England (*sic*) thinks is largely controlled by a very few men, not by virtue of the direct expression of any opinion of their own but by controlling the distribution of emphasis in the telling of facts: so stressing one group of them and keeping another group in the background as to make a given conclusion inevitable.**[56]

Part 2

Sound and vision

4

Rescued by Rover: British cinema before the Second World War

The final decade of the nineteenth century saw a number of key developments in mass communication. As we have seen, in 1896, the first popular, mass circulation daily newspaper, the *Daily Mail*, was published. In the same year, however, a more significant event took place – the first showing of a moving picture. The growth of the film industry – or the 'pictures' as they were popularly called – coincided with a shift in the leisure activities of British working people. The years between 1880 and 1895 witnessed 'probably the most rapid general improvement in the condition of the nineteenth-century worker'.[1] Changes in the economic circumstances of the working class, together with the reduction of the working week, led to the freeing up of time and money for leisure. Spare cash and free time led to an increased demand for popular entertainment and amusement. People started to go to the seaside in greater numbers, attend organized sporting events, such as football matches, and enjoy their evenings at the music hall. By the end of the nineteenth century, leisure was well on its way to being regarded as a 'right of all people'[2] and the cinema had quickly established itself as the most popular form of entertainment and recreation in Britain.

The early days

The first public showing of a moving picture in Britain is commonly regarded as having taken place in February 1896 at the London Polytechnic, Regents Street. The Lumière brothers' presentations were simple and direct, including films of events such as the arrival of a train at a railway station or a ship unloading its cargo.[3] The advent of the moving picture was the culmination of a number of technological developments in a range of fields including photography, optical instrumentation, lighting, animation and combustible materials in the nineteenth century. The nineteenth century saw inventions such as the light bulb, the electric telegraph, the telephone and the phonograph which were to provide communication with the means to be a 'mass' process. In the early 1890s, Edison pioneered the moving picture camera and invented the kinetoscope or peepshow. Peering into little black boxes to see flickering pictures, which included titles such as 'Love in a Hammock' and 'What the Butler Saw', became popular. However, it was with the development of the projected film that cinema began. Initially there were various opinions as to the possible application of the new medium. These ranged from using film as a means of preserving archives to a method of assisting in the teaching of science and surgery, with an emphasis on film as the preserve of the classroom and the laboratory. The first film pioneers did not foresee the role of moving pictures in telling stories to entertain and amuse people.

The early years were a period of experimentation. Moving pictures were exhibited in a number of venues and environments. In 1906, Hales Tours were started in Oxford Street where, for a small charge, customers sat in a false railway carriage and were presented with the illusion of travel by filmed scenery moving by the window. Bioscope Teas were fashionable in London where you could take a break from your shopping and enjoy 'a dainty cup of tea and an animated display'.[4] Mobile cinema cars toured all over Britain, showing films from the top of the car to open-air assemblies of people. It was in the musical halls and fairgrounds that film found its first home. Films were shown in the intervals between the musical hall acts or in side booths at fairgrounds.[5] The optical instrument maker, Robert Paul, who had shown his material at Finsbury Technical College on the same day as the Lumière brothers' pioneering show, was hired by the Alhambra Variety Theatre in Leicester Square, where for four years he showed his films. These included extracts from the performances of famous musical acts and topical news items, such as sporting events and royal visits, as well as the first British film with a distinct storyline or narrative, *The Soldier's Courtship*.[6] Filming topical events was made possible by the invention of a new lightweight camera by Birt Acres, who used his invention in 1895 to film the Oxford and Cambridge boat race and the Derby. It was at the fair that most people watched the new discovery. Travelling shows – or 'bioscopes' – brought films to people throughout Britain. One such travelling showman was John Codman, who screened films all over Wales, hauling his projector and screen as well as a 600-seat caravan theatre from one fairground to another, Competition was fierce – in 1907 as many as six travelling film theatres competed with each other at the Neath fair – as people flocked to see the magic of the pictures.[7]

The early film industry was characterized by what one writer has called a 'free booting, buccaneer spirit'. There were no established ways of doing things, no rules to follow and no large organizations dominating the market.[8] The trade revolved around pioneer inventors and travelling showmen. In the beginning there was a variety of film equipment and inventors were more interested in developing the equipment than in making films. Films were only made to sell the equipment to a 'motley crowd of magic lanternists, fairground showmen, itinerant theatre people and music hall magicians'.[9] The competition between this motley crowd was intense. Film-makers stole each other's plots, films and venues. Topical incidents, particularly during the Boer War, were often recreated for the screens and passed off as real events. The showmen resorted to gimmicks and razzmatazz to publicize their film shows, including parades of 'half naked' women which attracted the opprobrium of 'respectable' people.[10] The showmen's main aim was to make money. To do this they had to maximize their audiences and the early cinema became increasingly brash and lacking in taste as the obsession of audiences and film-makers to see everything in front of the camera grew.[11] The legacy of the showmen was to provide the industry with a reputation for squalor, sleaze and bad taste. It was seen as lacking respectability to the extent Alfred Hitchcock could observe that 'no well-bred English person would be seen going into the cinema'.[12] But the showmen ensured the industry would be firmly part of the emerging world of commercial entertainment in Britain.

Audiences enjoyed moving pictures for their novelty. The films were short and silent. The average length was no more than 40 foot, a running time of less than a minute. Their content was crude with the emphasis on movement and action, including items such as 'Sea Waves at Dover', boxing matches as well as trains going in and out of tunnels. Showmen like Codman to bring in the customers would make films of the local towns they visited – the chance for people to see themselves and their town proved highly popular. Films were often badly projected, poorly lit and roughly edited and the flickering images on the screen would often cause headaches. But they very quickly began to attract a huge following and the industry established itself as a lucrative trade. It ceased to be seen as a 'craze' which would disappear almost as quickly as it had come. To fully exploit its commercial worth, the industry had to clean up its act and move from being a sideshow to other forms of cultural entertainment and develop in its own right.

The moment of cinema

Theatre halls devoted solely to the showing of films began to appear from 1904 onwards. In 1907, there were around 250 theatres like the Balham Empire which ran a two-hour programme of films. Theatre owners found that the public preferred dark halls which allowed them to 'see the pictures and have a canoodle'[13] and from 1908 onwards there was a huge expansion in the number of cinema theatres in Britain. By 1914, it is estimated that there were nearly 4000 picture halls with over 600 located in the Greater London area.[14] These halls ranged from the specially constructed 'picture palaces', elegant and architecturally splendid, with names such as the Empire, Majestic or Jewel, which could seat as many as 2000 people, to the local 'flea pits' springing up in the provinces. By the eve of the First World War, the popularity of the new medium was underlined by the fact that overall annual attendance had reached 364 million for a population of just under 40 million.[15] Going to the cinema had become a natural pastime for many people.

Many of the newly established sites were comfortable and contained the most modern amenities, with marbled walls and ornate mirrors, plush carpets and uniformed attendants, catering for all the film-goer's needs. The theatres were only one of several developments before the First World War that enabled the industry to attract a wider audience. Exhibitors were forced to pay more attention to the production of films as people tired of the 'local scenes and the short slapstick comedies which were usually available'.[16] In 1903, an American, Edwin

Porter, an electrician and cameraman with the Edison Company, produced a film, a western called *The Great Train Robbery*. It was 10 minutes long, had a number of shots of different locations and a clearly defined story line. In Britain the narrative film was developed by Cecil Hepworth, who in 1904 produced *Rescued by Rover*. It ran for 7 minutes and used professional actors for the first time. The narrative film provided the cinema with a product that offered entertainment that could not be found elsewhere.[17] Increasingly, the industry became interested in the artistic quality and aesthetic merit of the film and the product became more complex. The silent era produced particular kinds of films – genres such as the western, melodrama, comedies, romances and travelogues – which became staple features of the cinema. The comic film was the most popular before the First World War; comic films constituted 38 per cent of all the films released in 1913.[18]

Theatre hall proprietors employed the whole gamut of techniques to promote their films, including posters, electric signs and announcements. In 1909, US companies adopted the 'star system' to build up a following for their films. The focus on the private lives and personalities of film stars became a central part of Western film culture as anonymity was dropped in return for large salaries and stardom. The first true British star was Gladys Sylvani, who appeared in Cecil Hepworth's film, *Rachel's Sin* in 1910. From the initial short screenings, film presentation developed into a set two-feature programme with newsreels, organ music and advertisements.[19] The silent newsreel – or 'animated newspaper' as it was called by many in the trade at the time – was part of the cinema from the early days but obtained prominence during the First World War. The French-owned *Pathe Gazette* and *Gaumont Graphic* pioneered the silent newsreel with competition from a number of small home-grown companies, the most important being *Topical Budget* until its demise in 1931. Each produced a bi-weekly newsreel which by 1911 had settled into a format of five 1-minute items on daily topical events. The kinds of topics the newsreels covered is illustrated by the content of Pathe's first issue – a sculling contest, a strike of Camden factory girls and Queen Alexandra leaving to visit Italy.[20] Celebrities, royal personages and dramatic occurrences, such as fires, accidents and public demonstrations, were prominent. Newsreels became very popular in the 1920s and 1930s, especially as there was no television or illustrated picture magazines and the newspapers' reproduction of photographs was still primitive.

The search for respectability led the film industry to address the need to control what was shown. Moral and social reformers had expressed their concerns about the influence of the new medium from the outset. They were worried that the cinema halls which packed in people close together in the dark would encourage lust and promiscuity. There was also the matter of health hazards; some of the audience would be so transfixed by the images that they would urinate in their seats. Many of the early theatres reeked of urine and disinfectant. Fire was also a risk at venues where celluloid was used. As a result, the 1909 Cinematograph Act gave powers to local authorities to grant licences for venues where films were screened. Under the guise of public safety local authorities started to use the licensing system to influence what was shown. For example, in 1910, the London Country Council banned a film of the world title boxing match between Jack Johnson and James L Jeffries. Johnson was the first black man to win the title – which may have had something to do with the LCC's decision to ban the film.[21] To stave off further official intervention and arbitrary interference from local authorities, and to show they were behaving responsibly in controlling what appeared, the industry put forward the idea of a board of censorship.

The British Board of Film Censors (BBFC) began its work in 1913. Its main task was to either classify or cut or reject the films submitted to it and the Board could either provide feature films with an 'A' certificate (adult only) or a 'U' certificate (universal, which meant adults and children) or withhold a certificate. The BBFC was set up by the industry, financed by fees from the producers submitting their films, and the head of the Board, the chief censor, was appointed by the Home Secretary. However, the Board had no legal status and producers were not obliged to submit their films. There were no written rules or code regarding the classification of films. The Board consisted of its head, the President, a secretary and four censors. BBFC certificates were only a guide to local authorities who could ignore them. In the absence of any formal code, it was the personality of the people who were in charge of the Board that was crucial in shaping its practice in the early years.[22] The first President was a former chief examiner of plays at the Lord Chamberlain's Office, but more significantly, the BBFC's first secretary was a former journalist and the secretary of the Cinematograph Exhibitors Association, James Brooke Wilkinson, who ran the Board until 1948. Under him the Board's work was shrouded in secrecy and with little outside scrutiny the partially sighted Wilkinson played a crucial role in determining the Board's approach to film censorship.

Only two specific rules guided the Board's work when it started in 1913 – no nudity and no portrayal of Jesus Christ. This reflected the fact that the main pressure from local authorities on the content of films centred around issues of morality.[23] However, the number of rules relating to film content multiplied and by the end of the year 166 films had been cut or banned.[24] In its first annual report the BBFC reported that its general principle was the elimination of 'anything repulsive and objectionable to the good taste and better feelings of the English audiences'.[25] The report listed 22 grounds on which films had been cut or banned. These included cruelty to animals, medical operations, indelicate sexual situations, vulgarity and impropriety in conduct and dress, drunken scenes carried to excess and scenes tending to disparage public characters and institutions. This list, as James Robertson points out, encapsulated the moral and social values of late Victorian and Edwardian Britain and was at the core of the Board's work until the Second World War.

The severity of the censorship operated by the Board surprised the film industry. It also failed to stave off local government interference. Local authorities became even stricter in their approach to film censorship and films passed by the Board were subjected to further cuts when they went before local censors. By the end of 1916, the Home Office proposed, with the consent of local authorities and fuelled by the worries of some of Britain's chief constables about the impact of cinema on crime, that a new Board of Censors should be constituted as part of the Home Office with legal sanction on any film producer or distributor who attempted to ignore censorship. Some British distributors had released pictures, primarily American films, without reference to the BBFC. The push for state censorship took place against the background of the first enquiry into the cinema in Britain organized by the National Council of Public Morals. This body involved many organizations known for their hostility to the cinema and during the enquiry which lasted for six months in 1917 evidence was taken from 47 witnesses, including the new head of the BBFC who explained the now 43 rules which if broken could lead to a film being banned or cut. Much of the evidence emphasized a link between the cinema and crime and juvenile deliquency.[26] Crucially, some senior policemen and the large majority of those working directly with the poor disagreed that the 'kinetic power of films' was responsible for crime and juvenile deliquency.[27] With much foresight the commission came to the conclusion that juvenile crime could not simply be attributed to one factor such as the cinema and it did not recommend – as some expected – that children should be banned from going to the pictures. The film industry was given a relatively good bill of health. It was recommended that censorship should be retained and the overall conclusions were favourable to the continuation of the BBFC's work.

BBFC grounds for censorship, 1926

The BBFC's codified grounds for banning or cutting films as given in the 1926 Annual Report were:

RELIGIOUS

1 The materialised figure of Christ.
2 Irreverent quotations of religious texts.
3 Travesties of familiar Biblical quotations and well-known hymns.
4 Titles to which objections would be taken by religious organisations.
5 Travesty and mockery of religious services.
6 Holy vessels amidst incongruous surroundings or shown or used in a way which would be looked upon as desecration.
7 Comic treatment of incidents connected with death.
8 Painful insistences of realism in death bed scenes.

POLITICAL

1 Lampoons of the institutions of the monarchy.
2 Propaganda against the monarchy and attacks on royal dynasties.
3 Unauthorised use of royal or university arms.
4 Themes which are likely to wound the just susceptibilities of our allies.

5 White men in a state of degradation amidst native surroundings.
6 Inflammatory sub-titles and Bolshevist propaganda.
7 Equivocal situations between white girls and men of other races.

MILITARY

1 Officers in British regiments shown in a disgraceful light.
2 Horrors in warfare and realistic scenes of massacre.

SOCIAL

1 The improper use of the names of well-known British institutions.
2 Incidents which reflect a mistaken conception of the police forces in this country in the administration of justice.
3 Sub-titles in the nature of swearing, and expressions regarded as objectionable in this country.
4 Painful hospital scenes.
5 Scenes in lunatic asylums and particularly in padded cells.
6 Workhouse officials shown in an offensive light.
7 Girls and women in a state of intoxication.
8 Orgy scenes.
9 Subjects which are suitable only for scientific or professional audiences.
10 Suggestive, indecorous and semi-nude dancing.
11 Nude and semi-nude figures, both in actuality and shadowgraph.
12 Girls' clothes pulled off, leaving them in scanty garments.
13 Men leering at exposure of women's undergarments.
14 Abortion.
15 Criminal assault on girls.
16 Scenes in and connected with houses of ill repute.
17 Bargain cast for a human life which is to be terminated in murder.
18 Marital infidelity and collusive divorce.
19 Children following the example of a drunken and dissolute father.
20 Dangerous mischief easily imitated by children.
21 Subjects dealing with venereal disease.

QUESTIONS OF SEX

1 The use of the phrase 'sex appeal' in sub-titles.
2 Themes indicative of habitual immorality.
3 Women in alluring or provocative attitudes.
4 Procuration.
5 Degrading exhibitions of animal passion.
6 Passionate and unrestrained embraces.
7 Incidents intended to show clearly that an outrage has been perpetrated.
8 Lecherous old men.
9 White slave traffic.
10 Innuendoes with a direct indecent tendency.
11 Indecorous bathroom scenes.
12 Extenuation of a woman sacrificing her honour for money on the plea of some laudable object.
13 Female vamps.

14 Indecent wall decorations.
15 Men and women in bed together.

CRIME

1 Hanging, realistic or comic.
2 Executions and incidents connected therewith.
3 Objectionable prison scenes.
4 Methods of crime open to imitation.
5 Stories in which criminal element is predominant.
6 Crime committed and condoned for ostensibly good reason.
7 'Crook' films in which sympathy is enlisted for the criminals.
8 'Third degree' scenes.
9 Opium dens.
10 Scenes of, traffic in and distribution of illicit drugs.
11 The drugging and ruining of young girls.
12 Attempted suicide by asphyxiation.
13 Breaking bottles on men's heads.

CRUELTY

1 Cruel treatment of children.
2 Cruelty to animals.
3 Brutal fights carried to excess, including gouging of eyes, clawing of faces and throttling.
4 Knuckle fights.
5 Girls and women fighting.
6 Realistic scenes of torture.

Source: Robertson, James (1985) *The British Board of Film Censors*, Appendix 1.

With a change of government in 1917, the threat of direct state censorship was staved off and in the years to come the government appreciated the informal set-up for censoring film content. The introduction of the BBFC and the building of modern cinema halls enabled the British film industry to overcome the reputation established by its low birth. Respectability was finally achieved in 1925 when the King and Queen attended the Marble Arch Pavilion to see their first picture. The cinema now started to provide amusement and information of higher quality to people from all walks of life. The trade adopted a tone that was to make it more appealing to the growing suburban audience and the middle classes became involved in the running of the industry.

The growth of a film industry

Compared to the United States, where financiers quickly saw the profit potential of film, British capital was slow to move into the film industry. British banks were put off from investing in the industry by the reputation of the peep shows and the concerns over what was shown. The City's contempt of the industry can be summed up by the remarks of the Governor of the Bank of England, Montagu

Norman, who, when a colleague told him that he was thinking of investing in the industry, said: 'Wyndham, you're surely not going to interest yourself in that awful film industry? It's no good, Wyndham, it's unsound. And those dreadful people are not of your class. Keep out of it!'[28] Film-makers were often dismissed as 'long hairs', 'corduroy wearers', and financially irresponsible. However, the lure of massive profits led many to swallow their prejudices. As one financier told a Cinematograph Exhibitors' dinner in 1920: 'Formerly it was difficult to raise even a small capital for a cinema enterprise. Today if you ask for a million you get half a million oversubscribed.'[29] Large-scale capital began to flow into the industry, directed almost totally to the exhibition side. In 1908, there were three exhibition companies registered in Britain with a total capital of £110,000; by the eve of the First World War the number had risen to 1833 companies whose combined capital amounted to just over £11 million.[30]

These companies organized their cinema halls into circuits. Electric Theatres was one of the first, with five theatres by the end of 1908. The Provincial Cinematograph Theatres (PCT) was founded by the financier, Sir William Bass, in 1909 with the intention of opening a cinema theatre in every town in Britain with a population of 250,000 or more.[31] It was responsible for constructing the first large-scale cinema theatre in Wales, the 648-seat Electric in Cardiff. By 1914, there were over 109 circuits throughout the country comprising approximately 20 per cent of all cinema theatres. The First World War saw a brief downturn in the growth of cinema theatres with, it is estimated, the closure of nearly 700 after the imposition of a tax on imported goods in 1915 and the introduction of the Entertainments Tax in 1916.[32] However, the immediate post-war years saw a boom in exhibition. Press magnate, Lord Beaverbrook bought a controlling interest in PCT which by March 1920 had increased its capital to £3 million. As more large-scale finance entered the industry, chain circuits tightened their hold over film exhibition and by 1929 capital in the industry had risen to £70 million with 167 circuits controlling about 1000 cinemas.[33]

The industry's expansion was accompanied by a process of rationalization. The restructuring has to be seen in terms of the unusual nature of the product. Film is a durable commodity which can be used over and over again until worn out. Films were sold initially at a fixed price, sixpence per foot, no matter what their content. This had implications for the creative process as there was no incentive to produce a high-quality product, either physically or aesthetically. It also meant that exhibitors were able to stockpile films and show them repeatedly. This open sale of films ultimately worked against the rapid growth of film production in Britain. It handicapped film exhibitors whose audiences became easily bored with the same films and demanded a wider range of product. The result was the emergence of a 'hiring system' which brought a new actor into the industry, the renter or distributor. Rather than films being sold they were now hired or rented to exhibitors. This allowed the exhibitor to show more films and led to demand for more films from the producers. The rationalization of the market for film was confirmed with the establishment of bodies representing the different parts of the industry – the Kinematograph Film Makers Association in 1906, the Incorporated Association of Film Renters in 1910 and the Cinematograph Exhibitors Association in 1912.[34] However, it was perhaps too late for British film production which had lagged behind foreign competitors from the start. According to one film historian: 'By the time the realisation dawned that the film industry would need larger infusions of capital and more rationalised modes of production, the Americans had swept the field.'[35]

From the outset, the British film market was dominated by foreign producers. As early as 1910 British film producers were unable to compete with their rivals in Europe and America. That year Pathe dominated the market with 36 per cent of all films released being from France; 28 per cent were American, 17 per cent were Italian while only 15 per cent were from British film-makers.[36] By the outbreak of the First World War, the American share of the British market had risen to nearly 60 per cent. The war saw off the competition from France, Denmark and Italy and, by 1923, Hollywood controlled between 85 and 90 per cent of the British market, making almost a third of its total foreign earnings from this country.[37] British film production experienced a steady decline. By 1923, only 10 per cent of the films released in Britain were made by British film-makers, falling to 5 per cent in the following year. In 'Black November' 1924, every British studio was idle. In 1925, only 45 British pictures appeared on British screens and in 1926 the number dropped to 37.[38] By 1926, the situation of British film production was desperate. Investors were not attracted to British films. The profits to be made from the industry was in showing American films and it was into exhibition rather than production they put their money.

There has been much conjecture over the reasons for Hollywood's hold over British film screens and the relative lack of popularity of British films with British audiences. The technical qualities of British films were seen as poor, described by film goers as 'stunted' and 'artificial' compared to the 'slick, polished, fast moving and often spectacular' product from Hollywood.[39] American actors were praised for their 'natural and lifelike' acting; according to one cinema goer: 'they seemed to have the knack of living the part they are acting, and the players in British pictures mostly seem to be "acting" the part they are supposed to be living'.[40] More significant was the apparent remoteness of British films from their audiences. The entertainment served up by Hollywood seemed to be in tune with British audiences. As one critic put it: 'American movies sometimes came nearer the actual attitudes of the British audiences than most British ones.'[41] Class was an important determinant in this respect. The 'intellectual' middle class was less likely to favour Hollywood film. At all stages of its development the film industry in this country had encountered considerable hostility. The social snobbery around the cinema led many to dismiss films as 'fodder for the mindless'.[42] American films, in particular, were singled out. But for the urban working class, American films offered a breath of fresh air from the rigid hierarchy of the British class system.

They presented a picture of a vibrant society in which, in spite of all that was wrong, things were being done, and could be done, to bring about change. Hollywood gained respect from British audiences for the ways in which they were prepared to tackle social issues. This contrasted with British films which were steeped in the theatrical tradition, dominated by upper- and middle-class accents and concerns and reluctant – or prevented from by the BBFC – to represent the social problems and issues of the period.

Rescued by the government

The decline of British film production caused the government to intervene directly in the industry. Pressure had begun to mount on the government to take action to save British film production in 1925 when a small number of mainly unemployed British filmmakers gained recognition from the Federation of British Industries (FBI) for the plight of their industry. The FBI launched a campaign for action. British industrialists accepted that British films had an important role to play in providing publicity for British goods at home and abroad. The government was concerned about the propaganda importance of film. Prime Minister Stanley Baldwin told the House of Commons of 'the enormous power which film is developing for propaganda purposes, and the danger to which we in this country and our Empire subject ourselves if we allow that method of propaganda to be entirely in the hands of foreign countries'.[43] Some British exhibitors and the American distributors were strongly opposed to any intervention in the film industry, while support came largely from British film-makers and the small number of British distributors. Exhibitors blamed the industry's problems on the block-booking system operated by American distributors. They could only book a popular film from the distributor if they also took a large number of other films. These other films were often booked unseen and sometimes even before they had been made, making it difficult for British films to obtain a large number of bookings. Attempts were made by the different sections of the industry to work out a voluntary system to protect British films but the scheme drawn up was rejected by the exhibitors.

The Cinematograph Films Act was introduced in 1927 with the aim of assisting British film production by controlling the discriminatory booking practices of US distributors and by placing a quota for British films of 7.5 per cent for distributors and 5 per cent for exhibitors. The quotas were set to rise gradually until they reached a maximum of 20 per cent for both in 1936. Certain types of films were excluded from the quota – for example, newsreels, advertising and educational films. There was the problem with what constituted a 'British film'. It was decided that to be registered as British, a film had to satisfy three requirements: the scriptwriter was a British subject, the studio scenes had to be filmed in a studio within the British Empire and a minimum of 70 per cent of the labour costs of the film went to British subjects.[44] A loophole which was to be exploited was that to qualify as British a production company did not have to be British controlled but simply have a majority of British directors. The Act had an impact even before it became law. In March 1927 John Maxwell, head of one of the Britain's distribution companies, set up British International Pictures and Isidore Ostrer brought together a number of distribution, production and exhibition companies to found the Gaumont-British Picture Corporation.[45] These were the first attempts at the vertical integration of the different sectors of the industry. The 1930s witnessed a growing concentration of power in the industry, as the attempt was made to create one or two large British film combines to challenge the major American companies.

There was a huge expansion and reorganization of the British film industry following the Act. Between 1925 and 1936 more than 640 film production companies were established, 395 of them during the first five years of the 1930s.[46] It was not all plain sailing. The advent of sound in 1929 saw the collapse of many of the new companies. An overall contraction of the capital of the companies registered on the stock market had occurred between 1927 and 1928, falling from £2.3 million to £254,000. The only company to make a profit during this period was Maxwell's British International Pictures which had made Britain's first talkie – *Blackmail*. The industry adjusted to sound and by the mid-1930s most of the major companies experienced a large increase in profits. Gaumont-British Pictures' profits rose from just over £462,000 in 1933 to £720,483 in 1935 while British International Pictures recorded a profit of around £656,000 in 1935.[47] Increased profits were translated into the construction of more studio space – most of the major British studios were built at this time. The growth in production facilities was matched by a spectacular cinema hall building programme. In 1926, 3000 cinemas were in operation, rising to 4448 by 1935, and reaching nearly 5000 by the end of 1938. Between 1932 and 1934 alone, 302 new cinemas were built. Many old cinemas were knocked down and replaced by grand, spacious picture palaces which went a long way to remove the image of the cinema hall as an old 'flea pit'. Oscar Deutsch's Odeons which popped up all over Britain in the early 1930s were the 'quintessence of modern architecture'.[48] Clean, bright, comfortable and simple, they were distinctive symbols of the decade and by 1937 his circuit amounted to more than 200 cinema halls. Deutsch was responsible for moving cinema going from the city centres to the suburbs in his mission to entertain the nation, thereby helping to broaden the appeal of films.

Increased prosperity led to the entry into the film business of the 'hard-headed financial bastions of the City'. With profits rising, the City tried to cash in on the boom. By the mid-1930s the purse strings of the British film industry were in the hands of large financial and banking institutions. The National Provincial Bank financed Gaumont-British while Oscar Deutsch's enterprise was backed by Eagle Star and British Dominions Insurance.[49] Other financial institutions with considerable involvement in the industry included Prudential Assurance, Equity and Life Insurance and the Law Debenture Corporation. In 1936, a group of leading businessmen, including the heads of Bovril, Wiggins Teape, and flour-milling tycoon, J. Arthur Rank, joined together to establish the General Cinema Finance Corporation (GCF) with the intent of helping to finance the resurgence of the British film industry. With more production companies, the opening or extending of studios, the building of new theatres, the 1930s can be seen as a significant period of expansion and modernization in British cinema history. The industry's growth was accompanied by a boom in cinema attendances and the rising popularity of British pictures.

The essential social habit of an age

In the 1930s the cinema dominated people's leisure to the extent that one historian called it the 'essential social habit of the age'.[50] People flocked to the cinema halls in large numbers. Attendances rose from 364 million in 1914 to 903 million in 1934 and by the end of the decade over 1000 million people were going to the cinema every year. In 1938, 20 million tickets were sold each week and 25 per cent of these people went at least twice a week.[51] For most people going to the cinema was simply the 'most exciting event of the week'.[52] But who were these people? As a pastime cinema going was dominated by the working class; it was, in the words of a survey of London life in 1934, 'par excellence the people's entertainment'.[53] The first survey of cinema admissions conducted that year found that 80 per cent of cinema goers went in the cheap seats. The loyalty of working people to the medium was not shaken by the deprivation and debilitation of unemployment. Over 80 per cent of unemployed people in Glasgow and Liverpool in the mid-1930s said they went to the cinema at least once a week.[54]

The cinema had a particular appeal to women and children. Jeffrey Richards notes that 'while a large proportion of the population at large went to the cinema occasionally, the enthusiasts were young, working class, urban and more often female than male'.[55] He cites a study of York in the 1930s which found that half of the cinema attenders were children and youngsters and 75 per cent of all adults going to the cinema were women.[56] Women's leisure prior to the First World War had largely been confined to the domestic sphere. The cinema allowed them to participate in a recreational activity outside the home and the industry was eager to take account of women's views in the selection of what films to show. This perhaps explains the popularity of the love story and romance in the films exhibited. A survey of Liverpool's cinema-going audience in 1929–30 found that 45 per cent of the films exhibited were romances.[57]

The success of British pictures

These audiences were watching more British pictures then ever before or since. The 1930s was a boom time for British pictures. In 1936, 212 British pictures were released, rising to 228 in 1937.[58] British pictures, stars and directors started to earn national and international acclaim. And, in 1933, money with the box-office success in Britain and America of Alexander Korda's film, *The Private Life of Henry VIII*. The film, costing £93,000 to make, earned over half a million pounds, much of it from the American market. On its first night at the Radio City Music Hall in New York, it set a world box-office record.[59] Its star, Charles Laughton, won an Oscar for his performance as the king. Other successful British films of the period included Alfred Hitchcock's *The Thirty-Nine Steps*, which was made in 1935, starring Robert Donat, and had a record-breaking five-month run in the West End. British film stars, such as Gracie Fields, George Formby and Jessie Matthews, began to emerge. 'Our Gracie' was not so much a film star as, in the words of the film historian Jeffrey Richards, a 'phenomenon'. The 'Lancashire Lass' became Britain's highest paid film performer and established an international reputation, becoming a Hollywood star in 1938 when Twentieth Century Fox signed her for four films at a salary of £200,000, described at the time as 'the highest salary ever paid to a human being'.[60] Fields was one of the first working-class stars of British cinema. From a music-hall background, she established her popularity in films such as *Sally in Our Alley* (1931) and *Sing As We Go* (1934), in the process making herself into a symbol for the nation during the Depression years.

The British film-maker who represented the 'success' of the industry in the 1930s was Alexander Korda. A Hungarian émigré, he had come to London in 1931 and soon established the reputation of his company, London Films. His first film. *Wedding Rehearsal*, was well received and he embarked on more ambitious projects. The success of *The Private Life of Henry VIII* enabled him to raise considerable funds from the City to further his ambitions. He spent a million pounds on building a massive studio complex at Denham in Buckinghamshire from which his company turned out blockbusters such as *Catherine the Great* (1933) with Marlene Dietrich, *The Private Life of Don Juan* (1934) with Douglas Fairbanks Snr, *The Scarlet Pimpernel* (1934) and *Rembrandt* (1936). Denham also produced the classics of British imperial cinema including *The Four Feathers*, *Sanders of the River* and *The Drum*. Korda's films were historical dramas and adaptations of the classics, something for which the British film industry established a reputation, both at home and abroad. None of these films – with the exception of *The Private Life of Henry VIII* – had much impact at the box office. Their success was with the critics rather than the audiences. But Korda's films did have success in America which was important in symbolic terms – it convinced British film-makers that they could achieve popular box-office success in America with their costume dramas and literary films. As the decade proceeded, a division emerged in the British cinema between the prestige productions, primarily aimed at the international market, which were a commercial flop at home and the domestic comedies, with Northern stars such as Fields, Formby and Will Hay, which did not travel well but were profitable at the home box office.

Even with the fortunes of British films and film stars at their highest, Hollywood still dominated what British people wanted to watch. British films accounted for no more than 30 per cent of releases in any one year in the 1930s. While the comedies of Fields and Formby and more serious films such as *South Riding*

(1938) and *The Stars Look Down* (1939) struck a chord with British audiences through the portrayal of recognizable working-class life, it was America's celluloid heroes and heroines who captured their hearts. The top stars throughout the 1930s were American: strong men such as James Cagney, Clark Gable and Walter Beery; comics such as Laurel and Hardy as well as musical performers such as Fred Astaire and Ginger Rogers and Shirley Temple. In comparison, many of the home-produced films were of 'dubious quality'. The 1927 Cinematograph Act led to the production of 'quota quickies' – films which satisfied nobody, only the quota target set by the government. Some surprised their makers and achieved box-office success and the quota films provided an introduction to the industry for directors, such Michael Balcon, who was to head up production for Gaumont, and Michael Powell, who became an important figure in the industry during and after the Second World War. But by and large they were the B movies of the day, mostly poor imitations of Hollywood films.

If we know what people watched in the 1930s, we know less about what they thought about what they were watching. There is no end of material about what government agencies, politicians, intellectuals and critics believed to be the effect of cinema-going. As for the ordinary film-goer, there is little documented about his or her experience of going to the pictures until the mid-1930s. There was, however, more to going to the pictures than just watching the films. It was a night out and the flavour of the night out is captured best in some of the novels about the period. Gwyn Thomas, the South Wales novelist, writes about the mixture of apathy, anticipation and humour in a visit to the local cinema, 'The Dog', in his novel, 'A Frost on my Frolic', at the beginning of the Second World War.

Visiting the local cinema

We make our way to the cinema at the end of our street. It is called 'The Laugh and Scratch' or simply 'The Dog' from the way people have of itching after a few minutes inside it.

We approach the portal of The Dog. It is not officially open yet. The man who stands at the entrance controlling the queue and sticking up posters is Talfan Phelps . . . he was out of work for so long that the shock of getting all these duties to perform in the porch of The Dog and a fine green uniform to do them in went to his head and he has become a chronic traditionalist and bitterly anti-radical, wishful only to apologise to the ruling groups for the sour things he thought about them during his years of idleness and under-feeding.

There is a rush of kids into the entrance, making towards the pay-box. These kids are not supposed to go in without parents or guardians. They see things just as peculiar at home as they do in The Dog but as they do not have to pay to look at home it does not make so deep or bruising an impression and that is why they have the rule about parents or guardians. The way they get around this at The Dog is either to sap and burrow and come up through three loose floorboards in the eight pennies or take any kid who is over ten or tall for his age and put him forward as a parent . . . Talfan makes the best of it. The flood passes him on its way to the box-office. He looks pleased to find bits of his uniform still sticking to his body when he finds himself in the clear again.

When Merlin Pugh the Operator up in his little box starts operating there is a shout from the audience . . . When Merlin started this job at The Dog his way with the projector and the rolls of film was not very bright. Sometimes we would sit for an hour with the place in darkness and nothing on the screen . . . and Merlin sitting in his box as complacent as you like projecting the whole of a seven reel film on the wall behind him, not conscious at all that relations between him and the public were in any way odd. Another method which he mastered was to show films backwards and we got used to the sight of a man right at the beginning of a film being buried, then shot, then drinking gaily with his friends, then working his way up to gradually being a baby, throwing in his mother's courtship as the final climax. Merlin even went so far as to defend this way of projection, claiming that it saved a lot of wear and tear on the nerves, there being no anxiety about what was going to happen to the principal character.

Source: Thomas, Gwyn (1953) *A Frost on My Frolic*, London: Victor Gollancz, pp. 135–44.

The slump

The 'boom years' of British film were short-lived. The bubble burst in 1937 with Korda's London Films being one of the first companies to run into financial difficulties. The company made a loss of over £330,000 in May 1936, and started to lay off people and cut salaries at the beginning of 1937. The sale of the Denham studio the following year effectively marked the end of Korda's influence over the industry. More significant was the collapse of Gaumont-British. In March 1937, the Gaumont studios at Shepherd's Bush and Gaumont Film Distributor closed when the company reported a trading debt of £100,000. Gaumont declared that it would no longer produce its own films and Gainsborough Pictures, representing Gaumont's production interests, was taken over by General Film Distributors (GFD). In 1937, only 20 British independent production companies remained.[61] As a result, the number of British films produced fell drastically, from 228 in the year ending 31 March 1938 to 90 in the following year[62] and in 1938 only half the available studio space in Britain was used.

The reasons for this decline have their roots in the rapid expansion of the early 1930s. Film companies had over-extended themselves with their efforts to follow Korda into the American market. The success of *The Private Life of Henry VIII* proved illusory and most of his subsequent pictures lost money in America. Others who tried had little success in entering the American market. According to one biographer, Korda 'gave the British cinema its first taste of international success and then undermined it all by trying to pull himself and the industry up too quickly'.[63] The industry's financial expansion in the 1930s was not built on secure economic foundations. There was excessive speculation in the industry and financial institutions, through ignorance of the workings of the film business and motivated by the desire of quick, short-term profit, threw money at all kinds of dubious and doubtful production companies. In the first 10 months of 1936 loans of £13 million were made to the British film industry and 'banks, insurance companies, legal trusts and motor manufacturers were falling over each other in their eagerness to stake a claim'.[64] The boom was based on nothing more than expectations and considerable losses resulted. Several producers simply took the money and ran, leaving the insurance company and banks to pick up the bill. Westminster Bank lost over £1 million in this way and one production company, with a capital of less than £100, was able to secure advance loans of over £200,000 for projects it never completed.[65] Investors fled the industry almost as quickly as they had arrived and with a number of court cases in 1939 the industry was left tainted by scandal.

There was increasing concern throughout the 1930s about the impact of 'quota quickies' on British film production. Many of these films were made for foreign, particularly American, distribution companies, to meet the stipulations of the 1927 Act. These companies were simply interested in cheap films and paid no attention to quality. Films at the Twickenham studios, one of the leading quota enterprises, were often shot in 12 days and at the ridiculously low cost of £1 per foot. Rates of pay were low and the hours were long. The better directors and camera operators left the industry or went abroad and there was some annoyance at the number of continental workers employed by British studios. Some argued that it was a deliberate policy adopted by American distributors to undermine the 'quality' of the British film. In 1936, the Moyne Committee met to review the working of the 1927 Act. After taking evidence from all sections of the industry, it concluded that the Act had assisted the development of the industry and recommended the continuation of the quota system with a number of changes. The 1938 Film Act did not implement all the changes suggested by Moyne, coming as it did in the midst of the slump that occurred after the Committee's deliberations. However, it did renew the quota system, with quotas for distributors and exhibitors rising. Measures to ensure the production of quality films were introduced. A minimum cost of £7500 for the production of a quota film was set down and a fair wages clause ensured that trade union rates would be paid to those involved in making quota films. The new legislation did not have much time to make an impact before the outbreak of war in 1939. It did, however, confirm that the government had a role to play in the development of the industry.

The rise of Rank

The slump in the late 1930s brought about a complete realignment of the British film industry. One man, the industrialist, J. Arthur Rank, was the main beneficiary and by 1941 he had taken control of much of the film industry. Rank, described as a 'genial, if enigmatic, Yorkshireman, driven in business by an unshakeable religious faith' had first become involved in the industry in 1933 when he financed the equipping of Methodist church halls and Sunday schools with film projectors.[66] His ambitions at the start were limited to assisting film to play a role in the spreading of the word of Christ. To this end, he became involved briefly in First National production company with Lady Yule, another millionaire who ran a film production company as a hobby, and together they built the Pinewood studios. Rank moved to the centre of the industry in 1936 when he joined the newly formed General Cinema Finance Corporation along with other leading industrialists. Rank slowly began to consolidate a position of power inside the consortium and in March 1936 played an important role in the take-over of the General Film Distributors, Britain's main distribution company, of which he was a financial backer. In 1937, he bought a controlling share of the Pinewood studios and the following year the Denham studios, merging both to form the Denham and Pinewood Studios Ltd. By 1939, Rank had control of Britain's main distributor as well as access to the best studios to make pictures. He now sought control of a cinema circuit. His target was the Odeon chain and from 1939 he began to buy shares in the enterprise, obtaining a seat on the Board in 1939. He did not, however, gain control of the chain until 1941 on the death of Oscar Deutsch at the early age of 48. In that year Rank sprung one of his greatest coups when he obtained control of the Gaumont-British cinema chain. Assisted by the untimely death of his main rival at ABC, John Maxwell, Rank was able to wrest away ownership of Gaumont-British from the Ostrer family who had fought off attempts to take over the company since 1937. As a result, by 1941, J. Arthur Rank exercised almost unchallenged influence over everything from the price of admission to the production of films in Britain. Rank was regarded by some as the man who saved the British film industry. He had come to the rescue of an ailing industry and provided finance to help it stave off total collapse. Others saw him as an opportunist who made the most of a set of fortuitous circumstances, including the death of his main rivals and the slump in the industry, which had allowed him to buy up assets at bargain prices. It is estimated that in return for an outlay of £1.7 million, Rank acquired assets of nearly £50 million.[67] At the outset of the war, he had built up a position of almost unchallengeable authority in the British film industry.

5

The golden age of the wireless: the early years of the British Broadcasting Corporation (BBC)

In the years between the wars, the wireless – as the radio was then popularly called – for the first time brought the sound of the outside world into British homes. Sound broadcasting before the Second World War was the responsibility of one organization, the British Broadcasting Corporation (BBC). The BBC began as a private company in 1922, formed by the leading wireless manufacturers to supply programmes to the growing number of people buying radio sets. At the outset broadcasting was a local service with stations set up in the main conurbations of Britain, such as Manchester, Birmingham and London, to serve the communities within range of their signal. These stations only broadcast for a few hours and their programmes were informal, irregular and relatively unstructured. Few people were employed to produce them and the total audience was no more than 149,000 people. By the end of the 1930s, the BBC had evolved into a large corporation employing over 5000 people. From its headquarters in London it broadcast to an audience of 9 million households, nearly 34 million people throughout Britain, and provided a regular schedule of programmes whose tone and style were instantly recognizable. The Corporation had become a national institution, firmly etched into the landscape of British society; along with the diplomatic service, Oxbridge and the City, it was seen as part of the 'British establishment'. In 1938, a national newspaper could describe the BBC as being as typical and representative a national institution as the Bank of England: 'reliable and responsible, the safe depository of the nation's cultural capital'.[1] In a very short period of time the BBC had transformed itself from just another 'ordinary commercial enterprise' into a major national institution whose influence, as one former employee stated in 1940, was comparable to that 'once exercised by the Court'.

The BBC's transformation is often presented as the personal achievement of one man, John Charles Walsham Reith, who dominated the BBC from its inception in 1922 to his resignation in June 1938. A man of exceptionally strong character and drive, he left a lasting impression on the BBC and British broadcasting. Reith, a man fond of nautical metaphors, held a firm hand on the BBC's tiller throughout his tenure of office. But to see the BBC and the form of broadcasting established in Britain between the wars as the product of one man is to misunderstand the nature of those times. Broadcasting was shaped as much, if not more, by the social, political and cultural factors of the period.

The development of the BBC was distinct from other media industries in that it was established as a 'public service institution'. The BBC was a compromise between the market-led free-for-all that characterized the growth of unregulated commercial radio in the United States and the highly regulated state control of broadcasting set up in the newly created Soviet Union. However, the form and shape of the BBC and what it broadcast were the outcome of a process of bargaining between the Corporation and a number of vested interests in British society, including the wireless set manufacturers, newspaper proprietors, news agencies and the military authorities and most significantly, the government, in the guise of the Post Office which had, under the Wireless Telegraphy Act of 1904, been given responsibility for the new medium. For some, the compromises and accommodations the BBC made in these negotiations diluted its commitment to the British public. One of the co-founders of the BBC, Peter Eckersley, argued that the search for acceptance from the powers that be, both the political elite and the cultural intelligentsia, led the Corporation, throughout the inter-war years, to neglect its relationship with the British people and renege on its declared obligation to them as a public servant. It 'had over-concentrated on securing its foundations' which 'prevented any clear conception of what was to be built on them'.[2] Reconciling the Corporation's commitment to serving the public and maintaining good relations with the powers that be has been the central dilemma of British broadcasting throughout its history. In the inter-war years the ways in which this dilemma was resolved during certain key events was crucial in shaping much of the policy and practice of the BBC that today we have come to take for granted.

Voyage into uncharted seas

Like the cinema, wireless broadcasting had its technical origins in the nineteenth century. Building on the work of scientists in the field of electromagnetic waves, Marconi demonstrated in an experiment in 1896 that signals could be sent between two points without connecting wires. On the basis of his success Marconi set up his Wireless Telegraph and Signal Company to develop the new means of communication. Wireless telegraphy was conceived of originally in terms of private communication between two points, such as ship to shore, not as a means of mass communication. In the early years, the ability of other listeners to pick up the signal and listen into such communication was regarded as a major drawback. An early parliamentary enquiry into radio telegraphy concluded in 1907 that 'the main defect which was first found in the working of wireless telegraphy resulted in part from the inability to control direction'.[3] The first step along the road to the development of wireless telegraphy as a means of mass communication came when Marconi began the transmission of speech in 1914. This coincided with the outbreak of war, during which the authorities came to realize the strategic importance of the new medium. For the first time the fleets of the world were directed from their home bases by means of ship-to-shore speech rather than dots and dashes. Wireless was now regarded as a national resource. Amateur radio was banned by the Post Office and the Navy granted a monopoly over the medium. At the end of the war the Navy fought to retain its control of wireless communication, emphasizing the danger interference posed to military communication. It urged the Post Office to resist the growing demand for the development of the medium from wireless enthusiasts and wireless manufacturers and in 1920 the Post Office banned Marconi's experimental transmissions. However, by this time a number of other bodies, including businesses, local authorities and amateur wireless operators were involved in the transmission of speech. Listening in to these messages was becoming a very popular pastime in Britain and it was out of this confusion of disparate sounds in the air that organized broadcasting grew.

Organized sound broadcasting first took off in the United States. In 1922, the American public spent over 60 million dollars on buying equipment to assemble radio receivers, which doubled to 135 million in the following year. To service this boom, transmitting stations were established across the length and breadth of the United States. By the middle of 1923, there were over 460 stations broadcasting on the same wavelength.[4] This uncontrolled growth caused considerable congestion due to the plethora of signals. It was commonplace for stations as they competed with one another to fill the airwaves with every form of entertainment and amusement, including the first radio advertisements, to try and blanket out each other's programmes. Those given the responsibility to introduce radio into Britain sought to avoid the 'chaos of the ether' which characterized the growth of commercial radio in America.

The Post Office, under pressure from wireless enthusiasts, lifted its ban on transmission in 1922 and granted licences to some of the large wireless manufacturers to broadcast experimentally. Marconi started regular nightly broadcasting on 14 February from Writtle near Chelmsford. Programmes were informal and usually put together minutes before being transmitted from the bar of the perhaps appropriately named Cock and Bull Inn.[5] In May, the first official wireless station was launched at Marconi House in the Strand, followed a few days later by the opening of a station in Manchester by Metropolitan Vickers. The Western Electric Company set up the Birmingham station which started regular broadcasting on 15 November. These three stations were to provide the regular programme service for the BBC when it came on air for the first time in November. The decision to bring all the wireless manufacturers together in the British Broadcasting Company was described as 'an expedient solution to a technical problem . . . the scarcity of the airwaves'.[6] In 1922, the 'wireless boom' was reaching the proportions it had attained in America and almost a hundred requests had been made to the Post Office from manufacturers and amateur enthusiasts wanting to establish a broadcasting station. The Postmaster General recommended that all those who wished to obtain a licence should cooperate with the Post Office to set up a service through cooperation rather than competition, forcing the wireless manufacturers to come together in one broadcasting company. The formation of a single company to direct transmission reflected official concerns about the impact of wireless listening on public opinion and the political process.

The launch of the British Broadcasting Company

The sensitivities of the British state to broadcasting are indicated by the number of official enquiries that have been held on the topic: several since 1922 including Sykes (1923), Crawford (1926) and Ullswater (1935) during the inter-war years. As the potential of the wireless to extend information on all kinds of topics to all kinds of people became more apparent, official fears about the impact of wireless listening increased. The years immediately prior to the First World War were some of the most turbulent in British political history. Widespread unrest spread fear through Whitehall that the country was on the verge of revolution.[7] The immediate crisis was swept away by the war and the government's decision to grant full male suffrage. By 1918 public opinion had become, in Reith's words, a 'new and mighty weight' in British politics.[8] A renewal of social unrest, including a police strike in 1919, exercised the thoughts of many in authority about the consequence of public opinion for parliamentary politics. The wireless, with its ability to provide information and knowledge to this new constituency, was seen as a potentially dangerous development. The Committee for Imperial Defence in 1921 stated the invention of broadcasting had 'incalculable significance for political stability'.[9] The introduction of sound broadcasting into Britain at a time of growing political tension ensured the state would play an important role in its development.

The arrival of the wireless also came at a time when there was a vigorous debate about the influence of mass communication on moral values and cultural life in Britain. Mass circulation popular papers – as well as popular weeklies, children's comics and pulp fiction – were seen as exercising an unhealthy hold over their readers and limiting, in the search for commercial success, the amount and nature of news in their columns. For many, they were undermining the role of the printed word as a means of promoting religious, cultural, social and political enlightenment. There was growing criticism of the impact of film on 'public taste'. A number of politicians, commentators and intellectuals, including John Reith, saw the trashy and vulgar products of the industry as a consequence of 'giving the public what it wants'. By pandering to public taste and providing cheap entertainment to pack in audiences, the film industry, they argued, was failing to give the newly enfranchised working class the necessary information and education to allow them to play a full part in the parliamentary process. Observers were quick to grasp that the wireless was a medium which could reach a vast number of people simultaneously and had 'immense potential as a cultural agency'.[10] The wireless not only made it possible to better inform and educate people to play a particular defined role in social and political life but also provided material to raise their cultural horizons. The wireless was seen by many as a possible antidote to the declining standards of the press and cinema.

For the set manufacturers, however, entertainment was the purpose of the wireless service. They wanted to sell sets, not to educate or enlighten, and entertainment was regarded as the key to commercial success. The new medium presented a direct threat to the interests of the press, film and theatre owners. If some saw the wireless as a 'craze' that would pass, others in the entertainment industries viewed the new competitor with much suspicion. To ward off competition from amateurs and smaller rivals and other media interests, such as Lord Northcliffe, who had first highlighted the potential of the new medium in 1920 when a larger than expected audience tuned into his staging of Dame Nelly Melba singing from Chelmsford, the larger wireless set manufacturers were happy to form the BBC cartel. Such a monopoly enabled them to consolidate their control over broadcasting and restrict competition by their agreement to fix the price of wireless sets between them. The British Broadcasting Company was formed in 1922 after much hard bargaining between the six leading manufacturers. Each put in £10,000 and nominated a director. The remaining smaller firms were represented by two independent directors. The company's income would come from two sources: an annual licence fee of 10 shillings levied on every receiver and payable to the Post Office, which kept half the fee, and a percentage of the royalties on the sales of sets. In return, the government granted the company an exclusive licence to broadcast for the next two years. A committee of inquiry, under Sir Frederick Sykes, was set up to oversee the expansion of the new broadcasting company. On 14 December, John Reith was given the job of the General Manager of the company. It was between the rock of the official view, represented by the Post Office, and the hard place of the set manufacturers and the entertainment industries that John Reith had to navigate his new vessel.

Reith at the helm

John Reith's values, attitudes and idiosyncrasies permeated the institutional development of the BBC. Reith's life, according to one biographer, was one of 'both tragic and baroque proportions'.[11] He was someone who believed in a world of absolutes and high standards. The son of a moderator of the United Free Church of Scotland, he was imbued with a strict and uncompromising code of Christian morality. He declared on his first visit to Marconi's offices in the Strand that the broadcasting of religion was the most important duty of the new medium. He would accept no lapses from the straight and narrow by employees of his organization. He insisted that female BBC employees resign when they married and male employees, as the BBC Chief Engineer, Peter Eckersley, found out, were dismissed if they divorced. However, he was a man full of contradictions. Intolerant of transgression in others, Reith's private life was not without its own lapses. He had strong opinions about what should be broadcast but there is little evidence he ever listened to the radio. He presided over and justified the growth of the new medium in terms of its contribution to the development of democracy but in his private dealings he was distinctly authoritarian. As one contemporary put it: 'he believes in irresponsible power and his temper is Fascist'.[12] Reith was a strong Scottish patriot and a believer in things Scottish but above all he wanted to be accepted by the English upper classes. An overriding dream throughout his life was to fulfil his public duty as the Viceroy of India. Vain, self-absorbed and self-pitying, he recorded his life in minute detail in a diary he kept throughout his days. These diaries show a man who suffered from depression, felt deep frustration and disappointment but also had deep insight into his failings. Yet Reith was to develop a vision of what broadcasting should be about and had the arrogance and self-belief to try to imprint his view on the BBC, the government and the British public.

Reith's control of the BBC was almost total. He came to think of the BBC as a national church in which he was Pope or even Messiah. The structure and ethos of the BBC established by Reith were to remain intact for several decades and are still apparent today. In terms of the governance of the BBC he established the power of the manager against those who were nominally accountable for the organization, first the wireless manufacturers and then the Board of Governors, who were appointed to oversee the operation when the BBC became a public corporation on 1 January 1927. Reith specified that only those with 'first class qualifications' should apply to work at the BBC. This meant that many jobs were taken by sons of clerics or those with impeccable establishment connections. For example, Roger Eckersley, brother of Peter, the BBC's first Chief Engineer, who became the first controller of programmes, was a noted socialite who taught Reith how to do up his bow-tie correctly. In 1935, the Ullswater Committee rejected the criticism that the BBC was dominated by a narrowly drawn elite on the grounds that only 60 per cent of the non-engineering graduates employed by the organization were from Oxbridge![13] Reith's BBC was a 'total institution' which George Orwell, a BBC employee during the Second World War, used as the model for the Ministry of Truth in his novel, *Nineteen Eighty-Four*. Mirroring Reith's authoritarian instincts, the BBC was hierarchical and top heavy with controllers rather than producers. The bureaucracy institutionalized Reith's obsession of recording everything by memo; the slightest passing comment was committed to paper and circulated in quadruplicate to a clutch of people identified by their acronym rather than name. Many of the institutional features of the BBC were a product of Reith's own highly personal style of management.

Reith might have had his own personal approach to management but he knew nothing about the workings of the wireless. However, it was not long before he outlined his philosophy of broadcasting in his book, *Broadcast Over Britain*, published in 1924. Reith was firmly against developing the new technology to provide public entertainment. In his opinion to have 'exploited so great a scientific invention for the purpose and pursuit of entertainment alone would have been a prostitution of its powers and an insult to the character and intelligence of the people'.[14] Rather, the wireless should serve to educate and uplift the public by seeking to 'carry into the greatest possible number of homes everything that is best in every human department of endeavour and achievement, and to avoid things which are, or may be, hurtful'.[15] Reith had no doubts about what constituted 'everything that is best'. One BBC producer summed up the views of his master clearly:

> We wanted to get people to know really good music – the classics, whether orchestral or instrumental or vocal. We put out talks and plays and broadcast really good music, which meant that if you were going to enjoy them you must sit quietly and think about them, not just to have something in the background which required no intellectual effort.[16]

The BBC under Reith would not compromise standards. As Reith put it: 'It is occasionally represented to us that we are apparently setting up to give the public what we think they need, and not what they want, but often they do not know what they want, and very few what they need.'[17] In other words, Reith knew what was best for the British public. His attitude to public education was very much in keeping with the tradition of Victorian reformers, such as Charles Knight and Matthew Arnold, who believed that education and the provision of knowledge about the moral, cultural and spiritual values of the British nation would turn working people into socially responsible citizens. Such knowledge would dissipate the need for radical social change and ensure that society would run more efficiently and rationally. Reith's broadcasting dream was built on the concept of 'public service broadcasting'. In his biography he sums up his views of such service when he writes that 'if there had been broadcasting at the time of the French Revolution, there might have been no revolution'.[18]

BBC bureaucracy in the 1930s

Administration had always been a bit of a stumbling block in the BBC, because Reith and Carpendale made it unduly strong: I believe they really thought that everybody who was doing a productive job was necessarily childish and irresponsible and needed controlling by someone who was concerned only with In and Out trays. But it reached its peak when the Internal Administration system was invented, and set up a sort of diarchy that ran right through the BBC.

This happened in 1933, when Nicholls became the first Director of Internal Administration. What it meant was that the head of every section, department, and branch had as his right-hand man an executive responsible for money, accommodation, staff salaries, and all the business and facilities side of his job, and this executive worked not for him or for his chief but for Nicholls.

This system of divided control lasted right through the pre-war phase and it made Nicholls, who became Controller (Administration) the most powerful figure in the BBC. Under that system, in my opinion, it became progressively harder to get the work done. The machine was manned by people who had every incentive to say No and none to say Yes, and who were suspicious of every demand because they did not know enough to see the reasons for it . . . It was during that period that only the enthusiasm and determination of the productive staff succeeded in overcoming the machinery and getting anything on air.

I always suspected that . . . our BBC executives dreamt of a BBC untroubled by broadcasts. Luckily there were always plenty of obscure people on the production side who did their jobs according to their likes and not according to the book. If everybody had followed the rules and accepted administrative Noes and delays, the BBC might easily have died of inaction before the war.

Source: Gorham, Maurice (1948) *Sound and Fury*, London: Marshall, pp. 53–4.

Public service broadcasting

The concept of public service broadcasting has changed over time and has been interpreted differently by every Director-General of the BBC and official enquiry into the state of broadcasting. While Reith played a central part in defining the concept, it was, as Scannell and Cardiff[19] point out, 'grafted onto an initial pragmatic set of arrangements between the Post Office and the British radio industry'. Two of the features central to public service broadcasting emerged from the negotiations to establish the company in 1922: the licence fee as a means of funding and the BBC's monopoly of broadcasting. Reith was to provide a framework within which these features, and his own understanding of public service, were woven into an ideological whole. In Reithian terms, public service broadcasting centred around four crucial elements. First, the BBC should have an 'assured source of funding'. In other words, the organization should not have to enter into any commercial arrangements in order to raise funds for its operation, essential if the BBC was to provide the 'best of everything'. If the BBC had to raise money through advertising revenue or profit-seeking, then its commitment to high-quality programming would be sullied by having to concern itself with public taste. Second, to reinforce its commitment to quality, Reith argued the BBC needed the 'brute force of monopoly'. Control of broadcasting should be 'unified' in the hands of one organization so that competition would not devalue the product on offer. It would ensure that general standards would be maintained throughout the country. For Reith monopoly was also the best way to overcome the technical and economic obstacles to the development of a broadcasting system that would ensure universal availability. Third, that broadcasting should be 'national', cutting across class, sectarian, local and social divisions. For Reith, broadcasting was a 'powerful means of promoting social unity'.[20] The broadcasting of rituals such as the King's speech was one example Reith cited as a way in which the British people could be brought together around a national event. Fourth, a sense of moral obligation. Reith saw high standards in terms of a mixture of 'middle class ethics, stern Christianity, patrician culture and school masterly morality'.[21] Reith's view of public service broadcasting was an amalgamation of the arrangements which had led to the setting up of the cartel and his notion of public service, which entailed the provision of programmes of high standards and moral purpose across the whole of Britain.[22]

Reith could not have exploited the concept of public service broadcasting without the support of a number of external interests, most importantly, the British State. The Sykes Committee, the first of many official inquiries into the state of broadcasting, clearly saw broadcasting in terms of a 'public utility'. As Sykes put it: 'the wavebands available in any country must be regarded as a valuable form of public property'.[23] Reith's vision of broadcasting based on a rejection of the market and direct State control corresponded to the 'turn and temper of the age'. During the First World War the conditions for acceptance of public corporations had been laid down. Health, insurance, the coal industry and food rationing had been organized and operated centrally as part of the exceptional measures enacted to fight the war. Civil servants who had been involved in the management of the centralized distribution of resources supported the government playing a more interventionist role.[24] There was widespread concern about the inefficiency of the free market in the distribution of resources. The Labour Party, emerging as a new political force in the wake of the death of Liberal England, advocated public corporations as a practical means of distancing themselves from capitalist production. With Sykes defining broadcasting as a vital national resource and the government providing financial support for the film industry, mass communication was acknowledged as distinct and different from other areas of industry and it was only a short step to recommending public ownership of the BBC.

Despite the broadly favourable environment, Reith still had to fight to establish the BBC. He inherited a number of agreements restricting what the BBC could and could not do. In setting up the company the Post Office had come under considerable pressure from the newspaper industry to prevent the broadcasting of news. The Newspaper Proprietors Association and the Newspaper Society, which represented the provincial press, joined together with the news agencies to lobby against the BBC developing its own news service. As a result, the company was not allowed to broadcast bulletins before 7 p.m. so as not to damage the market for the provincial press and the material used had to be supplied and compiled by the news agencies in return for an annual fee. Despite Reith's protests, with the exception of a number of national emergencies, BBC news remained a highly circumscribed form of journalism until the late 1930s. It was not until 1934 that the BBC established a regular news programme and began to employ its own network of correspondents. The newspaper industry also attempted to prevent the new company publishing details of its programmes in the press. This dispute led to the launch of the *Radio Times* in 1923, in which the company published details of its programmes.[25] Reith was able eventually to overturn the newspaper industry's restrictions on live coverage of public events such as the Derby, Cup

Final and the Boat Race. However, the first broadcast of the Derby proved to be a farce. The press had agreed the BBC could cover the 1926 Derby but on the condition it only broadcast the sound of the race. Heavy rain resulted in not only no sound from the hooves of the horses but little crowd noise as most people were inside taking shelter from the downpour.

Reith's most intense struggle was with the Post Office, the 'policeman of the ether', over its prohibition on the company dealing with 'controversial matters'. The licence awarded to the BBC incorporated official concerns about the impact of broadcasting on public opinion. It stipulated that the BBC had to broadcast programmes 'to the reasonable satisfaction of the Postmaster General'.[26] What this meant became clear in March 1923 following a talk broadcast by the BBC on a strike in the building construction industry, when the Postmaster General declared that 'it is undesirable that the broadcasting services should be used for the dissemination of speeches on controversial matters'.[27] The position was put more clearly when the Postmaster General in November 1926 introduced to Parliament the terms of the charter that would turn the BBC into a public corporation. He stated that 'once you let broadcasting into politics, you will never be able to keep politics out of broadcasting'.[28] Reith fought hard between 1923 and 1926 to secure the right of the BBC to report controversial matters, including the coverage of Parliament, official events such as the budget and the election addresses of the Party leaders in the 1924 election. The Sykes Committee supported him on the grounds that all subjects would ultimately give rise to some controversy. Reith sought to convince the government that the BBC could be trusted to report politics and controversial matters. He wrote in his diary later on the reporting of a particularly controversial issue, that 'they knew they could trust us not to be really impartial'.[29] The Crawford Report, set up following Sykes to establish the long-term future of broadcasting, fully supported Reith's view that the BBC should become a public corporation and recommended there should be a 'moderate amount of controversial matter' on the BBC. The report was published in March 1926 but before the government could consider its findings, the loyalty of the BBC was put to the test in its reporting of one of the most important events in British political history – the General Strike.

The BBC and the General Strike

The General Strike, which for nine days in May 1926 threw life in Britain into upheaval as the trade union movement tried to bring the country to a standstill, was significant in shaping the relationship between the BBC and the State. The General Strike divided British society. In the midst of the convulsions the BBC was the only source of information for most people about what was going on around the country and the company for the first time had the opportunity to produce its own news bulletins. This opportunity came at a delicate time in the organization's history – with the negotiations with the government over the renewal of its licence to broadcast. The BBC was keen to preserve its independent status during these negotiations. The General Strike, however, exposed the nature of the BBC's relationship with the government to sharp scrutiny. The arrangements made by the BBC to cover the event defined the nature of its 'independence' and laid down the framework within which broadcasters and ministers have negotiated ever since – a framework described as allowing the corporation 'liberty on parole'.

On 1 May, two days before the General Strike started, a message from the Prime Minister was broadcast. A 'stentorian voice' boomed out: 'Be steady, be steady' and after a pause, 'Remember that peace on earth comes to men of good will.' The message was repeated three times. It was not spoken by Baldwin himself but conveyed to the people of Britain by a BBC announcer, who was none other than John Reith.[30] For the duration of the General Strike the ties between the government and the BBC were very close. The government had the legal right to take over the running of the BBC. Within the Cabinet there were those, including the Chancellor, Winston Churchill, who argued strongly for the government to commandeer the BBC during the strike. Prime Minister Baldwin argued that the cabinet should 'leave the BBC with maximum autonomy and independence', realizing the propaganda importance of the credibility of the BBC and, more importantly, understanding that Reith had little room for manoeuvre.

For Reith, the General Strike was a chance to prove to the government that it could be trusted to report 'controversial matters' as well as maintain a commitment to impartial reporting. In the first news bulletin of 4 May, the BBC declared that it 'fully realized the gravity of its responsibility to all sections of the public and will do its best to discharge it in the most impartial spirit that circumstances permit' and it added that 'we shall do our best to maintain our tradition of fairness, and we ask fair play in return'.[31] In practice the BBC found that discharging its duty was not straightforward. Attempts by the Archbishop of Canterbury and the Leader of the Labour Party to broadcast were denied by the government, a decision taken against Reith's advice. His reason for supporting the broadcasting of the speeches, however, was nothing to do with a principled defence of impartial reporting but that they would have made no difference to the situation. Throughout the dispute Reith's BBC, in preparing the news, co-operated closely with the government. BBC staff moved into an office in the Admiralty for the period of the strike. Admiralty officials assisted in the preparations of the news bulletins and clearance for what was reported was needed from the government. On the other hand, the BBC sought to ensure that the news bulletins included comments from both sides and references were made to both the official government paper, the *British Gazette*, edited by Churchill during the strike, and the *British Worker*. Scrupulous attention was paid to distinguishing agency copy from official government statements and the organization sought to ensure what it reported was accurate. But accurate reporting of events did not equate to impartial coverage of the strike. There were significant gaps in the coverage. Besides not allowing certain broadcasts, the BBC failed to rectify errors in its reporting – for example, inaccurate figures for returns to work were not corrected.[32] It also assisted the government in its efforts to break the strike by broadcasting calls for volunteers and putting out every night editorials designed 'to have a soothing effect on the nation's nerve' by 'appealing to people to keep their heads'.[33] The editorials were often written by J. C. C. Davidson, the man in charge of the government's handling of the dispute.

The BBC during the General Strike interpreted 'impartiality' in a particular way. It did not publicly take sides but it did operate within a particular understanding of the political and moral order which led it to support the government. In a celebrated aphorism, Reith articulated the BBC's position in these words: 'Assuming the BBC is for the people, and that the government is for the people, then the BBC must be for the government in this crisis.'[34] The fact that the Strike had been declared 'illegal' reinforced Reith in his view that the BBC as a national institution 'had to assist in the maintaining of the essential services of the country, the preservation of law and order, and the life and liberty of the individual and the community'.[35] Thus 'impartiality' was applied only to political activity that fell within the parameters of what was legitimate and legal. Many argue that Reith had no choice other than to accept this state of affairs; a pragmatic decision to maintain the independence of a fledgling organization. While the preservation of the BBC was a consideration in Reith's decision, it is also fair to say the position Reith adopted during the General Strike was in accordance with his views – and that of other senior BBC staff – on the Strike. Reith might have had some sympathy for the strikers but he was not prepared to take their side against that of the government.

When the Strike collapsed on 12 May, Reith delivered a message from the King on the wireless and the tones of the hymn 'Jerusalem' were struck up. The BBC's role was praised by the government. Baldwin wrote to Reith stating: 'you and all the members of your staff may rest assured that your loyal service has earned the warm appreciation of the government'.[36] Supporters of the Strike were critical. The Labour MP Ellen Wilkinson, in a letter to the *Radio Times*, spoke for many working people. She wrote:

> The attitude of the BBC during the crisis caused pain and indignation to many subscribers. I travelled by car over two thousand miles during the strike and addressed very many meetings. The complaints were bitter that a national service to every class should have given only one side during the dispute. Personally I feel like asking the Postmaster General for my licence fee back as I can hear enough fairy tales in the House of Commons without paying ten shillings a year to hear more.[37]

The legacy of the BBC's performance during the Strike was far-reaching. The imprecision which had characterized the understanding between government and broadcasters in the negotiations about the role of the BBC prior to the Strike was replaced by a clear indication of the practical limits to the BBC's independence.

These limits were incorporated into the BBC's definition of 'impartiality', particularly regarding 'controversial matters'.

The government, however, did not lift the ban on controversial matters until 1928 which Reith saw as a betrayal. But the impact of the BBC's reporting of the Strike left its mark. For some, the Strike might not have collapsed without the intervention of broadcasting and, for the rest of the inter-war years, if not longer, the Corporation was treated with great suspicion by a large section of working people. Whatever the arguments around the role of the BBC in determining the outcome of the General Strike, broadcasting had, according to the BBC's official historian, established during May 1926 that it was 'a force in national life with enormous possibilities for good or ill'.[38]

The wireless audience in the 1930s

The wireless quickly established itself as a means of mass communication in the 1930s. The first struggle was to provide a service as technically perfect as possible, cutting out interference and producing good quality sound.[39] The first wireless set to be developed for the general public was the crystal set which came with headphones for listening. These sets were replaced by valve receivers which came with loudspeakers. The main preoccupation of the listener in the early years of sound broadcasting was with the reception rather than the content of programmes. The problem of 'oscillation' plagued the development of the wireless throughout the 1920s and nearly 75 per cent of all the correspondence received by the BBC during this time related to the search for interference-free reception.[40] Improvements in set design in the 1930s removed the problem and the first modern wireless set was the Ecko set produced by the E. K. Cole company in 1934, followed a year later by the Philco, the People's Set, produced by Philips. These sets meant that good quality sound was, for the first time, available to all at a relatively cheap price.

The price of radio sets fell throughout the 1930s; cheaper radio sets cost on average £1 to £3. However, they were still expensive for low-income listeners and as such the working classes were to be underrepresented in the radio audience until the introduction of the 'utility set' in 1944.[41] The arrival of a wireless set in many working-class households during the inter-war years was a major event. 'When we first get the wireless set from the shop there comes the first thrilling moment when the set is to be operated and the family delighted with the music. This, like the wedding day and the first ride on a bicycle, gives a thrill such as we seldom feel in this unromantic age.'[42] Those who could not afford to buy a set, used the relay exchanges which in return for a small rental could be wired to loudspeakers in the home.[43] This method of listening was cheaper in that there was only a rental charge and no payments for the use of electricity. It was also technically better sound reproduction and, according to the BBC's chief engineer, in one of the first examples of the BBC underestimating the capacity of its audience, 'the listener has no bother either in operating and maintaining a complicated wireless set which, to women especially, is often frightening and mysterious'.[44] The disadvantage was that the listener had no choice in terms of what she could listen to as the relay exchange decided what to broadcast. By the mid-1930s the mains-operated wireless set had become more accessible to all and its purchase in large numbers was one of the features of the era. It outsold all other electric appliances even in the most severe years of the Depression. By 1939, George Orwell could write that 'twenty million people are underfed but literally everyone in England has access to a radio'.[45]

Radio listening in the inter-war years was an activity confined to the home. It was not to escape the home until the advent of the transistor in the 1950s. There was, however, nothing inherent in the technology that demanded its domestic application. At the start people had no knowledge about how to listen to the new medium. The first type of listener was the young male with mechanical interests who saw the wireless as a hobby; something to fiddle about with in a shed with a 50-foot mast at the bottom of the garden. In the early 1920s wireless audiences could be large crowds as easily as family groups.[46] Wireless clubs were set up to support the new medium. They organized events whereby listeners could get together to discuss what they had just heard on the wireless. It was the manufacturers and sellers of wireless sets who promoted the household application of wireless, simply as a more attractive way of selling the medium. Its domestic use distinguished the wireless from the cinema, the other main means of mass communication in the inter-war years. The wireless played a significant part in changing the pattern of popular recreation by making home-based leisure for the whole family more attractive to working people. Being part of the household had consequences for wireless development, since it had to fit into family routines and the mundaneness of day-to-day life. This meant identifying a particular kind of listener – women. If the cinema was the first to shape its content to meet the needs of a female audience, the radio built its schedule and language around the home and the family which preferenced women who were at the centre of the domestic sphere.[47]

Developing a programme policy

The years following the BBC's transformation into a public corporation were taken up with the development of a programme policy that would reflect Reith's philosophy of public service broadcasting as well as attract popular support for the new medium. The struggle to define Reith's philosophy in practice was not simply a conflict with outside interests. Reith also had to overcome the opposition of many of his staff as well as the desires of the growing radio audience. At the outset Reith – and the BBC – paid no attention to what the audience wanted. The whole thrust was towards the education of the listener. However, as the wireless developed into a mass medium, the views of listeners became more important in shaping the BBC's output – particularly when they began to vote with their feet in the mid-1930s by tuning to commercial radio stations being set up on the Continent.

The relationship established between the first programme makers and their audience has played an important part in structuring the content of broadcasting ever since. The early years of broadcasting were steeped in mutual ignorance. As one programme-maker stated: 'We have to admit we are in the dark, for we simply cannot know what sort of music listeners have liked most or what sort of plays listeners most wish to hear.'[48] Letters were the main means by which broadcasters learned about their audience's views before 1936 which of course only represented the opinions of a small section of the listening public. The wireless and listeners' organizations, established to help people to learn how to listen to the radio, were active until the late 1920s in trying to make the BBC more accountable and responsive to their audience. For example, the Wireless League, in evidence to the Crawford Committee, suggested ways in which the BBC could be more democratically accountable. The decline of these bodies meant the removal of the public from the Reithian concept of public service broadcasting. From the late 1920s onwards, the BBC 'knew best' and built its programme policy around how it believed listeners should listen. They should be discriminating, switching off programmes they were not interested in rather than listening 'on tap'. According to the BBC the 'listener must recognise that a definite obligation rests on him to choose intelligently from the programmes offered to him'.[49] Listening to the wireless as background noise was disapproved of. As a result the programme output of the BBC in the 1930s discouraged the lazy listener or 'tapper'. There were no continuity announcements between programmes and no fixed times or lengths for programmes. Periods of silence were left between programmes with only the sound of the studio clock to indicate the station was still on air. The breaks were there to deal with the problem of programme overrun which was common in live broadcasting and to allow people to switch off as they made a decision about what to listen to. They were also there to help listeners to compose themselves after a particularly moving piece of music or to contemplate what they had just heard.

For much of the inter-war years, news and journalism hardly featured in the BBC's output. Dependent on the agencies for copy, fearful of the consequences of transgressing what was deemed politically acceptable by the government and anxious not to give offence to the listener, the news from the BBC was limited, complacent, conventional and dull. The fact that radio was live for most of this period accentuated these concerns and meant that the Corporation carefully policed what was put out as news. Particular attention was paid to ensure that nothing gruesome or harrowing appeared in news bulletins. Sensitive topics included the religion of persons mentioned in the news, royalty and illness – as well as 'anything that might stimulate feelings akin to Bolshevism'.[50] BBC news attempted to distance itself from the sensationalism of the popular press and as a result its conception of news values was narrowly drawn. So much so that if there were no quality stories of the 'normal type or standard for broadcasting' available, then the announcer would simply say 'there is no news tonight'.[51] Actuality or eyewitness news and studio interviews began to appear in the late 1930s – pioneered in BBC North where innovation took place away from the over-cautious centre – but were only developed during the Second World War.

Much of the information provided by the BBC during the inter-war years came from talks and features and documentaries. The Talks department of the BBC was set up in 1927 and was a crucial part of the BBC's operation until, under a cloud of recrimination and criticism and the removal of its first two directors, it was reorganized in 1935. Talks were the main way in which the Corporation reported on areas of controversy. The talk encapsulated Reith's objective to create an informed citizenry and brought before the microphone leading members of the British intelligentsia, including Wells, Shaw, Huxley, the Webbs, Keynes and Harold Nicholson. The talk took the form of a lecture, debate or discussion. A discussion was seen as 'good table talk' rather than conflict between opposing views. Attempts were made to develop an informal and inclusive form of talk but, above all, the talks were carefully scripted and vetted. But for all the precautions taken by the BBC, talks became the focus of accusations of political bias. These attacks mounted with the departure of the Labour government in 1931 and in 1935, the year in which its Charter was up for renewal, the BBC decided to forestall any further controversy over the output of the Talks department by tightening up its internal control mechanism. This caused a major row inside the BBC when proposed speakers for a series called *What Price Freedom?* were vetoed by management. The outcome was the removal of the key personnel in the Talks department. Their replacements were better known for their administrative than programme-making skills. According to one contemporary observer, the 'orthodox public school type', who knew the difference between a nod and a wink, was preferred.[52]

It was not only factual programming that was subject to careful control by the BBC authorities. Most of the BBC's output was music and entertainment – for example, in 1935, music alone made up 70 per cent of output.[53] Listeners wanted more entertainment and there was considerable demand for the broadcasting of variety and vaudeville acts. Reith recognized that music and entertainment had a part to play in wireless broadcasting, but his view of what was entertaining was very narrow. One critic in the early 1930s complained that 'the programmes are like elongated penny readings with orchestral variations and, when I look at this long list, my mind's eye sees the vicar in the chair and the local concert party in menacing preparation'.[54] Popular music in Reithian terms was light operetta and classical music. The 'stuffed shirt' attitude of the BBC also influenced the variety programmes put out. Comedy was circumscribed by a ban on jokes pertaining to a whole range of subjects including politics and politicians, clergymen, medical matters and human infirmities, Scotsmen and Welshmen (but not Irish).[55] Reference to the word 'bottom' earned one comedian a five-month ban. Vulgarity was carefully policed by the Corporation as it sought to earn respectability. But the clearest manifestation of the BBC's programme policy in the inter-war years was its Sunday output. Sunday on the wireless was a special day. Reith's Sunday was dominated by religious services in the morning and evening, with the station closing down for nearly two hours after the morning service, and a mixture of serious talks and music for the rest of the day. It was popular disenchantment with the BBC's Sunday that brought about change in the late 1930s in the amount and kind of entertainment provided by the Corporation.

Recollection of working in the BBC in the 1930s

Because of its official status the BBC had a congenital terror of the impromptu that was quite unknown to American radio: one remembers with a nostalgic shudder those high minded discussions on public affairs presided over by conscientious lady arts graduates from one of the older universities (the BBC took a long time to recognize red brick) which would begin with a cosy talk on the 'ground to be covered', followed by a recording of an appropriately patterned conversation which was then transferred to paper to be edited and scripted with a proper eye to balance, and finally, but only after several rehearsals to get the right intonations, read from the edited script to give an illusion of live and lively debate.

Source: **Williams, Francis** (1969) *The Right to Know*, London: Longmans, p. 125.

Challenges to Reithian radio started in 1934 when Radio Luxembourg came on air. It was soon followed by other commercial stations in Normandy, Toulouse, Lyon and Paris. Supported by sponsors such as Beecham's Pills, Kraft Cheese and Lifebuoy Soap, these stations offered record shows, band shows as well as the Littlewoods Pools Show. The stations targeted the British audience every Sunday with non-stop entertainment. What Reith called 'this monstrous stuff from Luxembourg'[56] attracted a large number of British listeners. The BBC was forced to respond to this challenge and in 1936 the Listener Research Department was established. The first listener survey found that 70 per cent of those interviewed wanted more variety programmes and from 1937 to the eve of the war, the Variety Department began to exert more influence over the BBC's programme schedule. Programmes such as *In Town Tonight*, *Monday Night at Seven* and *Band Waggon* represented a 'new found populism' in BBC entertainment.[57] These programmes, which included humour, show business glamour and attention-grabbing human interest stories, were the first programmes to receive a regular fixed weekly slot. They began to build large audiences and establish themselves as the BBC's best loved programmes of the 1930s.

The BBC's gradual move to giving its listeners more of that they wanted was also marked in the emergence of representations of working-class life in the output. Although there were no programmes specifically made for working-class audiences and the sound of working-class voices speaking for themselves was not heard until the Second World War, aspects of working-class life appeared in comedy shows such as *The Plums* in 1937 and features such as the radio documentaries produced by Olive Shapley for BBC North.[58] But in general the BBC conceived of its listeners in middle-class terms – for example, in 1938, the Corporation launched the first domestic serial, the forerunner to the 'soap', *English Family Robinson*, which dealt with the 'daily life of a typical English family', who 'lived in the suburbs, with a maid called Shirley and a car called Ella'.[59] In the late 1930s there was also an increase in listener participation with competitions and quiz shows being broadcast in greater numbers. The birth of the radio request show with programmes such as *You Asked for It* which played records requested by listeners also occurred in these years. Such programmes were a return to the BBC's roots. The early years of local radio were full of quiz shows, competitions, request shows, phone-ins and novelty programmes of one form or another that gave the listener access to the airwaves. It was this kind of material that was removed with the BBC's establishment as a public corporation. The 'lofty condescension' of the Corporation replaced the relaxed and friendly relations between broadcaster and listener that characterized the days of the company. For one contemporary: 'It is only since the BBC attained the status of a Corporation that it has become swollen headed and put uplift before laughter.'[60] At the heart of Reith's contribution to British broadcasting was the imposition of a certain set of cultural values on the whole of Britain and the centralization of these values at the expense of local, regional and national differences.

Centralizing control of the BBC

Reith never envisaged the development of local public service broadcasting in Britain. For him broadcasting was to be a 'national service', a means of bringing together all classes and peoples of Britain by providing them with a sense of belonging to one national community. Major national events such as the Boat Race, the F.A. Cup Final, the opening of Parliament and, above all, the rituals and ceremonies associated with the monarchy were used to provide people with the feeling they all belonged to one national community. Universal availability was central to the drive for a national service. Whether it was, as Reith said, the crofter in the North of Scotland or the agricultural labourer in the West of England, all should be able to tune in to 'hear the King speak on some great national occasion'. To achieve this objective the BBC embarked on a policy of centralizing control and production in London. The concept of public service broadcasting articulated by Reith was imposed on the local stations and the kind of broadcasting that emerged between 1923 and 1927 was 'deliberately eradicated by the policy of centralisation'.[61]

By 1930, the diversity of local stations had been submerged into the National Programme broadcast from London and the Regional Programme produced from six centres serving the Midlands, North, Northern Ireland, West, South and Scotland. It soon became apparent there was to be no parity between the Programmes. The National Programme was the senior service; it would provide the 'best in music talks and drama and entertainment' while the Regional Service would simply reflect everyday life in the regions. London was so confident of the superiority of its output that it insisted the Regional Programme take more and more of its programmes unless there was a good reason for not doing so. For Reith, the BBC's duty to serve the 'national community' was pursued to the exclusion of local interests. The dominance of London in the new network meant that its view of national life and culture prevailed. The national community was defined as being middle class, middlebrow, English and middle of the road, and programmes and policies were constructed accordingly. The 'voice' of the BBC became standardized; the 'BBC voice' which replaced the gamut of national and regional voices was the educated, middle-class speech of the Home Counties. The Home Counties dominance of the BBC was clear in the composition of the first Board of Governors. Every member lived in London or the Home Counties, among them a coal owner, an ex-headmaster of a major public school, a former comptroller of the Bank of England and the Conservative Party's Chief Whip in the House of Lords.[62]

Resistance to the reorganization of the BBC was minimal. Technical and economic considerations for the most part prevailed over concerns about the loss of local output. A national service was cheaper, more efficient and provided better reception. There was little public resistance to the changes although the Sheffield station mounted a public campaign against closure.[63] Opposition came from the local station managers whose concerns were articulated by Peter Eckersley. Eckersley was one of the founders of the BBC, the architect of the regional scheme as well as the person who oversaw the BBC's engineering feats which resulted in the whole of Britain being able to receive the wireless signals in a relatively short period of time. He was highly critical of the centralization of control. He had envisaged the reorganization in terms of providing a balance between London and the rest of the country, between metropolitan and provincial interests and needs. He accused the BBC of becoming more like a public school than a public service and believed the growth of 'corporate self consciousness' in the BBC made it more unsympathetic to its audience.[64] His dismissal from the BBC, ostensibly on the grounds of his involvement in a divorce case, should also be seen in terms of his attempt in 1929 to get the new Regional Directors together to oppose Reith's policy.[65] This was to be the first of many protests from the regions about London's development of programmes and policies in the 1930s.

Apart from Scotland and Northern Ireland, the new regions created in the 1930s made no sense in terms of people, places or culture. The North region, based in Manchester, included a third of the population of the British Isles, stretching from Newcastle upon Tyne to north Wales. The West, above all, highlighted the incongruous nature of the new regions. Based in Cardiff, it was set up to serve south Wales and the West Country. Both sides of the Bristol Channel were aggrieved by the service. The West Country voiced its dissatisfaction with programmes from and about Wales. The *Bristol Evening World* complained in

1931 about sharing a wavelength with Wales: 'The truth is that the West is weary of Wales. The West is not interested in Wales. The West wants wireless home rule.'[66] As for the Welsh, nationalist leader Saunders Lewis complained that the 'BBC administers Wales as a conquered province.' The 'Welsh Controversy', as it was referred to in BBC files, came to take up more of Reith's time in the 1930s as political and racial passions escalated, fuelled by Reith's intense dislike of Wales and the Welsh. Under pressure in 1937 a divorce was granted with the establishment of a separate Welsh region.

There were growing conflicts between the regions and London throughout the 1930s over London's insistence that the regions take 'top quality' programmes as the regions asserted the importance of their local output. The regions complained that, with the exception of Scotland, they were largely staffed by people from southeast England and treated 'as a dumping ground for failures among the London . . . staff'.[67] Dissatisfaction reached such a crescendo that the BBC sent the Director of Regional Relations on a tour of the regions. His report severely criticized the policy of centralization, blaming it for the grievances of the regions and he stated that 'the danger inherent in the power and range of broadcasting of achieving a uniform pattern of thought, of standardizing taste and values according to the authoritarian few and "expert" are too obvious to need elaboration'.[68] From 1937, the BBC did slowly start to move toward establishing regional advisory bodies. However, under Reith, the Corporation attempted to impose its metropolitan and middle-class view of nationhood and culture on British society. There was no doubt that the wireless was able to bring people together and give them a sense of belonging to the same nation by listening to the same programmes. Besides affirming a common heritage, radio programmes could also highlight the irreconcilable differences within Britain. Major national events could 'ostracise the individual rather than draw them into a wider network'.[69] Thus one woman could describe her feelings on Coronation Day in 1937: 'Drink sherry at midday meal, rest of family gloomy, decide broadcasting of big events brings feeling of isolation.'

6

Sing as we go: representing British society in the 1930s

The 1930s are often called the 'Devil's Decade' or the 'Hungry Thirties', a time when British society was bitterly divided between the haves and have-nots, between classes and peoples, a nation at war with itself. It is a decade that calls forth the images of hunger marches, unemployment, idleness, poverty, slums, ill health, the rise of fascism, class struggle in the Civil War in Spain and appeasement. In recent years this popular recollection of the 1930s has been challenged. Revisionist historians, such as Stevenson and Cook,[1] claim it was not a period of absolute misery and depression. Unemployment and hardship, they point out, were unevenly spread, concentrated mainly in the old industrial areas of the north, Scotland and, above all, Wales. Here the rate of unemployment, which never fell below a million throughout the decade, was particularly high. For example, in towns such as Brynmawr and Dowlais in South Wales, Jarrow and Gateshead in the north-east and Greenock and Motherwell in the Central Lowlands of Scotland, over three-quarters of the insured population were out of work in 1934. Outside these particular regions the picture was not of unremitting misery and social distress. For some, the 1930s were boom years; according to A. J. P. Taylor, many people were 'enjoying a richer life than any previously known in the history of the world: longer holidays, shorter hours, higher real wages'.[2] For those in work, the 1930s were not 'wasted years'; they were years of prosperity.

Stevenson and Cook argue that British society was not as divided by social conflict as the popular recollection of the 1930s would have us believe. Marshalling the evidence from official documents, such as police records, as well as pointing to the local and general election performances of the period, they suggest that Britain was relatively stable and comparatively unified. However, the stark evaluation of the figures for real wages and consumption and the uncritical assessment of official accounts hide people's experience and perceptions of these years. The 'high' quality of life was limited in class terms. The migration from areas of hardship and unemployment, such as the Rhondda Valley, to the bright lights of the rapidly expanding centres of light industry, such as Slough and Oxford, caused much disruption to families and communities. Working in the new industries was often tedious and monotonous, changing people's experience of the workplace. There was also an increase in political activism in the 1930s. Between 1935 and 1937, the British Communist Party sold nearly a million pamphlets and sheets[3] and the party's official paper, the *Daily Worker*, enjoyed its highest readership. In 1936, the New Left Book Club was launched by Victor Gollancz, and within a year the Club had 40,000 members and over 400 local discussion circles.[4] Members of the club were often ordinary working men and women, and, in 1936, with the outbreak of the Spanish Civil War, many travelled to Spain to enlist in the cause of the Republican government against the forces of fascism and authoritarianism. The conflict also saw many British intellectuals and writers becoming involved in a political struggle, which the poet Stephen Spender[5] described as 'a war of light against darkness'. In taking sides, some, such as the writer George Orwell, went to Spain to fight. It was during the 1930s that the foundations for the changes in British society that happened during the Second World War were laid.

For the sociologist Tom Burns, the notion of a united, stable nation is an illusion conjured up by the mass media. He talks of the 'imposed consensus of the 1930s' when the press, radio and cinema were used to project an image of national, social and cultural integration.[6] Burns highlights how mass communication was used to propagandize a particular appearance of British society. There was, whatever the 'reality' in the country, a growing unease in the corridors of power of the potentially disruptive forces that were gathering at home and abroad. The advent of new and more powerful means by which these forces could express themselves led the State to develop its capacity to use and manage the media. Censorship had always been a tool to manipulate opinion but the State in the 1930s developed new tools to project its particular view. Hence the birth of the Press Office at Number Ten, the establishment of the Empire Marketing Board and the growth of more sophisticated techniques of news management. To understand the role of mass communication in the 1930s it is important to examine two factors: the impact of the First World War on the development of censorship and propaganda *and* the rise of the documentary tradition in the inter-war years.

The Great War and modern media

The First World War (1914–18) was not simply a grand conflict in which millions of men went to their deaths to maintain the balance of power in Europe; it represented the collapse of the old Victorian order and the birth of the modern era. At the heart of the modern world were the mass media. The war coincided with the development of new and more powerful means of mass communication. Through the media, in particular, the emerging media of cinema and sound broadcasting, the Great War forged a direct link between government and public opinion, made more politically important with universal suffrage. From the mid-nineteenth century, with the repeal of the taxes on knowledge, the State sought to exert its influence over mass communication by other means. The market and the system of information control laid down from the 1880s onwards became central to the government's strategy for managing the media in the twentieth century. These mechanisms enabled the government to exert influence and control not directly over the journalist, but rather over the information which he or she gathered.

Hennessy, Cockerell and Walker[7] identify three pillars to the system of information control in British society that developed from the end of the nineteenth century. The first pillar consists of draconian legislation, encompassed in the Official Secrets Acts and the D-Notice laws, which made disclosure about government activities very difficult. Attempts to restrict the disclosure of official information began in the 1880s. The First Official Secrets Act was passed in 1889 but it was not until the years of tension preceding the First World War, when the government was able to exploit the 'German scare', that truly rigid controls on the flow of official information were introduced. Under the pretext of combating espionage, the Second Official Secrets Act was introduced in 1911. It made it illegal for anyone holding office under the Crown, from Post Office workers to civil servants and ministers, to disclose any information about the working of government deemed to be an official secret. What constituted an 'official secret' was not spelled out, thereby giving the government the power to decide. The legislation also made the recipient of an 'official secret' liable to prosecution. The result was that over the years a number of absurd prosecutions took place or were threatened under the Official Secrets Act. For example, in 1935, Sotheby's was threatened with prosecution when it sought to auction correspondence of Lords Nelson and Wellington from the 1830s – the government said it contained secrets.[8] The Secrets Acts were supported by two other pieces of legislation passed immediately before the war. In 1909, the Secret Service was founded with the aim of catching spies. However, its main role was to be a policing service for unwarranted disclosures or leaks. In 1912, the D-Notice system came into being. The notices – the 'd' stands for defence – cover areas of sensitivity, particularly but not always in relation to military matters, which the media should take special care in reporting. Prior to 1971, the D-Notice Committee, which included members of the armed forces, government and the media, would issue a notice in advance to the media on a topic they deemed sensitive. This system had no legal standing. It was – and still is – a voluntary system, in which the media cooperated in censoring themselves. For Hennessy and his colleagues, this system is an example of the 'British way of censorship', a 'nod and a wink' type of relationship between the 'good chaps' in Fleet Street and Whitehall which deny the public information about the workings of government.

The second pillar was the development of a news cartel. The Lobby, which was first established in 1884, became the primary mechanism for the reporting of government decisions and political issues. Lobby correspondents comprise nearly all the political reporters of major media outlets based at Parliament. They operate according to a set of rules which require that they do not reveal the workings of the Lobby to the outside world. These rules include not reporting what journalists see happen inside the corridors of Parliament and who says what to them – they can only indirectly refer to their 'source' as every conversation is on the basis of non-attribution. Such practices, Hennessy, Cockerell and Walker argue, run contrary to the professional ethics of journalism. In return, the correspondents are guaranteed a regular supply of information through government and Opposition briefings on the issues of the day. A large amount of government information is funnelled through the Lobby. The third pillar was the commercialization of official information. During the First World War the government started to establish an apparatus to 'sell' information it wanted to release. The apparatus consisted of press officers, official spokespersons, public relations advisors and information officers. The first body set up to perform this function was the News Department of the Foreign and Commonwealth Office which was established in 1916.[9] These three pillars were cemented into place during the First World War with the first systematic attempt to organize official information.

The Ministry of Information was set up by the government to promote the war effort through censorship, propaganda and psychological warfare – a task made more urgent with the arrival of more powerful means of mass communication, the cinema and the broadcast media. This established a direct link between the machinery of government and mass opinion.[10] The Ministry's objectives were to inform the public about the progress of the war, maintain morale at home and coordinate the propaganda efforts abroad. A Press Bureau was established to manage government relations with the newspapers. The Ministry was particularly successful in managing news about the huge casualties sustained by the British armed forces during the war and putting forward the best interpretation of what was happening to the British public.[11] The two men in charge of the Ministry's efforts were Lords Beaverbrook and Northcliffe – the two leading newspaper owners of their day. Their involvement in the coordination of government information highlights the close ties between newspaper owners and the political process during this period. The relationship that developed between the mass media and the government during the war had lasting consequences for the development of mass communication in the 1930s.

Developing techniques of news management

The Ministry of Information was disbanded in 1918. However, the experience of the First World War impressed on the government the importance of publicity and propaganda. The inter-war years saw the gradual growth of the government publicity machine. The Air Ministry was the first government department to appoint a press officer in 1919, with the Ministry of Health and War Office soon following their example. The Foreign Office had maintained its news department while the Department of Overseas Trade became involved in providing some trade news and organizing exhibitions. There was also a Government Cinematograph Adviser who oversaw a small stock of official film material.[12] Until 1926, the peacetime press and publicity work undertaken by the government was modest in scope. The establishment of the Empire Marketing Board (EMB) in 1926 marked the advent of a large-scale government propaganda and publicity machine.

The EMB was established by the Baldwin government as part of the conviction that imperialism offered a solution to the economic problems that beset Britain in the 1920s. The Empire was seen as the best opportunity for developing new markets for British industry.[13] Increasing trade with the Empire was to be promoted by the newly established EMB. Some government ministers also saw the promotion of the Empire as a means by which to counter the expansion of socialism in Britain. The Board was established with cross-party support, including from the Labour Party, such was the consensus around imperial values during the inter-war years. The EMB sought to persuade people to 'buy British', using all means of mass communication to induce people to change their purchasing habits which the EMB believed could only happen by 'bringing the Empire alive'.[14] The EMB only lasted until 1933 but, under the direction of Stephen Tallents, it showed itself to be highly innovative in the area of publicity. Tallents appreciated the importance of advertising and 'translated the message of the advertising profession into a language of government service'.[15] Posters and leaflets were designed and distributed in large numbers, including *A Book of Empire Dinners*, whose first print run of 10,000 was distributed within a few weeks, and leaflets such as *Why Every Woman Ought to Buy British*. By the time of its closure the Board had issued 10 million leaflets and pamphlets and 7 million copies of 50 different shop window posters.[16] One of the posters in 1931 – *Remember The Unemployed, They are Your Brothers* – attests to the domestic consideration in the 'Buy British' campaign. The EMB took out advertisements in the British press and employed a press officer to inform the newspapers of its activities. It appointed a representative of the BBC on its publicity committee and was able to persuade the Corporation to broadcast numerous talks relating to the Empire, including nine 15-minute talks on Friday evenings in 1932 on 'The Empire and Ourselves'.[17]

The Board was most innovative in its use of film. The Imperial Conference of 1926 believed:

> **the Cinema is not merely a form of entertainment but . . . a powerful instrument of education . . . and even when it is not used avowedly for purposes of instruction, advertisement or propaganda, it exercises indirectly a great influence in shaping the ideas of the very large numbers to whom it appeals.[18]**

Tallents set up, under the leadership of John Grierson, the EMB Film Unit. The Unit attracted several talented film-makers, including Paul Rotha, Basil Wright, Edward Anstey and the American Robert Flaherty to work for it. In films such as *Drifters* (1929) and *Industrial Britain* (1933), the Unit represented the heroic struggles of labour in a range of industries, including fishing, tea-picking and farming. These films were originally intended for showing to a mass public but the commercial cinema circuits refused to include them in their programmes. Grierson and his colleagues at the EMB pioneered a new form of British film, the documentary. Rather than use the cinema for escapist pleasure, their films had a social purpose. They sought to represent everyday life; realism was the 'appropriate mode of expression' for this type of cinema.[19] Hence the reluctance of commercial concerns to exhibit such films.

It was not only the EMB that became interested in film as a means of propaganda in the late 1920s. Private companies, such as Austin Motors and Cadbury's Chocolate, sponsored publicity and advertising films.[20] The Shell Group established a Film Unit and the Conservative Party was quick to realize the potential of the new medium.[21] In September 1924, the Party employed a travelling cinema van as part of its election campaign in Devon. By the early 1930s, the Conservative and Unionist Film Association had 10 cinema vans and a large collection of silent and sound films.[22] From 1929, a number of organizations affiliated with the labour movement became involved in the production and distribution of films. Organizations such as Kino Films, the Progressive Film Institute and the Workers Film and Photo League produced around 122 films between 1929 and 1939.[23] These films included titles such as *Peace and Plenty*, *Storm Over Asia* and *Voice of the People* as well as several films on the Spanish Civil War. The organizations distributed films relevant to the labour movement, such as Eisenstein's *Battleship Potemkin* and a number of other Soviet films. Some of these films were shown on the commercial circuit, through the independent chains such as that of Sidney Bernstein. But they were screened more usually at social and cultural gatherings, educational meetings and summer schools as well as political meetings and conferences. Miners Institutes were a favourite venue. As early as 1912 a bioscope committee had been set up at the Ogmore Vale Workmen's Hall and Institute in the Welsh Valleys and during the 1920s other miners' cinemas were founded across South Wales, the North of England and Scotland.[24] These cinemas did not only screen films made by the labour movement; much of their fare was made up of American films, popular on the commercial circuits. There were divisions within the labour movement about the value of film. A section of the movement, particularly among middle-class intellectuals associated with the Fabian Society, was critical of the cinema for its Americanizing influence.[25] However, by the mid-1930s, film had become a staple part of the political propaganda process.

The documentary tradition

The documentary film movement developed by John Grierson in Britain was part of a broader attempt to document the facts about life in Britain. The social impact of the economic depression of the 1930s led many writers, journalists, photographers, painters and film-makers to attempt to report and record accurately what was happening in British society. These documentarists were primarily middle class and their shock at discovering hunger and poverty in the North, the West and the Midlands of Britain, resulted in their trying to uncover more about these 'foreign communities' that existed outside the cosy confines and ivory towers of the South-east of England. Their efforts were an attempt to cross the rigid class divide that had been established in Victorian and Edwardian Britain. They were primarily left-wing, many being associated with the Communist Party. They believed that by documenting the facts and gathering information about life in these communities, they could contribute to increasing social awareness that would lead to political intervention to improve living conditions. One of the first efforts to document economic and social change in Britain was J. B. Priestley's *English Journey*, published in 1934. The book described the existence of three Englands – the 'old England' of squires and manor houses, cathedral closes and clergy and rural idylls; industrial England of the heavy industries, coal, steel and cotton and unemployment; and new England, the rising, bright and breezy world created by the new industries in the South-east and the Midlands. However, the most celebrated effort to capture the plight of these communities in novel form was George Orwell's *The Road to Wigan Pier*, published in 1937.

The written word was not perhaps as important in the development of the documentary movement as the visual image. Photographers, such as Bill Brandt and Humphrey Spender, captured these communities in stark black and white pictures.[26] One of the more important products of the documentary movement was the magazine *Picture Post*, which used photojournalism to provide more positive images of working people. Launched in 1938, the magazine aimed to be a British version of the American publication, *Life*, which provided documentary photographs accompanied by short commentaries. One of its founders, Stefan Lorant, an exile from Nazi Germany, used the photograph as a reporter's notebook to record the events and lives of ordinary people. Assisted by the development of smaller and less obtrusive cameras, the news photograph was already ceasing to be an illustration to a news story in the press and acquiring an intrinsic news value of its own. *Picture Post* used photographs to present a pictorial representation of events and problems. Originally aimed at an up-market audience, the magazine quickly attracted a large circulation, estimated to have reached a million a week by the eve of the war.[27] Its themes were popular cultural events, usually those close to the lives of working people. A more direct method of finding out what was happening in working-class communities came with the establishment of Mass Observation in 1937 by a poet and journalist, Charles Madge and an anthropologist, Tom Harrisson. Mass Observation was made up of volunteers, who provided detailed accounts of what they did on particular days. Teams of observers were organized to investigate specific events and habits of British life. The most ambitious project was the *Worktown* survey, funded by the publisher Victor Gollancz, which documented everyday life in Bolton in the late 1930s. Mass Observers, writing down what they saw and what they overheard, became figures of ridicule in sections of the press who characterized them as 'spies', 'eavesdroppers' and 'snoopers'.[28]

It was the medium of film that attained the pre-eminent position within documentary movement. In 1934, with the closure of the EMB, Tallents was moved to the General Post Office, taking Grierson and the Film Unit. Under the auspices of the GPO the documentary film movement blossomed. From 1933 to the outbreak of the Second World War, the Post Office spent more money on publicity than any other government department.[29] The GPO came to act as a central body for official government publicity, and, under Tallents, developed public relations activities which aimed to increase general awareness of government business. This coincided with Grierson's interest in using film to educate people to be citizens in the emerging mass democracy. As he stated in 1942: 'We are reformers, avowed and concerned with bringing alive the new materials of citizenship.'[30] Grierson and his colleagues were interested in 'high bravery of upstanding labour' and sought to capture the dignity of the lives of ordinary workers on film. Strongly influenced by Soviet cinema, the documentary film-makers placed the worker at the centre of the narrative, using the techniques of montage in film associated, above all, with the great Soviet director, Sergei Eisenstein. For the first time the daily routines of work and the workplace appeared on cinema screens. In Edgar Anstey's *Housing Problems* (1935), working men and women spoke directly to camera for the first time.[31] The documentary film-makers dispensed with the staged conventions of mainstream cinema and used ordinary people as actors and original scenes and events rather than studio reconstructions in their films. Realism and naturalism were central to the form, rooted in the belief that the camera never lies. They saw their work as a political statement and act – in other words, to report is to condemn.[32]

The documentary movement of the 1930s had a significant impact on the development of British film and television. British feature films and television programmes have borrowed and adapted from the rhetoric and work of the movement to the extent that their influence is seen as determining the way in which film-making is understood, discussed and practised in Britain.[33] But what was the impact of the movement in the 1930s? There are a number of questions that can be raised about the movement's representation of the working classes, their relationship with government and their audiences. While sympathetic to the unemployed and poor, the documentarists, the writers and photographers as well as the filmmakers, were trapped in their middle-class perspective of working people. They either portrayed the 'otherness' of the working classes or romanticized the struggle of these people. The 'otherness' was reflected in, for example, Orwell's obsession with the 'smell' of working people. Grierson talked of the dangers of travelling 'into the jungles of the Middlesborough and the Clyde' while Harrisson studied what he called 'the cannibals of Britain'.[34] In portraying the 'dignity of labour' the film-makers often concentrated on 'heroic images' of male workers. Critics referred to the 'patronizing', 'condescending' and 'sneering' attitudes expressed to ordinary people in these films. Some members of the movement, such as Paul Rotha, believed that the films did not go far enough, ignoring crucial questions such as wages, conditions of work and trade union activity and organization.[35] Much is made by modern critics of the use of an upper-middle-class voice to provide the narration, thereby contextualizing the voices of ordinary men and women in the films. But it should not be forgotten that, whatever their limitations, these images at the time had a profound impact on their audience. They were a radical departure from the representation of workers in mainstream British cinema which Ralph Bond, a member of the movement, described as providing 'servile comic relief'.[36] They are reported as having had an electrifying impact on their viewers who, unused to depictions of ordinary life, their lives at work and at play, would sometimes break into spontaneous applause.[37]

The sponsorship of the documentary film movement by the British State raises the issue of the impact of patronage on the work commissioned. Most of the films were commissioned by government departments or industry. Basil Wright's *Song of Ceylon* (1935) avoided any critical reference to imperialism and colonial exploitation, as it was produced by the GPO Film Unit in association with the Ceylon Tea Propaganda Board. *Housing Problems* (1935), which exposed the conditions of people living in London slums, was commissioned by the British Commercial Gas Association.[38] The gas industry, concerned about the London Country Council introducing electric light into council houses, sought to promote the message that 'gas is best'. Such patronage placed limitations on what could be shown and said. As one documentary film-maker acknowledged: 'The truth is that if we indulged in real social criticism to any extent, we would have immediately been without sponsorship and our whole experiment, which artistically a fine one, would have been finished. So we compromised.'[39] Grierson recognized the 'necessary propaganda limits' of working with government and industry but argued that bodies such as the EMB provided a 'unique degree of freedom'.[40] Compromise was perhaps inevitable with the Conservative Party in power. The result was that the documentary film movement operated within a narrow agenda for reform. The final point about documentary films in the 1930s is that they played to small audiences. Despite their influence on the development of British film, in their time they had little influence outside a small coterie of people. Very few documentary films found a following on the regular commercial cinema circuits. Most were seen in non-theatrical displays: either as a result of loans to groups or institutions, primarily schools, or through a 'roadshow' scheme using mobile projection units.[41] At most, it was estimated, that the GPO's films showed to 20 million people a year, a small fraction of the 903 million who annually went to see commercial films.

Representing the Depression

The attempt to document what was happening in Britain during the two wars clashed with the increasing resources devoted by government, and to a lesser extent other political interests, to the management and manipulation of mass communication. This clash can be examined in relation to the coverage of two of the key issues of the era: the impact of the Depression and the rise of international tension in Europe. Cinema was the dominant mass media of the inter-war years, with the output of the film industry higher than it had ever been in the history of the British cinema. But what images of Britain were represented in the cinema? The overwhelming evidence is that British films of the 1930s carried 'little of divisive issues or social problems'.[42] Unemployment was hardly mentioned. Attempts to engage with the economic and social realities of the day, in films such as *The Citadel*, *The Proud Valley* and *The Stars Look Down*, only occurred late in the decade, in 1938 and 1939, and even then these films did not include any reference to the political debate around the issues.[43] *The Stars Look Down* (1939), for example, was an adaptation of A. J. Cronin's novel but marginalized the central political theme in the novel, the nationalization of the mines.[44] Filmmakers avoided engagement with social realities. The representation of working-class figures and communities in the musical comedies of the two major box-office British stars of the period, Gracie Fields and George Formby, as well as in more serious films, such as *South Riding* (1938) and *Hindle Wakes* (1931), was narrowly drawn. Class division and antagonism were absent from such films. Unemployment was seen as something that was natural and which could be faced with cheerfulness and optimism and overcome by pulling together. Gracie Field's film, *Sing As We Go* (1934), provided an anthem for the Depression. 'Our Gracie', a Lancashire lass who overcame the trials and tribulations of life, singing in the face of adversity, became the embodiment of the picture the British cinema presented of the Depression.[45] The picture painted was of 'a profoundly stable and cohesive society'.[46]

Mainstream cinema and unemployment in the 1930s

Sing As We Go is essentially an optimistic film. The beginning of the film as released makes that immediately obvious. Depression threatens, the mills are closing down and unemployment looms. 'It's a damned bad day for Greybeck', everybody agrees. On being told by Hugh Phillips, the manager's son, that the mills won't re-open 'unless we can find a new cheap process', the foreman laments 'Aye, and just when we wor getting a damned good football team together again'. The mass of the workers bemoan the loss of the mill concert party and send Grace to see 'young Mr. Phillips' on their behalf since 'He's been rehearsing with us'.

When in Mr. Phillips' office, Grace seems intent upon cracking jokes, making plain her affection for him, and displaying her indomitable spirit. 'If we can't weave, we can still sing', says Grace, and 'We'll be able to practise while we're all queuing up for the dole'.

The script direction for the last piece of Grace's dialogue reads 'carrying it off bravely'. And it is precisely that spirit – 'bravery and fortitude in the face of adversity' – which is engendered in the subsequent scene when Grace reports back to the workers. On being told that 'It's no good. We'll have to pack up', an older man jeers, 'Well Grace, this lot's knocked the song and dance out of you'. 'No it hasn't, long face' she replies sharply. And turning to the crowd, Grace utters: 'Come on girls, come on lads. Let's leave the owd place in style. Give it a chorus. "Sing as we go" '. Linking arms together, the workers march out with a rousing chorus of the theme song to the film.

By this point the scene has been well and truly set: depression and unemployment are unfortunate occurrences: they deprive people of their livelihood and their social life; but they threaten both workers and bosses alike. Furthermore such setbacks need not take away personal dignity or pride in one's local culture. And it is possible to overcome adversity. Most of the rest of the film shows Grace just doing that . . . and in the process treats the audience to a rich array of comic escapades.

Only at the end of the film do we return to the problems of the mill. Yet it too is saved by a miracle of technological innovation, the sort of 'new cheap process' Hugh was talking about. The mill re-opens and . . . Grace leads the workers back in triumphant procession, at the head of a column which now includes a brass band. Everyone boisterously sings the theme song and some are waving the Union Jack. The band marches off and the workers follow on behind Grace until a new camera shot singles her out and brings her to the forefront of the screen. Gaily she continues singing, someone rudely brushes past her, but now she confidently calls after him: 'Who do you think you're shoving?' She fades from view to reveal the logo of Dean's Ealing Studios, yet another Union Jack, which fills the entire screen as the film comes to an end.

Source: Tony Aldgate's *The British Cinema in the 1930s*, Unit 7, Block 2, *The Historical Development of Popular Culture in Britain*, in the Open University *Popular Culture* Course, Open University, 1981.

What was shown in British cinemas during the 1930s was carefully controlled by film censorship. The power of the British Board of Film Censors (BBFC) was extended in the 1920s to include pre- as well as post-production censorship. The grounds for banning or cutting films were also broadened to include depictions of conflict between capital and labour; in the words of one censor, if a strike is 'the prominent feature of the story, we would consider the subject unsuitable'.[47] Industrial, social and political conflict was discouraged. Attempts to turn critical novels of the 1930s into films were stopped. Walter Greenwood's acclaimed novel and play, *Love on the Dole*, was rejected twice by the BBFC. Ostensibly the script was found by the censors to present 'too much of the tragic and sordid side of poverty'.[48] However, it was the scenes of confrontation between the police and demonstrators that were 'undesirable'. Another novel which starkly exposed the problems of poverty in the 1930s, *Means Test Man*, also never made it to the screen. The BBFC's policy on the depiction of industrial affairs is highlighted by its treatment of two films: *Tidal Waters* submitted as a script by Gainsborough Pictures in 1932 and *Red Ensign*, released in 1934. Both pictures centred on stories of industrial unrest. *Tidal Waters* was about the conflict between strikers and non-strikers in London docklands which culminated in a plot to sabotage a fleet of barges while *Red Ensign* centred on a dispute in a Clydeside shipyard which involved strikes and sabotage. The difference which enabled the latter film to be exhibited was that its hero was a crusading managing director, played by Michael Redgrave, who risks his own money to save the yard, prevent the sabotage of his ship and persuade his workers not to strike with a rousing, patriotic speech.[49] The BBFC prevented the making of any film that directly tackled class conflict and social unrest and encouraged films that promoted social harmony and the acceptance of the status quo. Such was the influence of the Board that its President could boast in 1937: 'We may take pride in observing that there is not a single film showing in London today which deals with any of the burning questions of the day.'[50]

The newsreels, while not directly subject to BBFC's jurisdiction, were also restricted in their reporting of contemporary events. Unemployment was represented as a difficulty that affected a small number of areas and which was being tackled by growing welfare provision. The hunger marches and demonstrations were reduced to issues of law and order and policing. The British Paramount story on the arrival of the marchers on the first 'Great National Hunger March against the Means Test' in October 1932, in Hyde Park, praised the police in their attempts to maintain order.[51] However, scenes of the police baton-charging marchers were disapproved of by Whitehall. Paramount, a newcomer to the British newsreel scene, filmed the demonstration against the stated wishes of the Home Office and, as a result, was denied access to the reporting of official events which, given the fierce competition between the companies to be first with the 'news', was a harsh penalty. The effect was to ensure that the company complied with the wishes of the government in its coverage of subsequent marches.[52] The newsreels ignored or marginalized the political message of the demonstrators. Even in 1936, when the Jarrow March took place and the coverage was a little more sympathetic, the focus was on the plight of the town of Jarrow and the story highly personalized around among others the local MP, Ellen Wilkinson, who in contrast with some of the other march organizers, such as the National Unemployed Workers Movement, was regarded as a 'responsible person'.[53] The British press, including *The Times*, the *Manchester Guardian* and the *Daily Mail* emphasized the irresponsible elements controlling events, labelling the marchers 'Moscow dupes' and 'pawns in a Communist game' and highlighting the threat they posed to public order.[54]

The new medium of radio was also subject to pressure to conform. Jonathan Dimbleby argues that, in face of the poverty and hunger of the Depression, the BBC was 'content to purvey the general goodwill of a country vicar at the vestry tea party'.[55] The Corporation was cautious in its treatment of unemployment, industrial relations and poverty. Its sensitivity was illustrated by the Ferrie incident in 1932. William Ferrie, a Communist trade union official, had been asked to give a talk in response to a commentary from a leading industrialist who claimed that the conditions of the working class had improved considerably in the twentieth century. Ferrie departed from his agreed script and was cut off. This confirmed the view of many British working people, formed by the BBC's performance during the General Strike, that the Corporation was biased.

Censorship of newsreel coverage of the Hunger Marches

An example of the kind of thing that may happen unless we have some hold occurred in 1932 in conjunction with the demonstrations by the so-called '*Hunger Marchers*'.

Some very unfortunate films were taken and exhibited which, by isolating small incidents, gave an entirely exaggerated impression of what was going on and made it look as if the Police were being unnecessarily violent and brutal. The Companies then operating were therefore asked to abstain from taking any pictures of the demonstrations and they willingly agreed except one – the Paramount Company – who took films and sent them to America where they were widely exhibited.

An opportunity of 'retaliating' upon the Paramount Company occurred almost at once when they asked for some special facilities to photograph the Lord Mayor's Show.

The facilities were refused and the Company were told in effect when they protested that if they would not put themselves out a little to help us, we should not be inclined to afford them any special assistance.

Home Office Minute (H. O. 45), signed by Sir Philip Game, Commissioner of Police of the Metropolis, 28 October, 1938

Source: Stead, P. (1988) 'Wales and film', in Herbert, T. and Elwyn Jones, G., *Wales between the Wars*, Cardiff: University of Wales Press.

The BBC very early on did attempt to grapple with the issues more seriously than other media. Between 1932 and 1934, there were a number of series looking at unemployment, housing conditions and the industrial scene. Produced by the Talks department, series such as S. O. S. (1933), *Time to Spare* (1934) and *Other People's Houses* (1933), allowed working people to speak for themselves. The broadcasting of eye-witness accounts and the personal opinions of working people, however circumscribed, represented a broadening of access to the means of mass communication. There was outcry at these programmes in the press and Parliament. Reith rejected a request by Prime Minister Ramsey McDonald to stop the series *Time to Spare*. However, in 1935, with the Charter up for renewal, the Corporation ceased to broadcast such programmes and closed the Talks Department, thereby ending the BBC's efforts to report the impact of the Depression. In the late 1930s only in the BBC regions were such programmes made. Programme-makers in Manchester, charged with the remit of representing the people of the region, made a number of innovative programmes on the lives of working people. Under the Programme Director of the Northern Region, E. A. Harding, a man banished from London for, in Reith's words, being 'a very dangerous person',[56] programme-makers, such as Olive Shapley and D. G. Bridson, developed the techniques of radio actuality and broadened the representation of working life. Programmes, such as *The Classic Soil* (1939), a comparison of working-class life of the day with that of 100 years previously, and

They Speak for Themselves (1939), made use of the actual voices of local working people. The output of the BBC North Region in the late 1930s not only pioneered many of the features of radio we take for granted today but also represented a considerable advance in social documentation of the period.

Reporting the rise of fascism

The other great issue of the 1930s was the rise of fascism, particularly in Germany. There was little critical debate or discussion in the mass media about government foreign policy, particularly the consequences of the Munich Agreement in 1938, a crucial point on the road to the Second World War. For most of the decade the press supported the government's policy of 'appeasement', keeping any criticism of the Nazi regime out of the newspapers and trying to minimize any talk of war. *The Times*, under the editorship of Geoffrey Dawson, led the efforts of the British press in backing the appeasement policy. His attempts to keep anti-German comment out of his paper were illustrated by his reaction to a temporary ban on his newspaper in Germany following his correspondents' reporting of the bombing of Guernica in Spain by Nazi warplanes in 1937. Dawson said he could not understand the reaction as he had done all in his power 'night after night, to keep out of the paper anything that might have hurt their susceptibilities'.[57] Dawson's rejection for publication of copy that carried criticism of Nazi Germany typified the attitude of many newspaper owners and editors to any journalist who sought to challenge government policy or report facts that contradicted the official line. Outspoken critics of appeasement, including Winston Churchill, were denied access to the pages of the British press. Even liberal and Labour-leaning papers, such as the *Daily Herald* and the *News Chronicle*, often cooperated with this policy. Vernon Bartlett, foreign correspondent of the *News Chronicle* and vigorous critic of fascism, found his newspaper refused to print his report on Munich.[58] The British press in the 1930s was eager to promote the 'feel good' factor in face of what was happening abroad and at home. In particular, newspapers played down international tensions – for example, the *Daily Express* at the beginning of 1938 told its readers *THERE WILL BE NO WAR THIS YEAR NOR NEXT YEAR EITHER*.[59]

The other mass media pursued the same approach to international affairs. Newsreels critical of government policy or Nazi Germany were suppressed or leaned on to ameliorate their comments. A Paramount newsreel in September 1938 covering the speeches of leading critics of the Munich talks was withdrawn after the Foreign Secretary asked the American ambassador to intervene with the parent company.[60] The BBFC banned the *March of Time* film, 'Inside Nazi Germany', in 1938; according to one censor, the film 'would give grave offence to a nation with whom we are on terms of friendship and which it would be impolitic to offend'.[61] Feature films on the topic were also carefully vetted by the Board. *Pastor Hall* was one of a number of films not passed for production by the censors. Submitted as a script in 1939, its portrayal of the persecution of Pastor Niemoller by the Nazis was declared 'inexpedient' for exhibition and 'anti-Nazi propaganda'.[62] The film was made on the outbreak of the war. Anti-Semitism was also a sensitive subject but the BBFC was not totally consistent in its treatment of the topic. The film, *Jew Suss*, which dealt with anti-Semitism in the eighteenth century, was passed in 1934. During the 1930s, films which were overtly critical of Nazi Germany were banned by the BBFC. From 1928 the BBFC had sought guidance from the Foreign Office on any film that had a foreign theme or setting.

The BBC ran into trouble in its coverage of foreign affairs in 1933 as a result of a commentary made by its then foreign correspondent, Vernon Bartlett, who was mildly critical of the government's position after the German withdrawal from the League of Nations. Prime Minister Ramsay MacDonald complained to Reith about what he saw as an infringement of the BBC's Charter which forbade editorial comment. Bartlett's services were quietly dispensed with. The event impressed on the Foreign Office the need 'to find some way of guiding the BBC's foreign comment more than we do'.[63] In 1935, the BBC was forced by the government to cancel a series of talks entitled *The Citizen and his Government* which included contributions from Sir Oswald Mosley, leader of the British Union of Fascists, and Harry Pollitt of the British Communist Party. The BBC was also prevented from revealing that the decision had been made as a result of government intervention.[64] The BBC's compliance granted the government a veto over the Corporation's reporting of foreign affairs. The 'independent expressions of views' of the European situation on the wireless were discouraged. As a result, the BBC's reporting of the major overseas events in the late 1930s, including the Spanish Civil War, the Czechoslovakia Crisis and the Munich Agreement, as well as the resignation of Anthony Eden as Foreign Secretary in 1938, was cautious and limited. Even if some contemporary comment expressed anxiety about the 'alarmist' and 'depressing' content of BBC News, the chief news editor for much of the period was certain that the Corporation had 'take[n] part in a conspiracy of silence'.[65]

Managing the news in the 1930s

The success enjoyed by government in laying down the framework within which much of the mass media represented and reported the key events of the 1930s was the outcome of the way in which politicians and government officials adjusted to the new politics of mass democracy. Universal suffrage was established in 1928 when all women were finally given the vote. Consideration of public opinion rather than the horse trading between a small cabal of political figures became the essence of politics in the 1930s. Some politicians, such as Lloyd George, were slow to grasp that public meetings and smoke-filled rooms were being superseded by the new media technologies as the most important means to build political support. Other political figures were quick to adapt to the new circumstances. Tory Prime Minister, Stanley Baldwin, had begun to appear in the newsreels in 1923, using the medium to appeal directly to the new mass electorate. Baldwin emphasized the theme of the stability of Britain compared with the chaos and problems abroad, stressing in a newsreel in 1936 that at home 'people as a whole have never been more prosperous, better cared for and more contented'.[66] The innovations of his successor, Neville Chamberlain, however, were to have a longer-lasting impact on British politics. He developed a system of news management to manipulate the press and other media.

The creation of the Press Office at Number Ten Downing Street in 1931 confirmed the growing importance of government publicity and propaganda. Ramsay MacDonald had appointed a press advisor in 1929 to counter the hostility of the press barons to his Labour government.[67] However, it was under George Steward, the Chief Press Relations Officer to the Prime Minister Neville Chamberlain in the 1930s, that the government began to coordinate the flow of government news and information to the media and the public. Steward introduced regular briefings for selected correspondents and more crucially centralized the release of all government information in his hands. Chamberlain briefed the correspondents on a daily basis and used the briefings to place his policy – and optimistic view of events – before the British press. The degree to which the correspondents were willing to report the Prime Minister's words verbatim surprised even officials in Whitehall.[68] The success of the briefings system led the government to establish a daily meeting between senior government officials and editors and owners during the Munich crisis. Arthur Mann, editor of the *Yorkshire Post*, and one of the few editors of a Tory newspaper who was critical of Chamberlain's policy, warned of the dangers of the press becoming too familiar with ministers. By entering into 'close relationships with Ministers of the Crown', journalists, he stated, would be incapacitated 'if called upon to criticise them in their representational capacity'.[69] This is exactly what happened in the reporting of the appeasement policy. Most of the British press responded to government overtures, abandoning their role of acting as a watchdog on behalf of the public and adopting a partisan role in favour of government policy.

The government's hold over the British media can be explained by a number of factors. The concentration of ownership of the British media enabled proprietors to exert extensive control over the media's output in the 1930s. This was most apparent in the British press where the 'press barons' exerted considerable influence over their newspapers. However, the interests of the press barons went beyond that of the newspaper industry. Lord Rothermere, the owner of the *Daily Mail*, the only paper that was consistently pro-Nazi throughout the inter-war years, owned one of the major newsreel companies. There was a close relationship between the Conservative Party and the owners and controllers of the newsreel companies. The Conservative Party was in government for most of the decade. The Newsreel Association of Great Britain, which represented the owners' interests, supported the party, and, in particular, Chamberlain at election times.[70] The business goals of the media industries, the press, cinema and newsreels, coincided with government policy. International tensions, the threat of war and unemployment undermined confidence in British industry and business. Under pressure from advertisers and wary of their commercial concerns, the newspaper industry stayed cheerful. The close connections between the film industry and the City as well as the business interests of the press and newsreels companies led them to ignore what was happening for their short-term commercial needs.

Projecting Britain

The overwhelming image projected of Britain by the mainstream mass media in the 1930s was of a relatively cosy, confident and comfortable nation. The poet Cecil Day Lewis described the tone of the newsreels as reassuring and upbeat and their content 'trivial with nothing to trouble the conscience'.[71] The emphasis was on British success and achievement, with sport, royalty and the military, industrial cooperation, the comings and goings of world leaders as well as the latest fashion and leisure pastimes receiving regular coverage. Domestic tranquillity was contrasted with vicissitudes of events overseas. A Gaumont-British story from August 1936 is typical of the coverage. Originally scripted under the title 'Wonderful Britain', the newsreel told its audience, after a round-up of events abroad, that

> in a spirit not of boastfulness but rather of gratitude we turn from these fitful scenes to fortunate Britain – still, with its tradition of sanity, the rock of steadying influence amid the eddying streams of world affairs. British industries have shaken off the chains that kept them fettered in the aftermath of the world war.[72]

The image presented by the newsreels was replicated throughout the mainstream media – press, radio and, above all, the cinema.

For some critics, the content of the mass media reflected the need for escapism in the face of the problems of everyday life during the Depression years. George Perry argues that British films in the 1930s helped to cheer up people by providing an 'escape from reality'. Perry's argument has been summed up thus: 'times were difficult, but the cinema provided fantasy and escapism for a country beset by difficulty'.[73] This view is supported by the popularity of stars such as Fields and Formby, who were much loved by the British public, as well as of the films of Ginger Rogers and Fred Astaire. However, to believe that the cinema had little significance other than to provide fantasy and dreams is to ignore their ideological role in the 1930s. British films projected a particular picture of the world which helped to 'organise the audience's experiences in the sense of fostering social integration and the acceptance of social constraints'.[74] They sought to promote social consensus and harmony through the projection of a particular set of values and a common collective identity – in the words of the social historian, Arthur Marwick, 'the cinema in fact reinforced the established order of things, either through sheer escapism or an affirmation of British values'.[75] Whether it was by distraction or direction, the British cinema projected the image of a united and contented nation.

The mass media in the 1930s addressed their audience as citizens of one nation, not as members of an antagonistic class, race, sex or ethnic group.[76] This is clearly illustrated by the most famous film made by the GPO Film Unit, *Night Mail* (1936). Directed by Basil Wright and Harry Watt, using the poetry of W. H. Auden and the music of Benjamin Britten, the film emphasized the theme of unity. The hero of the film is not the people, the rail workers and postmen and women who deliver the mail, but the train whose journey from London to Scotland unites the nation.[77] This was the aim of official propaganda throughout the inter-war years. Manipulated by Whitehall's 'good news machine', the media between 1919 and 1939 played an important role in the reinforcement of a particular construction of national identity. Tallents in 1932, in his pamphlet 'The Projection of Britain', outlined the appropriate components of this identity. It was not the 'social realist' image of the documentary movement but a 'class-based' and 'conservative' vision. It laid stress on the *English* virtues of decency, niceness, fair play, justice and order, gentlemanly conduct, bravery against the odds and moderation. Patriotism and pride, especially in Britain's imperial venture, were stressed. It was a nation where everyone knew their place and in which the lower orders were respectful of their betters. Stanley Baldwin was an incarnation of these values. In his speeches and newsreel appearances he stressed a picture of England and Englishness which was of 'a sensible and moderate people united behind their government, true to their historic traditions'.[78] His appearance as 'bluff country squire' fitted the image of the countryside and rural idyll which British propaganda has always presented as the essence of Englishness. Despite being one of the most urbanized and industrialized nations in the world, England has often been represented by rural images such as the village green, hedgerows, cottages, green fields, copses and streams. The 1930s saw an upsurge in popular interest in leisure activities associated with the countryside, hiking, rambling, camping and cycling. Corresponding images of Englishness were redolent in the output of the mass media.

What was the impact of official propaganda in the 1930s? Some contemporary observers point to the decline of political consciousness. The trivial content of the press, cinema and newsreels – as well as the advent of monotonous factory work and cheaper luxury items and amusements – is held responsible for the general apathy and domestic tranquillity of the inter-war years. The growth of political activism and consciousness in British society was confined to sectors outside the mainstream – the Communist Party, the New Left Book Club, the Peace Pledge Union and the Documentary Film Movement. But this does not mean that Britain was a more united country. The uniform message of the media did assist in the construction of a notion of 'Britishness' between the wars but it did not break down class and regional identities. The attempts to sweep debate under the carpet on some of the key issues of the day had a consequence for public confidence in the British political system by widening the gap between the rulers and the ruled. The failure to provide any critical debate on the Munich Agreement by the British mass media or to reflect the range of feelings of the British public on appeasement was critical in this respect. BBC Manchester's Olive Shapley, drawing on the work on Mass Observation, provided one of the few insights into popular feelings over Munich that appeared in the British media. Ordinary people were either confused or hostile to Chamberlain's policy. There was no consensus over government policy. The lack of critical discourse about policy to Nazi Germany and the other major issues of the inter-war years damaged the credibility of the British mass media in the eyes of the public.

7

Their finest hour: the Second World War and the British way of censorship

A set of powerful memories about the Second World War is deeply entrenched in British popular imagination. Since 1945 the insatiable interest in this period can be measured by the vast output of British books, TV, radio and films devoted to the war years. This interest amounts to a national obsession. Whether it is *Captain Hurricane* and comics such as *Victor* or *Valiant*, or Captain Mainwaring in the popular TV comedy, *Dad's Army*, the British people have been reliving 'their finest hour' through the mass media ever since 1945. Recollections of the war years have been shaped as much by the myths promoted by the mass media, particularly the cinema in the 1950s, as by the reality and experience of the war. The mass media were central to the war effort, almost as important as the fighting forces themselves. A war of national survival demanded the total mobilization of the population. It was the 'People's War' in which ordinary men and women played a crucial role. Distinctions between the 'home front' and the war front were swept aside as the conflict touched everyone's lives. The maintenance of morale and popular domestic support for the war was an overwhelming success for British propaganda efforts. Even Goebbels, the Nazi propaganda genius, expressed his admiration for Britain's particular talent for propaganda, censorship and psychological warfare. However, many British people were unaware of the government's total control over the wartime media, and the extent to which the values and attitudes of wartime Britain were shaped by the propaganda machinery of the British State has never been fully appreciated or acknowledged. The war had a profound impact on the nature of the mass media and their depiction of life in Britain. They underwent a process of 'democratization', which made them more sensitive to a broader range of social experiences and activities, including a wider representation of the views, aspirations and demands of ordinary people.

War and social change

Changes in the British mass media during the Second War World can only be understood within the context of the fundamental shift that took place within British society. British nostalgia for the Second World War is rooted in a particular national experience of war. In contrast to most of Europe, Britain was not occupied; there was no experience of total defeat and national humiliation which tore apart other nations. For many people the war years were 'the best years of our lives'. It brought comradeship, a sense of national purpose, excitement, drama and, most crucially for many, jobs. It was the war that swept away the scourge of unemployment and saw a crumbling of rigid class distinctions that pervaded British society before 1939. One woman wrote in her diary at the time that 'there is one thing, and only one thing about this war – it is an instant and complete leveller of "classes"'.[1] A vivid example of 'social mixing' was the evacuation of nearly a million children from the major urban areas to the countryside in the early days of the conflict. Not that the billeting of poor children from the slums on middle-class households in the shires always led to more understanding. Often it merely confirmed the middle-class image of the fecklessness of the working classes.[2] All the same, the war effort forced British social institutions to accept the interaction of different classes; whether it was in factories, the armed forces, the home guard, voluntary services or welfare organizations. For George Orwell, this was the recognition of the strength of 'patriotism' in Britain 'which is stronger than class-hatred'.[3] Others argue it represented a genuine shift in popular attitudes. The movement in popular opinion during the war has been documented and after Dunkirk and the end of the 'phoney war' in June 1940 popular resentment against 'privilege' and 'vested interests' grew rapidly. This was accompanied by the belief that things were not going to be the same after the war had finished.[4]

There was also an acknowledgement by those in power that to prosecute the war effectively, working people had to be promised more than the usual 'King and Country' rhetoric. In particular, they had to be promised something tangible in terms of the reconstruction of British post-war society. The Labour MP and First Lord of the Admiralty, A. V. Alexander, stated: "Our working men and women have responded magnificently to any and every call made upon them. Their reward must be a new Britain. Never again must the unemployed become the forgotten men of peace.'[5] These words appeared significantly on a caption shown at the end of the film *Love on the Dole*, banned by the BBFC during the 1930s, but released in 1941. The new public mood that emerged from the war years favoured 'pragmatic' economic and social reform. These aspirations received concrete expression in the Beveridge Report, published in December 1942, which laid the foundations for the building of the welfare state in post-war Britain. Throughout the war tension existed between popular and official attitudes to change. Many in government and positions of authority, particularly in the Conservative Party, while recognizing the need to mobilize people, sought to manage and restrict the pace of change. The mass media were at the centre of the conflicting attitudes to social change. While seeking to reflect popular feeling and play a role in the propaganda effort around building a new Britain at the end of the war, they were also subject to the censorship of a government cautious of change. The different media responded to the change in different ways; some were more outspoken and bolder than others in promoting the cause of change.

The propaganda effort

Propaganda played a central role in Britain's prosecution of the war. There was external propaganda aimed at enemy countries, in particular, occupied Europe, as well as the effort made to maintain the morale of the armed forces overseas. However, the maintenance of home front morale was crucial. There was pessimism in British official and government circles at the outset of war about the willingness of the British people to fight. This was to some extent a reaction to the wasted slaughter of the First World War and the false promises then made to the soldiers that on their return from the battlefield there would be 'homes for heroes'. The failure of these homes to appear had bred cynicism among working people concerning any talk of reward for their blood, sweat and tears. The inter-war years had also seen, in reaction to the devastation of the Great War, the growth of pacifism. Many felt that the experience of the 1914–18 war should never again be repeated. The rise of the Peace Pledge Union, which within a year of its launch in 1936 had over 120,000 members, represented a high degree of popular anti-war sentiment in Britain. But the most significant factor accounting for official nervousness about the will to fight was the sharpening of social divisions in British society in the 1930s as a result of mass unemployment and the unrest that it brought in its wake.

Class antagonism had been acutely felt in the 1930s. Fear of encouraging such antagonism, as we have seen, led to the policing of what the BBC could say about unemployment and industrial relations and references to social divisions and difference in the cinema were carefully vetted by the British Board of Film Censors. On the outbreak of war in 1939, those in authority believed that the experience of the 1930s had made the British worker so militant that he wouldn't fight and that class divisions would weaken morale. This fear was fuelled by Mass Observation reporting that among some sections of the working class there was a feeling that if the Germans came, things couldn't get any worse.[6] To combat these problems, the government had started to plan for wartime propaganda as early as 1936. The propaganda effort at home and abroad was to be coordinated by the establishment of a new ministry.

The Ministry of Information

The Ministry of Information (MoI) started to operate as soon as the war broke out in September 1939. By 1945, it had a staff of 3000, and its activities reached into all areas of life and every aspect of cultural production. The Ministry was split into 14 divisions classified in a number of broad groupings: press relations, news and censorship, publicity, cultural production, including divisions for film, literature and arts, radio and communications and administration. In addition, there were 12 regional offices. The early months of its existence were riddled with complaints and grumbles about the slowness and ineptitude of its operation. The American news magazine, *Time*, spoke for many when it complained:

> **Nobody could accuse British propaganda of functioning smoothly last week. It was clumsy, amateurish, slow starting, and gave an impression**

> **like that of a sincere but badly staged show in which the stagehands dropped things during big speeches, and the curtain came down at the wrong time.[7]**

Comedian Tommy Handley branded the MoI the Ministry of Aggravation. There were also concerns expressed inside government about what the role of the new Ministry should be in relation to other departments of state. The first Minister, Lord Macmillan, admitted to Parliament in October 1939 that he had 'considerable difficulty in ascertaining its function'.[8] Confusion over the MoI's role in the early years was compounded by the rapid turnover of staff at the top of the organization. A number of luminaries took charge, four in the first two years, including Lord Reith, but each left almost as quickly as they had arrived. It was not until Brendan Bracken took over in July 1941 that the Ministry was to have consistent leadership, which he gave it until the end of the war. In the early years the MoI achieved a reputation more as an irritant than a source of reassurance. This was made worse by the Ministry's initial attempts to mobilize popular support.

The Ministry's early attempts at propaganda were based on the assumption that the government had to build up the people's resolve. One MoI memo in 1940 expressed concern that 'the public may be subjected to a series of shocks, the effect of which . . . may be that nerves will be shattered and the will to victory be grievously impaired'.[9] The MoI therefore sought to bring 'restraint and sober determination' and attempted to promote 'an attitude of cheerful courage in keeping with the British character'.[10] Traditional themes of King and country and 'our past' were woven into the Ministry's efforts. From the outset there was recognition of the need to appeal to people from all walks of life but the tone adopted to address them was patronizing and rooted in the class attitudes of the 1930s. One early poster, 'Your courage, Your cheerfulness, Your resolution will bring Us victory' simply served to reinforce class divisions, between them and us, and failed to mobilize people. The press was vocal in its criticism of the poster: *The Times* called it 'an insipid and patronising poster'.[11] The MoI's estimation of the intelligence of the people is illustrated by its instructions on how to avoid panic in an air-raid shelter. They recommended that 'scared people sheltering during a raid should be made to sit quietly, be told their fear is only natural and given a cup of coffee after which they should be alright'.[12] The government had little interest in finding out how people felt and what they thought about the war. In keeping with the spirit of the 1930s they simply relied on exhortation and basic appeals to patriotism. Official propaganda at the start of the war was inept, lacking knowledge of public opinion and betrayed a complete distrust of the people. It was in Lord Reith's words, 'utterly ineffective'.

The failure of the early propaganda effort was highlighted by the fact that the first radio personality of war was not British but German. In the absence of adequate news at home many started to listen to the broadcasts of William Joyce (Lord Haw-Haw) from Berlin. In the autumn of 1939, one-sixth of the British listening audience, as many as 6 million people, tuned in regularly to his broadcasts and by January 1940, 25 per cent said they had listened to his programme the previous day.[13] His appeal to the British public was partly the result of curiosity and the lack of any real war news during the 'phoney war'. His lisping upper-class accent was also a source of amusement, hence his nickname. But he also played on the themes of class which had some resonance for his audience. Joyce's early success encouraged the MoI to reassess their efforts. Another impetus to change was the information that the MoI started to obtain through polls and surveys about what people were thinking. The Ministry's Home Intelligence Committee began to publish regular reports of popular attitudes which were to play a key role in guiding the propaganda effort during the war. Instead of 'guessing the mood' of the public, a range of modern techniques were deployed, including the use of the services of Mass Observation, Gallup (set up in the UK in 1938), and the BBC Listener Research Department (started in 1936), under the Ministry's control. Armed with a more realistic assessment of popular opinion and more knowledge about what people wanted, the MOI began to adapt its campaigns – although for most of the war the Ministry was nervous of too much innovation.

Letter to Ministry of Information from a member of the public, 1940

Dear Sir,

I am amazed at the way people are talking of late. I work in one of the biggest armaments factories and on all sides of me I hear discussions going on. I cannot put into words what they say about the BBC, and any opposition I make to what they say, they call me alsorts of fools for believing you, and I find nine out of every ten of them listen to Lord Haw-Haw, saying they can get more truth from him, and they want me to do the same. They are saying that this terrible defeat in Flanders is being twisted into a victory. It is a standing joke in the factory about your oft repeated phrase, 'all our planes returned safely'. According to them the government ought to be shot for what they have done to our boys, and though I don't know what they mean they say the Mayfair clique are leading our men to their doom. They said to me today for instance, how crafty they are in trying to camouflage Lord Gort's return here into something noble, they say that the stuttering officer who spoke in Gort's defence, was an example of the type of men who are leading us to-day. Really I am so bewildered by all they say that I do not know what to believe, am I to believe that Germany have got us in a trap like they say. I feel I must listen to German news now, or I cannot argue unless I know the two sides.

Yours truly
Miss Verney

Source: Yass, M. (1981) *This is Your War: Home Front Propaganda in the Second World War*, London: HMSO, p. 22.

MoI campaigns

A good example of the Ministry's adapting to the new situation was the Home Front Campaign on Food Rationing. In October 1939, the War Cabinet started to think about food rationing. It had to be done, but the question was how to do it. A decision was taken to gauge public opinion but the chosen technique for finding out was a tried and tested method of the establishment. They decided to take soundings – which often meant simply talking to reliable journalists of their acquaintance, or consulting members of their club, or ascertaining the views of their servants! Public opinion was seen as the aggregation of the views of journalists or of the interested parties.[14]

This approach did not last long and the Ministry turned to Gallup and Mass Observation to gather information about attitudes to food consumption and rationing. Based on the findings, the MoI and the Ministry of Food adopted new techniques of persuasion to encourage people to eat better and to prepare for food rationing. From the first poster ads – 'Twenty things to do with a carrot' – emerged a highly successful and sophisticated campaign. The new Minister of Food, Lord Frederick Woolton, quickly realized the possibilities of opinion-polling techniques and exploited all the means of mass communication to put his messages across. A former department store owner, ex-social worker and part-time freelance journalist, Woolton projected himself as an avuncular 'Uncle Fred' figure and employed many of the advertising devices we associate with radio today, including the use of the first 'radio jingle'.[15] Woolton's methods were innovative and extremely popular and they were carried over into peacetime when he put his skills to use for Conservative Central Office.

Another example of the Ministry's ability and willingness to learn from its mistakes was the campaigns on the role and contribution of women to the war effort. With most of the male population fighting on the front line, women played a crucial role on the home front. Whether as munitions workers, anti-aircraft battery operatives or transport workers, women were of vital strategic importance to the war effort. This was not at first grasped by the MoI which in 1940 launched a series of special broadcasts and pamphlets on the theme of 'The Kitchen Front'. The series included titles such as 'Being Brave' and 'Looking Our Best'.[16] Mass Observation was quick to get the message back to the MoI that this campaign was badly received. Most people considered such material to be patronizing, inept, clumsy and ill-judged. Traditional images of femininity were replaced by material which reflected the range of contributions women made to the war effort. For example, the 1944 pamphlet from the MoI, 'Fifty Facts about Women', discussed women in roles such as drivers, dustmen, postmen and engineers as well as in the forces, land army and factories. The BBC's decision not to use women as newsreaders during the war illustrated the discomfort within official circles – and beyond – about the part women played in the war effort. For the BBC 'matters are not so desperate that we are considering using women as newsreaders'.

What are we fighting for?

In August 1940, the MoI decided that the propaganda effort on the home front would have to change. It instructed that 'exhortation must be as far as possible abandoned. The word "morale" must not be used again. People must on no account be told to be brave. In future the Ministry would restrict its role to information and explanation.'[17] The emphasis was to be on the 'people's war' and the MoI began to stress not only what Britain was fighting against but also what it was fighting for. The War Aims Committee, set up in June 1940, to discuss the broader objective of policy, identified the themes of democracy and building a better post-war world. Morale had been severely dented in 1940 and 1941 by the Blitz and the reverses on the battle front. Weekly reports of the Home Intelligence Committee showed growing resentment about the way in which better off people were able to get around the rationing system and avoid the worst of the bombing raids. After one particularly damaging raid, people in the East End were reported as complaining that 'it is always the poor that get it'.[18] Cities such as Bristol, Birmingham and Coventry were reporting low morale in late 1940 as physical fatigue began to set in. Discontent within industry was growing with shortages of materials, hold-ups and inefficiencies and, as the war progressed, more and more working days were lost through strikes and industrial disputes. There was mounting gossip and rumour about waste, profiteering and corruption. Ill feeling toward the 'better off' was a trend that emerged from these reports. The government also found growing support among the British public that things should be better after the war. Popular feeling for a 'new dawn' and a 'better Britain' was increasingly manifest in the mass media. In January 1941, the photo magazine, *Picture Post*, ran a special issue, *A Plan for Britain*, which emphasized the need for change after the war. The MoI commissioned the Boulting Brothers to make a short film, *The Dawn Guard*, in which Bernard Miles, as one of the soldiers on sentry duty, tells the audience that:

> **We've made a fine big war effort and when it's all over we've got to see to it we make a fine big peace effort . . . we can't go back to the old ways of living, leastways not all of it, that's gorn forever and the sooner we all make up our minds about that the better.**

Such sentiments were also to be found in the mainstream cinema and the press. Vague platitudes about rebuilding Britain became practical suggestions with the publication of the Beveridge Report in December 1942.

The immediate impetus for the Report came from the TUC whose concerns about the inadequacy of health insurance led them to lobby the Ministry of Health in early 1941 with the result that Arthur Greenwood, a Labour Member of the National Government, established a committee, chaired by Beveridge and including representatives of all major government departments, to undertake a wholesale review of social security. The document proved to be a milestone in

British social history with its support for a cradle-to-grave system of welfare and care. The Report has to be seen in the context of the struggle to maintain popular morale at home. Beveridge emphasized this when he concluded his report with the words that 'the purpose of victory is to live in a better world than the old world . . . each citizen is more likely to concentrate his public effort if he feels that his Government will be ready in time with plans for that better world'.[19] The MoI gave the Report's findings much publicity and it was greeted with considerable acclaim. Gallup found that within two weeks of publication 19 out of 20 people surveyed had heard of the Report and that 9 out of 10 believed it would be implemented.[20] Beveridge went on the radio to explain his plans, promising improved benefits, better housing and free education and health for all and the BBC broadcast details of the Report in 22 languages.[21] The Report was integrated into the MoI's propaganda directed abroad, with the emphasis on it as another example of the democratic values that distinguished Britain from Nazi Germany.

One major exception to the favourable response was from inside the War Cabinet. Churchill had never been particularly keen on discussing post-war reconstruction. He regarded such discussion as a distraction from the task of winning the war and used his influence to prevent any airing of what he saw as a potentially divisive topic. Following the fanfare surrounding the publication of the Beveridge Report, the government machine lapsed into total silence. Leading members of the Tory Party, led by the Chancellor, Kingsley Wood, were hostile to Beveridge. However, Churchill faced pressure to address post-war reconstruction, not only from Labour members of the coalition government but also from reform-minded Tory MPs. There was also the question of dashing the hopes of the public raised by Beveridge if the government appeared unwilling to embrace its proposals. The Cabinet in March 1943 accepted many of the Report's recommendations in principle but declined to legislate – a decision supported by the leaders of both major political parties. Agitation for the changes envisaged by Beveridge continued for the duration of the war and in November 1943 a Ministry of Reconstruction was created, thereby acknowledging the growing importance of the issue. For the remainder of the war Churchill tried to limit discussion of post-war change to woolly and vague commitments. This led to increasing frustration and was a decisive factor in Churchill's defeat at the 1945 election when people in vast numbers voted for the Labour Party which, by the end of the war, had decided to fully embrace Beveridge's recommendations.

The British way of censorship

While the projection of Britain at home and abroad was an important part of the work of the MoI, censorship was its first priority. The largest number of officers employed by the Ministry worked in the field of censorship. Their primary task was to control news output. Lord Reith during his short tenure as Minister of Information stated that, 'news is the shock troops of propaganda'.[22] The monitoring and vetting of the content of the newsreels, BBC news and the press were given top priority. There was confusion at the outset over the operation of the censorship division. The MoI underestimated the 'voracity' of the news machine when it put into place its censorship plans but before long it had set up a sophisticated and relatively sensitive operation. Rear Admiral G. P. Thomson, chief censor for the duration of the war, talked of the success of his operation:

> Many people had an idea that the BBC broadcasts went out uncensored. This is quite incorrect though it might seem at first sight an extraordinarily difficult problem to cope with. The BBC were broadcasting throughout 24 hours over their various services . . . fortunately for censorship, however, although the BBC sent war correspondents to the fighting areas and also had correspondents resident in one or two important places, such as New York, they depended entirely for their *news* bulletins on the agency tape machines. And this news had, of course, already been submitted to and passed by the censorship.[23]

What appeared a daunting task for the censors was made easier by the structure of newsgathering deployed by the British media. The provincial and national press, the BBC and the newsreel companies were dependent on the Press Association (PA), a domestic news agency, and Reuters, an international agency, for much of their home and foreign news. Controlling news at source was further simplified by PA and Reuters being located in the same building in Fleet Street. Thus the MoI could exert a considerable degree of control over the news behind the scenes without damaging the credibility of the news outlets. The censors could exert maximum influence over news content without being detected.

The British government, despite having the power to take direct control of the mass media, rarely used the full range of its powers. The British way of censorship allowed the mass media considerable space to make their own decisions, some of which were to result in rows and fierce differences of opinion. In this sense the mass media were never the mouthpieces of government. While the MoI exercised guidance, film-making, radio broadcasting and newspaper production were left in the hands of the professionals. At the heart of the so-called 'voluntary system of guidance' was the understanding that:

> proprietors and editors of newspapers, controllers and programme planners in the BBC, film-makers and senior military personnel, ministers and top civil servants would, because they came from the same social background, share the same attitudes and thus cooperate readily in the proper prosecution of the war effort.[24]

While the media were constrained by formal links with the MoI, it was these 'informal understandings' which enabled the system of censorship to work – reinforced as the war years progressed by the growing sense of social unity in the face of a common enemy and around a better future for all. The British way of censorship allowed the government to exercise control of the media while maintaining a reputation for reliability and accuracy which was contrasted to that of its adversary, Nazi Germany. The MoI might have been disbanded in 1945 but the system built up during the war continued into the post-war period as the relationships and ways of doing business had been cemented in. The foundations of this system were apparent in the performance of each of the mass media during the war.

Film and the war

The day war broke out all cinemas in Britain were closed. Fearing massive loss of life from enemy bombers all venues where people gathered in large numbers were shut down. When the expected air raids did not happen, the government, under public and commercial pressure, allowed cinema halls to reopen. From that day on the cinema was to be the most popular form of entertainment in the war years. Despite an increase in the price of attendance, people flocked to the cinema in greater numbers than ever before. Average weekly attendances increased from 19 million in 1939 to 30 million in 1945.[25] As other kinds of popular amusement disappeared, particularly pleasures associated with the middle classes such as motoring and eating out, the film industry provided many people with their only form of entertainment.

But the cinema was not simply a source of pleasure. The MoI recognized its importance as a propaganda medium. The Ministry's Films Division played a crucial role in the maintenance of home front morale. The Division, like the rest of the Ministry's efforts, took some time to be put into place. At the beginning there was a rapid turnover of those in charge. The early heads of the division, including the historian, Sir Kenneth Clark, were not from a film background but rather the world of arts and literature. John Betjeman was employed as a script writer. Initially what film had to offer as a propaganda tool was not fully appreciated. Sir John Ball, the first head of the division, the former director of publicity and research at Conservative Central Office, only favoured the leading lights in the industry, such as Sir Alexander Korda, and focused efforts on the newsreels at the expense of the feature or documentary film. The first feature film of the war, encouraged but not commissioned by the MoI, was Korda's *The Lion Has Wings* (1939), a fairly crude piece of propaganda. It was the story of an RAF bombing raid of Germany and made use of newsreel footage, as well as an extract from a previous Korda film, *Fire Over England*, which featured a stirring patriotic speech from Flora Robson as Queen Elizabeth the First. But it embodied many of the themes and images that were to be taken up by the British war film of the Second World War. It presented an image of the good-natured, but rather eccentric, Englishman pitted against the regimented, fanatical and faceless Nazi. The main location shots were of small towns and villages which evoked the 'timelessness' of England; of old values and a settled way of English life, based on decency and hard work. The film suffered from a structural weakness in that it was 'resolutely upper and middle class in tone and values with little realistic evocation of the lives of working class people'.[26] Mass

Observation surveys found considerable hostility to it as a piece of propaganda. 'It was all propaganda', said one film-goer, 'nobody wants to see that sort of thing, it's not entertainment. They get enough of that on the news.'[27] The MoI decided that film propaganda had to become more effective. To this end, a new policy plan, Programme for Propaganda, was formulated, incorporating the lessons of Korda's effort. Film propaganda, according to the programme, 'will be most effective when it is least recognisable as such' and the films had to be entertaining if they were to be good propaganda.

In April 1940, Jack Beddington, a former director of publicity at Shell, joined the Films Division which he ran until the end of the war. He resuscitated the GPO Film Unit (renamed the Crown Film Unit) which played a significant part in film propaganda for the rest of the war. Documentary film-makers, such as John Grierson and Paul Rotha, accounted for nearly 74 per cent of all the films commissioned or produced by the Films Division between August 1940 and the end of the war.[28] Many of these films projected the part ordinary people played in the war. It was these films, and in particular those of Humphrey Jennings, which included *Listen to Britain* (1942), that defined the images of the nation at war presented to other countries and handed down to subsequent generations. Beddington was criticized in some quarters for using politically motivated film-makers, like the documentarists, but most of their work was made for non-theatrical distribution; that is films shown by 16 mm mobile units outside the normal cinema halls, where the audiences were relatively small compared to the commercial circuit. Informal pre-censorship of film ideas was exercised using guidelines which encouraged certain subject matters and forbade others. The MoI encouraged themes such as 'what Britain was fighting for', 'how Britain fights' and the 'need for sacrifice if the fight is to be won'.[29] All films were vetted for security reasons and cinemas were liable for prosecution if they showed anything deemed to contain material of use to the enemy. The Ministry also exerted control through the rationing and allocation of film stock. Some differences of opinion did emerge. Noel Coward's film *In Which We Serve* (1942) and Powell and Pressburger's *The Life and Death of Colonel Blimp* (1941) were only released after a struggle between the film-makers and the authorities. But overall, in the situation of total war and the struggle for national survival, the MoI and the film-makers were prepared to cooperate.

Cooperation was facilitated by the responsiveness of the MoI to the needs of film-makers. The war had a considerable impact on the ability of the film industry to produce and exhibit its work. Shortages of material and personnel as well as the requisitioning of a large amount of studio space for war purposes made a considerable dent in the industry's film-making capability. The MoI responded to the industry's calls for assistance and although the number of films made during the war declined (on average, 69 films per year), their quality was seen as an improvement on pre-war fare. The producer, Michael Balcon, believed the war assisted the industry to assert itself in face of competition from abroad, in particular, Hollywood. Propaganda pressures led the industry to pay more attention to the presentation of things British on the cinema screens and the MoI helped to lay down a financial foundation for the industry. Film-makers were also encouraged to explore narrative and visual style. The distinction between feature film and documentary broke down with the need for film to fulfil informational and entertainment roles. Personnel shortages meant more exchange between the two branches of the industry and the outcome was 'an intermarriage of style and address' which produced 'a new, specifically British quality in filmmaking'.[30]

Film-makers, despite censorship and the guiding hand of the MoI, were freer to tackle topics they could not touch in the 1930s. The new climate made possible the filming of *Love on the Dole* as the cinema portrayed a broader representation of life in Britain. The MoI helped finance films celebrating the role of women in the war effort such as *Millions Like Us*. The Second World War appeared to establish a new relationship between the British cinema and its audience. The cinema 'reflected the changing experiences of the population, evoked the currents of opinion in the country at large, and helped visibly to manifest a good many of the concerns that captured the public's thoughts and imagination in the years between 1939 and 1945'.[31] This did not mean the British cinema became a standard bearer of social reform. For radical documentarists, such as Paul Rotha, the war films stressed patriotism at the expense of 'social good purpose'.[32] The appearance of ordinary people in films during the war was not on their own terms but as part of a set of controlled images laid down by the MoI, which by and large reinforced a 'cosy image' of Britain at war. It should also be remembered that many of the films produced during the war did not deal with the conflict. Although the upsurge of patriotism led to people wanting to see more British pictures about Britain, they were also keen to escape from what was going on around them.

Regulating the press

Invasion fears in 1940 led to the Home Office acquiring draconian powers to regulate the press. Regulation 2D allowed the government to ban any publication containing material 'calculated to foment opposition to the prosecution to a successful issue of any war in which His Majesty is engaged' with no right of appeal.[33] The powers were not greeted with total enthusiasm by Parliament and their ratification was passed by the House of Commons with only a small majority. The legislation was first used in January 1941 to close down the *Daily Worker*, the official organ of the British Communist Party. The closure of the *Daily Worker* was part of a broader attempt to curtail the left-wing press in the early years of the war. The *Daily Herald*, *Reynolds News*, and, most significantly, the *Daily Mirror* and its sister paper, the *Sunday Pictorial*, were all under government pressure to conform to official policy. All these papers had been critical of government policy under the discredited Chamberlain during the 'phoney war'. When Churchill took over as Prime Minister in 1940, he brought his long-standing animus against the press to bear. The *Herald* and *Reynolds News* tempered their criticism with the entry of the

Labour Party into government but the *Mirror* and the *Pictorial* were more difficult to deal with. Churchill accused them of 'rocking the boat' and campaigning for a 'surrender peace'. In response to a series of articles in the autumn of 1940, critical of the government's conduct of the war, he fumed that 'they stood for something most dangerous and sinister, namely an attempt to bring about a situation in which the country would be ready for a surrender peace'.[34] Churchill warned that he would take 'firm action to deal with this menace'. However, the Prime Minister found the War Cabinet divided and his threats were not realized. But in response to informal pressure through the Newspaper Proprietors Association, the *Mirror* did, in the words of one of its directors, 'pipe down'.

Clashes between the government and the two newspapers were the result of the process of social change occurring in wartime Britain. Allegations that the newspapers were not committed to winning the war mask the real reasons for the hostility of Churchill and many Conservatives to the papers. While nearly every newspaper at one time or another criticized the government for blunders or mistakes in pursuing the war effort, the *Mirror* departed from the respectful tones of the rest of the press to firmly commit itself to the side of 'us', the people, against 'them', the appeasers and their hangers-on in government who through their pusillanimous behaviour had got Britain into the war. It supported Churchill for leader in its campaign for a more vigorous prosecution of the war but felt no obligation to suspend criticism on his accession to office. The *Mirror* believed it had a duty to speak out against government incompetence. Or in the paper's own words: 'in these critical times dead wood isn't even of use for the coffins of those martyred through muddle'.[35] Much of this incompetence the newspaper saw as arising from the 'snobbery and privilege' of the British class system. It campaigned for key jobs going to those of ability rather than of birth and railed against the 'brass buttoned boneheads, socially prejudiced, arrogant and fussy'.[36] This of course was not well received by those in office who felt such comments served to undermine discipline at a crucial time.

It was over the issue of post-war reconstruction that the *Mirror* touched the rawest nerve. In 1937, under Harry Bartholomew, the newspaper became a tabloid with provocative headlines and snappy, if trivial, news stories. On the eve of the war the *Mirror*'s readership stood at over 4 million, only behind that of the *Express* and *Herald*. However, the newspaper had 'no clear impression of who those readers were, of how they located themselves socially or politically'.[37] The war years saw the newspaper grow from strength to strength by developing a close relationship with its readership. A survey conducted in the autumn of 1941 found that the newspaper's appeal reached across all social groups and classes; in particular, the *Mirror* was read widely by factory workers, members of the armed forces, and women.[38] The reason for the newspaper's close relationship with its readers was the way it used its letters and advice columns to learn what they were thinking, in particular those in the armed forces. The *Mirror* came to reflect the thirst for change, campaigning boldly for a better Britain after the war. For Churchill and other Conservatives, these calls were a threat to national unity.

In March 1942, the confrontation between the government and the *Daily Mirror* flared up into open conflict with the publication of a cartoon portraying a sailor clinging to wreckage of a torpedoed ship adrift in the open sea with the caption: 'The price of petrol has been increased by one penny – official'. The cartoonist argued he was trying to draw public attention to the sacrifice involved in getting oil to Britain. Churchill and many of his colleagues, including Ernest Bevin, the only trade union leader in the war cabinet, saw the cartoon as an attack on the government for allowing oil companies to make profits at the expense of people's lives.[39] The War Cabinet decided to ban the newspaper under Regulation 2D but had to back down in face of the protest the move caused in the House of Commons and throughout the country. The *Mirror* was allowed to continue publication and this was the last attempt to use Regulation 2D to prevent the publication of material in the press that the government did not like. In the wake of this episode, the ban on the *Daily Worker* was lifted.

The BBC at war

It was during the Second World War that radio usurped the press as the main source of information for most people. The conflict was a 'war of words' with the BBC at its heart. The propaganda effort to maintain home front morale forced the BBC to become more responsive to the audience and the war saw considerable changes in its output. However, this did not happen overnight. In September 1939, the regional service was closed down and the national service, renamed the Home Service, became the only channel at the start of war. The initial output of wartime radio was dominated by official information, such as ministers explaining the work of their department, talks by various civil servants and experts on topics such as the blackout and *Making the Most of a Wartime Larder*, and announcements of rules and regulation covering matters, ranging from fuel consumption to blood transfusions.[40] There were also regular news reports intermingled with solemn music and stirring oratory which included renditions of 'Land of Hope and Glory', military bands, as well as readings from Shakespeare. What music could be played was a matter of concern and one BBC memo lists 80 banned German and Italian composers – 40 years later the BBC was to ban over 60 discs that mentioned death or dying during the Falklands/Malvinas conflict. Entertainment in these early days consisted entirely of records and the organ playing of Sandy Macpherson. In the first fortnight of the war, there were 45 sessions of *Sandy's Half Hour* which prompted many viewers to write to the BBC saying they would rather face the Germans than hear another half hour of Sandy's organ.[41] It was this kind of output that earned the Corporation the nickname of 'Auntie'. Such programming was unpopular with the audience: a BBC listener research survey, conducted a month after war broke out, found that 35 per cent of the public were dissatisfied with the BBC and 10 per cent did not listen to it at all. Mass Observation also found that during the 'phoney war' many people had little trust in the BBC.[42]

The opening of a service for the armed forces made the BBC rethink its programme policy. In January 1940, the Forces Programme began broadcasting on an experimental basis. The first transmission included music from the BBC Salon Orchestra, Mantovani, a song recital and only one dance band. This was very much in the tradition of BBC light music, defined in terms of light orchestral or palm court music. For an audience that sought its musical entertainment in dance music and the 'crooners', it was unpopular. The soldiers complained and their complaints grew when the Allied authorities closed down *Radio Fecamp*, an English-language commercial station in France, whose musical output was preferred by the armed forces.[43] The BBC had to respond to the demands of serving men and women. An official report at the end of January stated that the BBC would have to issue 'a self-denying ordinance against the more austere kinds of programmes and by experimenting frankly in the difficult technique of approaching simple men without boring them and at the same time without talking down to them'.[44] Copying the model represented by stations such as *Radio Fecamp*, the BBC set about producing more popular material for the forces, including more variety and dance music and hiring producers from commercial radio. The success of the Forces Programme was highlighted when the British Army returned to Britain following the debacle at Dunkirk and the service became a popular alternative to the domestic Home Service with 65 per cent of the civilian audience tuning in. The new service led to a significant increase in listeners' satisfaction with the BBC's performance. The division of the radio service was to have a lasting impact on the BBC's output. In 1945, the mixed programming model developed under Reith was discarded as BBC radio was split into three services: the *Light Programme* which concentrated on entertainment and popular music; the *Home Service* with a focus on talks, plays and news and the *Third Programme* which played classical music. The view of the mass audience where everybody was given what BBC thought was best for them, was replaced by the recognition that there are different aspirations, demands, needs and cultural values among the audience. Different people wanted different things and BBC only recognized this as the result of the experience of the war.

The BBC played a crucial part in the propaganda effort to maintain the nation's morale. The Listener Research Unit, set up against the wishes of Reith, grew in importance throughout war. Feedback from listeners and gauging popular attitudes to programmes became a feature of broadcasting as the BBC developed more sophisticated mechanisms and techniques for audience research. Listening panels were set up, sending in regular comments about programmes throughout the war. Programming was modified in light of knowledge of audience opinion and tastes. For the first time what people wanted played a part in the BBC's schedules. This was apparent in two key developments in BBC radio broadcasting. The first was the change in BBC News. Radio news underwent a radical transformation, establishing itself at the centre of the Corporation's output. A BBC spokesman acknowledged in 1944: 'Once the news was not of very great importance. Now it occupies the peak hours and has swept culture into the background.'[45] News bulletins brought in the largest audiences with between 30 and 50 per cent tuning in regularly. Special circumstances would see the audience rise to 60 per cent of British households with 80 per cent listening the night of the D-Day landings. Despite the restrictions placed on news by the censors and the handicaps under which wartime news reporting had to operate, the BBC established a reputation at home and abroad for reliability and accuracy. This is not to say that the BBC told the truth during the war but, relative to the overtly propagandist outpourings of German radio, it was more restrained and fair. By tuning into the national news programmes, particularly the nightly nine o'clock news, the sense of common wartime endeavour and purpose of the British people was most clearly expressed.

The second development was the Corporation's shift to more popular kinds of entertainment programmes. Entertainment was recognized by the BBC at the outset as important in helping 'to take our minds off the horrors of war'.[46] As the war progressed, the BBC broadcast more popular kinds of entertainment programmes. The popularization of radio can be seen in the changing balance between light and serious programming between 1938 and 1942. In 1938, serious music made up just over 17 per cent of total output whereas by 1942 this had dropped to just below 9 per cent. Variety and revue programmes, on the other hand, increased from 5.76 per cent of total output in 1938 to 14.73 per cent by 1942. Dance music rose from 4.67 per cent to 9.97 per cent in the same period.[47] There was also a change in the nature of these programmes. One significant change was the increase in audience participation. This was most apparent in variety shows, which included broadcasts of camp concerts and shows from factory canteens, in which workers were placed before microphones. *Workers Playtime* which brought together amateur and professional entertainers was particularly popular. Specific programmes were made for workers, including serials based on working-class family life such as *The Plums* and *At the Armstrongs*. These programmes were full of useful advice such as not to stay up late listening to radio or to get a good night's sleep to be ready for work the next day. Increased productivity and efficient labour practices were the rationale for the programme *Music While You Work*, which began broadcasting three weeks after Dunkirk. By 1943, nearly 7000 factories around Britain employing more than 4 million workers had loudspeaker systems to relay the programme. Promoting industrial efficiency was a key objective of BBC programme policy. There were many problems on the industrial front during the war, particularly in 1941 and 1942. Workers blamed management and management blamed the workforce. Discontent about the running of industry was the focus of the press coverage but was never reported by the BBC. The BBC concentrated on producing propaganda to maintain morale in the factories of Britain and improve industrial production to keep the front-line fighting forces going. A key radio personality in this area of programming was Wilfred Pickles who presented the series *We Speak for Ourselves*. Pickles went to different parts of the country, usually to meet ordinary people in their place of work, to show how they were standing up to the trials and tribulations of the war and willing to make sacrifices to beat the Nazis. Started in 1940, the series was, in Pickles' words, 'rank propaganda disguised as entertainment'[48] and by 1942, with the fear of invasion receding, much of the audience saw the programmes in this way and they were discontinued.

The most popular programmes of the war were from genres which had established themselves in the 1930s – comedy and talks. *The Brains Trust* was the most popular spoken word programme. It started in 1941 as a 5-minute programme at teatime on Sundays in which a team answered questions and queries sent in by listeners. The panellists included the biologist and novelist, Aldous Huxley, a professor of chemistry, Cyril Joad, and a retired sailor, Commander A. B. Marshall. The initial success of the programme came from the way these men approached the topics at hand and the conversation between them. It was certainly not the topic matter itself, which included questions such as 'How do flies walk on the ceiling?' and 'Why do cattle rise forelegs first?' The programme, broadcast entirely unscripted, became the first 'serious' radio programme to obtain a mass audience and was moved to a slot immediately after the nine o'clock news where it remained for the rest of the war, listened to by 1 in 3 of the British public. If the heads of the wartime British public were captured by *The Brains Trust*, their hearts went to the comics. Old favourites such as *Bandwaggon* returned, establishing the reputations of the comics, Arthur Askey and Richard Murdoch. But it was Tommy Handley's *It's That Man Again (ITMA)* with characters such as Ali Oop, the saucy postcard vender, Colonel Chinstrap, Sam Scam and Mrs Mopp that established itself as the most popular wartime programme. *ITMA* was irreverent, with little respect for authority, and relied on schoolboy humour and terrible puns. It thrived on innuendo and risqué wordplays, pushing back the restrictions that had held radio comics in check in the 1930s. It also expressed popular frustrations as it poked fun at bureaucracy and red tape. For its producer, *ITMA* was 'the closest radio had come to everyday jokes that ordinary people have always made'.[49]

The concerns and feelings of the ordinary man and woman were also articulated in the 'talks' of the novelist and playwright, J. B. Priestley. Alongside Churchill, he was the most popular broadcaster of the war. For several months, from 5 June 1940, Priestley, with his distinct Yorkshire accent, presented talks which departed from the carefully stilted prose that had come to characterize BBC broadcasting. Priestley spoke to and for ordinary people and BBC audience research found that 1 in 3 people on average tuned into his fireside chats.[50] At first, his talks were simple tales of wartime life but as he went on he started to discuss what life would be like in post-war Britain. He emphasized – albeit occasionally and in very general terms – that there could be no return to the conditions of the 1930s. Remarks on this theme brought sharp criticism from some in government who complained of the dangerous 'leftish' tendencies of the talks. In the autumn of 1940 he was taken off the air. The BBC said it was at the instruction of the MoI but the Ministry wrote to Priestley blaming the BBC.

The Second World War witnessed the integration of the working class into radio life. The changes were forced on the BBC and the Corporation never adapted to them with enthusiasm or commitment. While the BBC responded to needs of the newly identified audience, it was cautious about how far to go in representing the demands of working people, as the Priestley episode indicates. The government, while encouraging the BBC to respond to growing popular pressure, kept a watchful eye and tight rein over what was broadcast. In 1942, restriction was placed on *The Brains Trust* answering questions on religion, followed a year later by a government ban on discussion of politics. *ITMA*, and variety programmes in general, were criticized from within and outside the BBC for 'poor taste' and 'vulgarity'. But it was over the debate about post-war reconstruction that the BBC's caution and hesitancy in its representations of working-class life were most clearly manifested.

The BBC, in contrast to the *Daily Mirror* or even the film industry, was far more cautious in its treatment of reconstruction. It had to operate under countervailing pressures from the government – and in particular, Churchill, who did not want to see the matter discussed – and popular opinion wanting more discussion. The outcome was the combination of a new desire by the BBC to represent working-class aspirations and the old patronizing attitude that shaped the Corporation's sense of the working class in the 1930s. A memo written in 1941 on 'Reconstruction and the Working Man' encapsulates the BBC's wartime approach. In suggesting a series expressing the hopes and aspirations of ordinary people about the post-war world, a member of the Talks Department wrote:

> **I am not proposing that we should ask working men and women what social legislation they would like to see implemented after the war, for actual legislation proposals, even of the kind which bear directly on working class conditions, are better discussed by people with administrative experience and a knowledge wider than working people can hope to have of the whole political and economic fabric within which the changes have got to be made.[51]**

By and large, the BBC took its cue from government, and programmes examining aspects of post-war reconstruction were either shelved or made in a diluted form. For example, in 1941, a proposal was put forward for a series of programmes on the peace aims called *Democracy Thinking Aloud*. The programmes would have taken the form of a radio forum. Senior management were concerned about the proposal. The head of the Talks Department wanted it renamed *Where Are We Going?* and expressed the view that only speakers who supported democracy and the war effort could be included. Communists, fascists and 'active' pacifists would be excluded. The series – despite having the initial support of the MoI – was finally scrapped because of fears Churchill would dislike it.[52] It was eventually made several months later in a much more circumscribed version and called *Making Plans*. The BBC's decision to ignore the Beveridge Report after its initial enthusiastic coverage was a reaction to direct pressure from the government. The experiment to introduce regional accents into the output, particularly the reading of the news which was, for a time, read by Wilfred Pickles in his strong Yorkshire accent, was short-lived. The upper echelons of the Corporation were populated by people who shared the outlook, attitude and assumptions of the corridors of power. They were in tune with and responsive to what emerged from Whitehall and the Cabinet. However, the war highlighted that the BBC was not a monolith. Programme-makers – and during the war many liberal and progressive intellectuals swelled their ranks – were closer to the public through their contact with them in making programmes. They tended to share their audience's attitudes and as the war progressed, more space started to open up for programme-makers to broadcast alternative and dissenting views. By 1943, with public pressure building up, the BBC began to assert more independence from government. In 1944, the BBC broadcast two major series which dealt with aspects of the post-war order of most concern to the British public. *Homes for All* focused on housing while *Jobs for All* examined employment. These programmes gained large audiences but listener research discovered that many people found they were boring, difficult to follow and responded cynically to their discussion of the government's post-war plans. The motive of the BBC in broadcasting these programmes was not so much to provide a debate but to ensure it would not emerge from the war appearing to be an agency of the State.[53]

Part 3

The television era

8

The cosy duopoly: the development of television

Television began in Britain in 1936 when a service was established for 23,000 people living around the Alexandra Palace transmitter in London. Physically separate from the rest of the Corporation, for senior management – as well as most of the British public – it was not only out of sight but out of mind. Lord Reith summed up the general attitude of BBC management to television when he told one of his senior producers that 'television will be of no importance in your lifetime or mine'. The service operated with benign neglect until 1939 when it was closed down for the duration of war. It had struggled as a marginal operation, short of funds, a poor relative of radio. When it resumed in 1946, it was in an even weaker position in the Corporation. The BBC emerged from the war with an enhanced reputation built on the performance of the radio service in the 'war of words' between 1939 and 1945. From 1946, the television service struggled to establish itself in a hostile environment.

The new Director-General, William Haley, as well as other senior management in the immediate post-war period, were men and women who had learned their broadcasting skills in the world of radio. Their priority was to rebuild and develop the radio service after the war. Haley focused the resources and efforts of the Corporation on the reorganization of radio into the Home, Third and Light programmes and the rebirth of the regional service, suspended during the war. The Corporation invested time and money making new programmes for the reorganized and expanded service, especially in relation to news which, as a result of its wartime performance, the BBC was encouraged to develop more fully. The BBC's hierarchy, dominated by 'old radio hands', regarded television as an extension of radio; as 'illustrated radio' rather than a medium in its own right. As a result, the television service in the immediate post-war years was heavily circumscribed. It opened for an hour in the late afternoon, between 5 to 6 p.m., primarily aimed at women and children and then closed down until 7.30 p.m. when it reopened with news and weather. The news until 1948 was broadcast in sound only; an anonymous announcer reading the news behind a picture of the BBC clock. It was compiled by BBC Radio personnel who fought against relinquishing control of news to the television people. The service then ran to 10.30 p.m. when it closed down. The development of BBC TV was hampered in the first place by the bias for radio of the BBC hierarchy.

There were also three other factors that handicapped the early development of the service. First, the cost of producing television programmes. In 1939, 1 hour of television is estimated to have cost 12 times as much as 1 hour of the most expensive kind of radio programming. In the climate of austerity that pervaded Britain immediately after the war – it was not until the mid-1950s that rationing finally ended – the BBC was particularly cost-sensitive. During 1947, the fuel crisis led to the closure of television for several periods. The Corporation was also concerned about the political implications of asking the government for an increase in the licence fee to develop the television service. The political climate was far from friendly for the BBC after the election in 1945 of the Labour Party with its traditional suspicions of the Corporation. Second, the cost of television sets. In 1948, the cost of a 'budget set' was just under £50 at a time when the average industrial wage was no more than £7 a week and only 48,564 people out of a population of 50 million owned a set. By 1950, when 33 per cent of the population were able to receive the transmissions from Alexandra Palace, set ownership was still fairly low at 344,000. The third factor was the technology. TV sets at this time had 8-inch screens and the pictures were in black and white. The viewer had to sit in a darkened room to see the programmes clearly, a far from sociable activity. The incentive to view was consequently low. The transmitter at Alexandra Palace only had a transmission reach of 40 miles at the outset and hence could only be described as a local service for London. It was only through a supreme feat of engineering that BBC TV by 1955 came within reach of 92 per cent of the population. For the immediate post-war years, television existed in a ghetto with little support from inside or outside the BBC.

As a result, TV output during this period was dull, dreary and unimaginative. Many of the staples of radio were transferred to TV, in particular 'Talks' which constituted a strong part of the early output of BBC TV. Without the teleprompter, the speakers often looked shifty and furtive. When the news was eventually presented in vision, the specialist correspondents, all from radio, were dubbed 'the guilty men' by the press because they were constantly looking down at the script with occasional glances to the camera, giving them a furtive appearance. The influence of radio was most apparent in the development of TV news. The war had established the public's appetite for news but radio did not want to jeopardize its reputation for professionalism and integrity by putting its news reporting at risk with television. Hence from 1948 onwards BBC TV carried only newsreels which were a form of entertainment. The newsreels became more and more topical which caused bitter arguments between the TV service and Bush House, the home of the radio division. On 5 July 1954, the BBC broadcast its first TV news bulletin. BBC News and Newsreel was composed of an illustrated news summary followed by newsreel footage of events at home and abroad. There was no news-reader – by remaining invisible the BBC argued that the impartiality of the news was maintained as a news-reader's gesture might imply comment. The result was that the news was made up of an 'endless succession of captions and maps; still pictures were on the screen interminably and explicitly described'. The lack of imagination pervaded much of the programming, illustrated by programmes like *Inventor's Club* and *Television Dancing Club*. It is also indicative of the standards of early television that two of the main TV personalities to emerge from this period were characters from children's programmes, *Muffin the Mule* and *Mr Pastry*.[1]

The other notable feature of early television was the virtual absence of domestic political discussion and commentary. The BBC painstakingly avoided direct intervention in matters deemed political. Most of the political discussion on BBC television in the early 1950s was carried on by politicians with the conspicuous absence of BBC personnel. Party political broadcasts were common as were programmes such as *In the News* in which four politicians, chaired by a freelance journalist, commented on recent events. Occasionally politicians would be subjected to more critical interrogation in the programme *Press Conference* but then only by invited members of the national and provincial press. The BBC's own political programmes, including the early current affairs broadcasts and documentaries, focused on foreign and international politics. *Panorama*, which was to establish itself as BBC's 'flagship' current affairs programme, began life in 1953 as a fortnightly general information programme and when it became a 'harder' current affairs programme, the initial focus was on the 'world outside Britain'.[2] BBC TV was reluctant to cover domestic politics as a result of the Fourteen Day Rule which had been drawn up by the BBC and the political parties during the war and renewed in 1947 by mutual consent. Under the rule, no matter to be debated in the House of Commons within the period of a fortnight could be discussed by the BBC. The rule was not relaxed until 1956. The technology of television in the 1950s, with the emphasis on live broadcasts, made it difficult to get beyond stilted studio discussion. The lack of spontaneity and the absence of 'the person in the street' on BBC TV in the early 1950s can also be explained by the constraints imposed by the amount and weight of the technical equipment. It is perhaps the Potter's Wheel, shown during breaks in transmission that distinguishes this period – the early days of BBC TV were an intermission in the development of British television. Television's marginalization did not last long and it was brought in from the cold by a number of factors: the growing alienation from the BBC of its audience; the rise of official dissatisfaction with the Corporation; the consumer boom of the 1950s; and, most crucially, the arrival of competition in the form of Independent Television (ITV) in 1955.

Reithian values and social change

The war had arrested the exodus of listeners from the BBC to the foreign commercial radio stations. The experience of the war led the Corporation to recast its output to reflect the different tastes within the radio audience. However, behind the setting up of the Light, Home and Third programmes there was still the same cultural mission to improve the lot of the average man and woman by furthering their aspirations to middle-class values and culture. The Director-General Sir William Haley hoped that the new system would still help the listener to 'move on to more serious things' and 'move up the cultural scale'. The BBC's deeply entrenched conservatism was manifest in its television service. Many viewers had the same feeling that listeners had in the 1930s; the service was, as one viewer recalled, 'rather elitist and snobby . . . it was what they used to call "high brow" and very "plummy". It was as if you had to be on your best behaviour to watch, we used to laugh at it sometimes – the airs and graces'.[3]

The conservatism of the BBC was accentuated by the arrival of the juke box, the Milk Bar, rock 'n' roll, the comic magazine and other facets of the 'candy floss world' which critics such as Richard Hoggart were later to see as undermining the traditional way of British life. The 1950s were the 'age of affluence'. The post-war rebuilding of Britain that followed the austerity of the late 1940s stimulated demand and economic growth. People were hungry for new goods, pleasures and activities. They now had more money to spend and the result was a consumer boom. Aided by the abolition of restrictions on hire purchase, spending increased rapidly. By the end of the 1950s, four out of five British families were the hire purchasers of £1000 million-worth of goods.[4] Their material wants were shaped by the 'Aladdin's cave of American goods, American entertainment and the American style of living'. In particular, the decade saw the emergence of 'youth'. As young people found their own identity, whether as the 'teenager', 'angry young man' or a member of the 'beat' generation, new lifestyles emerged. This was nowhere better illustrated than with the development of 'popular music' as youth expressed itself through the music of American entertainers such as Bill Haley and the Comets whose disc, *Rock Around the Clock*, became an anthem for young people in the 1950s. The hedonistic world of consumerism and youth – a world of fun – was antithetical to the Reithian values of the BBC. For the BBC, the 1950s was a period of adjustment.

Another Beveridge Report

The urgent needs of social reconstruction and the reputation the BBC gained during the war led the Attlee government to delay setting up the required review of the Corporation until 1949. It then asked Sir William Beveridge, the 'father' of the welfare state, a high-minded Liberal MP with a Reithian sense of public duty, to head the committee of enquiry. The Committee's report, published in 1951, was not as many had expected. It was highly critical of the organization, accusing the BBC of being overly orientated toward London, overly secretive, self-satisfied and believing it had a divine right to broadcast. Beveridge expressed concerns about the Corporation's lack of public accountability and recommended the 'democratisation of broadcasting' and the establishment of 'national commissions' for Wales, Scotland and Northern Ireland with strong powers of their own. However, the report did accept that the BBC monopoly of broadcasting should continue and that the licence fee was the best method to finance broadcasting.

It rejected the introduction of advertising for television which, after the Committee's visit to the United States, one member stated was 'obtrusive and objectionable'.[5] Despite Beveridge's criticisms, the report found the alternative commercial system of broadcasting to be worse. However, the Committee's findings were not unanimous. One member dissented from the final report and issued his minority report. Tory MP, Selwyn Lloyd, while 'substantially in agreement with my colleagues on a considerable number of matters contained in their Report' wanted the BBC's monopoly brought to an end and advertising introduced as a means of financing British broadcasting. In making his case for the introduction of commercial broadcasting, Lloyd exploited the widespread concern about the BBC's monopoly. Critics of all shades of opinion were ranged against the monopoly: for some there was the danger of the 'power exercised over men's thoughts concentrated in a single organisation', others saw the 'excessive size of the Corporation being unwieldy', regional interests objected to central control from London and broadcasting professionals resented the power of the monopoly over their livelihoods. Lloyd appealed to them all when he stated:

> **I am not attracted by the idea of compulsory uplift achieved by the 'brute force of monopoly' to use Lord Reith's phrase. If people are to be trusted with the franchise, surely they should be able to decide for themselves whether they want to be educated or entertained in the evening?**[6]

The Beveridge Report was to have far-reaching implications for the development of British television. Lloyd's dissenting comments became the rallying call for the introduction of commercial television when the Conservative Party regained power in 1951. Beveridge, according to Curran and Seaton,[7] was to influence the development of commercial broadcasting in two significant ways. The report expressed the view that 'spot' advertising, the designated placing of adverts within programme schedule, was preferable to programme sponsorship on the grounds it gave the advertisers less power over what was broadcast. Sponsorship, it argued, could result in nothing appearing in a programme that was detrimental to the sponsor's product. The report's advocacy of the regionalization and decentralization of broadcasting to fully incorporate local interests into the service was also to have a significant impact on the establishment of commercial broadcasting in Britain. While supporting the continuation of the BBC's broadcasting monopoly, the Beveridge Report had sown the seeds for the development of commercial television.

Television and the consumer boom

1953 was a crucial year in British television history. It was the year of the coronation of Queen Elizabeth II and its coverage on TV brought the new medium to the attention of a large audience. It is estimated that nearly 56 per cent of the adult population of Britain, that is around 20 million people, watched the coronation. Nearly 8 million watched it in their own homes while another 10 million went to friends' homes to watch. Many rented sets for the occasion. Most significantly the TV audience for the coronation was far in excess of those who listened on the radio. The coronation established the potential and popularity of TV and in its wake a huge increase occurred in the number of television sets sold. In 1950, only 4 per cent of the adult population owned a television set; by 1955, this had risen to 40 per cent and in 1960, it had doubled to 80 per cent. This corresponded with an increase in transmission hours which rose from 6 hours a day in 1954 to 16 hours in 1963.[8]

The sale of television sets in the mid-1950s was also the result of rising prosperity. Real wages rose by 20 per cent between 1951 and 1959. Average weekly earnings for industrial workers grew by 34 per cent between 1955 and 1960 and by a staggering 130 per cent between 1955 and 1969. This corresponded with an increase in home ownership by manual workers of nearly 40 per cent by 1962 and perhaps for the first and last time the advent of full employment.[9] People as a result had more disposable income to spend on consumer durables such as cars, washing machines and refrigerators. This consumer boom led Prime Minister Harold Macmillan to speak for most of the country with his 1959 election slogan – 'You've never had it so good'. The feel-good factor was especially expressed in increased spending on leisure and entertainment; the television set became one of the symbols of status and modernity in the glitzy world of the 1950s.

The consumer boom had another impact on television – it whetted the appetite of advertisers for the medium. By 1955, it is estimated that 5 million TV sets had been sold. With the increased purchasing power in the economy, advertising expenditure began to grow steadily. A number of new products were launched with massive advertising campaigns. With cinema audiences beginning to fall rapidly and newspaper advertising increasingly regarded as less direct, business began to see television with its presence in the household as the best means to reach their customers. With the BBC resolutely opposed to opening the airwaves to advertisements, industry began to lobby hard for the introduction of a new TV channel on which to sell their products.

Campaign for commercial television

The Labour government had no time to act on Beveridge's recommendations, being swept from office in 1951. On taking power again, and motivated by his intense dislike of 'that Bunch of Bloody Communists', Churchill ignored Beveridge and embraced Selwyn Lloyd's minority report as the basis for reorganizing British broadcasting. Churchill's decision had been influenced by an extraordinary campaign launched to promote the commercialization of British television. The *News Chronicle* described the campaign as 'perhaps the most remarkable exhibitions of political lobbying this country had ever seen – for there has been no disguise of the commercial interests involved'.[10] In his book *Pressure Group*, H. H. Wilson outlines how an effective but small pressure group representing business interests and the advertising industry succeeded in influencing government policy.[11] However, the debate about the introduction of commercial television represented more than the ability of a pressure group to shape the direction of government policy. It also reflected a vast outpouring of dissatisfaction at the way in which the BBC had treated the British public during the inter-war years. The lid which had been so tightly kept down by Reith on public engagement in broadcasting, and had been slightly opened during the war, was blown off by the debate about commercial television.

The coalitions which went to war over the government's decision to end the BBC's broadcasting monopoly threw together some strange political alliances. The case for commercial television was made by the Popular TV Association which was supported by a range of personalities of diverse backgrounds and interests including historian A. J. P. Taylor, cricketer Alec Bedser, Canon Collins, then head of CND and the Earl of Derby. Political support came from across the political spectrum. On the Right, groups such as the Society for Individual Freedom and Aims of Industry, which had previously funded monitoring exercises of the BBC's output to draw viewers' attention to the Corporation's 'Marxist bias', were joined in their support of the Association by Liberals, those representing regional interests and disaffected BBC staff. The BBC's defenders were ranged together under the auspices of the National Television Council whose members included a former Tory Foreign Secretary, the Chair of the TUC as well as a Liberal peeress. The Council was backed by the bulk of the British press, fearful of the impact of a commercial TV channel on their advertising revenue, a large part of the British cultural establishment who feared the 'vulgarization' of television and the Labour Party. The Labour Party pledged to defend the BBC as part of its commitment to public ownership despite the fact that most Labour supporters and voters backed a new commercial channel.[12]

Besides throwing together odd bedfellows, the debate contained strange and bizarre arguments and exchanges. Some parts of the Tory Party feared that a fully commercial system would allow the British Communist Party to buy time on television to present its case. To placate their fears the government agreed to a complete ban on political advertising. Debate in the House of Commons became particularly heated with the mention of the name J. Fred Muggs. Muggs was the chimpanzee who had appeared selling tea during NBC's coverage of the coronation and had outraged many MPs. The government promised that no such event could occur on commercial TV in Britain. But perhaps the most telling contribution to the debate came from Lord Reith. In a bitter, splenetic and vituperative speech in the House of Lords he lambasted the idea of commercial television and served to remind everyone of the elitist and patronizing attitude of the BBC that many had grown to despise during the 1930s. For Reith, the introduction of commercial television was equivalent to the bringing into this country of dog racing, smallpox, bubonic plague and the Black Death.[13]

The 1954 Television Act

The 1954 Television Act was a watershed in the development of British broadcasting – it ended the BBC's monopoly. The 'competitor' as Independent Television (ITV) was to be known to BBC staff, was constructed around two aspects of the Beveridge Report – the preference of spot advertising over programme sponsorship and the decentralization of broadcasting. The Act prohibited the direct linking of a programme to an advertiser or his or her product. Restriction was further placed on the amount of advertising the new commercial channel could carry: 6 minutes per hour was the maximum and it had to be clearly distinguished from the programmes. The Act also created the ITV network. The government decided that ITV should be a regional system with the provision of commercial television in a particular region the responsibility of a single contractor for that region. Britain was divided into 14 regions with a central news service (ITN) owned by all the ITV companies to provide national and international news. Each franchise holder entered into a separate contract with the Independent Television Authority (ITA) and was answerable for the programmes in its region.

The whole network was to be regulated by the Independent Television Authority, whose members – like the BBC Board of Governors – were government appointees. The ITA was responsible for running the TV transmitters, awarding the franchise to a contractor to provide programmes in every region, monitoring the output with respect to 'impartiality', 'taste and decency' and ensuring the provision of the required amount of regional programming. It also ensured that the rules concerning advertising were enforced. The contractors had to pay a rental to the ITA covering the cost of running the transmitters and paying for ITA staff. The franchise holders financed themselves and drew their revenue from selling advertising. Finally, the Act laid down that a separate company should provide the national news for the whole network – the contract going to Independent Television News (ITN). The end result of all the campaigning was that the 1954 Act did not produce a truly commercial system of television in Britain. It was a hybrid system combining characteristics of commercial and public service television. The government exercised a certain amount of control over ITV which ensured that it became part of the public service system. After initial difficulties in the late 1950s and early 1960s, the Act provided the basis for the BBC and ITV to live together in relative harmony for the next 20 years.

Impact of ITV on British broadcasting

ITV's initial years were far from easy. In the beginning there were only 25 bids to run the 14 regional franchises. The regional network was slow to start. Five months after the Act only the London region was operational. Audiences were small, making it difficult to attract advertisers and the cost of programmes was enormous. It has been estimated that Associated Television (ATV), winners of the London Weekend franchise, lost £600,000 in the first seven months.[14] Many started to pull out of the business – for example, the newspaper owner, Lord Rothermere, sold his shares in ATV. However, as the transmitting system started to reach greater numbers and other companies came on air – Midlands region in February 1956 followed by the North-East in May – the growth in audiences brought a corresponding rise in advertising. It became quickly apparent to the franchise holders that the formula for success was to build large audiences to attract advertisers. In other words, programmes were a means of bringing in an audience for the advertisers and the bigger the audience, the more you could charge the advertiser. The experience of the early years meant that ITV companies would cling to this formula with its consequence of producing programmes of appeal to the greatest number.

By 1957, the ITV companies were seeing a change in their financial fortunes. Viewers, on gaining access to the ITV signal, started to tune into the new channel in large numbers and by the end of 1957 nearly three-quarters of the television audience were watching. With larger audiences, advertising revenue poured in to the extent that Lord Thomson, the owner of Scottish Television, could state in 1961 that holding an ITV franchise was 'a licence to print money'. The winds of change had started to blow through British broadcasting. First, the new channel brought in a new breed of people to run British television. The controllers of the ITV companies were in stark contrast to the stuffy bureaucrats who had managed the BBC for so many years. Lew Grade, who headed ATV, was a show business agent and theatre impresario, running the largest theatrical agency in Europe with interests throughout the world of entertainment. Sydney Bernstein, the boss of the most influential ITV franchise, Granada, came from a long-term involvement in the theatre and film industry. The cigar-smoking Grade with his penchant for publicity represented for many the brash and vulgar world of commercial television.

Second, ITV brought a new kind and style of programme to television. This was most apparent with three key developments in programme-making. ITN radically changed the nature of news on television. When ITN came onto the air on 22 June 1955 it tried to be a programme, not an illustrated bulletin, with personalized newscasters and a lack of deference in its interviewing style. Robin Day embarked on his robust technique of interviewing which was to become a feature of news and current affairs in later years. ITV also introduced more popular programmes including quiz shows, many from the United States. By 1957, there were eight quiz shows on ITV every week. The channel also introduced the first daily soap opera during its first week on air. *Sixpenny Corner*, the life and times of newly-weds Sally and Bill Norton set in a broken-down garage in the town of Springwood was short-lived: it was axed in June 1956 as a result of a lack of money. ITV also played an important part in advancing the reporting of politics on television. Partly because of the competition from commercial television, the BBC became less deferential in covering politics. During the Suez Crisis in 1956, the Corporation resisted pressure from Prime Minister Anthony Eden to control television in his effort to rally the nation behind the Anglo-French invasion of Egypt to regain the strategically important Suez Canal. Against the government's wishes, it gave the Opposition leaders air time and covered anti-government rallies. One consequence was the abolition of the 'Fourteen Day' rule. A more significant step forward was Granada's decision in 1958 to break with usual practice by covering the by-election campaign in Rochdale. ITN broadcast the first TV election report which, while not going as far as broadcasting what the candidates had to say, did provide pictures of the hustings for the first time. The BBC refused to follow ITV's lead, publicly justifying its stance on the grounds that it did not want to 'influence voters'; privately it was still fearful of incurring the displeasure of government. However, there was no comeback on ITV which successfully demonstrated that electoral reporting was not illegal under the 1949 Representation of the People Act as some had believed.[15] Both channels developed their electoral reporting during the 1960s, assisted by the growing realization among politicians of the power of the medium to appeal directly to the public.

Third, the ITV companies were new kinds of broadcasting organizations. They were large conglomerates with interests outside the television and media industries. While the theatrical production company, Moss Empire, held 26 per cent of ATV shares in 1960, other shareholders included Daily Mirror Newspapers, Sunday Pictorial Newspapers, Pye Electronics, Associated Electrical Industries, and provincial newspaper groups, such as Westminster Press.[16] With increasing profitability, the ITV contractors began to broaden their financial interests into other fields. Granada, for example, the oldest ITV company, rather than plough back profits into television, diversified into a range of other interests, including book publishing, motorway service stations, property and bingo halls. As a Head of BBC News in this period said: 'The wealth extracted from commercial television did not flow into the pockets of "the people" . . . nor did it go into improving the quality of programmes.'[17]

Perhaps the most telling impact of ITV was on the BBC. By late 1957 viewers were turning to the new channel in droves and by the end of that year the BBC's share of the audience, according to its own estimates, had plummeted to 28 per cent. For BBC managers what constituted an acceptable audience became a pressing concern, particularly as the licence fee was levied on all viewers. Many staff left the Corporation, attracted by the higher salaries offered by ITV. In a 6-month period between 1955 and 1956, more than 500 people quit the BBC. The increase in programme-makers' and artists' fees represented one aspect of how competition had led to a rise in the cost of making television. Limited by the licence fee and with commitments in other areas, the BBC was unable to spend as much on television production as the ITV companies. With the alarm bells ringing inside the BBC, changes were made in the management structure which were not only significant for the Corporation's revival but also for the development of programme-making innovations in the 1960s. The most important change was the appointment of Sir Hugh Greene as Director-General in 1960. Unlike others in BBC management Greene did not regret the ending of the BBC's monopoly. A maverick, out of step with his predecessors, Greene, who was to preside over the 'golden age of television', admitted in later years that without ITV he would never have been made Director-General.

Running the new network

ITV was put together in a hurry and much discretion was left to the ITA in interpreting the Act. Hence the ITV network never functioned as the Act envisaged. This was most apparent with the commitment to regional broadcasting, which was welcomed in the regions. When Scottish TV joined the network in 1957, the *Scotsman* newspaper described the opening night as 'the most brilliant collection of Scots artists ever to amalgamate their talents in a single production'.[18] Granada, winners of the franchise for the North from offices in London, relocated to a newly built centre in Manchester and under Bernstein made a conscious effort to identify the channel with the North. Programming policy reflected this objective, and programmes, such as *Coronation Street* which began in 1960, represented working-class communities in the North. Granada's output was in keeping with the resurgence of things northern which was also apparent in films and in the theatre of the early 1960s. Overall the ITV network made a major contribution to representing the regions in British broadcasting – for example, in 1960 the network produced 3750 hours of programmes outside London compared to 1220 hours by the BBC.[19] However, despite the achievements, there were several weaknesses in the way the ITV network functioned. First was the lack of equality between the regions. Four companies came to dominate ITV's output – ABC, Associated Re-diffusion, ATV and Granada. They held the most lucrative franchises, those with the larger and wealthier audiences. They had more money for programme-making and by agreement sold programmes to the less well-off regions giving them a greater share and say in running the network. The necessity of economic survival in the first shaky years of the network led the ITA to agree to the 'Big Four' having a guaranteed access to the national market for a certain number of hours each week. These companies were to produce in the early years over 80 per cent of British commercial television programmes, with Granada making 25 per cent of network programmes. The other companies were never able to break this stranglehold.

The second weakness was that while the new 'regions' might have made economic sense, they did not make cultural sense. There was little in common between Tyneside and Teesside in the Tyne-Tees franchise besides proximity. TWW, which held the franchise for South Wales and the West of England, had to make programmes for the audience in the West of England, the English-speaking Welsh and the Welsh-speaking minority, while Border Television had to serve the

Scottish Lowlands and the North of England. Certain areas were excluded altogether from the ITV map. North Wales, for example, with its distinct culture and language was served initially by Granada, who started broadcasting Welsh language television programmes in September 1957. To resolve this unsatisfactory situation, the ITA in 1961 invited bids for a contract to provide television programmes for West and North Wales. The fifteenth ITV franchise went to Television Wales (West and North) Ltd which began broadcasting in September 1962. Unusually the ITA insisted that the new company's shareholders be told that dividends were of secondary consideration. Without a secure financial base, facing competition from TWW and Granada, both of whose programmes could be picked up by the audience in North Wales, and with technical problems of transmitting throughout the area, TWWN collapsed in March 1963. The ITA, despite having identified the importance of cultural and regional considerations in the awarding of this franchise, did nothing to save the fledgling company. Face was saved when TWW took over the company but the episode emphasized the limited commitment to cultural identity in the setting up of the ITV network.[20]

Another area in which the ITV network operated in a way not foreseen in the 1954 Act was advertising. The ITA determined its rules on spot advertising shortly after it was established. There would be no more than 6 minutes of advertising every hour and they would come in the 'natural breaks' in programmes. But on starting broadcasting many ITV companies put on air whole programmes promoting products, known as 'shoppers' guides'.[21] The advertising magazine programmes or 'admags' such as *Shop in the South*, *For Pete's Sake* and *On View* were hosted by TV personalities talking about a range of goods on display in a familiar setting such as a shop or kitchen. The most popular, *Jim's Inn*, was located in a public house where a set of regular characters discussed different products every week. These programmes were not part of the 6 minutes per hour allocated to advertising and, presented as entertainment, they blurred the distinction between advertising and programming. Critics argued they were not in keeping with the 1954 Act but the ITA maintained that they were in accord with the spirit of commercial television and were clearly labelled as advertisement features. For the advertisers they substantially increased their ability to reach the ITV audience.

Programming policy also failed to develop in the way in which many expected. The opening night of ITV, 22 September 1955, is remembered for the moment everyone had been waiting for – the 'natural break' in which the first commercial ad, that for Gibbs SR toothpaste, appeared. What is forgotten is that much of the content of the first evening's viewing on ITV resembled that of the BBC – it included Sir John Barbarolli and the Halle Orchestra, excerpts from Oscar Wilde's *The Importance of Being Earnest* and Noel Coward's *Private Lives* as well as *Gala Night at Mayfair* introduced by a stalwart of BBC television, Leslie Mitchell. Granada on its opening night firmly associated itself with the tradition of the BBC. Although ITV did bring about innovation in British television programming, it also copied much from the BBC and was firmly attached to the notion of 'improvement' in broadcasting from the outset. It was the cash flow problems faced by the companies following the high capital costs of the launch that resulted in what the newspapers at the time dubbed 'the retreat from culture'. Ratings became the key to economic survival and ITV concentrated all its efforts on audience building. Popular shows that could win and hold large audiences, such as quizzes, sport, variety and American imports, became more central to the ITV schedule. By the late 1950s, only 12 per cent of ITV's peak time output could be categorized as 'serious television', compared to 36 per cent of the BBC's.[22] As one ITV boss put it:

> The public like girls, wrestling, bright musicals, quiz shows and real life drama. We gave them the Halle Orchestra, Foreign Press Club, floodlit football and visits to the local fire station. Well we've learned. From now on, what the public wants, it's going to get.[23]

The refrain 'giving the public what it wants' was to be the justification for amassing high ratings and large profits. The ITA, fearing the collapse of the system, prioritized economic survival at the expense of all other considerations, allowing these developments to occur. As a result, the ITA became closely identified with the interests of the ITV companies. Mass taste, however, did not satisfy everyone. It did bring profitability to the industry by the end of the 1950s; advertising revenue rose from £10 million in 1956 to £60 million by 1960 with over half the revenue being paid out to shareholders. TWW, for example, paid out a 110 per cent dividend in 1959.[24] But there was an increase in middle-class and highbrow concerns about the impact of ITV on British culture.

Cultural debasement

Fears about being swamped by things American have accompanied the growth of the visual media in Britain. Concerns were expressed in the early days of the cinema but it was in the 1930s that both Left and Right in Britain became united in their fear and loathing of the 'chewing-gum world' they saw as posing a threat to British cultural identity. Commentators as politically different as George Orwell and Evelyn Waugh were hostile to the spread of 'Americana' which they associated with amorality and vulgarity.[25] American programmes were first heard on British radio during the war. The *Jack Benny Show* and the *Bob Hope Show* were examples of US variety programmes popular with British audiences. They were live and unscripted which appealed to an audience brought up on the stodgy fare of the BBC. The introduction of these programmes corresponded with the arrival of US troops in Britain in 1942. The Armed Forces Network (AFN) was established with its own transmitter to give the 'boys over there' news and programmes from home. At least 10 per cent of British people listened in and fears were expressed about the influence of AFN on local people.[26] These fears were also apparent around the setting up of ITV.

The campaign to save the BBC's monopoly centred its efforts on the fears of Americanization. Christopher Mayhew, one of the leading critics of commercial television, claimed that the 'Americanization' of television, particularly with the introduction of advertising, would result in 'unending banality'.[27] As a result, the 1954 Act stipulated that a 'proper proportion of recorded and other matter had to be of British origin and performance'. Ever since, this had meant the proportion of non-British material on our television screens has stood at or about 14 per cent. After the start of commercial TV, Richard Hoggart, in his influential book, *Uses of Literacy*, attacked the homogenizing impact of American life on British society, especially the working class. For Hoggart, working-class culture was being bombarded and swept aside by the 'hollow brightness', 'shiny barbarism' and 'spiritual decay' of imported American culture.[28] Television, which had by 1961 established itself as the nation's main evening leisure activity, was increasingly seen as part of the Americanization of British life. American-style programmes such as *Take Your Pick, Emergency Ward Ten* and *People are Funny* as well as imported programmes such as *I Love Lucy, Dragnet* and *Gunsmoke* (originally called *Gunlaw*) were extremely popular, dominating the ratings in the late 1950s.[29] It was not just ITV serving up this fare; in response to declining audiences, the BBC began to introduce its own quiz shows, variety programmes and American imports. However, it was commercial television that was held responsible for opening up British broadcasting to the influx of American cultural imports and values. And because of the large audiences ITV had built up in the late 1950s, it became the focus of the official enquiry set up to examine the state of broadcasting in 1960 – the Pilkington Committee.

The Pilkington Report

The Pilkington Committee concentrated on two concerns relating to broadcasting in the late 1950s and early 1960s – the excessive profits of the ITV companies and the 'decline' in cultural standards. The importance attached to the latter reflected the fact that Richard Hoggart was the driving force behind the Committee. In addition to Hoggart, the membership of the Pilkington Committee included the archetypal BBC entertainer, Joyce Grenfell, the footballer, Billy Wright as well as a trade unionist, a headmaster, two industrialists and Mrs Elizabeth Whitley, described as a 'housewife'.[30] Unsurprisingly, the report, published in 1962, heaped praise on the BBC, rewarding it with the allocation of a new channel – to become BBC 2 – and was severely critical of commercial television. The report concluded that:

> The disquiet and dissatisfaction with television are, in our view, justly attributed very largely to the service of independent television. This is so despite the popularity of the service, and the well known fact that many of its programmes command the largest audiences . . . it is a success which can be obtained by abandoning the main purpose of

> **broadcasting . . . We conclude that the service of independent television does not successfully realise the purposes of broadcasting as defined in the Television Act.[31]**

The report criticized ITV programmes for being 'trivial' and of 'low quality', declared that much of the output was 'vapid and puerile' and singled out quiz shows as being potentially harmful and for the 'half wit'. It recommended a reduction in prize money and that prize winning should be tied more closely to ability and knowledge. The report was uneasy about 'the preoccupation in many programmes with the superficial and cheaply sensational', the focus on violence and the representation of 'low standards and behaviour'. There was criticism of the 'narrow range' of subjects dealt with by ITV, especially during peak hours and particular anxiety was expressed at the limited amount of serious programming, most of which was broadcast outside peak viewing hours. The regulatory body, the ITA, came in for the strongest criticism. The report believed the ITA had failed to exert 'effective control of commercial television' and held it responsible for the lack of programme diversity. It did not help the ITA that its chairman had, in his evidence to the committee, dismissed the view that television had any impact on society. Pilkington argued for the doing away of 'admags' and stated that in general the profit and loss approach of ITV did not 'coincide' with the 'best possible service of broadcasting'. Overall the report found that 'winning the largest number of viewers . . . is not the only, and by no means the most important, test of good broadcasting'.[32]

The Conservative government ignored most of Pilkington's recommendations, particularly the radical changes proposed in the relationship between advertising and programming, which included the ITA taking direct control of programme planning and scheduling, and advertising revenue being paid directly to the regulatory body. However, the 1964 Act did tighten official control over the ITV network. To deal with the criticism of excessive profits, the government imposed a profit levy. The additional payment was to be paid to the Treasury and, as Stuart Hood[33] points out, the fact that a Tory government introduced this tax highlights the extent to which the ITV companies were making excessive profits. The Act increased the powers of the ITA in determining the criteria for awarding ITV franchises and over the scheduling of programmes. Members of the Authority were represented on the Network Programme Committee which drew up the network schedule. As a result, the Authority could insist specific programmes were aired at certain times in the schedule, which meant serious programming appearing at peak hours. The ITA used its new powers to reallocate the ITV franchises in 1968. 'Granadaland' was broken up into two with Yorkshire Television (YTV) being awarded part of the old franchise; Rediffusion had its London franchise taken away on the grounds that its programmes were of poor quality and it was only interested in ratings and the Wales and the West franchise changed hands because of TWW's refusal to decentralize its operation from

London to the region. The ITA began to exert more influence on commercial television and with the inclusion of more serious programmes, such as *World in Action* and *This Week*, at peak times, the network's output began to resemble that of the BBC.

The Pilkington Report brought to an end the first phase of commercial broadcasting in Britain. Pilkington spoke with the same voice as Lord Reith. For some it was the last defence of Reithian values in British broadcasting and it is argued that its criticisms of ITV were 'elitist'. Pilkington's paternalism was seized on by the press. A *Daily Mirror* headline screamed 'Pilkington tells the public to go to hell' while the *Daily Sketch* warned of the dangers of 'Big Brother': it stated 'if they think you're enjoying yourself too much – well, they'll soon put a stop to that'.[34] These comments can be taken as special pleading given the involvement of the national press in the ownership of ITV companies; the *Mirror*, for example, was a shareholder in ATV. Behind the committee's statements about 'quality' in broadcasting there was nevertheless a genuine anxiety about what was happening to popular culture. It is too easy to characterize the Pilkington Report as a defence of paternalism against forms of popular expression. Hoggart and his colleagues can be accused of underestimating the audience, reducing them to passive recipients of trashy products and false consciousness peddled by advertising. They can also be accused of romanticizing the 'traditional way of life' of working people. But at the heart of the report is the concern about the commercial exploitation of popular forms of expression. By juxtaposing 'quality' and 'commerce' in its findings, the report clearly identified the main fault line in the debate about the impact of broadcasting on national culture. In this way, Pilkington, as an official report, made a unique contribution to British broadcasting history. The short-run impact was to see the cementing together of 'quality' and 'commerce' in the British broadcasting system.

The cosy duopoly

The 1964 Act moved the ITV network more closely toward a set of public service responsibilities and further away from commercial considerations. At the same time the BBC, in trying to regain the viewers who had crossed over to ITV, embarked on a more adventurous programme policy which departed from the Reithian tradition and took its lead from ITV. After an initial ratings war, the two networks settled down into a 'cosy' or 'comfortable duopoly' in which competition was regulated to suit the needs of both channels. For most of the period from 1964 up to the election of Margaret Thatcher in 1979, the BBC and ITV had roughly the same share of the viewing audience. Programmes were scheduled by the channels to suit each other and the dependability of the schedule meant that both could show current affairs and documentaries in the same slot, which was the only way in which many viewers would watch such programmes. Regulated competition meant that the BBC could protect its right to the licence fee while ITV was able to meet the programming commitments placed on it by Pilkington while maximizing profits. For some, this resulted in the standardization of the product dished up for the audience whose tastes were marginalized in the process. It was also to correspond to what many say was a 'golden age' in the development of British television.

It was the BBC, under Hugh Greene, that led a period of innovation in British television in the 1960s.[35] Greene, who ran the BBC until 1969, encouraged expansion at almost every level of programme-making. Thus came the advent of satire shows, such as *That Was The Week That Was*, which lampooned the establishment. Current affairs became more hard-edged. The setting up of BBC 2 allowed the Corporation to experiment in new forms of programming including the late night chat show, the most successful being *Late Night Line Up*, science programmes such as *Horizon*, as well as Kenneth Clark's *Civilisation* which, described as a 'milestone in television history', established a new television genre. Light entertainment experienced an upsurge with comedy programmes such as *Till Death Do Us Part, Dad's Army, Steptoe and Son* and *The Likely Lads*. The Corporation's reputation for drama was maintained by series such as the *Forsyte Saga* and enhanced by *The Wednesday Play*, a series of single plays focusing on contemporary themes, which caused much controversy in the mid-1960s with *Cathy Come Home* and *Up the Junction*. Playwrights such as Dennis Potter were able to develop their skills of writing for TV under a regime that encouraged artistic freedom. Greene also presided over radical restructuring of BBC radio, the most important change coming in 1967 with the start of Radio One, a response to the musical demands of the growing youth culture in Britain. Hugh Greene oversaw a revolution in the Corporation. For Greene, there was no issue that could not be dealt with by television and, favoured by the social climate of the 1960s, the BBC started to deal with issues not touched on before such as abortion, single parenthood and sex. Greene also attempted to redefine the BBC's attitude to 'impartiality and balance'. In a speech in 1965 he stated that:

> **There are some respects in which [the BBC] is not neutral, unbiased and impartial. That is where there are basic clashes for and against the basic moral values – justice, freedom, tolerance. Nor do I believe we should be impartial about certain things like racialism.**[36]

In practical terms, the policy was to cause considerable problems especially in the reporting of Northern Ireland but under Greene, the BBC shed its stuffy, old-fashioned image and played an important part in pushing back the boundaries of taste, challenging the social, sexual and moral mores of British society.

Greene's efforts did not go unopposed. The BBC was under constant fire from those who blamed television for 'declining' moral standards. Mrs Mary Whitehouse, who began her Clean Up TV campaign in 1966, later to become the National Viewers and Listeners Association, accused Greene of being responsible more than anyone else for the 'moral collapse which characterized the Sixties and Seventies'.[37] Greene for his part refused to see Mrs Whitehouse and never wrote to her; there was not 'any evidence that she represented anyone'.[38] However, he did have to see Tory MPs who supported Mrs Whitehouse and small battles were engaged over bad language, 'four letter words' and 'dirty programmes' on the BBC. In these battles the 'moral rearmers' were supported by Lord Reith, who wrote that Greene 'follows the mob in every disgusting manifestation of the age . . . the BBC is no longer on the Lord's side'.[39] But the debate was very tame. The political climate enabled Greene to pursue his assault on taste. The only major political controversy around a programme came with Peter Watkins' *The War Game*. Made in 1965, the programme explored in a mixture of fiction and documentary forms what would happen in Britain in the event of a nuclear war. Following government intervention, the BBC decided that it should not be broadcast – and it was not seen on British television until the 1980s.[40] For some this act of censorship by Greene contradicted his reputation as a director-general who supported artistic freedom. However, every director-general has to negotiate his or her own relationship with the British State depending on the social and political circumstances of the period in which they hold office. For Greene, the circumstances were favourable – it is even said that Prime Minister Harold Macmillan enjoyed the political satire of *That Was The Week That Was*! Like all other holders of the office, Greene had to know how far he could push back the parameters in which broadcasting happens and his close contacts with the establishment meant he knew how far he could go. His eventual demise came out of the breakdown in his relationship with Harold Wilson, who was elected Prime Minister in 1964. Wilson, next only to Margaret Thatcher, was the Prime Minister most bent on imposing his will on broadcasting and had taken against the BBC early in his first administration, seeing many of the senior personnel in the news and current affairs as opposed to his government. Throughout his second term of office Wilson regularly complained about the 'prejudice and bias of the BBC, compared to the meticulous impartiality of ITV'.[41] The sudden death of BBC Chairman, Lord Normanbrook in 1967 led Wilson, motivated by revenge, to appoint a former Tory minister, Lord Hill, as his replacement, with the objective of removing Hugh Greene from office. In 1969, after numerous disagreements with Hill, the Greene light for innovation in BBC programming was turned off.

9

Crisis? What crisis? The demise of British broadcasting in the 1980s and 1990s

In the mid-1970s the cosy duopoly in British broadcasting began to unravel. A number of pressures arose which were accentuated by the election of a Tory government under Mrs Thatcher in 1979. Pre-Thatcher pressures included the rising cost of programme-making, which, by the mid-1970s, was running ahead of the normal rate of inflation for the economy as a whole. Rapid changes in the technology of broadcasting, including the advent of cable, satellite and the video cassette recorder, were challenging the whole basis of terrestrial broadcasting. Politically the broadcasting institutions were criticized from all parts of the spectrum as the consensus which had shaped the development of post-war Britain started to collapse in the face of economic and social change. Political attacks on the broadcasting institutions initially had come from the Left, with criticisms of the coverage of industrial and political issues. The election of Margaret Thatcher issued a challenge to the ideological basis of broadcasting as the new government, committed to a free market ideology, came into conflict with the public service ethos of British broadcasting. De-regulation and privatization invaded the citadels of British broadcasting as well as sweeping through the commanding heights of the British economy. These pressures culminated in the late 1980s in a crisis for public service broadcasting which resulted in a fundamental shift in the whole ecology of British broadcasting.

The changing circumstances of British broadcasting are clearly manifest in the changes in the BBC in this period. In the 1960s – as the sociologist Tom Burns[1] captures in his study of the Corporation made at the time – the BBC was a self-confident organization, complacent and untroubled, assured of its place in British society. A decade after the publication of Burns's study a very different picture emerges from Michael Leapman's account of the problems that beset the Corporation in the 1980s.[2] He depicts an institution under siege, marked by internal conflicts and lacking direction. If Leapman's BBC was troubled about its future, under the present Director-General, Mark Thompson, it is concerned about its survival. Under the Blair government the Corporation has struggled to survive the political, regulatory and commercial battering it has been subjected to. Broadcasting today is undergoing a revolution comparable to that of the changes wrought in the press in the nineteenth century with the repeal of the taxes on knowledge. Reith's citizens are being replaced by Thatcher's consumers as the opening up of British broadcasting to market forces is radically changing the structure as well as the content of the broadcast media. The concept of public service broadcasting is becoming increasingly unviable in the new environment which is being shaped by the multi-channel, digital world (see Chapter 13). This chapter outlines the financial, political, technological and ideological developments that set the stage for this revolution.

Financial pressures

By the 1980s, broadcasting had become a big business. The BBC in 1986/87 had an annual income of nearly £1000 million, the largest proportion of which came from the licence fee. ITV, for the financial year of 1985, attracted around £983 million in advertising revenue and the 15 ITV companies made a profit of over £82 million before tax.[3] The broadcasters were at the heart of a UK information technology sector whose output in 1983/84 was estimated to be £3.25 billion; one of the most successful parts of the British economy. However, financial storm clouds began to gather above broadcasting in the 1970s in the form of rising programme costs. Inflation in programme costs started to run ahead of the normal level for the British economy as a whole. This put real pressure on the BBC whose main source of revenue came from the licence fee, a poll tax on viewers. Revenue began to fall short of spending. In the early 1970s the increasing cost of making television was met by the boost given to revenue by the introduction of a higher licence fee for colour TV. From the end of the 1970s the BBC funds were whittled away as the real value of the licence fee declined. Increases in the licence fee were always below what the BBC asked for and as a result throughout the 1980s the BBC was in continuous financial difficulty. In the 1970s, the ITV companies and the BBC spent roughly the same amount on their television services; by the mid-1980s, ITV contractors were able to spend one and a half times more than the BBC.[4]

The BBC's financial plight was increased by other pressures on the licence fee. When the BBC was a monopoly, the licence fee was an adequate source of funding. However, the arrival of commercial television meant that the Corporation had to compete for its audience. The response was to develop programme policy in the direction of some of the popular formats introduced by ITV. In the 1960s, the BBC was successful at doing this but at the cost of weakening the basis of its claim to the licence fee. It could no longer argue it provided a unique broadcasting service to the British public. As the programme output of commercial and public service television became similar, it was increasingly difficult to argue that viewers should pay for one service while they could watch the other free. In the early 1980s, the BBC, in the face of falling audiences, hired Michael Grade to compete more effectively with ITV. He decided to develop a more popular programming policy with the purchase of foreign soaps and serials, as well as the development of indigenous soaps and chat shows. In pursuing this policy the BBC competed with ITV for the right to cover events, especially sporting events, thereby helping to further increase programme costs. While such a policy succeeded in attracting more viewers, it further undermined the BBC's claim to special treatment in the form of the licence fee. This was pointed out by the then Home Secretary, Leon Brittan, over the BBC's decision to buy *The Thornbirds* from Australia and schedule it against ITV's prestigious drama *Brideshead Revisited*. Brittan wrote to the BBC about the decision, asking 'why should a broadcasting service funded by a tax on the public . . . squander its resources in providing fare that is indistinguishable from the run of material provided by commercial TV?'. He broadened his criticism by asking of what public benefit were programmes such as *Dallas, EastEnders* and *Wogan*. Such sentiments highlight the dilemma at the heart of the BBC's funding – if its audiences decline, then it becomes less easy for the BBC to present the case for an increase in the licence fee, while if it develops a formula to increase audiences by competing with ITV, then it undermines its claim to special treatment with the licence fee. This became more urgent at a time of rising costs and competition, added to in the 1980s with the arrival of new means of television distribution and different ways of paying for them.

Rising costs also exposed problems with ITV's funding – its dependency on advertisers. These costs were passed on by the ITV companies to the advertisers but this had the effect of increasing their dissatisfaction at the restrictions placed by ITV on advertising on the network. The amount of time for advertisements and the emphasis on spot advertising were criticized by advertisers, increasingly unhappy at the ITV's monopoly of television advertising. It is estimated that ITV's monopoly led to advertisers paying four times as much as they would under a market system. The concerns were accentuated by ITV's inability to deliver the audience. This was a product of the technological revolution which began to sweep through the world of television in the 1980s.

Technological change

For much of the post-war period, ITV and BBC dominated the television market. However, in the 1980s the development of new broadcasting technologies such as satellite, cable and video cassette recorder (VCR) began to threaten the cosy duopoly by providing new outlets for viewers. Viewers had more 'choice' over what they viewed and when they viewed it. These developments undermined ITV's and BBC's hold over the television audience as well as the output. The inroads into their audiences made by cable and satellite were initially relatively small. Cable never developed as quickly as was forecast in the early 1980s: by 1996, only 15 per cent of British households subscribed to the new service. Satellite also struggled to penetrate the television market. By 1992, 10–11 per cent of households with TV sets had satellite dishes.[5] However, backed by the resources of the News Corporation, satellite television in Britain was able to outbid the terrestrial companies and take key parts of their output from them, especially sporting events such as test cricket, Ryder Cup golf and a percentage of premier league football matches.

The fragmentation of the audience was at first associated with the development of the VCR. Available in 1971, the VCR became an important part of the broadcasting environment in the 1980s. By 1986, it is estimated that between 44 per cent and 51 per cent of households possessed a VCR, rising to around 59 per cent by 1990 and reaching 68 per cent by the mid-1990s.[6] VCRs allow the viewers to 'time shift' by enabling them to record material to view at a time of their choice. VCRs are also used to watch material, usually feature films, hired from rental shops. The ability of traditional broadcasters to control the television screen was challenged. While the amount of time that the average viewer spent consuming the output of cable, satellite and VCRs in the 1980s was minimal, it is estimated that each viewer devoted 6 per cent of his or her total viewing time on the output of the new technologies,[7] the growth of such services placed more pressure on traditional broadcasting institutions. The new cable and satellite industries were supported by the new political and economic climate surrounding broadcasting.

Fragmentation of the 'consensus'

The political consensus that had underpinned British broadcasting since the end of the war broke up in the 1980s. British television, as we have seen, was developed in the 1950s when there was a relatively high degree of consensus about the political direction which the country should take. In political terms the relative agreement between the front benches of the two major parties on many of the major issues of the day enabled broadcasters to tread the fine line of political balance and objectivity. In the 1960s, Greene had challenged the consensus by pushing back some of the parameters of taste but in the 1970s changes occurred in British political culture which caused some groups to feel marginalized by British television. Increasingly groups outside the national consensus became more and more critical of their representation on television. So-called minority groups such as trade unions, ethnic communities, women and the other nations of Britain complained about their lack of voice on the air waves or the misrepresentation of their views and ways of life. Charges of political bias were dismissed by the BBC with the hoary cliché that if they were being criticized from both the left and right of the political spectrum, they must be getting their reporting correct. Sitting comfortably in the middle of the road, however, became more precarious in the early 1980s with the rise of the Social Democrats. As the political consensus became more fluid, it grew less easy to define where 'balance' rested in the reporting of politics. More accusations of bias followed.

Concerns about the representations of minorities were raised in the deliberations and report of the Annan Inquiry into the state of broadcasting in 1977. In response to submissions from minority groups, the Annan Committee argued that space had to be developed on television for minority audiences. As the report stated: 'there are enough programmes for the majority ... what is now needed is programmes for different minorities which add up to make the majority'.[8] Annan broke with previous official enquiries in that it no longer saw the broadcast audience as a unified national entity but as a fractured collection of cultural interests. This view influenced the debate about the allocation of a new channel. In November 1982, Channel Four began transmission and represented a new form of broadcasting. The company was set up as a commercial entity to be funded by advertising under the regulation of the Independent Broadcasting Authority (IBA). But in many ways it was distinct from the rest of the ITV system. The channel was to be a 'publisher' not a 'producer' of programmes, commissioning material from the ITV companies, ITN, foreign companies as well as a certain proportion of its output from independent producers. The channel was required by the 1982 Broadcasting Act to produce material that would appeal to 'tastes and interests not generally catered for by ITV', that is, consciously to produce material for cultural and ethnic minorities, as well as 'encourage innovation and experiment in the form and content of programmes'. Responding to the climate of rapid social and political change, the channel was allowed to define balance across its whole output rather than within a specific programme. The arrangements for advertising were also different. Channel Four was paid for from an annual subscription from the ITV regional companies who in return were allowed to sell advertising for the channel in their own region. The channel was a compromise between the calls of Annan for broadcasting to respond to the needs of minority audiences, the demand from independent programme-makers to produce material for the network, the advertisers' search for new audiences and the government's desire to introduce more commercialism into British broadcasting.

The arrangements satisfied nearly everyone except the Welsh. In an unprecedented campaign of civil disobedience in the history of British broadcasting, Welsh people refused to pay their licence fees, damaged and closed down transmitters and went to prison in large numbers to demand a Welsh language TV channel. The government backed down in the face of such protests and amended the legislation to set up Sianel Pedwar Cymru (S4C), the only television channel in Britain to be created out of the demands of its audience. A separate broadcasting authority, S4C is required to commission Welsh language programmes from BBC Cymru/Wales, HTV and the independent sector to be shown in prime time in Wales. The remainder of the output is taken from Channel Four UK. The operation was funded by a levy on the advertising revenue of the ITV companies. Catering to the specific needs of the Welsh audience by S4C, as well as by Channel Four to a range of minority audiences, did not bring about an end to the political criticisms. They were now to come from a different quarter – the government.

Political attacks on broadcasters

Mrs Thatcher's relationship with the broadcasters began on a shaky footing. She had been suspicious of the broadcasters since her association with the Clean Up TV campaign in the 1960s. Her views on the media in general were motivated by the perceived slights she had received at their hands. We are told she regarded journalism as the 'haunt of the brittle, the cynical and the unreliable'.[9] She attributed great influence to television. Not only was television central to the projection and management of her image and that of her government, but she accused television of encouraging copy-cat rioting during the urban unrest of 1981, providing the 'oxygen of publicity' to terrorists and promoting the increase of pornography and violence in British society. While accepting the role of the free market in most aspects of life, she claimed in relation to television, particularly on issues of sex and violence, that she was a 'regulator'.[10] Her desire to provide a framework for the content of television brought her into conflict with the broadcasting institutions.

There were a number of skirmishes between Mrs Thatcher and the broadcasters in the early 1980s. She was particularly incensed when the BBC's *Panorama* broadcast an interview with a member of the Irish National Liberation Army, which had claimed responsibility for the assassination of her close confidant Airey Neave in 1979. There was also a dispute over *Panorama*'s footage of the IRA setting up a road block in Carrickmore that same year. Mrs Thatcher's first major conflict with the broadcasters came during the Falklands/Malvinas conflict. The BBC was singled out for criticism for the way in which it reported the war, particularly the efforts by the Corporation – or at least part of the Corporation – to report the war as impartially as it could. She criticized the BBC for not supporting 'our boys' and one *Panorama* programme, which reported dissent within Britain, was described by one of her parliamentary outriders as an 'odious and subversive travesty'.[11] The row that ensued was bitter and sowed the seeds of deep antagonism between the Prime Minister and the BBC which were to be reaped later in the decade.

In 1985, relations between the government and the BBC took a further knock over a programme, *At the Edge of the Union*, in the *Real Lives* series which concerned two politicians on opposite sides of the war in Northern Ireland – one was Martin McGuinness, who had been accused in the British press of being the chief of staff of the IRA. After the programme had been cleared for transmission by BBC management, the Home Secretary contacted the Chairman of the Board of Governors asking the BBC not to broadcast it. The governors agreed. The programme was stopped, provoking a nationwide strike by BBC journalists. The programme was broadcast later after a number of cuts. The *Real Lives* dispute brought into stark relief the tensions which had come to characterize the BBC's relations with the government. But they also sparked off a serious crisis within the BBC which eventually led to the resignation of the Director-General, Alastair Milne. Following the Carrickmore episode, Mrs Thatcher had declared that it 'was time the BBC put its own house in order'.[12] To this end the Prime Minister used the appointment powers of the government to put into place as governors people who would do her bidding. Tradition deemed that political balance should be maintained in appointments to the BBC Board of Governors. Mrs Thatcher's government – as it was to do in other walks of official life in Britain – broke with tradition and politicized the appointments process. The first indication of this policy came in 1980 with the retirement of Sir Michael Swann as Chairman. The obvious successor, according to time-honoured conventions, would have been the Vice Chair, the former Liberal MP, Mark Bonham Carter. Instead Mrs Thatcher chose the more Conservative-inclined governor, George Howard. As more vacancies came up, the government filled them with people it felt would be supportive of their policies, including William Rees Mogg, former editor of *The Times*, an enthusiastic supporter of Mrs Thatcher and bitter critic of the Corporation – one BBC insider stated that he 'loathed the BBC and everyone in it; he couldn't disguise the malevolence'.[13] Rees Mogg became Vice Chairman, thereby breaking with the tradition that the Chairman and Vice Chairman of the BBC should be of different political allegiance.

With its increasingly Conservative bias, the Board of Governors began to exert its influence inside the Corporation, challenging the Board of Management on a number of occasions. The cancellation of the *Real Lives* programme by the governors after an emergency viewing of the programme, overrode the decision to broadcast made by the management. The Director-General, Milne, and his Board of Management found themselves increasingly in conflict, often acrimoniously, with the governors over a range of issues from scheduling and programmes to editorial and legal matters.[14] Underlying these tensions was the governors' conviction – and Mrs Thatcher's – that the BBC was out of control and Milne was unable to exert the leadership required. Three episodes in 1986 were to create a political climate in which the attempts to remove Milne became a concerted campaign – Libya, a libel action by two MPs against *Panorama* and the Zircon affair.

The Conservative Party under the new and more aggressive chairmanship of Norman Tebbit renewed its political onslaught on the BBC. This time it extended its criticisms from news and current affairs programmes to include drama and fictional television. The series, *The Monocled Mutineer*, which dramatized events surrounding the mutiny of elements of the British Army at the end of the First World War, was deemed 'anti-patriotic' by Tebbit. The hospital series, *Casualty*, was criticized for being biased in its representation of the health service. Tebbit's most vitriolic spleen was reserved for the BBC's reporting of the US bombing of Libya which had involved the use of airbases in Britain. Conservative Central Office organized a campaign against what they perceived as the BBC's anti-US and anti-government bias, calling on its supporters to ring in and jam the BBC switchboard. Pressure was also put on the BBC over a libel case brought by Tory MPs, supported by Conservative Central Office, over a *Panorama* programme, *Maggie's Militant Tendency*. The BBC settled the case, paying out substantial damages to the two MPs involved. The decision was made only after the Board of Governors put pressure on senior management to abandon what the programme's makers believed was a strong case. The final and most damaging clash came over the *Secret Society* series made by the investigative journalist, Duncan Campbell, for BBC Scotland. One programme examined the Zircon spy satellite, the costs of which Campbell alleged had been withheld from Parliament by the government. In response to pressure from the government, the BBC Governors – including former MI5 employee, Daphne Park – banned the programme. The government went further when Campbell published an article on Zircon in the *New Statesman*. Police raids were made on Campbell's home, the offices of the magazine and BBC Scotland in Glasgow in a search for any material likely to support their claim that the Official Secrets Act had been broken. There was never any prosecution. For many, the raids were an act of intimidation against the media. For the governors, the fact that the programme had been commissioned was an indication of the failure of BBC management. Opposition to Alastair Milne remaining as Director-General reached its high point. Much of the press had conducted a campaign against the BBC throughout the 1980s, with consistent attacks on what it saw as political bias, financial profligacy and declining programme standards. There was a vested interest in performing this role as the Murdoch newspapers were part of the media tycoon's efforts to improve the opportunities for his broadcasting interests by pushing for the deregulation of British broadcasting. The pressure against Milne eventually led to his departure in January 1987. The assertion of pre-eminence by the Board of Governors was a watershed in the development of the BBC.

Ideological challenge to public service broadcasting

The political softening up of the BBC was part of a broader ideological challenge to public service broadcasting. The attack on public service broadcasting emerged initially within the ranks of the small, right-wing 'think tanks' which proliferated in the late 1970s and increasingly exerted a hold over the intellectual high ground as Mrs Thatcher consolidated her position in the 1980s. Thatcher's government, as Tom O'Malley documents, drew on the policies and perspectives developed and promoted by bodies such as the Centre for Policy Studies, the Institute of Economic Affairs and the Adam Smith Institute. These groups focused their attack on British television being 'in the hands of one public monopoly and a number of regional private ones'.[15] Samuel Brittan, brother of the man who oversaw British broadcasting as Home Secretary in the mid-1980s, Leon Brittan, was at the forefront of those arguing for the deregulation of broadcasting. Some of the views of these bodies were picked up and promoted by the advertising industry and those associated with the independent television production sector which was expanding with the growth of Channel Four. Both had their own vested interests in 'opening up' broadcasting. Not all the outpourings of these organizations were adopted by the government but they were influential in framing broadcasting policy.

In the early years of the Thatcher government these views played a marginal role in policy formation. While Mrs Thatcher personally had great sympathy with much of what they advocated, her position to act was limited by the balance of power within her administration. The BBC and public service broadcasting had many defenders. The Conservative Party's leading grandee and deputy Prime Minister, William Whitelaw, supported the continuation of the status quo and from his position at the Home Office was able to deflect or ameliorate any proposal for change. However, as the old 'one nation' Tories – the 'Wets' – were eased from their position of power inside the party, radical right-wing proposals for the restructuring of British broadcasting came to the fore. By the mid-1980s Mrs Thatcher felt she was in a powerful enough position to embark on a direct assault on the BBC and in March 1985 she set up the Peacock Committee into the financing of broadcasting.

The Peacock Report

The Peacock Inquiry emerged from the negotiations that had gone on over the renewal of the licence fee at the end of 1984. Mrs Thatcher was determined to explore alternative means of funding the BBC. Her favoured means – although not government policy at this time – was to make the BBC accept advertising. To this end, the committee was to be chaired by Professor Alan Peacock. Selected by Downing Street, Peacock was a committed free marketeer. He was joined by Samuel Brittan, as well as the Chairman of Rank Hovis McDougall, a former deputy chair of the Monopolies and Mergers Commission, an academic ennobled by Mrs Thatcher, a broadcaster with known affiliations to the Conservative Party and Alastair Hetherington, former editor of the *Guardian* and controller of BBC Radio Scotland. The Committee had a bias towards the Tory Party and was unrepresentative of society at large. With such a composition, it was expected that the Committee would recommend the financing of the BBC by advertising. However, to everyone's surprise, the Peacock Report did not support the introduction of advertising.

The Peacock Report, which established the framework for broadcasting policy in the late 1980s and early 1990s, was a document riddled with contradictions. At one level it staved off the more radical right-wing arguments for the reform of the BBC, preserving the licence fee and maintaining the BBC in its present form until the renewal of its charter in 1996. However, the report did lay down the basis for shifting British broadcasting from a system which emphasized public service to one which put profit and business at the centre of its endeavours. In the evidence to the Committee, an overwhelming body of opinion came down against advertising on the BBC which made it impossible for the report to support such a recommendation. Yet the whole thrust of the report was to consider broadcasting as a commercial activity rather than one which had social and cultural significance. According to Sam Brittan, the report 'planted the idea of a broadcasting market akin to publishing which will flower in time'.[16] Among the recommendations, were that both ITV and the BBC should over a 10-year period increase the amount of material they took from independent TV producers to not less than

40 per cent of its output; that BBC Radios 1, 2 and local radio should be privatized and financed by advertising; restrictions on cable franchises and pay per channel and pay per programme as options for TV channels should be removed; and Channel Four should have the option of selling its own advertising. Peacock also recommended that the basis for the allocation of the ITV franchises should be changed, with an auction system replacing the established allocation mechanism. For one observer, the report in policy terms meant 'laying the economic and managerial foundations for the restructuring of the BBC, deregulating ITV and Independent Local Radio (ILR) and creating new openings for market driven cable and satellite-delivered services'.[17] The Peacock Report represented a break with previous reports with its departure from the view that broadcasting was best organized as a public service.

The 1988 Broadcasting White Paper

The recommendations of the Peacock Report did not satisfy the government. Its rejection of advertising was at odds with Mrs Thatcher's publicly expressed desire to see advertising as the basis for financing the BBC and hence an embarrassment. In the immediate short run an election was looming, the Prime Minister was embroiled in the damaging Westland Affair, which diminished her influence inside Cabinet, and with strong opposition from the Home Office to her broadcasting policy, she left things alone. However, never a Prime Minister to accept any recommendation or advice that she did not agree with, she returned to broadcasting issues in the wake of her 1987 election triumph to ensure she obtained the 'correct response'. This time the government put forward its own ideas about broadcasting. The result was the 1988 White Paper – *Broadcasting in the 90s: Competition, Choice and Quality* – which was described by one critic as 'a detailed epitaph for a television system which had been the envy of the world'.[18] The document accepted many of the recommendations of Peacock but focused most of its attention on commercial television. For some, the shifting of attention onto ITV was a result of Mrs Thatcher's fury over the Thames TV programme *Death on the Rock* which highlighted the government's economy with the truth in its version of the events surrounding the assassination of three members of the IRA by the SAS in Gibraltar. But there was also some consistency in the approach of the White Paper to the reorganization of British broadcasting. By deregulating commercial, broadcasting – as well as satellite, cable and radio – and creating a new market-oriented ITV, the government sought to change the whole environment in which the BBC, now identified as the primary public service provider, had to operate. The government started to put a financial squeeze on the BBC and encourage internal reorganization of the management of the Corporation, with Mrs Thatcher's appointees to the Board of Governors asserting themselves. The BBC also had to respond to pressure on the production side by taking 25 per cent of its programmes from independent producers. There were, nevertheless, inconsistencies in government policy which reflected the differences inside government between the Home Office and the Department of Trade and Industry (DTI), which had become more involved in broadcasting policy as a result of being in charge of privatization. These differences were reflected in the White Paper and were exposed in the debate and lobbying that went on around its proposals. By the time the broadcasting bill was published in December 1989, the DTI had gained the upper hand. Douglas Hurd had left the Home Office to be replaced by a Thatcherite hard-liner and attempts to ameliorate the worst excesses of the White Paper diminished. The result was that the broadcasting bill did not substantially change from that envisaged by the White Paper.

The 1990 Broadcasting Act – reorganizing the ITV network

The 1990 Broadcasting Act brought about substantial changes in the running of ITV. The most significant – and controversial – change concerned the awarding of the franchises. The Act introduced a system of auction in which the highest bidder was awarded the franchise. However, the bidders, as part of the process of competitive tendering, had to draw up detailed financial plans and programme proposals for consideration by the Independent Television Commission (ITC), the new regulatory body which replaced the IBA and Cable Authority. The bidders had to satisfy the ITC that their programme proposals passed a 'quality threshold' and their business projections made sense. In 'exceptional circumstances' where the ITC decided bidders did not meet the requirements, then the right to operate a franchise need not be awarded to the highest bid. The requirements for programme quality were spelled out in some detail in the Act.

The outcome of the franchise auction was announced in October 1991 and the inconsistencies and absurdities of the system were clearly apparent. There was no contest for three of the franchises – Central, Scottish and Border. The amounts which successful bidders paid for the right to operate their franchise varied enormously – while Channel Television paid £1000 per annum for their franchise, Carlton paid out over £43 million for the right to broadcast weekly in London. The iniquities of these disparities were highlighted by Central TV having to pay only £2000 per annum for the right to run one of the most lucrative ITV franchises with an annual turnover of more than £314 million while Yorkshire TV (YTV) paid £37 million for a franchise with an annual revenue from advertising amounting to around £125 million.[19] It was calculated that YTV, Anglia and Tyne Tees paid over the odds to obtain their franchises. Out of keeping with the intention of the Act, the ITC only awarded 5 out of the 16 franchises to the highest bidder. The Commission used the exceptional circumstances clause to turn down eight of the highest bids on the grounds of their failing to pass the quality threshold. Overall ITV companies paid £350 million for their franchises. Ironically Mrs Thatcher saw one of her allies in the broadcast world, Bruce Gyngell at TV-am, lose the franchise for breakfast TV. This, as she said, was not supposed to have happened.[20]

Many of the new ITV companies who bid large amounts for their franchise faced the problem of meeting their annual payments to the government and providing a quality service. In a highly competitive market with costs still rising – particularly over the coverage of key sporting events – some companies ran into financial difficulties. In 1992, it became apparent that Yorkshire TV and Tyne Tees TV were having financial problems. Both had over-bid for their franchise and, in a climate of economic recession, advertising revenue was strapped. The ITC, in a special dispensation, allowed the two companies to break the rules of franchise ownership and merge to form YTT. The following year the newly merged company made a loss of £8 million, hampered by the amount it had to pay annually to the Treasury.[21] Other companies only avoided running into financial difficulties by embarking on huge programmes of cost cutting. HTV bid £20 million for the Wales and West franchise. Concerns about the company's ability to survive were allayed at the end of 1993 by an approach which one city analyst described as 'the most cost effective and efficient in the ITV network'.[22] Behind such City-speak was the reality of huge job losses and drastic financial cutbacks. For a while, the number of people employed by HTV fell below the figure the company stated in its franchise bid that was needed to provide a quality service. Many argued that the quality of programmes provided by HTV had declined – an ITC review concluded that 'HTV West's overall performance was weakened by the high proportion of co-productions with other ITV licensees and with satellite channels' which 'had the effect of diluting regionality and, in some cases, quality'. Viewers in the West Country reportedly saw much of the output as 'uninspiring'.[23]

One part of the ITV network particularly beset by problems in the 1990s was ITN. Under the old ITV system, ITN was the sole provider of news for the network, operating as a non-profit organization owned collectively by the ITV companies. Under the 1990 Act ITN retained its sole provider status for the next decade but subject to a review after the first five years. This introduced uncertainty about its long-term future. If the ITV companies were dissatisfied with its service, they could turn to another provider. ITN's uncertainty was accentuated by the organization becoming a 'profit-making' business – in spite of the financial success of ITN throughout the period between 1954 and 1991 which saw its turnover rise to £110 million.[24] From 1991 ITN had to compete to survive. Increased competition from the BBC put pressure on ITN and, with declining audience figures in the early 1990s, the company position was further weakened in a commercial system that demanded the delivery of large audiences for advertisers. ITN's position became more precarious. In 1990, it moved to a large new purpose-built headquarters but with the recession biting it was unable to rent space to other businesses, thereby losing an estimated £6.5 million per annum.[25] The cost of gathering news increased considerably in the early 1990s with a succession of 'big foreign stories'. The collapse of communism and its aftermath, Tiananmen Square and the Gulf War added considerably to the news budget. In 1991, the company had an overspend of £9.8 million – a figure inflated by what was described as a serious breakdown in the accounting processes at ITN.[26] The result was massive job losses, a move away from serious news towards a more tabloid, human interest format and a sell-out of a controlling interest in the company to a consortium led by the major ITV companies. ITN increased its audience share and improved its solvency with these developments but the pressure to further cut costs as well as reschedule its main evening news programmes to meet the programme needs of the ITV companies increased.

Part of the reason for the decline in employment in the ITV sector was the decision that 25 per cent of production should be taken from independent producers. This ruling also had an important impact on the kind of companies that emerged following the 1990 Act. Many ceased to be integrated production companies who made most of what they broadcast. There was a shift to the publisher-contractor model pioneered by Channel Four. A change also occurred in the kind of people in charge of the ITV companies. Programme-making experience counted for less as these companies searched for people with financial acumen to take the helm. This was starkly emphasized at Granada with what happened to David Plowright, who, first, as editor of regional news and ITV's flagship current affairs programme, *World in Action*, and then as chief executive of the company in the 1970s and 1980s, had helped to earn Granada the prestige it enjoyed for programme quality. Plowright's reputation had played a crucial part in Granada's beating off a strong challenge for the North-west franchise. But in January 1992, Plowright was dumped by Granada as in the new economic climate the balance sheet took precedence over programme quality. The new chief executive of the Granada Group, the owners of the TV subsidiary, had been brought in to cut costs and the television operation seemed as good a place to start as any. For many in the industry, Plowright's departure meant that 'all pretensions of good programme making in ITV now fall by the wayside'.[27] Money started to talk more loudly as accountants and money men proliferated in the running of the network.

The leading player in the new ITV system was Carlton Communications, which took over the London weekday franchise from Thames TV. Carlton's boss, Michael Green, described in the Sunday newspaper colour supplements as the 'most powerful man in British television', had been trying to buy into British broadcasting since the late 1970s. He failed in a bid for a franchise in 1980, was prevented by the IBA from taking over Thames in 1985 and had his application to run Britain's first satellite TV service turned down in 1986. In the 1990s, Carlton amassed more and more of the ITV network. Green became the Chairman of ITV and Carlton consolidated its hold over the network following the acquisition of Central TV. This represents a degree of influence over the network never previously achieved by any company. The rise of Carlton as ITV's leading force represented the triumph of commerce over creativity. Green was one of Mrs Thatcher's chosen broadcasters, donating to the Conservative Party's funds, and consistently advocating the opening up of British TV to 'market forces'. Carlton's attitude to programmes was summed up by its first head of programmes, Paul

Jackson, who emphasized the need for a more commercial approach with game shows, comedy and music at the top of his schedule. He stated: 'We won't have the latitude in future to find excuses for programmes that don't earn their keep. Programmes will not survive in the new ITV if they don't pay their way.' Jackson's concern with ratings reflected the increasing importance of money in shaping the output of the ITV network and for many of those who had learned their trade in the old ITV system it was confirmation that the new system is 'bereft of public duty and any public concern beyond their shareholders'.[28]

The Birtist Revolution – inside the BBC

Commercial television's conversion to the mechanisms of the free market left the BBC holding up the edifice of public service broadcasting. Despite staving off the attack on broadcasting under the 1990 Act, things were beginning to change at the BBC. The Corporation appointed Michael Checkland, the BBC's accountant, to replace the deposed Alastair Milne in 1987. The Board of Governors in making the appointment had overlooked seasoned programme-makers, including Michael Grade, who had done much to develop the BBC's output in the early 1980s in face of competition from ITV and the new entrants in the television market. Checkland's appointment coincided with the reorganization of BBC news and current affairs. A new Directorate was created, bringing together the operation of television and radio journalism under one structure. John Birt, the director of programmes at London Weekend Television, was appointed to head up the new body. By emphasizing its commitment to serious news and current affairs, the BBC believed it had found one way of distinguishing its role as a public service broadcaster. The creation of the News and Current Affairs Directorate was also a reflection of the battle inside the BBC. Mrs Thatcher's appointee, Marmaduke Hussey, had, soon after taking over as Chairman, attacked BBC journalism for having lost its 'integrity and independence', thereby mirroring the criticism levelled from without by Norman Tebbit and others in the Tory Party.[29]

Birt, himself, had previously expressed his criticism of the 'bias against understanding' which pervaded TV news journalism. He regarded TV news bulletins as being composed of too many short items and current affairs reporting not doing enough to provide a broad context for viewers to understand the issues of the day. On taking over at the BBC, Birt expanded the amount of time TV news devoted to the main news stories of the day as part of his 'mission to explain'. In addition, current affairs programmes such as *Panorama* were directed to be more focused in their choice of topic, concentrating on providing background to the day's main news events. Features output was increased with programmes such as *On the Record, Assignment* and the *Money Programme* specializing their reporting in particular areas. To complete his overhaul, more resources were thrown at news and current affairs. The changes were not popular inside the BBC. Many reporters complained about the increased 'centralization' of news and current affairs operation with management exerting more influence over the product. Others were unhappy about the decline of committed journalism. Journalistic enquiry was seen as taking a back seat to a more staid, careful style of reporting which avoided taking risks. For Birt and the management, these responses from staff were simply the complaints of those unhappy at change. Birt's changes must be seen in the context of an institution fighting for its survival in an increasingly hostile political and economic climate and the desire of the BBC governors to exert more control over BBC journalism, thereby ensuring that the Corporation would come into conflict less often with the government and the Tory Party over its reporting.

Birt's ambitions did not stop at heading up the BBC news and current affairs operation. In 1991, in an unprecedented departure for the BBC, he was appointed Director-General Designate during Checkland's last year of office. He took over the reins of the BBC in 1993 with the full support of the governors. The timing of his appointment was crucial in the development of the Corporation, coming in the run-up to the renewal of the BBC's charter in 1996. Birt had the task of negotiating the renewal. The political climate within which he had to operate had improved with the departure of Mrs Thatcher and the end of her private war against the BBC. Yet Birt continued to make far-reaching changes in the operation of the BBC – not only in relation to its journalism but also more critically in the financial and commercial operation of the Corporation. For some critics these changes further eroded the BBC's public service commitment.

The most fundamental change was the adoption of Producer Choice. Plans for the introduction of an internal market inside the BBC were announced in 1991. Within two years, Producer Choice was established at the centre of Birt's policy for the development of the BBC. The initial impetus for Producer Choice was the new requirement that 25 per cent of production had to be from independent sources. But it was also an effort to restructure the BBC to make it better able to respond to the competition from new media, such as satellite and cable, and a vital part of the BBC's strategy to convince the government that the BBC should have its charter renewed. Producer Choice would show the government that the BBC was not an inefficient bureaucracy but a lean and fit organization geared to compete in the market-place. As elsewhere in the public sector the internal market in the BBC saw the creation of cost centres which bought and sold their products, services and expertise to each other. This meant that producers and departments had control of their own budgets and could go outside the BBC for their needs, if they could be purchased at a lower price than offered in house. The argument in support of the Producer Choice was that costs would be reduced, efficiencies increased and programme-makers would have greater freedom. The new system was fully embraced by BBC management. According to one Auntie watcher, it was a 'major break' and 'dramatic change' in corporate culture at the BBC which saw managers respond positively to the 'strategy of making every decision in the Corporation subordinate to market forces'.[30] However, elsewhere inside the BBC the new system was less welcome.

For the staff – those responsible for creating the product – the internal market resulted in job losses. Between 1991 and 1993, the BBC shed 3500 jobs.[31] For many BBC employees who remained, the internal market reduced job satisfaction as journalists had to become budget managers, haggling for the best prices. A survey of staff in 1993 found low morale, lack of motivation and hostility to management.[32] Staff morale was not helped by attacks on them from the Director-General: on first joining the BBC, he said of the current affairs output, for example, that 'there's nothing I like'. Veteran reporter Mark Tully accused Birt of 'Big Brother leadership', ruling through fear and sycophancy and giving priority to cost-cutting at the expense of programme-making.[33] Michael Grade saw Birt's management style as 'pseudo-Leninist' while the playwright, Dennis Potter, dismissed him as a 'croak-voiced Dalek'.[34] Staff anxieties were heightened by the logic of Producer Choice, which meant that BBC departments that could not compete would be closed, thereby reducing the production basis of the Corporation. John Birt denied this would happen but he was not able to reassure staff. Finally, one of the direct consequences of the change was the increase in bureaucracy as more pieces of paper had to be signed in order to acquire and pay for the resources needed to make programmes. Birt's strategy was regarded as vindicated in 1994 when the government agreed to renew the BBC's charter – praise was heaped on the Director-General, one newspaper dubbing him 'The Man Who Saved the BBC's Licence'.[35] But many argued that Charter renewal had been attained at the expense of weakening the Corporation's commitment to public service broadcasting.

The future of the BBC

There is no doubt that the BBC invented the concept of public service broadcasting. The question is whether the present-day BBC is worthy of the public service legacy that it created. I doubt it more day by day.

Although the BBC arrogates to itself the benefits of the public service legacy, especially total access to licence funding, I fear that there is accumulating evidence that that legacy is being wantonly frittered away and that, more and more, the BBC is becoming just another broadcasting organisation jeopardising quality standards in the quest of the fool's gold of audience ratings.

The BBC is becoming a vehicle for massive exploitation by commercial organisations. For example, it is providing free sponsorship to companies that sponsor sport . . . The Committee was told by corporate sponsors that they would prefer the events that they sponsor to be transmitted by the BBC because the audience – and therefore, the free publicity that they obtain – was, for the time being, much greater than that provided by BBC's non-terrestrial rivals.

The BBC might say its public service ethos is safeguarded on its radio wavelengths. Last month, Duke Hussey, the BBC's chairman, said radio was the 'most distinctive part of the BBC, and the BBC must be distinctive to justify the licence fee'. However, BBC radio is not as distinctive as it ought to be, and is becoming less distinctive.

Radio 4 has many high standards . . . but constantly its standards are reduced or assailed. It has an exceptionally loyal audience. However, I know from correspondence that that audience is regularly affronted by what is being done to Radio 4.

What has happened to Radio 4 is nothing compared with what has been done to Radio 3. It was once the epitome of high standards, which were copied throughout the world, but has been so debased and vandalised that it is scarcely worth transmitting. It has been turned into a famous composers latest hits wavelength.

In television, it has already two major satellite channels that broadcast to millions abroad. BBC Prime is a subscription service; BBC World is funded by advertising. Those two BBC channels are no longer BBC channels; they are conducted in partnership with major commercial organisations, including Pearson here in Britain, the huge Cox Communications in the United States and Nissho Iwo in Japan.

The BBC claims that those services are financially ring fenced and not funded by the licence, but that is nonsense. On BBC Prime . . . many of the programmes transmitted are past or present successes funded by the licence payers. On BBC World, the news material is provided by BBC Worldwide News staff, again funded by the licence.

I do not criticise the BBC for that development . . . But those developments do raise questions about the BBC's future. On the one hand, its share of the domestic audience is falling and will continue to fall – the director general admits as much. On the other hand, the BBC's commercial activities will continue to increase and should continue to increase.

The BBC is no longer solely a publicly funded public service broadcasting organisation. It is an increasingly commercial organisation which, with decreasing justification, lays claim to public funding through a regressive tax which is increasingly the subject of public debate and controversy.

Source: Gerald Kaufman, MP, Chair of Select Committee on National Heritage in House of Commons debate reported in the *Guardian*, 19 February 1996.

Paying for the Beeb? – Renewal of the BBC's charter

At the end of 1995, the BBC's new draft charter and licensing agreement was published by the government. The position of the BBC was safeguarded for the next ten years with a review of the licence fee taking place in 2000. The agreement placed tougher decency standards on the Corporation, but by and large the document was a triumph for the BBC, so much so that one commentator could say that 'whole portions of the document read as if they have been written by the BBC's own policy unit, which has clearly conducted some very fruitful lobbying'.[36] However, two aspects of the new charter represented a break with the past. First, and most significantly, the BBC was allowed to be both a commercial and public service broadcaster. It acquired the right to provide services which 'are funded by advertisements, subscription, sponsorship, pay-per-view system or any other means of finance'.[37] Such a move recognized the importance of financing the BBC in the rapidly changing and more competitive broadcasting environment. While allowing the BBC to compete to maintain audience share, there were implications for the Corporation's commitment to public service broadcasting. Raising more money to support services from commercial activities made it more difficult to justify maintaining the real value of the licence fee. Particularly in light of rising public hostility to the licence fee – a MORI poll in 1993 found that 60 per cent of people favoured replacing the licence fee with advertising.[38]

Second, the agreement increased the power of the Board of Governors to appoint, not just the director-general, but all other members of the Board of Management and other 'key appointments' in the Corporation. Previously, appointments to the management board were the responsibility of the director-general alone, now his role is consultative. The selection of the governors remained unchanged; it still rested with the government. As Steven Barnett said, 'Everyone knows the system is flawed. And they are now being given astonishing powers to bring in anyone they want.'[39] The new agreement was seen as the culmination of Marmaduke Hussey's mission to bring the BBC under control. Under his chairmanship the BBC could be seen as becoming less independent and more subject to market forces.

Market forces – choice and quality?

Supporters of the 1990 Broadcasting Act claimed it would introduce more choice for the consumer and more competition between the broadcasters. This would, they argued, improve the quality of the product. Opponents said it would inevitably mean a decline in programme quality. As a result of the auction system, money and resources would be taken away from programme-making and the focus on profit at the expense of quality would mean that creativity and risk were sacrificed on the altar of the balance sheet. A debate was waged over the impact of the Act on the output of British television. This debate highlighted the difficulty of defining exactly what is meant by 'good television'. Everyone has a different opinion. While politicians may only judge quality in the narrow terms of how they are reported and represented on television, broadcasters appear to care more deeply about quality. However, the judgements of British programme-makers are shaped by their own professional codes and practices as well as their interests. The Campaign for Quality Television, which attempted to mobilize opposition to the Broadcasting Bill, was dominated by concerns which focused primarily on an updated version of the Reithian idea of educating the viewer. References to a previous 'golden age' of television conveniently ignored the failures of British broadcasting of yesteryear. Public notions of 'good television' only really manifest themselves in the terms of audience ratings. The more people watch a programme, the better the programme. Critical judgements of programme quality are found in newspaper guides to the day's television viewing with crude forms of ranking to indicate whether a programme is worth watching or not. There are also the musings of TV critics. However, in recent years TV criticism has declined as programme plugs and puffs find their way into the lifestyle sections of many newspapers.[40] Elsewhere special interest groups of one form or another attempted to make assessments of coverage in their areas and a number of academic studies have sometimes successfully worked their evaluations into mainstream discussion. Finally, there are official bodies who publish their reports on programme content, the most important in the 1990s being the ITC surveys of the output of ITV companies which allowed some comparison with past programmes. Judgements as to what is 'quality' are highly subjective and ultimately those who determine the discussion set the agenda for what is deemed 'good television'.

In the 1990s, concerns about programme quality increased. ITV was on the receiving end of criticism from several quarters. The ITC's first annual appraisal of the new ITV franchise holders in 1994 was critical of Carlton's output, arguing that there had not been many programmes of 'distinctive or of noticeable high quality' and demanded 'significant improvement'.[41] Carlton's contribution to the ITV network was the 'flashing blue lights' and 'surgical trolley infotainment' programmes, such as *Police, Camera, Action!*, *Blues and Twos*, *Animal Detectives* and *Special Babies*. Its attempts to produce new sitcoms often resulted in British remakes of American series, such as the *Brighton Belles* and *Married with Children*. The two crucial features of Carlton's programme policy – reflected to a greater or lesser extent throughout the ITV system – were the need to play the 'ratings game' and the fear of flops. Carlton's response to ITC censure was to ask Jackson to resign in December 1995 and invest more in producing quality programmes, including popular drama, such as *Branwell* and *Kavanagh QC*. However, the new commitment to programme-making has to be placed firmly in the context of the commercial aims of Carlton. Green always stated that he wanted high-quality programmes but the reality was that the overwhelming desire of his enterprise was to make profit and grow. For one observer, 'The primacy of the bottom line in the Carlton culture militates against the establishing of the creative atmosphere that could produce memorable programmes of quality.'[42]

'Light touch' regulation

The 1990 Broadcasting Act envisaged that there would be less regulation of British radio and television. The ITC would operate with a 'lighter touch' than its predecessor. However, throughout the 1980s there was a marked increase in the regulation of broadcasting. In the early 1980s, the Broadcasting Complaints Commission (BCC) was established to assess complaints made by members of the public or private organizations about the way in which they had been treated by television. While the number of complaints that the BCC received increased steadily in the 1980s, very few of them fell within the narrow remit of the body.

In 1988, another body – the Broadcasting Standards Council (BSC) – was created to monitor the portrayal of sex and violence and matters of taste and decency. Both these bodies were recognized by the 1990 Act which charged the BSC with the task of drawing up a code of conduct for broadcasters to follow in their representation of sex and violence. Ignoring her own commitment to less regulation and public opinion – for example, on sex and violence the great majority of people surveyed by the ITC found nothing offensive on Independent Television – Mrs Thatcher presided over the growth of regulation of British broadcasting. It is more appropriate to describe the changes in the ecology of broadcasting under Mrs Thatcher as 're-regulation'.

Certain sections of British broadcasting, however, were able to exempt themselves from regulation. This is most apparent with satellite broadcasting where Rupert Murdoch's Sky gained commercially preferential treatment. Sky was able to merge with its competitor BSB in November 1990 without any intervention from the government, despite the breaking of the competition rules. The new company, BSkyB, did not have to conform to the programme requirements, as the BBC and ITV had, to provide news and current affairs and children's programmes; there was no requirement to broadcast European-made material or commission original material. BSkyB paid nothing for the right to operate its service while News International, the parent company, was exempted in the 1990 Broadcasting Act from the cross-media ownership rules which prevent newspaper companies taking more than a 20 per cent share in an ITV company.[43] Through political patronage Murdoch was not only able to extend his ownership of the British press but consolidate his entry into the more lucrative broadcasting market.

10

Carrying on: the British film industry since 1945

The British film industry emerged from the Second World War with an enhanced reputation. Some of the best British films ever made were produced during these years. Films such as *Henry V, This Happy Breed, Millions Like Us, The Bells Go Down* and *The Life and Times of Colonel Blimp* achieved both critical and box-office success and cinema attendance rose sharply during the war. By 1945, the film industry appeared to stand on the verge of increased prosperity and international success. However, the post-war period saw a radical change in the role of the cinema in British society and by the 1960s the British cinema had developed 'from being a very influential mass medium and an important business in its own right' to becoming 'a minority entertainment and a sideline of the leisure industry'.[1]

The decline of the British film industry since 1945 has been the subject of much debate, with the familiar concerns of the inter-war years to the fore: the influence of Hollywood, the monopoly control of a small number of British interests, the problems of distribution and the lack of stable domestic production. Only now this debate lacked the intensity of former years as cinema gradually ceased to be a significant means of mass communication. Attendances declined, the number of British pictures made fell and the business collapsed. The change in the cinema's fortunes is often attributed to the arrival of television. Television played an important part in the fate of the industry but the decline of British film also has to be seen in the context of other changes that were happening in post-war British society. The 'consumer boom' of the mid-1950s led to a restructuring of the leisure habits of most British people, which marginalized the role of cinema in their lives. The structural weaknesses in the industry became more apparent as it was subjected to competition from other forms of popular entertainment and amusement. The failure to build an established industry with the necessary acting and technical skills, financial management, political influence and investment was clearly exposed from the mid-1950s onwards. But perhaps the most critical factor was the failure of government to develop a realistic and consistent policy toward film. It is these factors, rather than the inability of British film-makers to appreciate the cinema as an art and entertainment form, that prevented the development of a national cinema in Britain. Occasional revivals in the fortunes of the industry, such as in the 1960s and 1980s, have flattered to deceive. Rather than represent any significant change in the fortunes of British film, they have only served to confirm the industry's increased dependence on television and foreign finance.

In peacetime

The promise of success for the British cinema appeared to be confirmed by developments in the early post-war years. Cinema audiences reached their peak in 1946, with the total number of cinema admissions that year at 1635 million.[2] There followed a gradual decline in cinema attendances between 1946 and 1955, when annual admissions dropped to 1182 million. But 32 per cent of people during this period still went to the cinema once a week and cinema attendance in Britain was still more extensive than that in other countries, with on average 28 admissions per head in England, Scotland and Wales in 1950 – this compared with 23 in the United States and no other country achieved more than 20.[3]

The finances of the industry were relatively healthy. The shares of the two largest British cinema chains, Gaumont-British and Odeon had risen by 1000 per cent since 1940.[4] The Rank Organisation announced in 1947 that it would spend more than £9 million making British pictures.[5] Under the new Labour government financial assistance was provided for British film-makers. In 1948, the National Film Finance Corporation (NFFC) was established with the aim of making loans available to British film-makers. The NFFC working capital of £5 million was far from substantial but a number of successful pictures, such as *The Third Man* and *The Happiest Days of Your Life*, were made with government money. The result was that, according to Board of Trade figures, the production of British feature films increased between 1945 and 1949. The number of first feature films rose from 28 in 1945 to 66 in 1949.[6] The year 1946 was declared a 'momentous year' by *Picturegoer* magazine as British films outgrossed their American counterparts at the box-office.[7]

The late 1940s was also a highly creative period in the history of British film production. There were classic adaptations, including David Lean's *Great Expectations* and Laurence Olivier's *Hamlet*. Gainsborough's romantic pictures, such as *The Wicked Lady* with Margaret Lockwood, enjoyed success as did Carol Reed's *The Third Man*, which starred Orson Welles. Perhaps the most successful films of the early 1950s British cinema were produced by the Ealing Studios. Ealing had come to prominence during the war under Michael Balcon who had taken over as head of production in 1938. Their pictures were associated with realism and social responsibility, combining the documentary tradition with simple and well-told tales. The stories usually featured 'ordinary people', often with regional accents. For Balcon, Ealing during the war was a 'happy marriage' of the documentary movement and progressive film producers.[8] However, in the immediate post-war years Ealing became associated with another kind of picture – the comedy. The 'Ealing Comedies' included films such as *Whisky Galore* (1949), *Kind Hearts and Coronets* (1949), *Passport to Pimlico* (1949), *The Lavender Hill*

Mob (1951), *The Titfield Thunderbolt* (1953) and *Ladykillers* (1955). Ealing's pictures obtained 'more success abroad than anybody else's' by their characterization of England and Englishness in the immediate post-war years.[9]

Rapid decline

A sharp downturn in the British film industry occurred in the mid-1950s. In 1955, disaster struck with 'a spiral of declining audiences, closing cinemas, cut-backs in domestic production and further audience losses'.[10] By 1960, annual cinema admissions had fallen to 501 million: a fall from just around 22 million admissions per week to 9 million within five years.[11] The rapid box-office collapse was accompanied by the disappearance of a large number of cinema halls; 4851 cinemas were open in 1951 but by 1960 this figure had fallen to 3034. The closures were disproportionately felt by the smaller cinema halls and as a result the two largest combines increased their hold over the exhibition end of the industry. By 1962, they controlled 41.5 per cent of British cinema seats compared to 33 per cent a decade earlier.[12] A decade later attendances had fallen to 163 million, the number of cinemas had contracted to 1482 and a crisis existed in British film production.[13]

Film historians identify the very affluence of British society in the 1950s as a cause of the decline of the film industry. The increase in real income, the growth of home-ownership and domestic consumption, the diversification of leisure activities, including the increasing popularity of motoring, reduced the amount of time and money spent on going to the pictures. The late 1940s saw people going to the cinema in their droves as a result of the lack of anything else to do. The cinema was a refuge from the austerity that characterized Britain as it struggled to rebuild itself after the ravages of the war. The newly found affluence allowed people to turn to other activities. One crucial change, identified by exhibitors at the time, that affected the British cinema audience, was the increasing number of women going out to work. Women had been the backbone of the cinema during the inter-war years but their flight from the pictures, especially the afternoon programmes, led ABC in 1958 to launch a new advertising slogan 'Don't take your wife for granted – take her to the pictures'.[14]

The rise of television also had a significant impact on the film industry. The new medium is seen as crucial for three reasons. First, and most obviously, the rise in the demand for television sets correlates with the decline in cinema attendances. The number of TV licences grew from around three-quarters of a million in 1951 to over 10 and a half million by 1960.[15] People were clearly choosing to consume their visual entertainment in the confines of their living-rooms rather than go out to the local cinema. Second, television began to buy up the rights to show films. In 1958, the Film Industry Defence Organisation (FIDO) was established to prevent the showing of British films on television. The body attempted to buy up the television rights to British films and organize boycotts of those in the film industry, both domestic and foreign, who sold such rights to TV companies.[16]

This proved to be a costly venture. But more significant in the failure of FIDO were the divisions in the industry within Britain and between British companies and Hollywood. By 1964, British television secured not only the rights to broadcast a large number of Hollywood films but also the output of major independents such as Ealing.[17] Third, major British film combines became involved in the television industry. The introduction of commercial television in 1955 considerably increased their involvement – ABC was one of the first network companies and Rank was part of the Southern Television franchise.[18] The participation of film companies in commercial television further weakened their commitment to making and showing films. The decline of commitment is clearly illustrated by the changes in the relationship between the Rank Organisation and the film industry in the 1950s.

Rank and the British film industry

Stimulated by the surge of public interest in British films during the war years, Rank built on his already important position in the film industry to establish his organization as a multi-million pound international enterprise. With assets valued at around $200 million, the Rank Organisation for the first time provided the British film industry with the capacity to challenge the power of the Hollywood studios.[19] Rank benefited from the boom in cinema attendance in the 1940s. With cinemas packed seven days and nights a week, Rank's profits from exhibition grew enormously. The increased demand for British pictures brought about by the war saw Rank enter into film production in a large way. The size of the Rank Organisation, with its ownership of a large number of studios, renting facilities and cinema theatres, meant that it could afford to sustain losses and take risks. As a result, Rank encouraged the creative talents of directors such as Powell and Pressburger, Launder and Gilliat and David Lean. He allowed film-makers to develop their ideas, skills and techniques without interference from the finance and money men. According to one of his biographers, Rank's 'greatest virtue of all was undoubtedly the fact that he knew nothing about making films'.[20]

With guaranteed profits from the exhibition side of the industry, Rank supported a renaissance in British pictures during the war. However, to ensure that success continued, Rank realized that British pictures had to be distributed to wider audiences, and, as Korda had done in the 1930s, Rank embarked on trying to break into the American domestic market. He stated in 1943, the 'whole future of British films is bound up in the question of overseas trade'.[21] In March 1944, Rank set up a world-wide distribution company, Eagle–Lion Films Ltd, and in June he entered into a deal with United Artists to distribute Rank's top-budget pictures in the United States. This relationship was short-lived as a result of the internal problems that beset United Artists; in 1945 Rank switched to Universal. The immediate post-war years saw the Rank Organisation buy up theatre circuits in Canada, Australia, New Zealand, South Africa as well as the major theatres in the West Indies.[22] Rank also distributed and part-financed Ealing Films. Towards the end of the war the dominant position of Rank led the government to commission an inquiry into the state of the film industry. The Palache Report, published in 1944, was critical of American influence and monopoly tendencies in the British film industry. It called for a financial system that guaranteed independent production. The report was dismissed by Rank and Korda – as well as others in the industry – and its findings were not acted on by the government which in the midst of the war had more pressing priorities.[23] But the stinging criticisms of Rank in the report highlighted strong animosity within government and political circles and the industry towards Rank.

The year 1947 started on a high point for Rank. British films were beginning to achieve some box-office success in America – Olivier's *Henry V* and Rank's big-budget *Caesar and Cleopatra* were showing profits while Universal's first set of British film releases were doing better than expected, including the film that was to be the British hit of the year, *The Seventh Veil*. Rank introduced a monthly documentary series, *This Modern Age*, into his cinema programmes to compete with the American *The March of Time*, and established a Children's Film Division to supply material for the popular Saturday morning shows. Rank embarked in an optimistic mood on a tour of the United States to sell British films to the sceptical American exhibitors. However, clouds were already gathering on the horizon. Rank lost £1.7 million on film production between 1945 and 1946.[24] While the film *Caesar and Cleopatra* was doing well in America, its astronomical budget, including the high cost of publicizing and advertising the film, meant that it never went into profit.[25] Rank's attempt at a million-pound musical, *London Town* (1946), failed at the box-office. These two films, besides losing a large amount of money, raised doubt about Rank's reputation. More damaging was the failure to break into the American market. Rank's films, despite all his efforts, could not overcome the prejudices of American exhibitors, who were reluctant to book British films on their circuits. By the end of the year it was clear that Rank had failed and with audiences at home becoming more discriminating, the Organisation's financial problems began to mount.

In August 1947, matters were made worse by the introduction of a tax on luxury goods. This hit the importation of American films and to fill the gap left by the lack of availability of Hollywood films, the government appealed to Rank to increase production. In November, he responded with an ambitious £9 million programme which involved the production of 43 pictures in addition to the children's films, animation, newsreels and 'B' pictures the Rank Organisation was already making. The money came from the exhibition side of the Rank operation which meant that for the first time the most profitable part of the enterprise was being used directly to support the most hazardous. The outcome was a disaster. Despite the boom in British film production, which reached a high point in the spring of 1948, it was evident that the British film industry could not fill the gap. They still had to compete with the American studios who had stockpiled pictures in the event of the imposition of a duty and also re-issued a number of films.

Some good films were produced but overall the quality of British films was mediocre and they were not popular with film-goers. Audiences were picking which pictures they wanted to see rather than indiscriminatingly visiting the cinema. Rank's efforts were further stymied when the government revoked its duty on American films the following year, realizing that it had failed to stop a drain of hard currency from the country. The lack of popularity of British films was emphasized in that 'American distributors were taking as many dollars out of the country as before from the re-issues and from stockpiled films'.[26] To compensate Rank, the government raised the quota for British films shown at the cinema to 45 per cent. However, this proved as ill-conceived as the import duty. The level was too high, placing more pressure on British film-makers. It meant that exhibitors had to take every British film made, irrespective of their quality and distributors exploited the situation by increasing the prices of hiring films. The dwindling audiences increased the concerns of exhibitors who were trying to find new ways to attract people into the cinemas. The result was that exhibitors began to disregard their quota obligations.

The impact of these decisions on Rank was considerable. Not only had government actions undercut his efforts to sell his films to the American market, but the costs incurred in trying to increase production pushed the Rank Organisation to the verge of financial collapse. Losses on film production for the year in 1949 amounted to nearly £4.7 million.[27] Rank's overdraft with his bankers rose to £16.25 million and the situation required drastic action. Cutbacks were made – the documentary series, the Children's Film Division as well as a film school established for British film-makers at Highbury were closed down. Film production throughout the industry was severely curtailed and as a result many studios closed – in February 1949, only 7 out of 26 British studios were in operation and the number of people employed by the studios had declined from 7253 in March 1948 to 4104 in March 1950.[28] Under Rank's accountant, John Davies, the bottom line became fiscal responsibility and solvency. Rank had been committed to the British film industry and sought to represent the British way of life, as well as certain moral values, on the cinema screens of the world. He had entered the industry committed to the social benefits of the cinema as well as its commercial rewards. This made him sympathetic to film-makers. The financial crisis of the late 1940s brought this philanthropy to an end. The balance sheet became the only concern as the Rank Organisation struggled to avoid financial ruin. Strict limits were placed on film budgets and the Rank Organisation moved away from film production to concentrate on exhibition and distribution. Film-making was only motivated by the need to fulfil the quotas required for the showing of British films at their theatres. By the end of the 1950s Rank had ceased to be the 'public-spirited' tycoon who believed in the production of quality film and the long-term survival of the British film industry. He had become a more hard-nosed businessman whose interest was financial gain. While his profits from exhibition remained constant throughout the 1950s, his production programme gradually dwindled. For the year ending March 1958, Rank had made only 14 films and by March 1961 only 6 out of the 81 British films registered with the Board of Trade were made by Rank or that other major producer of the 1940s, ABPC productions.[29] By the mid-1960s film was only a small part of the Rank Organisation which now made the bulk of its profits from the duplication and photocopying business.

Government policy in the 1940s

The crisis in the British film industry in the late 1940s – and Rank's demise as a force in the industry – can be attributed to a number of factors. Rank placed some blame on the film-makers who produced films that 'were not of the quality to ensure even reasonable returns'.[30] However, Rank's support of profligate producers, such as Gabriel Pascale, the man behind *Caesar and Cleopatra*, and Filippo Del Guidice, whose company Two Cities had produced during the war successful films such as *In Which We Serve* (1942), indicated poor judgement. Both men were extravagant in film-making, producing big budget pictures which no one in the post-war years wanted to see. The attempt to break into the US market proved costly. Not only did it drain resources but it ultimately soured relations with the American studios and resulted in increased competition in the British domestic market. But Rank believed that, more than anything else, he had been betrayed by government policy.

The new Labour administration in 1945 represented the 'first government of ordinary picturegoers in British history'.[31] Several members of the new Cabinet saw the propaganda value of cinema, influenced as they had been by the documentary movement, while others were concerned with the interests of those who worked in the industry, especially as represented by the Association of Cine-Technicians (ACT). The Labour government was also suspicious of Rank's strong commitment to the Conservative Party.[32] The result was that the new government directly intervened in the running of the industry, establishing the NFFC and the Eady levy. The levy was introduced in 1950 as a means of raising finance for film production. Exhibitors agreed, in return for tax concessions, to pay a levy on the price of each cinema ticket to British producers on the basis of their share of box-office earnings.[33] The system was voluntary until 1957 when it became a statutory obligation. However, the economic difficulties that beset the Labour government in the reconstruction of Britain following the war had more consequence on the development of post-war cinema than the small-scale measures enacted to support the industry.

The Attlee government embarked on a radical overhaul of most aspects of British life from health care to education. The condition of Britain in the immediate post-war years did not create a favourable environment for implementing such change. Fuel and food crises, bad weather and, above all, a massive national debt as a result of fighting the war all contributed to the government's difficulties. The substantial balance of payments deficit meant that Britain had to negotiate a huge loan from the American government. To secure this loan the government had to promise to introduce a number of economic measures, including a reduction in imports.[34] In June 1947, the Chancellor of the Exchequer announced the need to drastically reduce the import of luxury goods. American film companies were estimated in 1947 to have taken £70 million out of Britain, and, without consulting the film industry, a 75 per cent tax was imposed on foreign films. The consequence of the tax was to alienate Hollywood and encourage the British film industry to launch a production programme which was beyond its financial and creative means.[35] Traditionally governments had taxed entertainment as an easy means of raising revenue. The Entertainments Tax, introduced during the First World War as a short-term measure, had hit the film industry hard in the 1930s. The tax was doubled in 1942 and in the year 1946–47 is estimated to have taken over £41 million out of the industry.[36] The tax was taking out of the industry nearly 10 times the amount of money needed to break even.[37] An official report in 1949 supported the industry's claims that the tax was having a crippling effect but its findings were ignored. The government was reluctant to give up such a good source of income but, as Rank predicted in 1945, the tax, while a golden egg for the Treasury, was killing the goose that produced it.[38] Besides taxation, inconsistency in government policy had a detrimental impact on the film industry in the late 1940s. Within a year of the introduction of the tax on imported films, the government changed its policy completely. Following an agreement that the Americans would reinvest a certain amount of their profits in the United Kingdom, the tax was revoked. The result was a flood of US feature films into the country which washed away British producers' efforts to increase production and plunged them into financial crisis. In the face of these problems the government's efforts to support the industry through the NFFC, the Eady levy and the film quota were nothing more than short-term palliatives.

British cinema and the age of affluence

The financial retrenchment in the British film industry in the 1950s was accompanied by an artistic decline. The economic reorganization of the industry, with Rank's demise and the crisis in funding, imposed constraints on British film-makers. It was increasingly difficult to raise capital other than for commercial certainties. The mid-1950s marked the end of an era in British film-making. Korda, who had returned to Britain after the war, died in 1956 while Ealing Studios closed in 1955. The film-makers who were free to explore their creative talents under Rank found less scope in the new environment. Some, such as Andrew Mackendrick, the director of classic Ealing Films including *Whisky Galore* (1949), left the country to work in Hollywood while others, such as Thorold Dickinson, whose films gained critical success in the 1940s, quit the industry altogether.[39] Michael Powell and Emeric Pressburger, whose films during the war marked the high point of the output of what some have described as the 'golden age of British film', made their last picture together in 1957. The new environment encouraged 'safe, innocuous films'.[40] While the films of the late 1940s had tried to address and tackle some of the issues and anxieties of their era, characterized by austerity, social upheaval, reconstruction and rationing, British films of the 1950s are accused of complacency. Some films, such as *Sapphire* (1959) and *Violent Playground* (1958), did address racism and juvenile delinquency but on the whole film-makers avoided difficult topics. They were unwilling to challenge the dominant mood of the period, summed up by Harold Macmillan's phrase 'you've never had it so good'.

British cinema of the 1950s thrived on nostalgia for the war, the good, clean fun of Norman Wisdom, the smutty innuendo of the 'Carry On' films and the 'Doctor' series as well as the spine-chilling thrills of Hammer horror films. The preoccupation with the war years was reflected in the peculiarly British – or rather English – war film. These films were usually set in prisoner-of-war camps, recreating the world of the public school and the traditional class divisions of British society. Everyone was a 'jolly good chap' and stiff upper lips quivered everywhere. Films such as *The Colditz Story* (1955), *The Wooden Horse* (1950), *Reach for the Sky* (1956) and *The Dambusters* (1953) were very different from the war films of the Second World War. The pain and agony of war and the effects of war on the individual and community were replaced by adventure stories with the emphasis on bravery, camaraderie and heroism. It was a cinema of 'chaps, prangs and team spirit'.[41] The war films are regarded by some as 'evidence of a strong reaction against contemporary change, a nostalgia for the fixed hierarchical society of the armed services and the firm, unquestioned virtues (fortitude, loyalty, courage) of the war period'.[42] People in the 1950s also wanted to shake off the austerity of the previous decade and enjoy themselves, laugh and have fun – and with the increased affluence they were prepared to spend money looking for laughter and amusement. Comedy in the cinema was extremely popular. Norman Wisdom was the biggest comic star of the period. He made his first film, *Trouble in Store*, in 1953 and every year until 1958 Rank churned out his films. Box-office success in Britain was matched by Wisdom's films doing well abroad, even in the most unlikely of places, such as Iran and Eastern Europe. The series of Wisdom films was indicative of Rank's approach to film-making in the late 1950s. Under John Davies, the Rank Organisation would simply repeat the formula if a film was a commercial hit. This reduced the risks in film production and lessened Rank's dependency on producers and directors.[43] Hence the production of six 'Doctor' films, adapted from the novels of Richard Gordon and the 23 'Carry On' films, which were produced regularly between 1958 and 1980, frequently topping the box-office earnings for British films. The formula approach was also adopted by Hammer which had appeared on the British film scene in the mid-1950s with the Quatermass sci-fiction pictures, adapted from television. However, it was the company's horror films, the Frankenstein and Dracula pictures, which first appeared with *The Curse of Frankenstein* (1957) and *Dracula* (1958), that became a feature of the British film industry. With a small cast, tight budgets, over-exposed studio locations and limited story lines, the horror formula proved successful for Hammer until the mid-1970s.[44]

The popular acclaim for these films can be attributed to a number of factors. Norman Wisdom's films were in keeping with comic tradition of Sid Fields and George Formby. The combination of slapstick and sentiment, with the little man, ungainly and incompetent, overcoming the odds to win the hand of a pretty girl, has consistently won over British film audiences. The success of the 'Carry On' and 'Doctor' films has been attributed to their use of sexual innuendo, which has its roots in the tradition of variety and musical hall.[45] This kind of humour thrived in the sexual conservatism of British society and the strict censorship of sex and sexual matters in film exercised by the BBFC. The vulgarity of the films has been compared to the seaside picture postcard humour of Donald McGill which was popular with working-class holiday makers during the inter-war years.[46] The recognizable stereotypes of the films have also been identified as part of the appeal. The popularity of the Carry On films, for example, is accounted for by their derogatory representations of the educated, middle classes, which 'fare badly in comparison with the stereotypical commonsense masses', and their mild anti-establishment tone, in particular, the lampooning of those in authority who attempt to prevent people enjoying themselves and having fun.[47] If such films were popular with ordinary film-goers, they were treated with opprobrium by the critics. The French film director, François Truffaut, is believed to have had these pictures in mind when he said that there is 'a certain incompatibility between the terms "cinema" and "British"'. The British director, Lindsay Anderson, described the output of British cinema at the time as 'snobbish, anti-intelligent, emotionally inhibited, wilfully blind to the conditions and problems of the present, dedicated to an out-of-date, exhausted national ideal'.[48] It was Anderson and his colleagues in the 'Free Cinema' movement who brought about radical change in British cinema.

The new wave – social realism and British films

'Free Cinema' describes a series of film programmes shown at the National Film Theatre between 1956 and 1959. They were small budget films, mostly funded by the British Film Institute, and nearly all documentaries. They allowed new directors, in particular Lindsay Anderson, Karel Reisz and Tony Richardson, all of whom went on to establish international reputations as film directors, to develop their talents outside the commercial pressures and constraints of mainstream British cinema. These documentaries explored the social changes brought about by the increasing affluence of Britain in the late 1950s, and in particular their impact on working-class communities. Reisz's *We Are the Lambeth Boys* (1959) was shot in a youth club in a working-class community of south London; *Momma Don't Allow* (1956) was set in a jazz club while Anderson's *O Dreamland* (1953) presented a view of the amusement arcade world of Margate. The changing nature of leisure in urban Britain as well as the newly emerging youth culture figured prominently in the work of the Free Cinema movement. While adopting the documentary approach, the Free Cinema directors were more concerned with style, commitment and art as a personal expression than Grierson and his colleagues. For Anderson, the essential difference between Free Cinema and the 1930s documentary tradition was the former's commitment to 'poetic realism' in contrast to Grierson's focus on actuality.[49] They sometimes employed cinéma-vérité techniques and impressed on the viewer an immediacy which made them stand out from mainstream cinema. In their assault on the mainstream culture, and their interest in social and cultural change, the movement reflected the intellectual and artistic revival characterized by the emergence of the 'angry young men' of the theatre and literature.

The Free Cinema movement made little impact on mainstream British film production in the 1950s. However, the release of the film, *Room at the Top,* in 1959 is regarded as a turning point in the development of post-war British cinema. The film, directed by Jack Clayton from the novel by the northern writer, John Braine, introduced a 'new wave' of British films which examined completely new areas of social and personal experience, presented a more realistic picture of working-class life and developed new, more realistic techniques of film-making. Laurence Harvey starred in *Room at the Top* as Joe Lampton, an ambitious young man working in local government in a northern town, who marries the daughter of a wealthy industrialist in order to better himself. The film captures the progress of Lampton from his working-class roots through middle-class respectability to career success. The hero's emotional trials and tribulations and his social alienation are central to the film. The explicit way in which the film dealt with class is seen as marking it out. However, the depiction of class tensions in 1950s Britain in *Room at the Top* is consistent with a number of other films of that year. The Boulting Brothers film, *I'm Alright Jack* (1959), for example, was a satire on the irresponsibility of both capital and labour as destructive to the nation. The film is mostly remembered for Peter Sellers's character, Fred Kite, the snobbish, racist and bloody-minded trade union official. But perhaps the significance of *Room at the Top* was that it was the first attempt to break out of the straitjacket in which the BBFC had confined British cinema's portrayal of sex and sexuality. It contained explicit sex scenes and the BBFC's decision to provide the film with a certificate represented a radical change in attitude.

Room at the Top was followed by a number of highly acclaimed films, which centred on northern working-class communities. Labelled 'kitchen sink dramas' as a result of their focus on the psychological dynamics of personal relationships, these films included *Saturday Night and Sunday Morning* (1960), *A Taste of Honey* (1961), *The Loneliness of the Long Distance Runner* (1962), *A Kind of Loving* (1962), *This Sporting Life* (1963) and *Billy Liar* (1963). These films were more open and honest in dealing with issues such as homosexuality, prostitution, racism, juvenile delinquency, changing marital roles, the breakdown of the family, and abortion. It was a 'socially committed' cinema. There was a preoccupation in the 'new wave' British cinema with the effects of mass production and mass commercialized culture. The spiritual crisis that many saw as accompanying the material improvements in people's lives is a recurring theme.[50] The 'candy floss' world of modern mass entertainment is the context in which these films operate. The focus was on the rise of the rootless, classless youth culture as a response to the decline of traditional working-class communities and consciousness. In this sense the 'new wave' films shared the same concerns as Hoggart and other intellectuals about the changes that were happening in working-class Britain. Richardson, Reisz and Anderson as directors and producers of many of the more successful 'new wave' films highlight the influence of 'Free Cinema'. The use of unknown regional actors, location shooting, improvised performances, working-class characters and the expression of a point of view are also legacies of the Free Cinema movement.[51] The rejection of the staged studio system of the commercial cinema, which for Tony Richardson meant 'artistic impotence', in favour of a more immediate, documentary-style realism was a characteristic of the 'new wave' British films.

Most of the leading lights of the 'new wave' came from a middle-class background and had close ties to the British theatre. Both Anderson and Richardson had spent a large amount of their time directing in the theatre. This has led some to question how far the 'new wave' represented a revolution in the development of British cinema. They argue that Free Cinema was very much in the theatrical tradition of British cinema. New wave directors are criticized as theatre directors who dabbled in film-making, and the writers, many of whom were novelists or playwrights, are dismissed for adapting pre-existing material for the cinema.[52] Most of the northern kitchen sink dramas were adapted from novels. Their social commitment is seen as consistent with that of the 1930s documentary movement: that is, 'the university educated bourgeois making "sympathetic" films about proletarian life, not analysing the ambiguities of their own privileged position'.[53] John Hill[54] points out that while these films did help to open up British cinema with their innovatory content and more socially enquiring approach, they were less than radical. Their view of the world was shaped by the discussion around 'affluence' that prevailed at that time. Their ability to go beyond the parameters of this discussion was limited by the economic factors of film production in the 1960s.

The economic organization of British cinema in the 1960s

The growth of 'new wave' pictures has initially to be seen in the context of the economic decline of the British film industry in the late 1950s and early 1960s. Innovation was encouraged and permitted as the industry scrambled about to find means of making its product more attractive. The 1950s saw the introduction of Cinemascope and 3D pictures as cinema tried to stave off the challenge of television. The decline of Rank's involvement in film production witnessed a shift in the pattern of film finance. Between 1958 and 1962, of the 37 most popular films, 28 were independently produced.[55] It was not only the 'new wave' films that were made by independents but also those of the 'Carry On' team, Hammer and the Boulting Brothers. This development was welcomed as film producers escaped from the clutches of the major studios. However, the notion of a newly found freedom for British film-makers can be exaggerated. Economic pressure still shaped the kind of films that could be made, the most obvious constraint being the continuing control of exhibition and distribution by a small number of large conglomerates. The realities of film production were that no film could succeed unless it was booked by one of the major cinema circuits. Central to raising money was the 'distributor's guarantee' which enabled production companies to obtain bank loans and often independent producers had to go to the majors to raise some of the money they required. Independents were in practice 'heavily circumscribed' by the power of the major conglomerates and, as Michael Balcon commented, 'without virtually limitless resources the independent producer is a myth'.[56]

The production company that raised the money for most of the 'new wave' films, Woodfall Productions, was set up by Tony Richardson in partnership with the Canadian producer, Harry Saltzman. The company raised money from many sources but overwhelmingly from America. From the early 1960s American interests began to heavily invest in the British film industry, it is estimated that by the mid-1960s 'anything up to ninety per cent of the films made in Britain derived their financing at least in some part from American sources'.[57] The extent of such American backing had implications for the content of British films. Screenplays were written for the US domestic market where British pictures began to play well, particularly on the growing arts cinema circuit. The 1960s revival was determined by the needs and interests of American finance: one producer admitted to the Monopolies Commission in the mid-1960s, that many British films 'inevitably . . . dance to the American tune of the people who put up the American money and I think undoubtedly the character of the film is changed by this factor'.[58] The dependency on US money was responsible for the emphasis on the plight of the north of England and the 'Swinging London' of Carnaby Street. Top pop groups, Britain's most successful cultural icons of the 1960s, were exploited by the film industry – Cliff Richard and the Shadows appeared in *Summer Holiday* (1963), The Dave Clark Five in *Catch Us If You Can* (1965) and The Beatles in the films, *A Hard Day's Night* (1964) and *Help* (1965), both directed by the American-born Richard Lester. A number of American directors came to Britain to produce pictures, including Joseph Losey, who made two of the most sharply observed films on class and sexual mores in Britain, *The Servant* (1963) and *Accident* (1967).[59] The cheap film-making facilities in Britain in the 1960s, brought about by the Eady levy and favourable exchange rates, led Albert 'Cubby' Broccoli, in partnership with Harry Saltzman who left Woodfall in 1962, to make the James Bond films, which started with *Dr. No* in 1962. Financed by United Artists, these films made considerable profits. The 1960s revival in British cinema was financed by American money, influenced by American interests and assisted by American directors and producers. The extent of American involvement in the industry by the end of the decade raises doubts about how far it was still possible to refer to a British film industry.

The Brits are coming – the Thatcher years

American interest in the British cinema dried up in the 1970s as Hollywood was plunged into financial crisis after some of the studios made big losses, and the cost of filming in Europe rose. With American money now flowing out of the country, there was a decline in the production of British feature films – the number of British quota films fell by nearly 50 per cent between 1971 and 1979.[60] Cinema attendances began to decline rapidly, after steadying out in the first half of the decade, and in 1981 they reached a low point when only 63.8 million visits were made to the cinema. It was also a bad year for British-made films – only 26 were released.[61] The film industry was also hit by the Thatcher government's attempts to free British industry from government regulation. The three main means by which the British state had supported the film industry were abolished. The quota system was done away with in 1983 and the Eady levy finally scrapped by the 1985 Films Act. Both according to the government represented 'an unreasonable burden on the cinema exhibition industry'.[62] The government attempted to privatize the NFFC, which by the end of the 1970s had assisted in the financing of 750 British feature films. The Corporation was replaced by the British Screen Finance Consortium. The NFFC's debt to the government was written off and the new body received £7.5 million over a five-year period at the end of which it was expected to become self-sufficient. Three private investors – Channel Four, Rank and Cannon – agreed to provide loans. However, the private investors, with the exception of Channel Four, did not renew their commitments to British Screen, which failed as a commercial enterprise. The government's failure to revitalize the industry by opening it up to the free market meant that the problem of film finance became more intractable during the 1980s. From 1986 investment in the industry declined drastically, from £270.1 million in 1986 to £49.6 million in 1989.[63] In 1989, the government had to swallow its ideological pride and inject more capital into British Screen.

The crisis in the film industry in the 1980s was hidden at first by the success of a number of British movies in America. During the bleak year of 1981, the film *Chariots of Fire* won several Oscars, including Best Picture. The unexpected success of the film saw British films becoming fashionable. In 1982, Richard Attenborough's *Gandhi* followed up the success of *Chariots of Fire* by sweeping the Oscars. The emergence of other British pictures, including *The Killing Fields* (1984) and *Local Hero* (1983), seemed to bear out Colin Welland's claim, made at the 1981 Hollywood Oscars Ceremony when he received his award for Best Screenplay, that 'the Brits are coming'. There was also a revival in cinema attendances in the middle of the decade. But this was also deceptive. The all-time low for cinema attendance in Britain was reached in 1984 when 58.4 million admissions were recorded. By the end of the decade this figure had risen to 94.6 million.[64] It was, however, still lower than any recorded figures for the whole of the 1970s and meant that even low-budget British films could not recoup their costs of production in the domestic market. The international success and box-office acclaim accorded some British pictures in the early 1980s led to over-optimism by the government in its assessments of the future of the industry. Norman Lamont, who introduced the 1985 Film Act into the House of Commons, predicted that the British film industry was 'on the threshold of a strong commercial future'.[65] The reality was that the revival in the 1980s – like its counterpart in the 1960s – did nothing to reverse the deep-seated fragility of the industry.

The continued weakness of the industry was manifest in the companies singled out by Lamont as being 'notable examples' of the strength of the industry in the early 1980s. The three companies cited – Thorn-EMI, Virgin and Goldcrest – had all within three years of the statement ceased to be involved in film production.[66] The decline of Goldcrest in particular illustrated the long-term weakness of film production in Britain. The company had been more closely associated with the 1980s revival than any other enterprise. It had been involved in the success of *Chariots of Fire* and *Gandhi* as well as the production of *The Killing Fields, The Ploughman's Lunch, Another Country* and *Local Hero*. However, in 1987, after losing more than £15 million on three high-budget productions – *Absolute Beginners, Revolution* and *The Mission* – the company was sold off. Its failure again highlighted the risks attached to investing in film production and from 1986 it became much more difficult to attract finance from traditional sources. American money was available but on the whole the Americans preferred to invest in making their own films in Britain rather than in British film production. With government sources drying up, City institutions reluctant and American finance unpredictable, the only stable source for film finance in the 1980s was British television.

Film and Channel Four

By the 1980s, British television had become the medium in which, according the British director, Mike Leigh, 'all serious film-making was done'.[67] The advent of the video cassette recorder (VCR) resulted in many people watching films on their television screens at home rather than at the local cinema. The UK box-office market in 1990 was worth $430 million whereas the video rental and purchase market totalled £890 million. Television showed 2294 films in 1989 spending £93.6 million acquiring them.[68] Channel Four, in particular, played an important role in maintaining British film-making. The channel was committed to a policy of investing in film production, not simply for broadcast but also for general cinema release. In the first 12 years of its existence, it invested over £90 million in the production of 264 films.[69] At first, films were wholly funded by the channel, including Hanif Kureshi's *My Beautiful Laundrette* (1985), but from the middle of the 1980s the rising costs of production, as well as the channel's proven production record, meant that involvement in co-productions became more common. Some of Channel Four's films were highly profitable, most notably the *The Crying Game* (1990) and *Four Weddings and a Funeral* (1994). The success enticed other British television companies into film production. The BBC's output included *Truly, Madly, Deeply* (1991) and in 1994 the Corporation pledged itself to release five films annually for general release. ITV companies, including Granada, Central and Thames produced 20 films between 1985 and 1989. By the end of the decade the television money accounted for nearly 49 per cent of all UK production – a substantial increase on the 4 per cent recorded in 1982.[70] The capacity of Channel Four to produce so many films – at one stage nearly half the films produced in Britain involved Channel Four finance – was the result of a commitment to the cultural importance of film production and the particular funding arrangements under which the channel had been created. Protected from commercial pressures by its funding through the levy on ITV companies, the channel was able to subsidize *Film on Four* to the extent the film channel received nearly 7 per cent of the Channel Four's overall budget.

However, Channel Four's significance for British film was more than economic. It enabled the development of an environment in which independent film production became viable and allowed a diversity of film-makers access to audiences for their films through the small screen.[71] Making films for the small screen had an impact on the aesthetics of film. In particular, Channel Four films have been characterized as having a specific aesthetic style. In the words of one critic, they 'often juxtapose what is foreign, strange, or sinister with the safe haven of the drably domestic' and address 'potentially disturbing themes' within 'structures of reassuring normalcy'.[72] Directors such as Mike Leigh, Peter Greenaway and Stephen Frears are associated with the Channel Four film, with their focus on what the channel's chief executive, Jeremy Isaacs called 'our preoccupations here in Britain'.[73] However, some directors have been critical of the channel's influence on British film-making. They argue that the small screen reduced the artistic ambition of British directors. Lindsay Anderson accused Channel Four of being responsible for 'some of the new British films being a bit lacking in the ambition one associates with a cinema film'.[74] Charges of timidity of both style and technique as well as the politics of the channel's small screen cinema are made. It is possible to criticize a number of Channel Four's films: some did seem to yearn for the nostalgia of the heyday of the political and social consensus of the early 1950s while others anchored themselves in an unchanging micro world of British domestic life. But there were films which engaged directly with the political and social upheavals wrought by Margaret Thatcher on British society. For example, *The Ploughman's Lunch* (1983) dealt with the corruption of the world of politics and journalism while Karl Francis's *Giro City* (1982) examined local government corruption and censorship. Other films also made political observations – Mike Leigh's *High Hopes* (1988) examined growing class tension, *My Beautiful Laundrette* (1985) and *Sammy and Rosie Get Laid* (1987) focused on greed, racism and injustice while Ken Loach's *Defence of the Realm* (1985) was set in the world of the national security state.[75] The Channel Four film was, above all, an 'art film': exploring, as one observer describes, the issues of 'individual identity, sexuality, psychological complexity, anomie, episodicness, interiority, ambiguity and style'.[76]

Television's support for British film industry

When Paul Turner takes his place among the glitterati and the backslappers at the Oscars ceremony it will be thanks to an industry which was once thought to be the death of the movies.

'Thank God we have television', says the director whose Cardiff production company has two full-time staff and a nomination in the best foreign film category.

Hedd Wyn, the story of a Welsh poet who fails to return from the First World War, probably has little chance of winning. However, the mere fact that it was made is some sort of triumph at a time when only 47 British films are turned out each year, with an average of about £3.94 million each, against Hollywood's £19.2 million.

The budget for Mr. Turner's little seen film, financed by S4C, the Welsh Channel 4, was £500,000 with a final cost of £700,000.

'If you don't get the money from television then you have to go to private money and you'll never get it for a worthwhile project unless it's a surefire commercial success', said Mr. Turner, who has made eight films with television money.

Mr. Turner's success is a detail in a picture which shows investment in British films plummeting from £425.7 million in 1984 to £185 million by 1992. The Americans also deserted the British industry, cutting their finance from $142.23 million in 1984 to £67.8 million in 1992.

The cinema going public is increasing from 53 million in the early eighties to 103 million in 1991, but it is not the British industry which benefits. US films had a 90 per cent share of the UK box office in 1991.

There are some signs that the American money is returning, despite a withholding tax which removes 25 per cent from a non-European Union artist's salary.

But the bedrock of support in Britain, which has won more than 30 per cent of the Oscars in the past 20 years, is television. Channel 4 fully or partly finances between 12 and 15 films a year, at up to £1 million or more a time.

'One of the galling things is that our films do much better in the cinema abroad than in the UK', said David Aukin, Channel 4's head of films. 'They can find a market because they are different, with a signature.'

The BBC spends £5 million on 10 co-productions a year, including the screen version of Roddy Doyle's *The Snapper*, which was first shown on television last year but has since been a cinema hit. 'If television money was removed from what's laughingly called the British film industry, there wouldn't be one', said Mark Shivas, BBC head of films.

Source: Ellison, Mike (1994) 'But for TV support, industry would be gone with the wind', *Guardian*, 19 February

The involvement of television, and in particular Channel Four, in the world of British film production was an unplanned consequence of the development of British broadcasting policy in the 1980s. As a result, British television's funding of film production rested on a fragile financial base. The weakness of this support was clear with the new climate introduced into broadcasting in the late 1980s. Change in the arrangements for collecting the ITV levy in 1988 and the 1990 Broadcasting Act made it less attractive for television companies to invest in film production. Channel Four, under the new commercial pressures, moved away from film production in the 1990s.[77] Throughout the 1980s and 1990s, the development of British cinema was characterized by the intensification of the relationship between television and film, at both the financial and aesthetic levels. That television companies are now making films for themselves rather than buying the rights from film companies has implications for what is meant by film. Television in the 1980s has been credited as 'the only factor which appears to have prevented the wholesale collapse of the British film industry'.[78] But even with television's involvement British film-making remained a 'fragile business'.

Re-defining British cinema

The British film industry has experienced a revival of fortunes since the dawn of the new millennium. This has been most apparent in the growth of cinema audiences. In 2007, more people were attending than at any other time for 40 years. A total of 162 million tickets were sold at the box office, a rise of 4 per cent, after two years in which attendances had declined. The growth in cinema attendances in 2007 was attributed to a range of factors including the poor summer weather and the rise of blockbusters such as Harry Potter and the Bourne film series. Rising attendances have been accompanied by British films attaining international box office success as well as critical acclaim. The early years of the millennium saw romantic comedies such as *Bridget Jones's Diary* (2001) and it sequel *Bridget Jones: The Edge of Reason* (2004) gross $254 million and $228 million world-wide. Richard Curtis's *Love Actually* (2003) followed up the success of *Four Weddings and a Funeral* and *Notting Hill*, cementing British cinema's reputation for romantic comedies with Hollywood's leading ladies. Films such as *Bend It Like Beckham* (2002), *The Queen* (2006), *The Last King of Scotland* (2006) and *Atonement* (2007) brought acclaim to the industry, as well as Oscar nominations and awards, including Helen Mirren's best actress award for *The Queen* and *Atonement*'s several nominations. In 2005, Nick Park's *Wallace and Gromit: The Curse of the Were-Rabbit* won best animated feature. Well-known directors such as Mike Leigh and Ken Loach have maintained their critical standing, winning awards at the Venice and Cannes film festivals for their films *Vera Drake* (2004) and *The Wind That Shakes the Barley* (2006). Other signs of success include the increasing amount of money spent on making films in the United Kingdom; aided by the new tax relief for British film the aggregate spend of £747 million made 2007 the fourth-highest production year on record.[79] The gritty social realism of the 1960s is still found in films such as *This is England* (2008) but it is the blockbuster series made in Britain and funded by US money that have brought the British film industry most recognition. Companies such as Working Title secured financing and distribution deals with US Studios, producing films such as *Mr Bean's Holiday, Hot Fuzz, Atonement* and *Elizabeth: The Golden Age*, and in collaboration with US studios, *Harry Potter and the Order of the Phoenix* and *The Bourne Ultimatum*.

The success of British film since 2000 has coincided with a radical re-structuring of how the industry is run. In 2000, the UK Film Council was established to promote the British film industry. It took over sole responsibility for the public funding of film from bodies such as the British Film Institute and the Arts Council. The aim of the Council was twofold: to sell Britain as a 'film hub' of locations and services to the global film industry and nurture regional film within the UK.[80] The new chairman of the council, film director Alan Parker, told the industry in 2002 that it was necessary 'to abandon forever the "little England" vision of a UK industry comprised of small companies delivering parochial British films'. To survive in an increasing competitive global market, Parker argued it was necessary to reposition the British film industry to attract worldwide distribution and larger audiences. He called for a 'radical re-invention' based on making Britain more attractive to international film-makers and boosting regional film-making in England and across the UK. To promote the UK as an international production centre, the Council took over the running of the British Film Commission and the British Film Office in Los Angeles which had been opened in 1998. Deals made with the BBC and other television companies, and connections were forged with the Film Exports Group, which was part of the Creative Export group at the Department of Culture, Media and Sport (DCMS). The territorial re-structuring of the industry had begun in 1997 with the formation of film bodies for Scotland, Wales and Northern Ireland. In 2000, this was extended to nine English regions. The new regional screen agencies were responsible for educational activities, training, promotion, archiving, production and film culture in their areas.

The Council's early years were beset by difficulties. Accused of cronyism for dishing out grants to companies in which some of its directors had interests, the number of films produced in the UK fell by 40 per cent in 2001. However, a gradual revival has started; the amount spent on film production grew from £534 million in 2002 to £840 million in 2006.[81] Changes in the definition of what constitutes a British film may have helped this revival. In 1999 and 2006, the official definition of a British film was altered to take more account of the cultural dimension of the industry as well as the Film Council's new strategy. Prior to 1999, a film could be denied British status if more than 7.5 per cent of its running time was filmed or recorded outside of the UK. This was replaced by the requirements that a certain percentage of labour and expenditure costs were

British. In 2006, the DCMS introduced a cultural points test reflecting the content of the film, where it is made and those involved in making it. In 2008, it was reported that British film enjoyed a 'huge boost', experiencing a rise of 50 per cent in global ticket sales which raked in nearly £1.65 billion.[82] It appeared that British film was booming. According to the then Creative Industries Minister Margaret Hodge:

> **The UK film industry is thriving, with huge audiences worldwide flocking to see British movies. We should be proud of the great successes of the last year with the award triumphs of *The Queen, The Wind that Shakes the Barley* and *The Last King of Scotland* demonstrating that UK film commands critical respect, as well as a healthy share of the global film market.**[83]

Appearances are deceptive. While public demand to see more films and, in particular more British films, has increased in the last decade or so, the British film industry is still controlled by global corporations and American products. The distribution side of the industry is dominated by five companies: Fox, Buena Vista, UIP, Warner and Columbia Tri-Star which accounted for almost 80 per cent of the market in 2006. The most successful British pictures are distributed by Miramax (owned by Disney), Murdoch's Fox or Polygram, a subsidiary of Phillips. Four studios, Disney, Universal, Warner Brothers and Pathé make most of the pictures released in Britain every year. In 2006, 84 per cent of the UK box office was made up of American films. Most of Britain's movie halls are in the hands of American firms which dictate the films that are screened and determine public taste. While 60 per cent of British people attend the cinema once a year, it is via television that people watch most of the films they see. In 2007, the total audience for film on television was 3.1 billion, 19 times larger than the cinema audience and three times larger than the estimated audience for film on DVD/video. British films attracted around one-fifth of the television film audience. The video rental market, including DVD and VHS transactions fell to £297 million in 2007 from a peak of £476 million in 2002. This was due mainly to the rapid decline of the over-the-counter rental market in the wake of competition from multi-channel television, piracy and in particular, the lower cost of retail DVDs. Sales increased in the same period.

The collapse of Film Four Ltd in 2002 was a blow to the efforts to make films; sustaining the British film industry in the 1980s and early 1990s, Channel 4 started to lose money in the late 1990s following its efforts to focus more on the international market. The then controller of Channel 4, Michael Grade, had convinced the government to let the channel siphon money paid to ITV, as part of an advertising airtime deal, into film production. Films such as *Very Annie Mary, Parole Officer, Birthday Girl* and *Lucky Break* failed in commercial and critical terms.[84] Film Four recorded a £20 million loss in 2001 and its sales and distribution operation was shut down and its commissioning budget cut back by nearly two-thirds.[85] Britain's flagship studios Pinewood-Shepperton posted a 26 per cent fall in pre-tax profits in 2007. Fewer movies are being made in the UK despite the country's continuing reputation for technical excellence, first-rate actors and top-notch studios.[86] The number of international co-productions shot in Britain has shrunk as films have had to pass the cultural test, to prove their British credentials. Making more British films has been at the expense of attracting more international finance. Culture and economy collided, as to qualify for a subsidy and tax breaks, a film must now have a British subject and be made in Britain. Failure to pass the test has resulted in a decline in the amount spent on employing British production facilities, talent and locations. Much of the British film industry is not what it seems: people are employed by foreign concerns and many of the pictures we associate with 'Britishness' such as *The Queen* and *The Last King of Scotland* are produced by overseas studios, in these case Pathé and Warner Brothers respectively. Since the removal of the Eady levy in 1985 and the further opening up of the British market, the British film industry has collapsed as indigenous production companies have disappeared. The last time people attended the cinema in such large numbers, companies such as British Lion, Rank and Thorn-EMI were still struggling along as studios. Today the industry is dependent on foreign enterprise and finance to an extent never previously experienced.

11

Goodbye to Fleet Street: the slow decline of the British press since the Second World War

The rise of television in the immediate post-war period as the dominant means of mass communication coincided with the rapid decline in the popularity of British cinema. The impact of television on the British press was less dramatic in spite of the dire predictions of total collapse that accompanied the newspaper industry's battle with commercial television for advertising revenue from 1955 onwards. After emerging from the war in a buoyant state, the British press has ever since gone through a gradual decline, accompanied by radical changes in the structure, ownership and content of newspapers. In terms of the structure of the British press, the national daily newspapers have strengthened their hold over the industry at the expense of the Sunday, provincial daily and local weekly press. Within the national press there has been a polarization between the popular and quality press with the disappearance of the middle-market, middlebrow newspapers. The rise of the tabloid newspaper, epitomized by the hold Rupert Murdoch's *Sun* established over the mass market, has radically changed the nature of 'popular journalism' in Britain. There has also been the development of a new kind of newspaper – the free sheet – which besides competing for advertising revenue in the provincial newspaper market has also come to represent a challenge to the traditional values and practices of journalism. All this has occurred within an increasingly competitive environment as newspapers have fought over a decreasing number of readers. At the same time a further concentration of ownership has occurred in the national and regional press in spite of the greater diversity promised by the 'Wapping Revolution' which saw the application of new technology to the newspaper industry in 1985. These developments were slow to manifest themselves as a result of the protected environment created for the newspaper market by the Second World War.

The rationing of newspapers

The Second World War brought an end to the circulation wars that had dominated the British press in the 1930s. The war and rationing kept costs down and profits up. Paper and newsprint rationing reduced the size of newspapers. The average size of a newspaper, up to 1956 when rationing was scrapped, was four pages, one-third of the number of pages of newspapers in the 1930s.[1] The cutback in pages was not accompanied by a reduction in the cover prices of newspapers.

Sales rose rapidly with the circulation of the national daily press rising from 9.98 million in 1937 to 15.6 million in 1947.[2] The bulk of the increase in circulation was accounted for by the success of two newspapers, the *Daily Express* and the *Daily Mirror*, which between them accounted for almost half the total circulation of the national daily press at the end of the war. Sales rose as a result of the thirst for news of what was happening at the Front, which led readers to buy at least two daily newspapers in their search for enough to read. The reduction of pages caused advertisers to spread their spending across the press, thereby supporting the weaker newspapers. The result was that the period up until the mid-1950s can be described as 'boom years' for the British press, highlighted by the 1947 Royal Commission on the Press which found that of 225 newspapers surveyed, only 7 were not making a profit. The owner of the *Daily Express*, Lord Beaverbrook, drew attention to the complacency of the British press during this period, claiming that this particular state of affairs brought new freedoms – freedom from competition, advertising revenue, newsprint and enterprise.[3] Few in the industry shared Beaverbrook's concern and the British press was not enthusiastic about the government's decision to do away with rationing in 1956.

The lifting of the controls that had held change in check between 1939 and 1956 resulted in the short term in a crisis which forced a number of national newspapers to close down. In the long term the British newspaper market became subject to intense competition, punctuated by short periods of stability. The intensity of the competition is explained by the stagnation of the post-war newspaper market; total sales of national newspapers have fallen gradually since 1945. From the introduction of commercial television the total circulation of national newspapers in Britain has dropped by almost one third. The decline became most notable in the 1990s; a survey found that only 59 per cent of young people between the ages of 16–24 enjoyed reading a newspaper.[4] For any newspaper to increase its sales, it had to be done at the expense of other titles. In such a climate of intense competition radical changes occurred.

The growing importance of national newspapers

The steady decline of the British press since the end of the Second World War has not been evenly spread across the industry. Today 10 national daily newspapers are printed in Britain, excluding the *Daily Record* which is published only in Scotland. Other newspapers are distributed nationally on a daily basis but for one reason or another are not classified as part of the national press. In 1959, the six most popular newspapers sold 14.2 million copies every day; by 1992, that had dropped to 11 million; the total circulation of national morning newspapers fell from 16.71 million in 1957 to 13.58 million in 1994.[5] This decline has not been as significant as in other parts of the British newspaper industry. Sunday newspapers, provincial morning and evening dailies and the local weekly press have suffered a more drastic reversal of their fortunes. The Sunday newspaper, traditionally the backbone of the British press, has seen a decline in its circulation by almost a third since the end of the 1960s. In 1969, the total sales of the four most popular Sunday newspapers were 21 million; by 1992, the five most popular Sundays could only sell 13.4 million copies.[6]

The decline in the provincial press has been even more pronounced. In 1945, there were 29 morning daily newspapers in Britain; by 1992, this had dropped to only 18.[7] Five major provincial morning newspapers closed between 1948 and 1961 in cities as far apart as Glasgow, Nottingham, Brighton, Manchester and Birmingham.[8] There was a similar pattern in the provincial evening newspaper market. In the 1960s, newspapers reached 90 per cent of local households; by the 1980s, the figure had fallen to 60 per cent. Paid weekly newspapers had dropped from a total circulation of 16.03 million in 1957 to 7.4 million by 1994. Overall the decline in the newspaper industry in Britain has been most pronounced in the Sunday and provincial press which means that the national newspapers have strengthened their market share and influence since the end of the Second World War.

The decline of mid-market national newspapers

If the national daily newspapers have strengthened their hold over the British newspaper industry, then within the daily press there has been a shift of power. The immediate casualties of the lifting of newspaper controls were the middlebrow, middle-market newspapers. In 1960, the only remaining daily newspaper that supported the Liberal Party, the *News Chronicle*, closed down overnight. The abruptness of the closure was highlighted by the fact that subscribers of the newspaper were given no warning and instead received through their post-box a copy of the Conservative *Daily Mail*, with which the *Chronicle* had been merged. The circulation of the paper at the time of its demise was 1.16 million, equivalent then to that of the *Daily Telegraph*. The *Chronicle* was soon joined by an even more famous daily newspaper – the *Daily Herald*. After all the trials and tribulations of the circulation wars of the 1930s the newspaper, still closely identified with the Labour Party, was closed in 1964. The *Herald*, when it died, also had a healthy circulation, over 1.25 million readers. The demise of these two popular, left of centre, daily newspapers was reinforced in 1967 by the closure of the *Sunday Citizen*, which had begun life as the popular Victorian Sunday newspaper, *Reynolds News*. The total circulation of these newspapers when they folded was near to 3.5 million, a sizeable proportion of the national newspaper market. Their closure represented the death of the centre-left press in Britain and deprived a large number of readers of their preferred newspaper reading matter.

The closure of these newspapers was part of a larger process which saw the disappearance of several other titles between 1960 and 1971, including the *Sunday Graphic* (died 1960), *Empire News* (1960), *Sunday Dispatch* (1961) and the *Daily Sketch* (1971). These newspapers were all located in the middle ground of the British newspaper market. They were characterized by a lower middle-class readership as well as moderate circulations compared to the other popular papers of the day. In 1948 the middle ground readership band accounted for 60 per cent of Fleet Street's circulation but by 1965 it had dropped to 47 per cent and by the end of the 1970s it had fallen to a mere 15 per cent.[9] Since 1956 there has been a polarization within the newspaper market. On the one hand there are the 'quality' or 'prestige' newspapers. These are up-market newspapers with low circulations but with readership profiles which figure prominently those who are well educated, work in the professions and have high incomes. On the other hand, there are the 'popular' or 'tabloid' newspapers which have large mass circulations but a readership which is primarily drawn from the less educated, low income earners of the manual working classes. In size and content these papers were clearly distinguishable from one another: the 'qualities' were broadsheets whose content can be described as 'highbrow' or 'serious' while the 'populars' were tabloids dominated by entertainment or 'human interest' stories.

A number of reasons have been put forward to account for the decline of the middle-market newspapers. Television, for example, has been singled out by many to explain not only the transformation of the British press but even its death. The middle-market papers with their focus on 'topical exposure in their news coverage' and the 'vivid use of pictures' were seen as especially vulnerable to television.[10] For others, the decline is associated with changes in reader interests, in particular the loss of the 'thinking working class reader'.[11] Poor management, old-fashioned presentation and layout as well as political commitments out of keeping with the politics of these years have also been mentioned as possible explanations.[12] However, the primary reason must lie in the economic structure of the industry, and in particular the re-imposition of the importance of advertising in determining the fate of the newspaper industry.

Increased power of advertisers

The opening up to competition of the newspaper market in 1956 brought about drastic changes in the economics of newspaper production. The 'flamboyant prosperity' of the previous decade brought about a rise in wage rates which led to a drastic increase in the costs of production. On top of this, newsprint rose from £53 per ton in 1955 to £250 by 1977[13] and extra journalists had to be employed to fill the additional pages. These increased costs had to be covered and in the 'brave new world' of newspaper production after 1956 the cover price of newspapers rose drastically. It doubled between 1960 and 1970 and again between 1970 and 1975[14] with a consequent decline in the purchase of newspapers. By 1974 only three dailies and three national newspapers were making a profit. These changes also returned the British press to its state of dependency on advertising revenue. However, competition for advertising had become tougher as a result of the presence of commercial television which from its beginning has taken advertising revenue away from the press. In 1956, the press accounted for more than 90 per cent of money spent on media advertising. By the mid-1960s, when advertising revenue had trebled, this share had declined to 65 per cent and by 1990 TV accounted for 32 per cent of total advertising.[15]

The regional press accounts for the bulk of advertising revenue while the national press share of advertising revenue has remained fairly steady throughout the 1990s at 16 per cent. But, with rising costs, advertising revenue for the British press has become increasingly the crucial factor in determining the difference between profit and loss.

The introduction of market research into Britain in the 1950s had a profound impact on the development of press advertising. The rapid expansion of market research is indicated by the growth in membership of the Market Research Society which in 1947 had only 23 members but by 1972 the number had risen to 2000.[16] Market research changed the way in which advertisers spent their money. Up until the Second World War spending was ultimately determined by the reach of a newspaper, what Northcliffe referred to as a newspaper's reputation for 'pull'. It was a crude measure based primarily on mass readership. Market research substituted a more detailed definition of a newspaper's readership profile built on the potential purchasing power of readers. Newspapers which could attract readers with higher purchasing power had more appeal to advertisers. As a result advertisers became more discerning. This explains the ability of newspapers such as the *Financial Times*, the *Guardian* and the *Independent* to survive on small circulations. Their readers are better off and therefore have more purchasing power. It is estimated that the 'quality press' depend on advertisers for 70 per cent of its income.[17] By contrast, the popular press realizes around 35–40 per cent of its income from advertising. The polarization of the British press into small circulation, elite quality newspapers and the mass circulation, popular papers is explicable in terms of the changes wrought in advertising by the advent of market research. The demise of the middle-market papers was a result of their inability to provide advertisers either with a small number of readers with high purchasing power or attract readers in sufficiently large number to reduce their dependence of advertising. The *News Chronicle*, the *Daily Herald* and the other newspapers that died in the 1960s and 1970s did so, not because they could not attract readers, but because of the lack of adverts. Advertising largely explain why some papers thrive with relatively small circulations while others with much larger circulations sometimes have difficulties. Large circulations are more important to popular papers while 'high quality' readers are likely to attract advertisers to elite papers. Thus the *Financial Times* can be profitable with a circulation of around 100,000 while some popular papers, like the *Daily Sketch*, selling more than a million copies, failed.

The overall impact of advertising on the structure of the newspapers market is underpinned by the fact that the vast majority of newspapers – national, regional morning and evening, local weeklies as well as trade and specialized publications – sell at a loss. Sales do not cover costs and profit is determined by advertising receipts. This gives advertisers considerable influence over the British press. Such influence is often conceived crudely in terms of direct pressure brought to bear on the editorial content. Advertisers have their political bias and do sometimes bring it to bear. For example, the radical *Scottish Daily News* was told by one advertiser that he 'was not going to keep a newspaper which, the first time I get a strike, will back the strikers'.[18] Political prejudice has been manifest in advertisers' decisions concerning 'papers of extremist outlook'[19] but more important has been the indirect influence of advertising. The shape and content of newspapers have been determined in the post-war period by the need of advertisers to reach particular target groups. The development of special features and sections in quality newspapers allows advertisers to target their product more directly which also explains the rapid growth of specialized magazines over the past couple of decades. According to a former women's editor in Fleet Street, the growth of women's features in the press is related to the growth of advertising they generate.[20] There has also been an increase in 'advertising features' or 'advertorials' as they are called in the industry which are written about certain aspects of a business or product for the purpose of attracting advertisements. In the local press they are used to solicit ads from suppliers or customers of the firm profiled while in quality newspapers they often take the form of special reports on particular countries with advertisements from the government, banks and trading companies of that country. The growth in advertising-sponsored features has been noticeable in the quality press during the post-war period, blurring the boundary lines between editorial and advertising content. For one critic, '[the] structure of the modern newspaper, particularly the so-called "quality" newspaper, has thus evolved in a form that organises readers into market lots, packaged in suitable editorial material, for sale to advertisers'.[21] In other words, it could be said that the sovereign editor of the nineteenth century has been replaced by the sovereign advertiser of the late twentieth century. The influence of advertising is most clearly demonstrated in the rise of the 'free sheets', newspapers which are totally dependent on advertisements.

Advent of the free sheets

Within the provincial press a shift of power has occurred with the advent of a new kind of newspaper – the 'free newspaper' or 'free sheet'. The declining circulation of the daily and weekly paid newspapers outside London was accompanied by the expansion of free newspapers. The number of such newspapers increased from 185 in 1975 to 1156 by 1990 with a distribution of 43.5 million copies.[22] Free newspapers, when they began in the 1960s, were solely devoted to advertisements with little news and no connection to the communities in which they were distributed. However, as they expanded, they came to take on more of the features of the local newspaper. Free sheets have varied enormously in their content, ranging from the Birmingham *Daily News*, which was launched in 1984 as the first daily metropolitan free newspaper staffed by around 40 journalists with regular features and columns, to the *Cheshire and District Standard* which, when it was established in 1987, marked a milestone in modern British newspaper history by being the first newspaper to be published without employing any journalists.[23] While PR puffs and stories which are simply a plug for advertisers constitute much of the news reported in free sheets, financial success improved their news reporting. But the total reliance on advertising has significant consequences for the way in which these newspapers operate. They are more open to pressure from advertisers and are less accountable to their readers. There is pressure to reduce costs which often means small, poorly paid and inexperienced editorial staff are valued less highly than the telephone sales people who are the heart of the enterprise. The result is that free newspapers are dependent on local news agencies for their news or if this is deemed too costly, the increasingly vast outpouring of information from the PR departments of local organizations becomes the sole source of their news content.

The most crucial aspect of the growth of the free sheets has been their impact on the paid-for local press. Local paid-for newspapers had been in decline for a number of years. In 1977, the Royal Commission on the Press commented on the lack of competition within the provincial press. The product had become staid, unimaginative and parochial and sales were falling. Advertisers were complaining about the hold local monopolies exerted over the provincial newspaper market and the rates they were charging for advertising. Advertisers responded to the competition provided by the free sheets with alacrity. The free sheets reduced the cost of advertising, guaranteed access to readers which other newspapers might not be able to reach and helped to target the audience more clearly by their delivery to particular households. By 1990, the free sheets' share of advertising in the regional press had risen to 35 per cent. A survey in 1989 found that concerns about people not reading the newspapers delivered through their post-box were unfounded. In fact, the free sheets were more read than all other newspapers: nearly 77 per cent of those surveyed stated they read free newspapers while 73 per cent read Sunday newspapers, 67 per cent national morning papers, 43 per cent local paid-for weekly newspapers, 29.5 per cent local evening newspapers and just over 13 per cent regional morning newspapers.[24] The rise of free newspapers corresponded with a rapid increase in the decline of local paid-for papers. In 1975, there were 1140 paid-for local newspapers which by 1986 had fallen to 867.[25] Circulation of local paid-for weeklies was hardest hit, falling from 11 million in 1977 to 7.6 million a decade later.[26] The 'free revolution' had an impact on the editorial quality of the local press. In face of competition from the free sheets the paid-for newspapers were not able to increase their cover prices and had to depend on increasing advertising and cost cutting: weeklies raised 14 per cent of their revenue from sales compared to 38 per cent for regional dailies.[27] This meant that commercial interests came to play a greater role than editorial concerns in deciding what is published by the paid-for local press. Increasingly there was a drift to lifestyle features to attract advertising revenue at the expense of the range and quality of the stories published. It is not only the local press that has seen a change in editorial quality since the end of the Second World War, the national popular press has also undergone a radical transformation.

Rise of the tabloids

Popular journalism has undergone considerable changes in the post-war period. The most crucial development was in 1969 when Rupert Murdoch beat off competition from Robert Maxwell to buy the *Sun* newspaper from the International Publishing Corporation (IPC). Formerly the *Daily Herald*, the newspaper was re-launched in 1964 after the Odhams Group had been taken over by Cecil King's IPC. There was a change of name and format and the market research directed the 'new paper born of the age we live in' to target the 'steak eating technocrats' of Harold Wilson's new age of white-hot technology.[28] However, the steak eaters did not bite and the newspaper continued to lose money, eventually being sold at a knock-down price with no strings attached. The original sale to IPC was on the condition that it would continue to support the Labour Party. Murdoch brought in Larry Lamb as editor and turned the newspaper into a tabloid, basing the design of the paper on the *Mirror* which had become a tabloid in 1935. The aim was to make the new paper 'bright and breezy' and easy on the eye with large headlines, wide columns and lots of pictures. The front page advertised the delights that awaited the reader inside which for the first edition included 'Beautiful Women – *Sun* exclusive' and 'The Love Machine – *Sun* exclusive', a serialization of Jacqueline Susann's sequel to *The Valley of the Dolls*. Sex was to be a selling point and on page 3 appeared a half-dressed 'Swedish charmer' as well as a news story about a man described as a 'walking lust automat'.[29] The formula was to prove a success and by 1977 all the popular newspapers had gone tabloid.

The success of the *Sun* profoundly influenced the development of popular journalism in Britain. The hold the newspaper exercised over the market corresponded with the 'metamorphosis of relatively healthy popular journalism into the junk food of the mass mind market'.[30] The roots of 'junk journalism', however, had been set down long before the arrival of the *Sun*, in the newspaper wars of the 1930s. Two newspapers set the pace, the *Mirror* and the *Express*. The former, under the guidance of Harry Bartholomew, was transformed into Britain's leading newspaper. Bartholomew took over the paper in 1934 when its sales were 720,000 and by the time of his departure in 1950 they stood at 4.5 million. The formula for success was the paper's bold and brash make-up, eye-catching headlines, racy style and coy pin-ups. Bartholomew believed that most people preferred to look at rather than read newspapers. He insisted that no news story should be more than 100 or so words and that the production of mass-selling newspapers was all about display and presentation.[31] Bartholomew, like his rival at the *Express*, Arthur Christiansen, was a 'journalistic technician'.[32] They had little interest in politics or current affairs but rather sought to simplify news in a way which would reach ordinary people. By the end of the war they had guided their newspapers to the top of the circulation tree based on a menu of sensation, scandal, human interest and readily accessible and well-presented popular journalism. Their efforts were not about educating people but producing an 'exciting newspaper' which provided its readers with an 'escapist view of the world' or as Christiansen said: 'Make the news exciting, even when it was dull. Make the news palatable by lavish presentation . . . the viewpoint is optimistic.'[33] The changes wrought by Murdoch and the *Sun* in the 1970s and 1980s must be seen in the context of the developments made in editorial techniques in the popular press in the 1930s.

20 things you didn't know about the *Sun*

- In *September 1982* the *Sun* stole an article from the *Mirror*'s Scottish stablemate, the *Sunday Mail*. *Sun* editor Kelvin Mac-Kenzie wrote apologizing: 'Yes, we did steal your idea and regrettably, we also seem to have stolen three-quarters of our facts from you as well. It will not happen again.'
- As early as *August 1979* the Sun had to apologize to its readers for printing a picture of four babies twice and claiming them to be octuplets.
- *January 29, 1980*: the *Daily Star* complained that the *Sun* stole its front page exclusive lead on child killer Mary Bell being freed.
- *March 4, 1982*: The Press Council condemned the *Sun* 'for bringing discredit on the British Press by publishing pictures of the Princess of Wales bathing and sunbathing in a bikini on holiday in the Bahamas, while she was five months pregnant. It was a gross intrusion into her personal privacy.'
- *September 16, 1982*: The *Sun* claimed to be the first British paper to see Princess Grace of Monaco lying in state. It was the *Sun* lying in state – only Monegasque citizens were allowed to see her.
- *September 17, 1982*: The *Sun* printed 'quotes' from the injured Princess Stephanie, who was in fact under sedation at the time. The report's author knew nothing of the interview until it was published.
- Later that year, two Southampton soccer players were accused of raping a Swedish girl and then released. The *Sun* printed a 'quote' from one of them, Steve Moran. Mr Moran did not speak to the *Sun*.
- *March 1983*: The *Sun* blatantly looted a *Mirror* story about Prince Andrew's visit to Barbados. In April the *Sun* apologized to the *Mirror* saying it had 'gone too far in lifting *Mirror* material'.
- *August 8, 1983*: The *Sun* claimed a 'world exclusive' interview with Marica McKay, widow of Falklands hero Sergeant Ian McKay VC. The *Mirror* had the exclusive. The *Sun*'s was made up. The Press Council later called the *Sun*'s invented story 'a deplorable, insensitive deception on the public.'
- *August 22, 1983*: The Press Council said the *Sun* 'produced no evidence for its allegation that at the trial of the spy Geoffrey Prime, the Attorney-General held back mention of the accused man's involvement with a child sex organization to avoid embarrassing security chiefs.'
- *October 24, 1983*: The Press Council said the *Sun* 'seriously misrepresented the activities of the Northern Friends Peace Board by suggesting it was part of a campaign orchestrated and financed by the Soviet Union with the direct purpose of weakening the West.'
- *December 12, 1983*: A complaint was upheld that the *Sun* invaded the Royal Family's privacy in publishing information about Prince Andrew and Koo Stark, supplied by a former Royal servant. The Queen took action to halt publication.

- *January 12, 1984*: A complaint was upheld for 'taking and publishing a sad and distressing photo of the late David Niven shortly before his death. It was a gross invasion of privacy.'
- *April 12, 1984*: Guilty of gross intrusion into Brigitte Bardot's privacy for using a telephoto picture of her relaxing topless by her private pool.
- *May 1984*: *Mirror* Political Editor Julia Langdon, then with the *Guardian*, had an article lifted wholesale from *Woman* magazine by the *Sun*.
- *July 10, 1984*: England batsman Graham Gooch won £25,000 libel damages in the High Court over an 'exclusive' interview that never took place, with a headline that he couldn't care less about the plight of English cricket.
- *March 6, 1985*: A complaint was upheld for a 'seriously misleading' report on a union leader's outburst.
- *May 1985*: The *Sun* broke all records – being condemned or criticized FOUR times in one month by the Press Council.
- *May 8, 1985*: The *Sun* was criticized for mentioning a black rapist and murderer's colour.
- *May 9, 1985*: Criticized for 'publishing an unsubstantiated front page lead story alleging an IRA plot to kidnap Royal children'. Again, on the same day, the *Sun* was criticized for another front page lead story that Princess Diana's brother was selling his home because police warned him he could be a terrorist target. No such warning was given.

Source: The *Daily Mirror*, June 1985.

The Second World War brought about a demand for more serious journalism and the *Mirror*'s ability to identify with the demands from the working classes for change enabled it to acquire a pre-eminent role in the popular newspaper market. The *Express* was never able to regain its former position after its support for appeasement and ignoring 'faraway countries' such as Czechoslovakia. In the 1950s, the *Mirror* became politically identified with the changes in post-war Britain introduced by the Labour government. Hugh Cudlipp, who took over control in 1952, believed that the paper should give voice to working-class opinion. Cudlipp had the ability 'to translate serious political issues into terms that even the politically illiterate can understand'.[34] Throughout the 1950s and 1960s the newspaper made serious efforts to include material to enlighten people which distinguished it from the general thrust to entertainment in post-war popular journalism. Under Cudlipp's direction, the paper reached its high point in 1967 with sales standing at 5.28 million. The *Mirror*'s capacity to perform such a function was in part due to a lack of competition. But from 1969 the competition in the popular newspaper market became more vibrant, led by Murdoch's *Sun*, whose circulation rose steadily, reaching the 3 million mark in 1973 and surpassing that of the *Mirror* in 1978. The rise of the *Sun* initiated a circulation war which is still going on in the tabloid press today.

The circulation wars saw the steady erosion of the values of popular journalism as papers moved further down market to compete with the *Sun* and attract readers.

The amount of news and information in the popular press continued to decline, to be replaced by an endless spewing out of sex, nudity, exposés of the private lives of people (and not only those in the public eye) and countless stories about the comings and goings of the Royal Family and the characters of soap operas. Prominence has also been given to other means of selling newspapers including games such as bingo and promotions reminiscent of the 1930s. The decline in the amount of news coverage has led some to query whether the tabloids can any longer be considered as newspapers. Rather, they are entertainment sheets. Sex in particular has come to play a prominent part in selling the tabloids. Nudity was introduced into the *Sun* with the 'Page three' girl and sexual titillation and voyeurism are a stock part of the output. The fabrication of news has increasingly become part of tabloid journalism as all inhibitions are dropped in the effort to outgun the *Sun*. In the late 1980s the emergence of the *Sunday Sport* saw a further decline in popular journalism. Launched by the former porn king, David Sullivan, the newspaper was a mixture of 'tits, bums, QPR and roll your own fags' promoting sex and 'happy to make up' stories such as 'Pensioner Killed by Killer Sprout', 'Hubby Turns Wife into Egyptian Mummy' and 'Peeping Tom Aliens Spy on Our Sex Romps'. By 1987, the paper was selling over half a million copies and its success allowed Sullivan to set up a daily version which located itself at the bottom end of the market. The *Sport* was happy to parody and have a joke at the expense of the values of the tabloid press but it is clear that it 'established new ground rules for what is printable in a national newspaper'.[35] The downward slide brought about drastic revision of news values and what constitutes a 'good story'. In 1988, the *Daily Star*, launched by the Express Group in 1981 in response to the changing mass market, briefly followed the *Sport* along the same path. Mike Gabbert, the 'brains' behind the *Sport*, was hired to re-launch the 'bonking mad *Star*' which published stories with a bonk or yuck angle and more 'raunchier' material. This effort fell flat on its face as readers turned away from the newspaper and key advertisers such as Whitbread and Tesco cancelled their contracts.[36] The newspaper soon retreated from 'bonk journalism' but the success of the *Sport* has made its presence felt in the popular newspaper market where the papers see themselves as having to produce more of the same if they are to maintain their competitiveness. Press scandals and sensational reporting are, as we have seen, nothing new in the British press but in the 1980s there appears to have been a qualitative change.[37]

The increased amount of entertainment is at the expense of space devoted to 'political affairs'. There has been a general decline in political, economic and social news in popular newspapers since the mid-1930s. Content analysis of the popular press found that there had been a 'marked reduction in the amount of public affairs news and analysis'.[38] By 1976, public affairs news took up less space than sport in the popular press. Journalists such as investigative reporter John Pilger bemoaned the demise of serious journalism in the popular press which they feel has been 'hijacked' by 'Murdochism'. Murdoch is seen as responsible for producing a whole generation of journalists who believe that 'sexism, racism, voyeurism, the pillorying of people and fabrications are "what the British public wants"'.[39] The failure of the attempt to launch a left-wing Sunday tabloid, *News on Sunday (NoS)*, with a commitment to serious challenging and campaigning journalism confirmed many people in this assessment of what the public wanted. The newspaper only survived for a short period in 1987, never able to obtain a readership exceeding the sales figure of 500,000 which greeted its first issue. However, the failure of *NoS* did not necessarily prove that a left-wing tabloid devoted to a more serious form of popular journalism is not viable. The paper's failure has been attributed to a variety of factors: bad management, poor marketing, a commitment to political correctness and ideological purity at the expense of news values, an inexperienced and naive news staff and an ignorance of the readership of tabloid newspapers. However, the bottom line is that the newspaper was undercapitalized – the £6.5 million raised from trade unions and Labour local authorities was insufficient to sustain the newspaper through its first few weeks.[40] The depoliticization and trivialization of the popular press have serious implications for the democracy in Britain. Serious political coverage today is by and large confined to the quality press. The vast number of people who read the tabloids have little access to information through their newspapers that enables them to fulfil their role as active citizens in the democratic process. But perhaps the greater challenge to British democracy lies with the fact that the ownership of the British press is increasingly concentrated in the hands of a smaller and smaller number of people.

Concentration of ownership

In 1948, the general newspaper market was dominated by newspaper groups that had risen to power during the inter-war years. The intense circulation wars of the 1930s had brought an increased market dominance of the three leading companies. By 1948 Beaverbrook Newspapers (16 per cent), Associated Newspapers (14 per cent) and Kemsley Newspapers (13 per cent) had come to control 43 per cent of the circulation of national newspapers.[41] The top three newspaper groups' share of the market was to remain stable at this figure until 1961, after which it began to rise until 1974 when two-thirds of the market share rested in their hands. However, by this time the old newspaper groups had virtually disappeared; only Beaverbrook Newspapers remained amongst the top three. The Daily Mirror Newspaper Ltd had in the early 1960s bought out the Kemsley's magazines holdings, Amalgamated Press and Odhams Press, the publisher of the *Daily Herald* and the *People*, and renamed itself the International Publishing Corporation (IPC). It was the market leader controlling 30 per cent of the national daily press but IPC's hold over the market was increasingly challenged by Rupert Murdoch's News International. Murdoch entered the British newspaper market in 1968 when, after a bitter struggle with the owner of Pergamon Press, Robert Maxwell, he bought the *News of the World* which by the end of the Second World War was the best-selling newspaper in the world with a circulation of over

8 million. With the *Sun* News International was able to increase its share of the popular newspaper market in the 1980s. On the basis of this success Murdoch was able to enter into the quality market with his purchase of *The Times* and the *Sunday Times* in 1981. In 1987 he added *Today* to his list of British newspaper titles and by the end of the 1990s News International' owned 1 in 3 newspapers sold daily and on Sundays. By 1988, nearly 60 per cent of the national daily and Sunday newspapers sold in Britain were owned by the three leading chains.[42] Murdoch's News International was joined by Robert Maxwell, who after years of having been shunned by Fleet Street was able to purchase the Mirror Group Newspapers (MGN) in 1984, and United Newspapers which, under the guidance of Lord Stevens, had bought up the press holdings of Trafalgar House which had taken over Beaverbrook's Express empire in 1978. United was also a major owner of regional newspapers.

The trend to concentration of ownership was also apparent at the provincial level. The most noticeable advance was made in the local weekly press where the five largest publishers increased their holding from 8 per cent of the circulation to 27 per cent between 1947 and 1988.[43] In 1988, the top five companies owned 54 per cent of regional evening newspapers and 73 per cent of regional morning newspapers. In all, 60 per cent of the local press was owned by 10 companies, while if you take the top 15 companies, they accounted for 80 per cent of the sales of all local newspapers. Much of the concentration of ownership at the local level was through take-overs. In some cases large companies exchanged titles in order to bring about their domination in one locality. For example, in 1991–92 Reed International, then the second largest publishers of local papers in Britain, did a swap with Thomson Regional Newspaper (TRN), then the largest publishers, of a series of weekly titles in Tyneside for the *Blackburn Telegraph* and other titles in Lancashire. This helped Reed to consolidate its hold in the North-west while TRN did likewise in the North-east.[44] Such regional concentration meant that many readers no longer had a choice of the evening, morning or weekly newspaper in their town or locality. The concentration was also seen in the new free newspaper market. Started by individual entrepreneurs free sheets were bought up by the local newspaper chains, primarily as a way of staving off the competition to their titles. By 1988, the top five chains owned 38 per cent of the free newspaper market – with the top two owners of free sheets being Reed International and TRN.[45] In some places every local newspaper was owned by the same newspaper chain.

Cross-media ownership

The growing concentration of ownership in the British press has been accompanied by a change in the nature of ownership. The newspaper groups that controlled the press at the end of the Second World War were very much steeped in the world of newspaper production. Newspaper publishers have always had interests in related publishing and print concerns. Hence Northcliffe's newspaper empire included a string of magazines and comics while most of the press empires of the inter-war years held onto interests in paper and printing companies. However, in the post-war period there has been a radical shift in both the extent and kind of interests in which newspaper chains and conglomerates are involved. Faced with the intense competition in the industry from the late 1950s onwards, newspaper groups have diversified into other media interests as well as non-media areas. This occurred during periods of relative economic prosperity in the industry and has assisted the press to weather the 'down swings' in their business. Diversification has been a feature of the newspaper industry in post-war Britain.

The first major shift of newspaper companies into other media areas occurred in 1955 with the birth of ITV. Newspaper interests accounted for almost 44 per cent of the shares in one of the major network companies, Associated Television, with IPC taking nearly a 30 per cent interest in the new ITV company.[46] Investment in the smaller regional companies by newspaper groups was more pronounced. Thomson took a massive 55 per cent holding in Scottish Television while Associated Newspapers held 37.6 per cent of Southern Television and the News of the World Group 28.3 per cent of Television Wales and the West (TWW).[47] Newspapers were also quick to invest in local commercial radio when the government ended the BBC's radio monopoly in 1971. Throughout the post-war period the newspaper groups have swallowed up many of the major publishing firms. But there has also been a diversification outside of traditional media-related industries. Leisure provision has become an important part of newspaper groups. The Thomson group acquired interests in the package holiday business and Pearsons, the owners of the *Financial Times* and the Westminster Press, a chain of regional newspapers, also owned the Tussauds Group, Alton Towers, Chessington World of Adventures and Warwick Castle.[48] Other non-media interests that press groups bought into included oil and gas businesses, air and road transportation, furniture and plastics, and insurance and finance. The old narrowly focused newspaper groups of the inter-war years are no longer. Today newspapers are simply a small cog in a larger commercial enterprise. Since the 1970s, non-media conglomerates have bought into the media, including the press, which has been a rapidly expanding part of the British economy. For example, in 1981, the American oil company Atlantic Richfield bought the *Observer* which they were to sell on to Tiny Rowlands' Lonrho. The property company Trafalgar House purchased the Beaverbrook papers, including the *Express* titles in 1978 before selling them to United Newspapers in 1985. In 1977, the Royal Commission on the Press pointed out that 'rather than saying that the press has business interests, it would be truer to argue that the press has become a subsidiary of other interests'.[49] In the post-war years the press has become integrated into British finance and industry. So much so that today there is no national newspaper or major regional newspaper group that does not have a tie through cross-ownership to interests outside publishing and the media.[50]

There has also been an internationalization of ownership of the British press. Foreign involvement in the British media can be traced back to the development of news agencies in the nineteenth century and the early days of the cinema. Also Lord Beaverbrook set a trend for Canadian entrepreneurs to intervene in the British press. His steps were followed by Roy Thomson in the 1950s and Conrad Black, the owner of the *Daily Telegraph* until his demise in 2005. Prior to the 1950s, foreign involvement in the British press was the exception rather than the rule. Today it is prevalent. Rupert Murdoch, the UK's largest national newspaper owner, was an Australian citizen who became a naturalized American. His British newspapers are only a small part of a global media empire which stretches from Australia and Asia to America and the Pacific Islands. His media interests in America include newspapers, film companies and most importantly, Fox Television, which has established itself as a major television network in the United States. This is where the serious money is to be made in the global media industry and Murdoch's expansion into the American TV market has been financed by the profits his newspapers have made in Britain. Thomson, the largest regional newspaper owner in Britain until 1996, is a Canadian multinational with its headquarters in New York and Toronto. It owned newspapers throughout Britain but especially in Wales and Scotland. The bulk of its profits earned in Britain over the years were reinvested within the USA and Canada – in its newspaper chains, book-publishing interests, data and information systems and non-media interests such as oil and travel.[51] British newspapers have increasingly found themselves outposts of large international business empires whose core interests lie elsewhere in the world. Thus the trend in ownership of the British press since 1945 has been towards concentration, conglomeration and internationalization. But what does this mean for the management, content and readership of the press?

Changing style of ownership

There is much disagreement over the relationship between ownership and the character of newspapers. At least three perspectives on this relationship have been identified: pluralist, instrumentalist and structuralist.[52] The 'pluralist' view is that proprietors cannot easily exert control over their newspapers. Their interests have to be balanced against the professional interests of editors and journalists as well as the interests of the readers. Competition between newspapers is seen as working against attempts to impose a particular viewpoint or ideology on a newspaper. Both journalists and owners want to triumph over their opponents. As Mike Molloy, the former editor of the *Daily Mirror* put it: 'journalists want to beat the opposition and owners want to destroy it'.[53] Thus, in the highly competitive environment, no major newspaper owner can simply use a newspaper to put forward his opinion or advance his own political agenda. The cost in running a newspaper simply dictates against such practice. On the other hand, 'instrumentalists' point to the fact that power in a newspaper is ultimately held by the owners. They have the final say, making the key decisions on long-term policies, levels of investment, closures, mergers and the hiring and firing of senior people. Editors and journalists only operate within the framework laid down by the owner. Thus, Lord Matthews, former owner of the *Express Group* could say in 1977 that 'by and large the editors will have complete freedom as long as they agree with the policy I have laid down'.[54] This view is reinforced by Lord Stevens, the chairman of United Newspapers, who stated that it would be

> very unlikely that I would have a paper that would support the socialist party. That isn't what some people would call press freedom but why should I want a product I didn't approve of? I believe it is in the best interests of United Newspapers in terms of its profits and shareholders to support the Conservatives.[55]

The 'structuralist' approach argues that this view is too simplistic; simply reducing the content of newspapers to no more than an instrument of powerful interests. Such a view, they argue, underestimates the way in which the economic necessity of the market forces owners to go in directions they might not otherwise want to. The search for markets, advertisers, and the fear of competition are all factors that structure the character and shape of newspapers. Beaverbrook could tell the 1948 Royal Commission that:

> My purpose originally was to set up a propaganda paper, and I have never departed from that purpose all through the years. But in order to make the propaganda effective the paper had to be successful. No paper is any good at all for propaganda purposes unless it has a thoroughly good financial position. So we worked very hard to build up a commercial position.[56]

Beaverbrook's view was echoed by Cecil King in the 1950s who went further in seeing the economic logic of the newspaper market as eroding a newspaper's commitment to political causes. King argued that 'newspaper circulations are vast assemblies of people of all social classes and all varieties of political views' and that any owner or controller 'who tried to campaign for causes profoundly distasteful, even to large minorities of his readers, would put his business at risk'.[57] King did not heed his own words. In the 1960s, he sought to be a kingmaker in Labour Party politics and his personal vendetta against the Labour Prime Minister, Harold Wilson, led to his dismissal as the head of IPC in 1968. The conglomeration of the industry meant that some of the new bosses of newspapers were responsible to boards of directors and other interests who could dismiss them.

The post-war newspaper industry is regarded by many as witnessing the ascendancy of the entrepreneurial proprietor, more concerned with profit than political influence. Business is seen as coming first and the old style of interventionist proprietorship becoming a thing of the past. The new-style owners were not seen as motivated by personal, political or ideological concerns but with commercial success. The new spirit of 'business first' is seen as epitomized by owners such as Roy Thomson who told the 1961 Royal Commission on the Press that his purpose was to run a newspaper as a business, to make money. He left his editors to get on with the job of putting out the paper, as long as the newspaper brought in a profit. He stated that he did 'not believe that a newspaper can be run properly unless its editorial columns are run freely and independently by a highly skilled and dedicated professional journalist'.[58] The downfall of Cecil King is seen as confirming the end of the era of the authoritarian proprietor. He overstepped his powers and was sacked. In the new conglomerates the proprietor was only the chairman of the board, a first amongst equals. However, the non-interventionist, enterprise-driven proprietor, if he existed at all, does not adequately describe the nature of ownership since 1945. Competition did at certain points in the history of the post-war press, as it had in the 1930s, curtail the interventionist tendencies of owners. For a period in the late 1960s and early 1970s, a time of political consensus in Britain, there was an increase in the delegation of editorial responsibility. But even in companies such as Thomson it was more apparent at the regional than the national level. It is true that Thomson had motives other than strictly commercial ones. He poured a vast amount of money into supporting the loss-making *Times* newspaper, before he sold it to Murdoch in 1981. Personal prestige played a role in his commitment to such a loss-making enterprise. Thomson did also intervene in the political stance of his newspapers. He did not believe that any newspaper that supported the Labour Party could succeed and in 1974 informed his then editor of the *Sunday Times* that he would be unhappy if it came out in favour of the party at the general election.

The late 1970s and early 1980s saw the re-emergence of the 'press barons' style of newspaper management. The highly personalized nature of newspaper ownership was characterized by the feud between Rupert Murdoch and Robert Maxwell. On taking control of the MGN, Maxwell exerted his personality over all his newspapers, including the *Daily Mirror*, to promote his own views and causes. In 1987, he tried to launch a new London daily newspaper to compete with the *Evening Standard*; the London *Daily News* folded five months later. Maxwell became tired of the newspaper industry and turned his attention to cable television in Britain, buying into the emerging industry, and then went on to acquire three football clubs. Maxwell's interest in newspapers was a small part of a number of other media and commercial activities in which he was involved. Similarly, Murdoch's press empire in Britain is a small component of larger commercial and media interests. This contrasts with the press barons of the inter-war years whose primary interests lay in their newspapers. They accumulated newspapers and then used them to promote their own political policies and personal whims. The modern 'media moguls' are as interventionist as their predecessors but, above all, they are finance men. They use their muscle to acquire publications, turning loss-making properties into profitable concerns.[59] Their political objectives are seen as secondary to their financial needs which have been of more significance in determining the shape and direction of their newspapers. Their activities have allowed them to obtain a near stranglehold on the British press and their power was illustrated by Tony Blair travelling halfway around the world in 1995 to court Rupert Murdoch's support for the Labour Party. This power was consolidated in the mid-1980s by changes in the British press which enhanced the ability and capacity of management at the expense of the rest of those working in the industry. In the process, the 'Wapping revolution' brought about the 'death of Fleet Street'.

The Wapping revolution

Sunday 26 January 1986 was a decisive moment in British press history. That day Rupert Murdoch moved his press operations from Fleet Street to Wapping and shifted the balance of power between the contending forces in the newspaper industry. The print unions, primarily the National Graphic Association (NGA) and Society of Graphical and Allied Trades (SOGAT), had built up a powerful position in the newspaper industry. High wage settlements, closed shop agreements, control over access into the trade, and working practices which allowed claims for shifts not work had been negotiated by the print unions. In the 1950s, weak management, in a time of high prosperity in the industry, had made wide-ranging concessions in the face of the threat of industrial action. Printers were crucial in the production process and their withdrawal of labour could paralyse the whole operation. Newspaper production was labour-intensive, with labour amounting to between 40 and 50 per cent of the cost of putting out a newspaper.[60] Such high costs were seen as making a substantial contribution to the decline of the newspaper industry. New technology promised to reduce costs of production and the attempts to introduce it were resisted by the Fleet Street unions. In late 1978 and early 1979 *The Times* and the *Sunday Times* had been shut down for nearly a year with the owners, Thomson, losing an estimated £40 million. Anti-trade union legislation brought in by the Conservative government in the 1980s created a more receptive climate to the introduction of such change. The harbinger of Wapping was a dispute in Lancashire when a local entrepreneur, Eddie Shah, employed non-union labour using new technology to print local newspapers. Serious confrontation resulted between Shah and the print unions. The NGA picketed Shah's plant to prevent the distribution of his newspapers but was fined £500,000 for illegal picketing under the new legislation. Shah on the basis of his success went on to set up a plant in London and launched the *Today* newspaper using new technology.[61]

Murdoch planned the move of his newspapers from Fleet Street to Wapping in London docklands in great secrecy. The high security plant was secretly installed with new print technology and Murdoch, taking personal charge, moved all his newspapers under one roof at what was dubbed 'Fortress Wapping'. The printers chose to strike and were dismissed without redundancy payments. Financial inducements and the threat of dismissal enticed most of the journalists to cross the picket lines and work at Wapping. The Wapping dispute proved to be a long and violent confrontation. Murdoch's plant was fortified with razor wire around the perimeter, security men patrolling constantly, surveillance cameras and armoured buses were used to bring in workers. But with the support of the new trade union legislation, backed by Mrs Thatcher and her government, Murdoch's decision to move to Wapping was successful. Soon most other national newspapers left for the Docklands and Fleet Street ceased to be the centre of newspaper production in Britain.

The introduction of new print technology was justified on the grounds that the reduction of costs would result in greater diversity in the newspaper industry. The workforce of most national newspapers was slashed immediately after Wapping. Lower costs promised an end to the high entry barriers into the industry. The Wapping revolution, it was argued, would stimulate the appearance of more newspapers and magazines and extend access to new groups. Some new newspapers were established. Besides Shah's *Today* and *Sunday Today*, the *Independent* came onto the market in 1987, set up by a group of journalists alienated by the machinations of Fleet Street proprietors, followed by the *Sunday Correspondent* and, in competition, the *Independent on Sunday* as well as a number of other Sunday papers, including the *Sport*. This growth in British newspapers had been unparalleled since the height of the Northcliffe Revolution. However, most of these newspapers folded very quickly. The *Correspondent* collapsed in 1990, the Today Group was sold to Murdoch in 1987, after losing £28 million a year under Shah, and eventually closed down in 1995. The *Independent* remains as a daily newspaper but is no longer independent of the newspaper chains, as MGN took a controlling stake in 1993 and it eventually fell into the hands of the Irish businessman and newspaper owner, Tony O'Reilly. The reality of the new technology was somewhat different from the promise. The overall structure of the British newspaper industry did not change radically. The start-up costs and running cost of national newspapers are still prohibitively high. If anything, the Wapping revolution consolidated the power of those already in the market: the established press chains. The power of the print unions was broken, industrial relations transformed and proprietors were able to exert greater influence over their newspapers.

Freedom versus responsibility in the Street of Shame

The new dawn in the 1990s saw the circulation wars in the popular newspaper market spill over into the quality press. In 1993, Murdoch slashed the cover prices of his newspapers. The price of *The Times* was cut to 30 pence and within a year the newspaper increased its sales by 42 per cent. Its main competitor, the *Daily Telegraph*, saw sales for the first time fall below the million mark. In response the newspaper's owner, Conrad Black, dropped the price of his paper which initially helped it to regain sales. Murdoch, however, retaliated by cutting the price of *The Times* to 20 pence, the price at which the *Sun* sold. The newspaper which suffered most in the midst of the price war was the *Independent* whose editor, Andreas Whittam-Smith, was critical about what was happening. 'Two right wing ideologues . . . have set about destroying the quality newspaper market. Men like

Murdoch and Black want control. They care nothing for the plurality of opinion, nothing for liberal values.'[62] It was the price squeeze on the *Independent* that forced it into the arms of corporate interests. Murdoch and Black, to obtain commercial gain, were able to run their newspapers at a loss in the short run by subsidizing them from their other media interests around the world. Prices returned to 1993 levels after sales gains had been made.

Crossing the picket line at Wapping

Like most people, I saw on television the journalists going to work for Mr Murdoch in his new plant at Wapping. Blurred figures filing down between the barbed-wire – I couldn't make out a face to recognize – they all shared an attitude: hunched-up; heads down between shoulders collars up in the drizzle.

'The Caudine Forks' said a memory from Latin lessons. After that battle, the victorious Samnites made their Roman prisoners walk under a yoke. Yes, they must have walked like that.

So I went along to see for myself. Mr Murdoch, it seems, assumed that his printworks would be assaulted by waves of typesetters with fixed bayonets, supported by light armour and by suicide car-bombs driven by Shiite machine-minders. Roll after roll of razor bladed wire form a defence in depth. Ten-foot steel gates, electronically controlled, are covered by swivelling television cameras. Police, supported by private security men, guard the entrance. There are ramps to block vehicles, searchlights, half-visible men photographing visitors from an empty factory next door.

A German correspondent, amazed, writes that it is like the East German border, a film set which just can't be for real in a Western country. He isn't quite right, for it is even more like a police station in South Armagh. The old East End of London, for those who built this grotesque and horrible place, is bandit country where the natives are hostile.

The natives? A handful of pickets stand near the entrance, from the night shift who would have been producing the *Sun* if they had not been sacked. A taxi arrives. A young woman reporter, in a fur coat, digs frantically into her handbag to find her pass, trying not to see the picket who approaches the taxi window. 'Can I have a word with you? Judas did it for only 30 pieces of silver. Going to sleep well tonight, are you?'

Her shoulders go into that pathetic hunch; she crouches as the taxi moves on into the defence zone. Presently, two buses come out very fast, lights out, curtains drawn. The picket says his three sentences again, but nobody stops. There are a few boos and groans, and the buses tear away down East Smithfield.

Those buses contain my colleagues, the journalists of News International who have been defeated. Mr Murdoch did not mess around with them. He ignored all his house agreements with journalists, and told them to choose: go to Wapping and be rewarded with a £2,000 rise and private health insurance, or be sacked instantly and without compensation. Most of them went to Wapping, some cynically, some wretchedly. A few still refuse.

Source: Ascherson, Neal (1986) *Observer*, 2 February. Reprinted in his book (1988) *Games with Shadows*, London: Radius.

The bitterness of the competition in both the popular and quality newspaper markets throughout the 1980s and the 1990s was accentuated by the fact that newspapers were competing for declining readership. This is most marked in the tabloid press. Between 1961 and 1986, aggregate tabloid sales dropped from 12.43 to 10.27 million.[63] The increasing hysteria of the press has to be seen as a response to the nature of competition. Public opinion, however, toward the tabloid press – and newspapers in general – changed. Amused interest in the tabloid press turned to overt hostility. A number of factors were responsible for the backlash – but the invasion of the individual's privacy by the press played a central role in changing public attitudes. Public confidence in the British press was at an all-time low. In 1991, the number of people expressing confidence in the press had dropped to only 14 per cent of those polled, lower than most of Britain's other social institutions, such as the police, courts, armed forces and education service.[64] Declining confidence brought forth renewed calls for the tightening of the regulation of the newspaper industry.

Criticisms of the performance of the press are not new. In 1949, the Royal Commission established the Press Council as the central plank of a system of voluntary self-regulation. The Council adjudicated on complaints brought to its attention by parties who felt they had been aggrieved by newspaper reports. However, the Council proved itself to be impotent in the face of the rising number of complaints in the 1980s. This has been attributed to a number of factors: the Council lacked sanctions to enforce its decisions, it was ignored by newspaper editors and had no independent means of funding. There was no agreement within the industry over what constituted the highest professional standards, and the Council spent most of its time reacting to contentious reporting in the press. It is also the case that most of the complaints to the Council were from organizations or professional people. The man- and woman-in-the-street were by and large unfamiliar with the body; a poll in 1976 found that only 21 per cent had ever heard of the Council.[65] By the end of the 1980s, the government, in response to public criticism as well as outcry from Members of Parliament, many of whom were most concerned about intrusions into the privacy of the Royal Family, announced the setting up of an enquiry into the regulation of the Press. The Calcutt Commission did not recommend statutory control but the Press Council was closed and replaced by the Press Complaints Commission (PCC) which drew up a code of practice in negotiation with newspaper editors. The PCC was better funded and involved the direct participation of the industry. Calcutt gave the British press 18 months to show that a voluntary system could work when the Commission would review the situation.

The next Calcutt Report in 1993 recommended the introduction of statutory controls and privacy legislation. In its first year the PCC did have some impact – the process of adjudication was speeded up and the press did appear to behave more responsibly. But 1992 was an *annus horribilis* for the Royal family and the British political establishment. A stream of sensational stories about the doings of

Charles and Diana as well as the sexual misdemeanours of a number of leading politicians, including the minister in charge of press policy, made the PCC look 'ineffectual, if not somewhat ridiculous'.[66] Calcutt believed he had no alternative. However, he was not supported by the government who rejected his call for more control. The government was reluctant to embark on more draconian legislation in the climate of financial, personal and political sleaze which had developed since the 1992 election. Public attitudes to the Royal family had also become more critical; many of the newspaper reports appeared vindicated by divorce, admissions of adultery and tales of extravagance by the Royals. In such circumstances placing restrictions on the press which might make it more difficult to report on the activities of those in authority was more contentious.[67] The result was that self-regulation remained. A new, high-profile head of the PCC was appointed, Lord Wakeham, the former Cabinet minister, and some proposals were made to compensate individuals who had their privacy intruded upon. The tension between allowing the freedom of the press to expose wrong doings and the need to curb the irresponsible excesses of the tabloid press remained.

The incorporation of the European Convention of Human Rights into British law as part of the 1998 Human Rights Act had an impact on the situation. It guaranteed a 'right to privacy' and permitted the courts to have more involvement in defining the boundaries beyond which the press should not intrude into people's personal lives. In 2001, the *Daily Mirror* published pictures of super-model Naomi Campbell leaving a Narcotics Anonymous meeting. A long court battle ended with a House of Lords ruling in her favour. Campbell only received £3,500 in damages but her case established that newspapers could be sued for 'misuse of private information'. Other celebrities used this right to protect their privacy including Michael Douglas and Catherine Zeta Jones who sued over the publication of unauthorized pictures of their wedding in *Hello!* magazine.[68] A privacy law was slowly emerging and was extended with Max Mosley's case against the *News of the World* in 2008 for publishing pictures and a story about sado-masochistic sex sessions.[69] The ruling in favour of Mosley rejected the *News of the World*'s public interest defence, drawing a clear distinction between matters which may be of interest to the public and matters which are in the public interest.

Mosley was awarded damages of £60,000 plus costs for the invasion of his privacy but his claim for exemplary damages was rejected. This cannot be seen as a deterrent to a newspaper indulging in such activity. The cost of the legal action for the *News of the World* was almost offset by the additional revenue generated by the story.[70] It is estimated that the Mosley scoop added as many as 200,000 sales in the first week and £1m to the bottom line in terms of increased circulation and advertising revenues. The video of the Mosley sex sessions was more successful than the printed story, helping to establish the *News of the World* as a global brand on the internet, succeeding in bringing the paper their greatest ever number of hits. Claims that 'the press is less free today' came from sections of the industry after the Mosley judgment. The development of the law regarding privacy under the European Human Rights Convention has not necessarily brought about the end to press intrusion into people's lives but simply made that intrusion more expensive.

The long goodbye?

There has been a steady contraction in the newspaper industry since the Wapping revolution. The number of newspaper titles has fallen and circulation has dropped. Since 1985 the sales of national daily and Sunday newspapers have declined by 41 per cent, a drop of nearly 16 million copies.[71] The popular or tabloid market has suffered the most, with a fall of over 3 and a half million readers between 1985 and 2006. The sales of the *Daily Mirror, Daily Express* and *Daily Star* have more than halved. The *Sun* has lost nearly a quarter of its readers. The only daily newspaper to have increased circulation is the *Daily Mail* whose sales have risen by just over 470,000. In 1998, the *Mail* overtook the *Mirror* to become Britain's second best-selling newspaper. The collapse of the popular Sunday press has been more spectacular. The *People*'s circulation, which reached a high point of over 5.3 million in the 1960s, plummeted to 729,000 in 2007. Declining circulation has also impacted on the most successful part of the newspaper business in the 1980s, the free sheets. Their number peaked in 1986, rapidly declining between 1989 and 2004 during which the numbers of copies distributed weekly fell from 42 to 29 million. Despite the launch of successful titles such as *Metro*, the *London Paper* and *London Lite*, there are 200 fewer free titles than 20 years ago. The collapse of paid-for local newspapers has been more pronounced; a reduction in titles of 56 per cent between 1948 and 2005. The fall in the number of titles reflects that newspaper reading is a less popular activity. In 2006, 42 per cent of 18–27-year-olds read a daily paper at least three days a week, compared with 72 per cent in 1986. As older readers vanish, they are not being replaced.

Disappearing readers, dwindling sales and declining titles have been accompanied by fewer journalists. Job losses in the national newspaper market are a consequence of the introduction of new technology. Salary levels are relatively modest, with half of Britain's newspaper journalists earning less than the national average wage. The number of newspaper journalists has not kept pace with the increase in the size of the British newspaper which has grown considerably since the mid-1990s. More space, sections and supplements have resulted in a substantial increase in workloads. The development of online editions has further added to the demands made on staff. Most national and regional daily newspapers have set up online editions. The decline of printed newspapers is attributed to the increasing popularity of the online editions. Uncertainty, however, has characterized the emergence of online newspapers. Doubts have been expressed about the commercial opportunities presented by the new technology. Finding a way to make money from online editions is proving difficult; most online news sites are losing money and have to be supported by printed editions.[72] The involvement of the newspapers is as much a response to the increasing use of the internet by the potential readers of the future – younger people. The challenge posed by online advertising is another major impetus.

The British press underwent a radical shift of political allegiance in the 1990s. From an overwhelmingly pro-Tory editorial bias at the 1992 general election, the national newspapers changed their allegiances to Labour five years later. New Labour leader Tony Blair enjoyed considerable editorial support in the General Elections of 1997, 2001 and 2005. The most significant change was the backing Labour received from Rupert Murdoch's newspapers which had resolutely opposed the party prior to Blair's acession to the leadership. Support at election time did not make for comfortable relations between government and the press. In his last days in office Blair described the press as 'a feral beast, just tearing people and reputations to bits', adding that the distinction between comment and news had become so blurred that it was rare to find newspapers reporting precisely what a politician said.[73] Many regard modern newspapers as out of control, all powerful and 'damaging the national psyche'.[74] Blair's press secretary Alastair Campbell, blamed the press for 'turning people's natural and healthy scepticism into a near phobia of politics driven by . . . relentless negativity'.[75] His words echo those of former *Financial Times* journalist John Lloyd who argues that a 'culture of cynicism' pervades British journalism and poses a threat to democracy.[76] He singles out the mendacious, tendentious and superficial way in which the press reports the major issues of the day as the central problem. This shift in the party allegiance of the British press does not represent a political transformation. It is British politics that has changed, with the Labour Party moving its policies further to the centre–right under Tony Blair. Support for private enterprise and the 'free market' remains a characteristic of most of the national press.[77] The increased focus on non-political news in the press, with the growth in coverage of lifestyles matters, fashion, house and home, travel, money and finance, food and wine, media and entertainment reflects the increasing pressure newspapers are under to attract readers. Critical copy, scandals and salacious gossip and speculation reflect the desperate competition that has pervaded the newspaper industry since the early 1990s.

A rapid turnover of editors and owners has characterized the post-Wapping newspaper industry. The beginning of the 1990s saw the greatest turnover of editors in the history of the British press.[78] The extent of market competition meant that editors were given little time to revive the fortunes of their titles. Owners also fell by the wayside in their struggles to compete. Many 'famous names with long pedigrees have vanished' as well as the old family concerns that pervaded the regional press.[79] Conrad Black sold the Telegraph group in 2005. Newspapers were further integrated into multimedia empires with intimate ties to British business and capital. Constant changes, as well as competition from other, new sources of information and entertainment such as the internet and 24-hour rolling television news, made the industry appear precarious. With fewer people reading newspapers, the speculation has been that Britain's oldest media was dead. *The Economist* magazine asked the question 'who killed the newspaper?'[80] However, the picture of decline that pervades the industry in the early twenty-first century belies the fact that there are considerable profits to be made from the newspaper business. With advertising revenue buoyant, profits will remain 'exceptionally high' compared to other industries.[81] Growing competition from the internet and other new media, as well as global recession, pose a threat to continuing profitability, but as long as money is to be made from their sales, newspapers will, no matter what form, shape or size, continue to exist.

Part 4

The digital world

12

Dumbing down? Declining standards and structural change in the contemporary media

The contemporary history of the British media cannot be separated from two fundamental transformations: the revolution in communications technology in the late twentieth century and the rapid commercialization of the media industries. New media such as cable, satellite, the internet and other digital technologies are eroding the terrestrial-led broadcasting system which has dominated the post-war years. We are entering a new epoch in the history of mass communication. Our experience of these technologies and their impact on our daily lives and consumption of the mass media are discussed in more detail in the next chapter. In this chapter we look at how the structure and content of the British media have changed. The rapid commercialization of the media industries and the increasing concentration of their ownership in the hands of large corporations whose primary aim is to make money have accompanied the emergence of the new media technology. New media technology is contributing to the formation of a global culture with the instant transmission of images simultaneously to all parts of the planet. This occurrence has serious implications for national societies and cultures. The British mass media are ever more 'global' in their outlook. They are becoming anchored in a global culture and part of global media empires that operate internationally rather than nationally or locally. It is perhaps incorrect to talk today about the 'British' media. The phenomenon of 'globalization' is, however, paradoxical. Pressures are building up on national media systems from local as well as global change. There has been a growth in local, community and regional media, serving local audiences and interests. Unprecedented migration across the planet had led people to exploit the possibilities offered by new technology of accessing their media back home. Globalization is associated with a resurgence of attachment to locality and the rise of local media.[1]

Much of the debate about the British media in the global era has focused on what has been seen as deleterious change in their content. 'Tabloidization' is seen as spreading to all parts of the media, with the last bastion to capitulate the broadsheet press whose conversion to smaller formats in the 1990s marked their 'dumbing down'. Public service broadcasting is entering a new downward spiral as a result of the further de-regulation of the broadcasting industry and increased competition from the proliferation of new channels. Several commentators have referred to a 'crisis in British journalism' generated by the transformation in media technology and economy.[2] Debate about declining standards was central to the fiasco of the Hutton Inquiry which the BBC's Director-General described as the 'biggest crisis for BBC journalism in 80 years'.[3] But incidents such as the ITV telethon deceptions, the answer phone insults broadcast by Russell Brand and Jonathan Ross on BBC Radio 2 and the misuse of the Queen to promote a BBC documentary also raise questions about the performance of contemporary broadcasting. Reality television has been subject to a barrage of hostile criticism with programmes such as *Pop Idol, The X Factor, Strictly Come Dancing, I'm a Celebrity, Get Me Out of Here* and, above all, *Big Brother* described as 'cheap self-exposure by rather silly young people seeking publicity at all costs'.[4] Falling standards are linked with the growing pressure to be competitive in a highly competitive global media market. The relentless search for readers, listeners and viewers is trivializing the output, marginalizing the serious and encouraging entertainment to thrive at the expense of information and education. Concerns about the 'dumbing down' of the British media are often articulated in terms of the 'Americanization' of content, style and form but matters of quality in journalism and the media are today connected with the rise of new forms of media manipulation, collectively labelled as 'spin', which are seen as further distorting and misrepresenting what is communicated to the public. The growth of professionals, agencies and techniques in the field of image-making, advertising and public relations is a feature of the contemporary media scene. As the information environment spins out of control, new technology is seen as enhancing the ability and capacity of the 'spin doctor' to influence what the British public sees, hears, reads, surfs and blogs.

Concentrating media ownership

The British media in a global era are owned by a smaller number of large media corporations whose primary aim is to make money. The concentration, conglomeration and globalization of British media ownership have been features of the post-war years. From the late 1990s the pace has quickened. Familiar British media companies have been swallowed up by larger interests, often foreign and non-media. The contemporary national newspaper industry is almost fully integrated into a handful of media empires. This has been done by a process of mergers, take-overs and acquisitions. Most of Britain's leading national newspapers have changed hands in the last decade. Murdoch's News International controls around 40 per cent of the sales of national newspapers. With the Daily Mail and General Trust Group and Trinity Mirror, these three companies account for over three-quarters of national circulations. They have been joined by the Barclay Brothers, who took control of the Telegraph Group in 2005; The Guardian Media

Group, which grew with the *Guardian*'s take-over of the *Observer* in 1996 and Richard Desmond who seized control of the ailing Express group in 1999. They own 98 per cent of the national newspaper titles. The frenetic exchange of national newspaper titles since the new millennium means that only the *Daily Mail* and the *Guardian* have experienced stable ownership.[5]

A similar pattern characterizes the regional newspaper market. Four companies emerged in the 1990s – Newquest, Northcliffe, Johnston and Trinity Mirror – to dominate the local weekly, daily and Sunday newspaper markets, controlling an estimated 65 per cent of their circulation in 2006.[6] This came about as a result of the 'precipitate sale' of regional newspaper holdings in the 1990s.[7] Most of the large multi-media empires vacated the local newspaper industry. Thomson, after 35 years in the industry, sold its newspaper titles in England and Wales to Trinity Holdings and its Scottish paper to the Barclay Brothers and Northcliffe Newspapers, part of the Daily Mail and General Trust Group. This sale triggered a wholesale clear-out. Reed Regional Newspapers was sold by the multinational Reed-Elsevier in 1995 with a management buy-out of £205 million proving successful. Financed by a New York investment house, the new company was called Newsquest. In 1996, EMAP – the East Midlands Allied Press – joined Thomson and Reed in quitting the regional newspaper industry. EMAP had grown from a local newspaper group into a multi-media enterprise with interests in the magazine industry, commercial radio and publishing. It sold its newspaper titles to the Edinburgh-based company, Johnson Press. The total circulation of EMAP's titles of around 2 million should have been submitted for official approval but the deal, as a result of a loophole in the Fair Trading Act, was not submitted to the Monopolies and Mergers Commission because no one title had a circulation of more than 50,000.[8] The huge Westminster Press was put up for sale by the multimedia conglomerate Pearson in the same year, to be acquired by Newsquest which paid £305 million for some of Britain's best-known evening and morning titles, including the *Bradford Telegraph and Argus* and the *Darlington Northern Echo*. This time the purchase was referred to the Monopolies and Mergers Commission and approved, despite the change of titles giving Newsquest a monopoly of the newspapers in certain areas of Britain. United Press Newspapers announced in 1996 that it wanted to sell some of its regional papers in London and South Wales. It stated that it wanted to concentrate on areas where it had a critical mass, in this case, its stronger titles in the North of England. The only major regional newspaper chain not to get out of the market was the Northcliffe Newspaper Group.

The outcome of the 'all change' policy in the local newspaper market is a further concentration of ownership. The decision by the large multinational companies to sell was motivated by their belief that newspapers will never be able to generate the profits that are realizable from the electronic media.[9] For them the key motivation is obtaining a reasonable return for their shareholders. High dividend pay-outs in the short run outweigh considerations about the long-run future of the industry. For a number of years the large local newspaper groups had been downsizing, rationalizing and milking their titles for greater returns. When this process came to an end, they moved on. The new owners, particularly Trinity and Johnson, are primarily interested in newspapers. Both had better records than the large groups on editorial matters and industrial relations. However, their commitment to the industry was overridden by the desire to drive the business forward. They attempted to run their business by organizing their publications in regional clusters, seeking to achieve economies of scale by standardizing their product and concentrating their resources, personal and printing. As part of the efforts to maximize profits, cost cutting was introduced into the industry. In 2003, Sly Bailey took over as chief executive of Trinity Mirror and by delivering a reduction in operating costs increased the profit margin of the regional newspaper division tenfold.[10] The corporate character of firms traditionally committed to regional newspapers had changed. As they expanded, companies such as Trinity and Johnson became more focused on meeting the rising expectations of shareholders, thereby weakening their commitment to editorial standards and operating their newspapers in the interests of the local community.

The profitability of regional newspapers – by 2005, Johnston Press experienced profit margins of 30 per cent whilst Trinity Mirror was not far behind with 28 per cent – reawakened the interests of larger corporations. In 1999, America's largest newspaper group, Gannett, bought out Newsquest. The top 20 publishers now account for 95 per cent of the circulation of the weekly press in the UK. But the circulation of what they own has slipped. A sharp decline in regional newspaper sales was recorded in 2004, followed in 2005 by a drop in advertising revenue. With 80 per cent of revenue now accruing from advertising, the response to a profit warning was to make further cost cuts. A further decline in sales resulted. While decline is not evenly spread in the regional market – weekly paid-for papers with a strong editorial commitment to their locality have fared better – the focus on profits through maximizing advertising revenue and costs cutting has been in the face of declining titles and circulation.

Since the 1990 Broadcasting Act the ownership of the ITV network has become more concentrated. Mergers and take-overs have gradually accounted for the demise of the 15 companies that constituted the network. With the exception of Scotland, where the franchises are held by the Scottish Media Group, Northern Ireland which remains in the hands of Ulster TV and the Channel Islands, the rest of the network is controlled by one company. ITV became a single company in 2004 when Granada and Carlton were given permission to merge. Its commitment to the regions has waned. As part of standardizing the ITV 'brand', manifest for viewers in a uniform logo for all regional stations, regional programming has been cut back. One of the new company's first acts was to appoint an 'editor of the ITV regions' based in London. The number of hours of regional programming, especially regional news, has been reduced. This retrenchment deepened when Michael Grade defected from the BBC in 2006 to take over as ITV's Managing

Director. Cutbacks in religious, children's programming and drama were now accompanied by a withdrawal from news. ITV could justify the reduction of non-news output as research had shown that they were not that highly valued by audiences. Local and regional news, however, has always been greatly appreciated. In 2007, proposals to reduce the number of regional ITV news services were agreed and ITV's commitment to the regions, once the *raison d'être* of British commercial television, began to wane. Faced with declining advertising revenue, further hit by the downturn in the economy in 2008, ITV has began to argue that a proportion of the licence fee should be used to support its regional commitments, which it increasingly finds an irksome burden.

Concentration of ownership has featured in other media industries. Two large conglomerates, EMAP and IPC, have dominated the ever expanding magazine market; the old-established names of British publishing rest in the hands of five large, mostly foreign, companies while the British film industry, as we have seen, is dominated by global firms, primarily American, who have controlling interests in the exhibition, distribution and production sectors of the industry (see Chapter 10). Similar trends are to be seen in the music, advertising and new media industries. Six major companies dominated the British music market, consolidating their hold in the late 1990s by increasing their share of the market to 80 per cent.[11] The advertising industry has had a long tradition of American involvement since J. Walter Thompson set up an agency in London in the 1920s. In the 1950s and 1960s, US companies acquired many of Britain's best known companies but following Saatchi and Saatchi's take-over of the US giants Compton and Ted Bates in the 1980s, UK agencies have attained worldwide prominence with WPP becoming the world's largest ad agency.[12] The media giants are also buying into the new media industries that are emerging, with familiar names such as News International, Virgin, Google, Microsoft and AOL dominating the early days of the market for internet content.[13]

Rupert Murdoch's News Corporation has further extended its geographical reach and range of media interests in recent years. It is involved in a range of media activities across the globe, in places as far apart as Australia, America, Fiji, Spain, Germany, Latin America, India and South-east Asia. In Britain, Murdoch's interests extend across the media, with television and newspaper assets complemented by his ownership of the Britain's second largest publisher, HarperCollins, as well as his acquisition of *MySpace* for $580 million in 2005. In 2006, BSkyB bought nearly 18 per cent of ITV, causing a furore of complaint from a variety of sources about the growing influence Murdoch was exerting over the British media. His competitors, such as Richard Branson at Virgin and film-maker David Putman, believed the extent of his influence posed a 'threat to democracy'.[14] Their views were not shared by the Blair government, which aware of the problems that market distortion can create, believed that encouraging the growth of larger media companies is an essential ingredient to increasing the competitiveness of the British media in the world market. Their focus was on the economic performance of the media industries – in 2005, it was estimated that the UK's 'creative industries', which included other activities besides the media such as arts, fashion and design, accounted for £53 billion or 8 per cent of GDP.[15] Their aim was to increase the industry's profitability in the global market rather than ensure that a diversity of expression appeared in the media.

The integration of British media and cultural production into the web of the global media marketplace can be seen most clearly in television. Britain is a major market for US media television products and their share of the British television output has almost doubled since 1983, from around 12 to about 20 per cent.[16] More significantly, the rising costs of television production have led companies to cooperate internationally in sharing the costs of making certain kinds of programmes, especially dramas. These deals have consequences for the nature of the product. Peter Golding and Graham Murdock argue that the increasing reliance on international co-production for drama imposes a variety of constraints, 'as partners search for subject matter and narrative styles that they can sell in their home markets'.[17] In particular they see the agreements producing an 'Americanized product' which lays stress on the formula of fast-moving action, simple characterizations and unambiguous endings.

Wall-to-wall *Dallas*?

There has been a revival in the concern that British cultural identity is threatened by the increasing flow of American media products into the country, the increasing prominence of US production values and the growing foreign ownership of British media interests. Television has again been at the centre of these concerns. British television has always prided itself on the small amount of foreign material on television screens. The ceiling was set at 14 per cent. But over the years it has become apparent that American programmes figure most strongly in prime time viewing hours when most people are watching. At key moments in the history of British television, US imports have played an important role in building prime time schedules. ITV in the 1950s relied on serials such as *Dr. Kildare* and *Gunsmoke* to establish its popularity. In the mid-1980s, when competition between ITV and BBC started to increase, an unseemly struggle took place between the BBC and Thames to secure the rights to *Dallas*. Channel Four has relied on US programmes, especially sitcoms, such as *Roseanne, Friends* and *Frasier*, to promote its schedule. Such a strategy has allowed British television to concentrate its effort in producing high-cost, prestige programming such as costume drama. In the words of one ITV executive, 'British television rode to success on the back of American programmes; it's been a matter of buying ratings while making our own prestige.'[18] In addition to American shows there are also a huge number of programmes on British TV which are a British version of American formats, in particular, game and quiz shows which have been adapted years after passing their sell-by date on US television. The strong showing of US programmes on British television is not simply a matter of their popularity; it is also the result of their low cost. It has been estimated that the BBC in the 1990s paid on average around £38,000 per hour for programmes brought in from abroad, primarily American products, while it cost £48,000 per hour to produce its own drama. The pressure to reduce costs in a more competitive and business-orientated market increased the flow of cheaper, American products into Britain. The new cable, satellite and digital stations depend more on cheap American imports, threatening that the content of British television will become 'wall-to-wall *Dallas*'.

The debate about the 'Americanization' of British television has to be put into context. Over the years it has been guided by an assumption of the superior quality of British programmes. However, it could be argued that the quality of American imports was higher than much of the home-grown fare. Innovation and creative energy were found in the work of Steven Bochco whose series, such as *Hill Street Blues, L.A. Law, NYPD* and *Murder One*, gained popular and critical acclaim. The strength of American comedy was reflected in the plethora of programmes shown on British television – including *Roseanne, Frasier, Cheers, Friends, M.A.S.H., Rhoda* and *Taxi*. Chat shows such as *Oprah* also proved to be more wide-ranging than their British counterparts. Programmes such as *Lou Grant* were not only good entertainment but also adopted a critical and challenging approach to many of the issues of the day. Since 2000, US imports have become more stylized. Cop programmes abound with series such as *CSI, Law and Order, Cold Case, Without a Trace* and *The Wire* showing on a variety of channels. Daytime television is full of repeats of old US series such as *Quincy ME* and *Columbo* and crime shows with old stars such as Dick Van Dyke in *Diagnosis Murder* and Angela Lansbury in *Murder, She Wrote*.

British television has had some success in selling programmes to the lucrative US market. Traditionally the BBC and ITV have traded costume dramas such *Brideshead Revisited, The Six Wives of Henry VIII* and *Upstairs, Downstairs* which exploit the stereotypical images American audiences have of Britain. Since the late 1990s a range of other genres have been successfully exported by British television to the US and other world markets including programmes such as *Who Wants to Be a Millionaire, Walking with Dinosaurs, The Office, Teletubbies, Bob the Builder* and *The Weakest Link*. Sales of television products in a variety of forms increased by 83 per cent between 1998 and 2003, establishing Britain as the world's second leading exporter of TV products behind the US. The capacity to sell programmes, DVDs and videos, formats and licensing agreements has been facilitated by support from the government and fundamental changes in the regulatory environment.

De-regulation

The ability of these companies to grow in size and the expansion of trade in British media products are due to the relaxation of the rules and regulations governing the media. Control of the British newspaper industry has been largely by self-regulation.

Mergers and takeovers have been subject to the Fair Trading Act of 1973, which required that any merger that may be prejudicial to the public interest be referred to the Monopolies and Mergers Commission. Under the legislation, responsibility for monitoring what is happening rests with the Office of Fair Trading (OFT). The OFT's interpretation of the Act favoured prospective buyers of newspapers at the expense of the public interest. The political will is to push such mergers through – so much so that Rupert Murdoch has bought five newspaper titles without having ever been referred to the Monopolies and Mergers Commission.[19] In 1999, New Labour replaced the Monopolies and Merger Commission by a new Competition Commission to rule on mergers and acquisitions. While the government justified this move as 'taking politics out of the ownership debate',[20] it was also possible to see this move as prioritizing commercial considerations.

Take-overs of broadcasting companies have been more difficult due to the broad range of statutory controls under which broadcasting has developed – rules governing standards, impartiality, diversity and the range of programming as well as ownership. The 1990 Broadcasting Act relaxed some of these rules regarding ITV but still maintained control over who could own what. No newspaper group could hold more than a 20 per cent stake in a company or group that held an ITV franchise or the new Channel 5 or national radio, while ITV licence holders are restricted to a 20 per cent stake in national and local newspapers. ITV companies were allowed to own more than one franchise – provided they were not adjoining or both major franchises. These restrictions were watered down in the 1996 Broadcasting Act; newspapers which had no more than 20 per cent of national circulation were able to increase their holding in ITV companies while broadcasters were allowed to expand up to 15 per cent of the total television audience – including an increase in their interest in cable and satellite companies. The adjustments were justified on the grounds 'that fundamental changes are taking place in the media industries throughout the world' and relaxation was necessary 'to enable British TV to compete effectively on an international stage with large multi-media organisations in the United States and Europe' and 'play an active part in national and international markets'.[21] The relaxation of the cross-media ownership rules represented the success of the lobbying efforts of the large newspaper groups and ITV companies. The British Media Industry Group (BMIG) was at the forefront of their efforts. At first the government was cautious, not wanting to cross swords with Murdoch whose growing interests in Britain would be threatened by the increased competition such changes could bring. BSkyB and Murdoch's newspaper titles had been exempted from the legislation. However, the government relented – possibly because of the lack of support given to John Major by the Murdoch press in his re-election as Tory Party leader in 1994. Despite the successful lobbying of BMIG, press groups, with the exception of News Corporation, struggled to enter the broadcast industry in the late 1990s – in fact United Media withdrew from ITV as well as selling off its press interests. The 2003 Communications Act removed most of the remaining limitations on cross-media ownership, including allowing non-EU ownership within the British broadcasting market, thereby opening up the way for the emergence of ITV plc and the extension of Murdoch's interest across the industry. Policing the new arrangements was a new regulatory body.

Birth of the 'super-regulator'

The establishment of the Office of Communication (Ofcom) in 2003 represented a new development in the history of regulation of the British media. It took over the functions previously discharged by several regulators, including the Independent Television Commission (ITC), Radio Authority, Oftel which had previously regulated the telecommunications sector and the Broadcasting Standards Council (BSC). Only the BBC remained outside the new regulatory arrangements, although on certain matters such as meeting 'the highest general standards' in respect of 'the contents of the programmes', 'the quality of the programme making' and the 'professional skill and editorial integrity applied in the making of the programmes' and maintaining independent production quotas the Corporation is subject to Ofcom.[22] Besides regulating media ownership, Ofcom is responsible for the rules governing media content. Responding to the rapidly changing technological environment (see Chapter 13), the regulatory regime seeks to be sufficiently flexible to respond to the rapidly expanding amount of content and content providers in the digital era. To facilitate this aim, three tiers of regulation were introduced: the first tier sets minimum standards for all broadcasters while tiers two and three consist of quantitative and qualitative provisions for public service broadcasters. The main thrust is to further limit the obligations placed on broadcasters. Commercial operations such as Sky and other cable and satellite are only bound by broad rules such as those governing taste and decency. More is demanded of those channels with public service responsibilities such as BBC, ITV, Channels 4 and 5 but Ofcom's initial expectation was that the broadcasters themselves would monitor their performance.[23] Ofcom nevertheless was involved in levying fines on ITV and BBC for the misuse of premium rate phone services and conducting unfair competitions, drawing attention to serious institutional failure in the case of the former.[24]

Unlike previous regulators who defined their role in terms of both cultural and economic objectives, Ofcom's responsibility is to 'facilitate a thriving communications market'.[25] On the surface the new regulator commits to balancing the needs of citizens and consumers and promoting choice and competition in the communications industries. The reality is that Ofcom's primary commitment is to advance commercial competitiveness. This was illustrated by the absence of any reference to the role of the media in developing and sustaining citizenship in the initial legislation leading up to the 2003 Act. It was only after a concerted campaign and a prolonged battle in the House of Lords that the new regulatory body was obliged to 'further the interests of the citizen'. Promoting the interests of the citizen has been subordinate to furthering the wants of the consumer.[26] Ofcom has struggled to incorporate citizenship into its operation. This is, for example, clear in the way in which it has allowed ITV plc to withdraw from its regional commitments. The 2003 Act stipulated detailed requirements about the amount and scheduling of regional programming. However, the super-regulator has allowed ITV plc to marginalize regional programmes on the network, appearing to accept the company's argument of commercial necessity rather than the region's requirement for its own programming.

The 2003 Act left Ofcom's relationship with the BBC unresolved. Calls have been made for the BBC to be brought under Ofcom and the super-regulator has undertaken several studies of the future of public service broadcasting in the digital era. The renewal of the BBC Charter in 2006 produced a heated debate about the services the Corporation provides as well as its financing and governance. What is the appropriate use of the licence fee in a rapidly changing broadcasting environment needs to be discussed. Ofcom has suggested several possible ways forward including the distribution of the licence fee to other broadcasters to provide public service content. The highly sensitive nature of this debate has been accentuated by the nature of the licence fee settlement as part of the renewal of the Charter; it was less than the BBC expected and has produced cutbacks, job losses and a major re-evaluation of the services that the Corporation supplies. In the meantime there were radical changes in the way in which the BBC is governed. New Labour proposed a new board, the BBC Trust, should replace the Governors. It argued that the Trust would be more 'representative' of society and avoid the failure of the Governors who were seen as too close to BBC management and unable to represent the wider public interest.[27] That the government maintain the right to appoint Trust members indicates their conception of representation was fairly narrow. New services would be assessed through a public value test, previously conducted by ministers, and competition matters would be part of the considerations that would determine approval of new services. The Trust started operating in 2007 and soon rejected proposals for the BBC to develop local television services.

Return of the local?

The fragmentation of the media audience has seen the growth of specialized media responding to niche markets and particular interests. De-regulation has brought about changes in local and regional media. At the local level, the British newspaper industry has experienced an 'eruption of change' since the 1990s. The resurgence of the Scottish press system is one example. Scotland has always had a tradition of a strong, national newspaper industry. Distance from London enabled it to escape the 'nationalization' of the British press in the early twentieth century. Scottish editions of London papers were printed to compete with locally produced products. By the 1970s, they had left the field to the Scottish press, dominated by the *Daily Record* which had a circulation of around 800,000 in Scotland. Nearly 90 per cent of the papers read by Scots were produced in

Scotland. The Wapping revolution led to attempts by London papers to break into the Scottish market by returning to Scottish editions. Most significant was the *Sun* which on 23 January 1992 shocked the Scottish nation with an edition that carried on its front page a giant St Andrew's cross with the headline: *RISE NOW AND BE A NATION*. The *Sun* stated that after 'thinking long and hard' it has come to the conclusion that 'Scotland's destiny lies as an independent nation within the European Community'. The *Sun's* conversion was not an indication of a political change of heart but of the strength of the Scottish newspaper market. Since the devolution of law-making powers to a Scottish Parliament in 1997 the *Sun* has increased its circulation in Scotland at the expense of the indigenous newspapers. By 2006, it surpassed that circulation of the *Daily Record* which has plummeted, along with that of Scotland's four indigenous daily newspapers which have experienced a decline of around 30 per cent in their sales since the late 1970s.

Locality also found a voice in the development of commercial radio in the 1990s. From the end of the Second World War, radio was rapidly superseded by television. Two factors played an important role in ensuring that radio had a future as a medium of mass communication. In the 1960s, technology brought about the cheap, portable transistor radio. This allowed radio to move from the living room onto the streets of Britain where it became closely associated with the growth of 'youth culture'. The transistor could be taken anywhere and listened to at any time with consequences for what was broadcast. Continuous pop music in demand from the 'baby boom' generation became the ideal output for the radio.[28] The BBC was slow to realize and respond. It was 'pirate radio', such as Radio Caroline, which started broadcasting from a ship in the Thames estuary in March 1964 that was at the forefront of the changes in the output of radio. By 1967 it was clear the pirates were making serious inroads into the BBC's audience. As a result the BBC launched Radio 1 to satisfy young people's radio needs.

In the same year, the BBC started local radio when Radio Leicester went on air. This was to replace the regional network which was eventually phased out in 1983. Within five years the IBA had responded to the BBC's initiative by launching independent local radio. In 1973, Capital Radio and the London Broadcasting Company, a news operation, opened.[29] The history of independent local radio in the 1970s and 1980s was uneven. Some stations were successful, others failed and a number of closures and mergers took place. The economic recession hit the sector's advertising revenue and the legal requirements placed on independent local radio in editorial and technical matters – for example, to provide certain kinds of programming, in particular a news service, and maintain equipment which conformed to high standards – affected its operation by keeping costs high. Such requirements failed to provide many stations with a distinct image which would attract advertisers and cater for a range of interests and groups in the community. The result was the return of pirate stations serving smaller groups and communities. Initially such operations were confined to stations serving hospitals, university campuses and housing estates. But soon more than 50 community radio stations, mostly serving the ethnic communities in Britain, were on air. Attempts by government to shut down such stations proved futile – as soon as the pirate was closed it was able to re-establish itself in another location. Operating costs were low, as bedrooms, garages and warehouses became the studios for such enterprises. Unimpeded by regulation, these stations could deliver the niche markets advertisers were looking for by providing an output that attracted the listeners.[30]

The 1990 Broadcasting Act re-organized radio in the British Isles. A separate authority to regulate radio was established and independent radio was no longer obliged to provide a range of programming. A host of radio stations were established at the local and regional level, bringing the total of independent radio stations to 150 as well as three new national commercial radio stations. Licences were granted to Talk Radio, Virgin Radio and Classic FM. By contrast, the BBC had 38 local stations and one new national service, launched in 1990, and revamped in 1994 as Radio 5 Live, a 24 hours a day news and sport service. In 1994, the audience for commercial radio surpassed that of the BBC, with the combined advertising revenue of commercial radio increasing from £60.8 million in 1992 to £178.5 million in 1995.[31] On the surface the de-regulation of British radio would seem to offer diversity of programming. However, diversity is in reality limited by a number of factors. Most of Britain's local stations are owned by a small number of larger companies. Companies such as Radio Clyde, which controls virtually every major radio station in Scotland, dominate large areas of the British Isles and commercial considerations make such companies play safe in terms of the content of their stations. Output is dominated by talk and music and there is a remarkable similarity to what is heard over the airwaves across the UK. As the NUJ put it: 'Travel from London to Bournemouth, and whichever commercial radio station you tune to, you will hear the same format, the same records and even the same voice saying, "We promise not to talk over your favourite records".'[32] The 'localness' of the stations is further diminished by the practice of taking feeds from other stations in the region owned by the same organization.[33] Local commercial radio is also under threat from the new national stations which have increased the competition for advertising revenue. The outcome has been the amalgamation of local stations in certain areas to increase the size of the market for advertising. Larger regional stations developed at the expense of the local community stations. Some of the latter have gone bust, including Sunset Radio, the first community ethnic station, in 1993.

The BBC in the 1990s pledged more money and commitment to regional production for the television network. BBC production in the nation-regions of Scotland, Wales and Northern Ireland as well as the regions of England fell dramatically during the second part of the 1980s. Total regional production fell by 23 per cent between 1987/88 and 1991/92, a situation which John Birt described on taking over as Director-General as 'indefensibly low'.[34] A BBC-commissioned survey of the audience – published as *People and Programmes* – found that many regarded the BBC as metropolitan and middle class and failing to provide a range of programmes to cater for all groups in society. This was at a time of renewed interest in local, regional and nation-regional broadcasting in Britain. Dubbed the 'new regionalism', local media development was seen as important, not only in assisting cultural representation but also in promoting economic activity. Spurred on by Channel Four, local production became part of the development strategies of a number of cities and regions throughout the United Kingdom.[35] In 1994, the BBC allocated £75 million to regional production, designating centres of excellence in Birmingham, Bristol and Manchester and moving two departments, Youth and Entertainments Features and Religious Programmes from London to Manchester. But there was much controversy over Birt's regional initiative. Critics argued that the initiative did not encourage regions or nations to produce material about life in their part of the world to show to the rest of Britain. The thrust was to shift London programmes – and the production values that accompany them – to the regions and nations of Britain. For the former head of BBC World Service, John Tusa, the new BBC regional policy was a sham – 'in practice the only beneficiaries have not been the audience but the bureaucrats policing the system and British Rail's Intercity as producers and presenters roam the regional headquarters of the BBC making programmes that are truly regional in name only'.[36]

The lead-up to the renewal of the BBC charter in 2006 saw a more concerted effort by the Corporation to devolve broadcasting to the regions and nations. A commitment was made to decant a proportion of BBC programme-making from London to Manchester; the new BBC centre at Salford Quay would host children's programming, BBC Sport and Radio 5. This devolution, according to DG Mark Thompson, represents the promise of the 'biggest injection of regional investment we've ever made'.[37] It builds on successful network development in the regions and nations such as BBC Wales's remaking of *Dr Who*. However, it is not without its opponents, many of whom are within the BBC and resistant to moving out of London.[38] There are also concerns that the BBC as an organization has still not come to terms with the new realities created by the devolution of some political power to Scotland, Wales and Northern Ireland. The King Review, commissioned by the Trust in 2008, highlighted the failure of BBC News and Current Affairs to adequately and properly report the devolved political landscape of Britain.[39]

The relationship between the local and the global in British media development in the 1990s was clearly illustrated by the attempts to launch the new television channel, Channel 5, which began broadcasting in 1997. The new channel, to be financed through advertising, was initially conceived of as an antidote to metropolitan bias of British terrestrial television. The IBA, the then regulatory body for commercial television, stated in 1989 that it would look favourably on the channel developing a 'distinctive non-metropolitan identity' as well as encouraging 'local sources of programme supply'.[40] However, the majority of bidders for the new franchise had little or no interest in local broadcasting. They represented the large, global corporations who saw the franchise as a potentially lucrative investment. Gradually these players withdrew as they assessed the prospects of the channel. As a result, only one bid was made. That was rejected by the ITC in 1992 on the grounds that the bidder would not be able to maintain the service for the duration of the franchise. The franchise was re-advertised and awarded in 1995 to a consortium of existing broadcasters, including Pearson and MAI. The success of Channel 5 was dependent on the commercial backing of the large global media players. According to Robins and Cornford, the experience of Channel 5 'shows how local and regional media have to accommodate to the forces of globalization'.[41] The global corporations are the real shapers and shakers in the industry and their commercial interests and muscle determine the environment in which other players operate. Regional and local interests have to come to terms with this reality.

The decline of investigative journalism

The growth of a more commercial media dominated by a smaller number of firms that privilege profit is associated with a decline in the standards of journalism. One of the main justifications for journalism is that it provides citizens with the necessary information they need to participate in political life and make informed decisions between different policies and political parties. The Royal Commission on the Press in 1977 identified the role of journalism and the media as to 'inform their readers about the world and interpret it to them' and 'act as watch-dogs for citizens, by scrutinizing concentrations of power'. The Commission acknowledged that the press seeks to entertain as well as inform but 'it is the performance of these serious functions which justifies the high importance which democracies attach to a free press'.[42] These functions act as the *raison d'être* of journalists; and are called forth by most journalists wherever they defend themselves and their profession against criticism. The way in which journalism and the media perform these functions has been subject to criticism throughout the history of mass communication but since the late 1990s the ability of the media and journalism to act as a 'watchdog' has been challenged by technological change, the new structure of broadcasting which works against serious and challenging journalism and programming, the concentration of ownership in Fleet Street and other parts of the British media, the increasing competition between media and the decline of resources, manpower and time available for campaigning journalism.

Parts of the British press established a reputation in the post-war period for campaigning journalism. The high point was reached in the 1970s with the *Sunday Times* Insight team, which specialized in the exposure of corruption, incompetence and illegality. These efforts were matched in television by *World in Action* and *This Week*. Crusading journalism had blossomed in the political atmosphere of the 1960s when authority was regularly challenged. This was the press and broadcasting fulfilling its role as the 'fourth estate' to its utmost.

A decline in the nature and amount of investigative journalism in the British media has been a feature of recent years. In the popular press such journalism has become confined to digging up dirt and revealing secrets about the private lives of the Royals, MPs, footballers and rock stars. The resignation of Paul Foot in 1993 brought to an end the *Daily Mirror*'s tradition of hard-hitting, political investigations. In the quality press, competition and new owners have acted to curtail investigative work. Harold Evans, the editor of the *Sunday Times* in the 1970s, had considerable freedom to develop crusading journalism under Roy Thomson. His successors have had less room for manoeuvre with Murdoch. More than 100 journalists, including most of the leading reporters of the pre-Murdoch era, left the *Sunday Times* between 1981 and 1986.[43] Conglomerate ownership has further enmeshed newspapers into a web of financial and industrial interests, making it more difficult to investigate some issues for fear of producing information damaging to their corporate bosses.

Unable to compete with television to provide the news, the press has focused more on features and colour pieces. Anthony Sampson[44] has complained about the decline of critical reporting in the quality press:

> **Investigations have been almost abandoned. There are no new Orwells or Priestleys, to inspect the rest of the country or to describe what happens behind the servant's entrance to the hotel or across the railway tracks. Instead there is an explosion of columns providing comment without facts, discussing friends, parties and other journalists.**

The result is an end to 'the time when investigative journalism was largely led by the Press'.[45] Television took over the mantle of campaigning journalism but the changes in broadcasting have emasculated the tradition. The demise of the ITV system has witnessed the decline of the traditional centres of such journalism: Thames TV's *This Week* disappeared from the screens with the company's loss of the franchise for the London region, Yorkshire TV's financial plight brought about the curtailment of its documentary output while ITV flagship current affairs programme, *World in Action*, had 'to operate in an inclement environment and at a less hospitable time' before vanishing from the schedules in 1998.[46] The new competitive climate driven by ratings has made it more difficult to mount serious investigative journalism in prime time. *World in Action* in its heyday had always been scheduled opposite BBC's *Panorama* ensuring that the audience had to watch current affairs. ITV's new attitude to challenging journalism was summed up in the comments of one senior executive who said in 1992 that 'If *World in Action* were to uncover three more serious miscarriages of justice while delivering an audience of three, four or five million, I would cut it. It isn't part of the ITV system to get people out of prison.'[47]

Panorama and Channel's Four's *Dispatches* continue to carry exposés but the new current affairs programmes such as ITV's *The Big Story, Tonight with Trevor Macdonald* and 3D and BBC's *Here and Now* were more magazine in format, often with three items in half an hour. Most of the stories were discrete investigations – as Bob Woffinden points out, they tended to be 'self contained, complete stories' which 'creates discontinuous journalism: there is no continuing flow of inquiry, no persistent invigilation of a subject'.[48] That many were produced by independent companies meant that once the programme is broadcast the knowledge gained by the journalists on the topic was lost. Independent companies are less likely to take the risk of lengthy investigative journalism as a result of their lack of resources and financial and institutional insecurity. Investigative journalism was compromised by the increasing involvement of private companies in the sponsorship of ITV programmes. But the commitment of public service broadcasters to current affairs and investigative journalism has also waned. *Panorama* wandered around the schedule for a period, shifted from weekday prime time to a Sunday night slot before settling down to a Monday evening. Serious programming has decreased in prime time, to be replaced by a new genre, factual entertainment, with the BBC pioneering programmes such as *Airport, Driving School* and *Hotel* which, according to the BBC, are 'observational documentaries . . . revealing new facets of contemporary Britain'.[49] The reality is that news, current affairs and other forms of serious television are increasing part of a ratings-driven, entertainment-oriented television culture.

The world of infotainment

Today we are living in an era in which there is a keen sense that standards are in decline in every aspect of our lives, educational, political, sporting, cultural and even climatic. Falling standards, as we have noted, have always been part of the discourse of popular culture and the media but they are acutely expressed in present times. Dumbing down is seen as a defining feature of the contemporary British media, and in particular television. Bob Franklin has described how 'entertainment has superseded the provision of information; human interest has supplanted the public interest; measured judgement has succumbed to sensationalism; the trivial has triumphed over the weighty; the intimate relationship of celebrities . . . are judged more newsworthy than the reporting of significant issues and events of international consequence'.[50] The ascendancy of entertainment that Franklin identified in the late 1990s is now further entrenched in the media. Broadsheet newspapers today are beginning to resemble their tabloid counterparts. Most of them have adopted a smaller size, whether tabloid or 'compact' or 'Berliner' as in the case of the *Guardian*. Features have been extended to incorporate subject matter such as work, media, pop music, parenthood, lifestyle, childhood and other kinds of 'soft news' which have not traditionally featured in the pages of the quality press. The layout and style of the broadsheets came to resemble that of the popular press; screaming, bold headlines with shorter words, more and bigger colour pictures and less text and more white space.[51] Today's *Guardian* carries fewer stories on its front page than the *Mirror* did in the 1960s. Their front pages are full of bold, colourful blurb, drawing the reader's attention to stories on the inside pages that previously would not have been given space. Celebrity columnists writing about their own lives – the 'me' column – are more commonplace. Giveaway CDs and DVDs – and more recently wall-charts – have been used to add readers. News is increasingly seen as lost among a tsunami of trivial and sensational copy and the personal opinions of a growing number of celebrity columnists.

Television is also pursuing a more populist and tabloid news agenda. ITV's evening news contains more lifestyle and celebrity stories and BBC news coverage has been criticized for containing more 'Madonna than Mugabe'.[52] The changing news agenda can be seen as a response to the declining interest in news; viewing figures for television news dropped by more than 10 per cent between 1994 and 2002.[53] Younger people are turning from newspapers and television to the internet for their news. But even more are turning to the new 'reality' formats that have come to dominate British television in the twenty-first century. The rise of factual entertainment formats is seen as 'emblematic of the dumbing down of British television'.[54] Programmes covering cookery, crime, fashion, gardening, property, DIY and makeovers and animals came to dominate the schedules. For critics they represented a shift in the balance between entertainment and information. They were supplemented by reality television programmes such as *Big Brother*, a Dutch format which triumphed around the world, making considerable financial gain for its creator, Endemol. Shows such as *Pop Idol, The X Factor* and *Strictly Come Dancing* are able to command huge audiences, emptying the pubs and becoming the centre of popular discussion. The winners of *The X Factor* and *Strictly Come Dancing* – as well as the ups and downs of the contestants – are newsworthy, sometimes headlining nightly news bulletins. Police and emergency services programmes such as *Caught on Camera, America's Most Wanted, Blues and Twos, Police, Camera, Action* and 999 are also a popular form of factual entertainment. The combination of 'authentic' footage of police chases and emergency rescues with eye witness testimony, narrative fictional style and commentary from experts or authoritative presenters has brought ratings success for a format that has been labelled as 'trauma TV'.[55] With ordinary members of the public becoming celebrities and ordinary viewers determining the outcome of programmes, many believe a shift is taking place in the relationship between audiences and those who produce television. Viewers were seen as 'empowered', an opinion reinforced by their participation in chat shows such as *The Jerry Springer Show*. The reality, however, was highlighted by the recent phone-in scandals when it was shown that the votes of many of those who called in had no bearing on the outcome of the contest.

The rise of the spin doctors

Debates about the quality of journalism have to be seen in the context of the growing resources devoted by other social institutions to the manipulation and management of the news. Since 1945, there has been a growth in 'promotional culture'. There has been a steady rise in publicity, advertising and image management in most areas of public life. During the 1980s and 1990s matters started to spin out of control as the distinction between official publicity and party propaganda in the government information services became increasingly blurred. In addition, political parties and pressure groups became more reliant on using the mass media to present their policies. The mushrooming of the amount of money, time, resources and efforts devoted by political parties and interests to packaging politicians and policies highlighted a qualitative change in the nature of British politics. What are referred to the 'dark arts of political persuasion' were taken to new heights under Tony Blair's New Labour government.[56] The men behind Blair's electoral triumphs, Peter Mandelson and Alastair Campbell, are credited with the establishment of the 'public relations state' in which news management and information manipulation are central to the operation of government. Spin doctoring has a long history but it was with the arrival of television in the 1950s that it took the first step on the road to becoming central to the nature and conduct of British politics.

Television was able to deliver a captive, mass audience to the politician. Whereas politicians of the pre-war years travelled the length and breadth of the British Isles to convey their message to the public, the rise of television allowed post-war politicians to sit in the comfort of a television studio to reach an audience the size of which their predecessors could only dream. At first they were wary of the new medium. Churchill dismissed television as the 'idiot's lantern'. A private screen test showed that he was not telegenic and he abandoned efforts to use the medium for his political advantage. Eden was the first prime minister to grasp the importance of television. He used to broadcast directly to the nation and helped to develop the party political broadcast (PPB). During the 1955 general election, the PPB was the only kind of TV coverage on offer. The BBC reported nothing else about the campaign. However, Eden illustrated that television was a double-edged sword for politicians – as Michael Cockerell[57] shows, he was the first political figure to highlight 'that those who live by the box, can also die by the box'. He tried to use television to rally the nation during the Suez Crisis. However, the conditions of his broadcast – poor lighting forced Eden to wear glasses for the first time, and occasionally he stumbled over the script – made it 'not a happy experience'. Eden appeared vulnerable and more human than prime ministers should. His credibility was damaged for the rest of the Suez Crisis. Politicians subsequently became more concerned about how they looked than what they said to camera.

Such concerns were translated into the emergence of a huge political public relations industry. Prime Ministers and leading political figures began to master the skills and techniques that an effective TV performance demanded. Harold Macmillan realized that TV was about images and impressions and he exploited his visits abroad and meetings with world leaders for domestic political advantage. The image of 'Supermac' was born – television created a picture of a prime minister who was quiet, calm, in charge, unfazed, always reminding people that they had never had it so good while jetting off to the far-flung corners of the world to soothe international tension by personal diplomacy. The 1959 General Election was the first contest fought by television. The restrictions on political broadcasting had been set aside and nearly three-quarters of the British population had television sets. In the new media environment the Labour campaign was masterminded by Tony Benn, who focused on building up the Labour leader, Hugh Gaitskell, as a prime minister-in-waiting. Despite the success and slickness of the Labour campaign, in the personality stakes, Gaitskell proved no match for Supermac. Macmillan's final TV election address drew the highest viewing figures of the campaign. It gained considerable praise in the press, even from the Labour supporting papers, such as the *Daily Mirror* which described it as a 'real corker'. The most dramatic part of the broadcast was singled out by Edward Heath as the moment when Macmillan walked over to a globe, spun it around and said 'Let me tell you what I am going to do about the rest of the world.' The impact was considerable and by the end of the election Macmillan was the best-liked and best-known prime minister in British history. His party won an overwhelming victory and Macmillan's use of television was seen as crucial.[58]

Between 1959 and 1974, political parties adjusted to using the news media, especially television, to build up the image of politicians and package their policies. The adjustment included a considerable increase in spending on election campaigns, the employment of party pollsters and publicity agents as well as advertising agencies to present the party's TV commercials, posters and newspaper advertisements. In 1964, Labour PM Harold Wilson made use of a variety of presentational skills and techniques to conduct his campaign, which included American-style showbiz rallies. An election rally held at Wembley in 1964 brought together Welsh male voice choirs, jazz bands, colliery brass bands, African drummers as well as a range of pop and show business stars to support the Labour cause.[59] Wilson drew on the television performance of John F. Kennedy in the United States to present an image of a vibrant, young and dynamic, man-of-the-people leader. He introduced the 'soundbite' into British politics. Television with its limit on time preferred short, concise slogans rather than long discursive outlines of policy. By the 1990s the average length of a soundbite on the main evening news bulletins had dropped to 23 seconds.[60] The 'quantum leap' in packaging politics came with Mrs Thatcher's arrival in Downing Street.

Mrs Thatcher has been dubbed the most 'media-conscious' British prime minister – she was described as 'the mistress of the pre-planned, carefully packaged appearance'.[61] She was groomed for television. Her media advisor, Gordon Reece, paid careful attention to how she looked and sounded. She had lessons to 'relax and lower her voice' – 'think low, before you answer a question', she was told by Reece, because 'you become more tense and nervous and your voice automatically becomes higher'.[62] Reece also advised her on what to wear on television and about her hair style and make-up. Planned 'photo opportunities' were carefully arranged and 'uncontrolled' television appearances were avoided at all costs. Reece stressed that what was said on television was not as important as what a person looked like. He rationed her television appearances and drew up a list of interviewers by whom she would not be interviewed. He also brought into the campaign team the advertising agency Saatchi and Saatchi. They applied the techniques of market research to ascertain voting intentions and voter attitudes, including the use of 'focus groups' which were to become as essential ingredient in the way in which her successor, Tony Blair, sold the policies of New Labour. Political adverts and broadcasts were tested on these groups and if found successful were incorporated into the Conservative campaign. Tim Bell, the Chairman of Saatchi, who handled the 1979 and 1983 elections for the Tory Party, based the campaigns on 'the emotional attitudes which emerge when ordinary people discuss polities'. He talked of the 'hours of discussion about finding the right tone, which had to be "warm, confident, non-divisive and exciting"'.[63] The result was slick advertising, emotional television appeals, selective photo opportunities and highly packaged and presented issues and personalities. The electoral triumphs of the Conservative Party in the 1980s led the other political parties – as well as pressure groups – to copy the formula. Under Tony Blair, 'spin' and PR became pervasive in British politics. Not only was daily politics put into a perpetual campaigning mode but the machinery of the State was also deployed to promote the government's achievements and present positive images of ministers and their activities. As a result, government information was professionalized, centralized and politicized.[64]

The growth of the Whitehall 'good news machine'

The growth of PR has been a source of great contention in central government. Government information has been the responsibility of the Central Office of Information (COI), established by the Attlee government in 1946 as a successor to the wartime MOI. Unlike the MOI the new body was non-political, with no ministerial head and no policy-making function: it simply had the task of informing the citizens of government actions that impinged on their daily lives. However, the birth of the COI was surrounded by the suspicion that the new body would serve as a propaganda tool for the party in power. The *Daily Express* told its readers that public relations officers would be 'propaganda agents for the party in power and with the best of intentions could never be anything else' and that the new system was a 'direct menace to one of our fundamental freedoms'.[65] These suspicions were never removed, despite the fact that for the public the COI was only associated with the presentation of the Highway Code and drink-driving campaigns. They, however, returned in full force in the 1980s as a result of the widespread changes of government information practices undertaken by Mrs Thatcher.

The government publicity machine underwent a complete overhaul in the 1980s under the directing hand of Bernard Ingham who throughout the period was Press Secretary to Mrs Thatcher. Ingham reorganized the Whitehall 'good news machine' to centralize the flow of government information through the press office at Number Ten thereby marginalizing the COI. In 1989, Ingham, in an unprecedented step, was appointed head of the Government Information Services (GIS), a job formerly held by the head of the COI, a civil service appointment. At the same time expenditure on government publicity grew rapidly. By 1990, the government had become the largest advertiser in Britain, surpassing Unilever and Proctor and Gamble, by spending £98 million that year.[66] Ingham also made vigorous use of the Lobby system to promote the government's position. Changes in the Lobby system since the 1950s, including the growth of the collective, 'off the record' briefing of journalists, the drawing up of a set of rules of attribution and the use of the body as the main conduit for the release of government information, have turned the body into a more 'passive purveyor of government messages'.[67] Ingham was an assiduous briefer of the reporters, using the conventions of the Lobby not only to set the political agenda for the day but also to orchestrate campaigns against political opponents of Mrs Thatcher inside the Conservative Party and the Cabinet. The political manipulation of the Lobby brought about increasing criticism of the system, from both journalists and politicians. In 1986, three newspapers, the *Guardian*, the *Independent* and the *Scotsman* withdrew from the Lobby, stating they would no longer abide by the system of non-attribution and 'off the record' briefings. Ingham's response underlined his basic hostility to the press. He refused to cooperate with reporters of the offending publications and dismissed 'investigative reporters' as a 'small effortlessly self-regarding clique'.[68] A greater surprise was the response of the media – a vote of Lobby members found a majority of them supporting the system. The matter was resolved following Mrs Thatcher's fall when the new PM's Press Secretary was able to convince the newspapers to re-enter the Lobby. John Major's Press Secretary also relinquished heading up the GIS, thereby allaying the fears of the concentration of power in the hands of Number Ten. Robert Harris, Ingham's unofficial biographer, describes how Ingham as the PM's personal media advisor, the government's official spokesman and the head of the information service had in all but title become Britain's minister of information.[69]

The centralization of information and the emphasis on 'selling' policy were returned to in the Blair's years. As Director of Communications at Number Ten, Alastair Campbell, a former Fleet Street political correspondent, brought the government information services directly under the control of the Prime Minster. The resources, spending, manpower and attention paid to framing information and news to favour government policy increased considerably. Behind the claim to be modernizing the government information machine to meet the demands of a rapidly changing media and information environment, the Blair government is criticized for driving a 'coach and horses through the established tradition of government neutrality' over the provision of information.[70] An unprecedented number of special advisors were appointed to by-pass uncooperative civil servants and an unprecedented number of civil servants in senior information posts were replaced or resigned.[71] This shift was accompanied by an exponential growth in the number of information officers employed by government. Setting aside those working in public relations and special advisors, the number of press officers employed by government increased from 300 in 1997 to 1815 by 2006.[72] Spin came to characterize the Blair government, and what was perceived as the cynical, bullying and contemptuous attitude that New Labour's spin machine adopted to civil servants and the media was satirized in shows such as Channel 4's *The Thick of It* and epitomized by the email sent by one New Labour spin doctor stating that September 11th was a good day to bury bad news. By New Labour's second term, central control had been established by Number Ten which vetted the content of all major speeches, press releases and policy initiatives as well as determined their timing, how they were announced and who could make appearances in the media.[73]

The exceptional control Blair exercised over the flow of government information was not without its critics in the media, Westminster, the civil service and inside the Cabinet. The outcome of the discontent was a number of enquiries into the performance of the government's information service, culminating in the Phillis Inquiry. Set up in 2003, following the reporting of 'Cheriegate' which concerned the involvement of the prime minister's wife with an alleged 'conman' who was the partner of her 'lifestyle guru', the review examined the effectiveness of the government information service, the relations between special advisors and civil servants and the appropriate boundaries that should exists between them.[74] Phillis's Review coincided with the Iraq War and the furore over what was reported by a BBC journalist as the 'sexing up' of a government document that provided the pretext for going to war. Tension between the government and the BBC over the reporting of the government's case for invading Iraq had been rising before Andrew Gilligan's report. His claim led to the complete breakdown of relations and a subsequent official inquiry into how the BBC and government handled subsequent events. While the inquiry exonerated Campbell, he had resigned before its publication. The evidence amassed had undermined Campbell's credibility as well as his relationship with the media. His master was also damaged, becoming a 'lame duck' for the remainder of his time in office. Spin was declared not to be central to the administration of the new Prime Minister, Gordon Brown, a declaration apparently supported by the recommendations of the Phillis Review which argued for a streamlined service headed up by a permanent secretary and aided by a political advisor.[75] Many were critical of the report which they saw as providing approval for the further centralization of the information service and it was not long before criticism emerged from officials within the government's information machine that it was 'business as usual'. Many were sceptical of Brown anti-spin stance, particularly after the botched attempt to spin an early election in 2005.

The Hutton Inquiry whitewash

The Hutton Inquiry was a major event in the history of the BBC's relationship with the State. It was established to examine the claim made by the BBC in a report on the Radio Four *Today* programme that the government had misinformed the public in presenting the case for going to war in Iraq. The report by Andrew Gilligan that the government had 'sexed up' the intelligence to mislead the public into believing that Iraq had the capacity to deploy weapons of mass destruction within 45 minutes led indirectly to the death of Dr David Kelly, a weapon inspector, who was the alleged source of the story. The PM's spin doctor Alistair Campbell had made the rounds of the media, famously bursting into Channel Four News when on air, to demand an apology and retraction. The government released Kelly's name. Hutton, a former judge, found in favour of the government, exonerating them from all culpability, either in embellishing the case for war or in the circumstances leading up to Dr Kelly's death. Hutton reserved all his criticism for the BBC and its journalism, concluding that the allegations made by Gilligan were 'unfounded' and the BBC's editorial system was 'defective'. Such an outcome was described by most of the press as a 'whitewash' and the gap between the evidence gathered by Hutton which was published in full on the net as witnesses gave their evidence, including the Prime Minister, and Hutton's conclusion further undermined public trust in Britain's political institutions. Polls found that the public overwhelming believed the BBC.

Hutton's findings had considerable repercussions for the BBC and critical journalism in the UK. The Director-General and the Chairman of the BBC resigned and reporter Andrew Gilligan left the Corporation. Greg Dyke and Gavyn Davies had been supporters of the Labour Party and the failure of the BBC Governors to support them was described as 'spineless'. BBC staff felt that their managers had been 'too conciliatory' in response to the government following publication of the report. Morale was further dented by the series of internal inquiries set up by the BBC. Everyone involved in the story was subject to an internal disciplinary procedure, the Charter renewal submission was delayed and the BBC complaints procedure was overhauled. Tension mounted as a report in the *Observer* (28 March 2004) stated that some senior staff threatened to 'walk out' because of the 'Politburo style' nature of the internal inquiry. The Neil Review into the BBC's handling of the affair made a variety of recommendations to tighten up stories based on single sources, the conduct of two-way live interviews and the handling of external complaints. In the run-up to the renewal of the BBC's Charter in 2006, the Corporation seemed to bend over backwards to put its house in order – despite the fact that public opinion appeared to support the BBC and its reporting. The failure of corporate nerve would return to haunt the BBC as even relatively innocuous incidents such as the comments made to Andrew Sachs by Russell Brand and Jonathan Ross could quickly escalate into judgements about the BBC's editorial processes.

Source: Kuhn, R. (2007) *Politics and the Media in Britain*, London: Palgrave, pp. 192–9; Wring, D. (2006) 'Politics and the media', *Parliamentary Affairs*, 58(2): 38–86; Temple, M. (2008) *The British Press*, London: McGraw-Hill, pp. 159–64.

The notion that spin would end with Campbell and Blair's departure was always implausible. So engrained into the body politic were the 'dark arts' of spin and public relations they had become an essential ingredient of the world of journalism. PR consultant Julia Hobsbawm draws on a survey by the PR industry to state that 80 per cent of financial news and between 40 and 50 per cent of general news is directly influenced by PR.[76] *Guardian* journalist Nick Davies documents the rise of 'churnalism' whereby journalists recycle, often uncritically, PR material.[77] His assertion is supported by research that has found that 'nearly one in five newspaper stories' and 17 per cent of broadcast stories examined in 2006 were taken, either wholly or mainly, from PR material or activity.[78] For one leading British journalist, much of the content of newspapers and broadcast news is 'suggested, or in the extreme actually written by public relations people'.[79] PR and spin are not confined to the reporting of politics: publicist Max Clifford is the most prominent figure in a blossoming industry which promotes celebrities and their 'kiss'n'tell' stories. Sport, travel, lifestyle and a range of other kinds of stories are influenced by PR professionals. David Miller and William Dinan[80] have documented how the PR sector grew 11 times in real terms between 1979 and 1998. The rise of the profession is a response to the gaps that have grown in the capacity of the news media to collect information. Larger newspapers with more sections and supplements, more television and radio bulletins including the arrival of 24-hour rolling news and online pages which need constant updating have added to the demands made of the journalist. More space to fill more quickly means the media and journalism are increasingly reliant on PR-generated stories and have little time to check their veracity. Technological change, commercial pressures and the expansion of media outlets have brought about what could be described as the colonization of journalism by the PR industry. The appointment of the head of a PR firm first as head of Ofcom and then the Number Ten Policy Unit under Gordon Brown attests to the growing influence of the PR professional on the politics and media in Britain.

Consumers or citizens?

A new commercial media order has developed rapidly since the dawn of the new millennium. The de-regulation of broadcasting in the first decade of the twenty-first century is comparable to the repeal of the 'taxes of knowledge' in the mid-nineteenth century which freed the press from the shackles of the State but tied them to the limits of the market. The increasing concentration of ownership of the British mass media is entrusting considerable power to people whose interests in local and national communities are minimal. The decline of public service media, highlighted by the growing commercialization of the BBC, the demise of ITV and the increasingly market-driven nature of the press are potentially detrimental to democracy and culture in Britain. Echoing – and sometimes evoking – the warnings of nineteenth-century critics, such as Matthew Arnold, many argue that insufficient attention has been paid to the cultural implications of technological and economic change. The relentless search to maximize profits is not only driving out information at the expense of more entertainment but also is a direct threat to literary culture and reading. The extension of visual communication is changing the nature of public discourse, contributing to a reduction in educational standards, diminishing the attention span and encouraging apathy, isolation and passivity. But perhaps more crucial is the view that commercialization is changing the relationship between the mass media and their audiences: no longer are we seen as citizens but as consumers. The increased emphasis on consumerism threatens the mass communication system that has evolved in Britain.

13

Living in a digital world: experiencing mass communication in the twenty-first century

New technologies are changing the media's relationship with their audience. People have more power over the way they consume the output of the mass media than ever before. The remote control allows them to channel hop, producing a more promiscuous pattern of television viewing. The VCR enabled them to watch programmes when they wanted to. The capability to fast forward helps to avoid the bits you do not want to see, particularly the adverts. Sky Plus lets people to build their own personal schedule of TV programmes. You can now watch TV programmes on your cell phone and listen to radio on your iPod. Television viewing has been revolutionized as programmes are downloaded, bought in DVD box sets and accessed at any time on a variety of platforms. The ability to interact with the media has developed with the growth of home computers, the computer games console and the CD ROM. The growing demand for 'interactivity' is not only an indication that people do not simply act as passive consumers of media products but also implies that a new relationship between consumer and producer, between the supply and demand for information and leisure facilities, is emerging.[1]

The new media technology is multimedia in its application, further blurring the divisions between media. We have seen how film and television became more interlinked in the post-war period and the close ties that developed between the press and broadcasting with the considerable amount of press coverage and comment on the world of television. Traditionally, the media of mass communication have been separate and their services distinct. Today they can be accessed or downloaded from a variety of platforms. Not only is television content viewed on a range of new platforms but newspapers and magazines can be read online. There is a 'convergence' of media forms as TV and radio sets, telephones and computer are brought together into one operating platform. Another dimension of interconnectedness is the internet, an informal network which connects computers world-wide, allowing those with email addresses to talk to each other unimpeded by gatekeepers as well as providing the individual user with access to a vast amount of material via the so-called information superhighway. Internet use has mushroomed since 1990 with the development of the World

Wide Web and in addition to traditional media putting their products on the net, individuals can post their own content with personal blogs and social networking sites such as *MySpace, YouTube* and *Facebook*.

The advent of digital technology is quickening the pace at which the barriers that have traditionally separated the media from one another are broken down. Broadband enables users to download material more quickly and share larger files over the net – one outcome is the growing problem of piracy. It is easier to obtain illegally distributed broadcast and music content as file sharing becomes more commonplace. Digital technology makes possible the processing of more information, more rapidly, more reliably and at lower cost. The development of television up to the 1990s was restricted by the 'scarcity of the airwaves'. A broadcast TV signal uses 2000 times the bandwidth of a telephone call.[2] Digital technology has increased the number of services delivered using the same spectrum capacity. Thus 10 channels can be transmitted in the space previously used by one. This applies to all information technologies, whether television or radio or the telephone. The ability of digital technology to process more information, more quickly is due to the optic fibre cable which can send information at the speed of light. As a result the range of information-related activities in which people can participate in their own homes has grown exponentially – everything from telebanking, home shopping, video games, databases, telephone services, teleworking and the simulations described as 'virtual reality' or 'second life'. The outcome is an explosion in the supply of information and media.

Encouraged – or forced, depending on your perspective – by the government's decision to switch off the analogue signal which supports terrestrial television from 2008, the British public has embraced the new digital technology. Over 85 per cent of the UK households now receive digital services over their main TV sets. They are now living in a multi-channel world in which an ever increasing number of channels and services are available to them. The expansion of television channels is reflected by the actual increase in size of television sets, growing an inch a year with the arrival of plasma screens and HDTV! Much hype has accompanied the development of the new technology with fabulous claims made about the changes that will follow in its wake. There are also growing suspicions about the impact on society. The fears that have accompanied the growth of the mass media are today found in the concerns about who stalks the information highway and the dangers they pose to impressionable young minds. Calls are made from all sections of society to regulate access to the internet and other kinds of interactive services. Continuity is a feature of the digital world: the mainstream channels remain the major providers of content and the appetite for nostalgia and repeats pervades the digital screen. As with previous media technologies, the hype surrounding the 'new media' often obscures the fact that their development is not driven by clear understanding of their applicability to everyday life. Corporations are still searching for a business model which will allow them to make money from the new services. It is not until the new technologies respond to a particular need of the public that their potential can be fully exploited. New media technologies can have a fundamental impact but it is still not clear how, when and in what way.

The great leap forward

The arrival of new media in the 1990s was accompanied by much excitement. The Conservative government believed that the digital world promised many changes. The then National Heritage Secretary Virginia Bottomley in announcing government proposals on digital broadcasting in August 1995 painted the picture of the brave new digital world seen in government and corporate circles:

> **We stand on the verge of a revolution. Digital broadcasting could transform the viewing and listening habits of the nation, as well as providing thousands of new jobs . . . Digital television will allow a huge expansion in the number of channels and of the range of programmes which will be available to British viewers. There will be more variety and choice.[3]**

The promise of an exponential growth in the number of channels and services available has materialized. Within the last decade there has been a boom in the number of channels on British television. The terrestrial channels that dominated the broadcasting landscape in the 1980s have been joined by a variety of digital, cable and satellite channels. Sky started in the late 1980s broadcasting to a few hundred thousand viewers across Europe; today it has over 9 million subscribers and has been joined by several rival operators such as Virgin, BT Vision and Freesat who make available the choice of more than 2000 digital television and radio services, including foreign stations.[4] In 1997, BBC1 and ITV, the two main terrestrial channels, attracted 62 per cent of the available audience, compared to nearly 10 per cent for all the satellite and cable channels combined.[5] By 2006, the share of the two main channels had fallen to 42 per cent while the satellite and cable drew an audience share of 33 per cent.[6] The rise of the new stations has been primarily at the expense of terrestrial commercial television with ITV, Channels 4 and 5 experiencing a sharp decline in their audiences and income. The proportion of advertising revenue received by the digital channels has increased; by 2008 they accounted for 32.8 per cent of the advertising spend on television.[7] The BBC's audience share has held up better. The new stations have in a very short time made a considerable stride forward in establishing themselves as a feature of the new broadcasting environment.

This development has not been easy; many stations have come and gone during the television boom of the last decade. Few of the stations are highly profitable. Sky is an exception; its operating profits rose to £724 million in 2007, nearly four times that of ITV. Sky developed its service through the careful cultivation of channels devoted to sport and films. Rights to the live coverage of major sporting events such as test match cricket, club rugby union and premiership football matches have been bought up by the company to be shown on various Sky channels. Sky's overall audience share is relatively small; its various channels only accounted for around 7 per cent. However, the broadcaster accounts for the bulk of the spending on programming by the growing digital sector; estimated in 2003 to be 80 per cent of that spent by the sector.[8] This has enabled Sky to distinguish itself from many of the other new stations which rely heavily on US imports, repeats and the development of US formats for the British market. This dependency is illustrated by Channel Five's recent launch of its digital stations Fiver and Five US. Sky is not an exception to the emphasis digital television places on showing old British television programmes and US or US equivalent shows – hence the surfeit of traffic cop shows, reality TV programmes and talk shows on Sky1, 2 and 3. It is the Sky Sports and Sky Movies channels that have helped the company to rapidly increase their number of subscribers.

The development of subscription television is a feature of the contemporary broadcasting environment. Advertising revenue and the licence fee were the primary mechanisms by which British television was financed. The result was that most people watched their favourite television programmes for free. Since the late 1990s subscription or pay per view television has become a major source of revenue in the television industry, with 'pay per view' growing at what one commentator has described as 'breakneck speed'.[9] People are willing to pay to watch major sporting events and Hollywood blockbusters. The success of Sky's business plan is underlined by the recent arrival of a rival sports broadcaster, Setanta. This does not mean that people are willing to pay for all kinds of programmes. Certain channels have succeeded as a result of the kind of product they offer – in addition to sports and film, pornography, cult television programmes and games have an audience who are willing to pay for the pleasure they get from watching. However, when asked if they are willing to pay for their television, most of those surveyed state they are not. The success of pay per view television depends on the exclusive right to the product. It is unlikely that the British public is willing to accept a television system solely based on the pay model. Nevertheless this sector of the market is likely to continue to grow.

Pornography and the new media

Pornography is estimated to account for 25 per cent of the internet traffic in the UK. The new technologies of third-generation mobile phones are using pornography to boost market dispersion. Digital channels such as the *Fantasy Channel* and the *Adult Channel* are connected to websites which feature more explicit images and content as well as links to hardcore sites. Amateur porn sites such as *Voyeur-web* and *Porntube*, a copy of *YouTube*, post thousands of new videos every week. The amount of internet porn increased 1800 per cent between 1998 and 2003, rising from 14 million to 260 million pages. Pornography is also increasingly part of the mainstream media. AOL Time Warner, producers of cartoons and children's programmes, as well as up-market print media such as *Time*, is the owner of internet service providers which make available access to pornographic sites and material. The company that owns the Express newspapers also owns top shelf magazines, adult TV channels and sex chat phone lines. On *MySpace* teenage girls with names such as 'nastygirl' post provocative photographs of themselves, attracting the interest of outlets such as *Playboy* magazine which in 2006 issued a casting call for a 'Girls of MySpace' nude photo shoot.

Source: Sarikakis, K. (2004), *British Media in a Global Era*, London: Hodder, pp. 108–9; Keen, A. (2008) *The Cult of the Amateur: How Blogs, MySpace, YouTube and the Rest of Today's User-generated Media Are Killing Our Culture and Economy*, London: Nicholas Brealey Publishing, pp. 155–9.

What's occurring on digital?

The growth of the number of television channels has not been accompanied by an increase in the choice of what is offered to the viewer. Over the years certain television programmes and genres have retained their popularity with the audience no matter how they are delivered. Crime dramas have been a staple feature of the schedules since television began in Britain. Soap operas such as *EastEnders, Coronation Street* and *Emmerdale* are today's most popular programmes, regularly attracting nightly audiences of more than 8 million. These soaps are broadcast by BBC1 and ITV which produce British television's most watched programmes – although in recent years Channel 4's reality television format, *Big Brother* has brought high viewing figures. The top twenty most watched programmes on British television are home-made productions with BBC's *Dr Who* and ITV's *The X Factor* joining the soaps as the best-rated programmes. The viewing figures for terrestrial programmes are huge, compared to those of the new digital channels.

The new channels cover a range of specialist, niche programming, including news, shopping, cartoons, children, history, music, sport, films, food, lifestyle, adult viewing and music. In recent years stations have appeared that attempt to serve particular groups or communities. Channels such as Men and Motors, Nuts TV and Dave are geared to the younger male. Dave is one of the most popular digital stations, gathering an average daily reach of 3.2 million. This contrasts with the BBC1 daily viewing figure of 24.9 million and ITV1 of 20.1 million. Dave's share of the British television audience of 1 per cent is large compared to most of the other digital channels; for example, Men and Motors average daily audience is 168,000, UKTV Food (548,000), The History Channel (318,000), Discovery (434,000), The Cartoon Network (416,000) and all of Sky's movie channels attract a total audience of 2.45 million.[10] Most digital channels attract a daily audience of considerably less than 1 million. The total daily viewing for the hundreds of digital channels that exist is 30.9 million, less than that of BBC1 and ITV1 combined. In addition, the majority of the most popular digital channels have been established by the terrestrial broadcasters: BBC3 (3 million), BBC 4 (1.29 million), ITV2 (4.6 million), ITV3 (2.7 million) and ITV 4 (2.5million), More 4 (1.9 million) and E4 (3 million) and Channel Five's Fiver (1.7 million) and Five US (1.2 million).

Another indicator of the influence of the terrestrial broadcasters on digital viewing habits is the kind of programme that digital stations broadcast. Television viewing in the digital world is a familiar experience. It consists for much of the time of watching offerings that used to be popular on terrestrial television and US imports. Digital channels appear to be re-packaging back copies of favourite formats. Dave, for example, airs old series of BBC's *Top Gear* and *Dragons' Den* and Channel 4's *Whose Line Is It Anyway?* The overwhelming characteristic of digital programming seems to be nostalgia. A glance at an evening's viewing[11] finds ITV favourites from the 1970s such as *Robin's Nest, Man about the House* and *Bless This House* on Bravo or BBC's crime drama favourites such as *Hetty Wainthrop Investigates, Shoestring* and *Between the Lines* on Alibi. One digital channel, UK Gold, is devoted to re-broadcasting old British television fare. The prevalence of US imports is illustrated by episodes of the sci-fi programme *Star Trek* appearing on several channels (Virgin 1, Sky 2, Bravo). The CSI crime thrillers are one of many US programmes that are littered throughout the schedule and with *Law and Order, NCIS, Monk, Numbers, Life, Cold Case, Without a Trace*, as well as the reality police series such as *Police, Camera, Action, Road Wars, Street Wars, Police Patrol, Criminal Minds, Nothing to Declare, Traffic Cops, Animal Cops* and *Cops Uncut*, they attest to the popularity of the crime genre. The amount of original programming generated by digital services is relatively small and much of it tends to be cheap and sensational. The tabloid nature of many of the digital channels is captured by the language used to title programmes, which helps to appeal to the viewer as he or she flicks through the schedule – for example, *Extreme Championship Wrestling* (Sky Sports 3), *Most Shocking Criminal Behaviour* (Virgin), *Extraordinary People: The Boy with a Tumour for a Face* (Fiver), *Deadliest Catch* (Discovery), *Megastructures* (National Geographic), *America's Fattest City* (Sky Real Lives) and *World's Most Extreme Homes* (Real Estate TV). Channels such as Virgin are scheduling late night soft porn such as *Sexcetera* to increase their ratings in what is with so many channels a highly competitive world.

Digital switchover

In 2005, the government made the decision to complete a full nationwide switch to digital by 2012. People will have no choice but to go digital as the analogue service is closed down. The 2006 White Paper designated that the BBC should have a leading role in building the digital infrastructure, promoting the transition and even assisting other channels in their preparations for the change.[12] That

Britain's public service broadcaster is playing this role indicates the failure of the market to develop digital terrestrial broadcasting. The government had hoped that ITV would deliver digital terrestrial television (DTT) in Britain. However, ITV Digital collapsed in 2002. There are three main distribution platforms for the delivery of digital television – satellite, cable and DDT. Licences to operate a multiplex service were awarded by the government in 1998. Sky had built up a formidable position since the launch of a satellite digital service in 1998, benefiting from its position as broadcaster and owner of a platform which allows it to set the price other companies pay to gain access. There were more than 200 channels on the Sky platform.[13] The cable platform, managed by NTL and Telewest, lagged far behind. The terrestrial platform, owned by the ITV companies Granada and Carlton, had a more limited channel capacity and struggled to attract subscribers.[14] Ondigital, as it was initially named, spent a considerable amount to gain the rights to broadcast nationwide football (that is Championship football nowadays – Sky had the rights to the Premiership) and developing and distributing set-top boxes in competition with Sky to allow people to access its service.[15] The technical quality of the service in some part of the UK was very poor. Huge losses, estimated at more than £1.2 billion, destroyed the business, leaving Sky in a dominant position in the digital distribution of television.

The collapse of ITV Digital released frequencies which were taken over by the BBC and, in collaboration with Sky, Freeview was launched. This was an important step on the road to digital conversion. For a one-off payment of £99, viewers gained access to a smaller number of channels, 28 in all, provided by BBC, ITV and Sky, which helped to improve the technical quality of the service. Since 1998, BBC has slowly increased its number of digital channels. Alongside the retransmission of the old terrestrial networks, BBC 1 and 2, and BBC News 24 and BBC Parliament, it added children's channels CBBC and Cbeebies in 2001, an arts and documentary channel BBC 4 in 2002, and an entertainment and drama channel BBC 3 in 2003. Freeview grew rapidly, and in 2007 overtook Sky as the largest digital television service, serving 8.4 million homes. Having helped to establish the multiplex, the BBC had become a major player in the digital world. The free-to-air provision of digital programming provided a new element in the pay per view future originally envisaged for the new services. It provided the BBC with an opportunity to establish a public service component in the digital world and reinvigorate its service by extending its capacity to cater for minority audiences.[16] However, the BBC's entry into its digital commitments put increased pressure on the licence fee, spreading its resources ever more thinly. Critics have questioned whether the BBC's licence fee should be used to develop an industrial policy that benefits all the television industry, including the large commercial operators.[17] The BBC, however, was in the best position to address the government's growing concern about the number of potential 'digital refuseniks'. Reports in 2001 showed a 'significant minority of people', 32 per cent of the public according to one poll, who did not want to switch to digital.[18] The extent of the opposition to switchover, and the possible political consequences of having to impose the service, troubled the Blair administration and passing responsibility to the BBC to be the key driver of digital terrestrial television eased these anxieties.

The decision to shut down the analogue signal is an 'enormously complex, costly and controversial project' which, as Des Freedman notes, has never been subject to a sustained public debate.[19] The government has put forward several justifications for embarking on digitalization, often contradictory and continually shifting. Announcing the date of the analogue switch-off, Culture Minister Tessa Jowell claimed that the 'overwhelming majority' of viewers 'are demanding it'.[20] With people having to convert to digital television, there is little evidence to support Jowell's claim that public demand is driving switchover. Other justifications used are the extension of consumer choice, the expansion of market opportunities for Britain's creative industries, the greater efficiency of the digital signal and the inevitability of technological change. In its 2006 guide to digital switchover, the government asserted that switchover will 'ensure the UK continues as a world leader in broadcasting'.[21] These economic and technical justifications are presented as unproblematic but in practice they are subject to differences of opinion. If they were unambiguous, then it is surprising that commercial interests have been so slow and reluctant to lead the transition. Britain's switch to the digital world is led by government, not consumers or citizens or corporations and according to one commentator, it is 'a clear example of coercive, determined, political government'.[22]

Death of the television industry?

The growth of satellite, cable and terrestrial digital television is a challenge for the contemporary broadcasting industry. However, the threat it poses pales into insignificance compared to the 'unparalleled consumer power' unleashed by the internet.[23] The internet threatens to usurp the central place that broadcasting has attained since 1945. It allows the ordinary man and woman to retrieve content in a variety of radically new ways and opens up the possibility to individuals for 'self expression, conversation and creative work'.[24] Digital technology enables viewers, listeners and readers to consume content when and where they want. As long as there is an appropriate computer and a phone line, then online media can be accessed from anywhere in the world. High speed broadband connections have enhanced the capacity to watch television, video and films online. With every individual possessing the opportunity to build their own viewing or listening schedule, channels are radically changing the way in which they plan their programming. Technologies that allow this to be done are now available to everyone; digital video recorders such as Sky Plus, iPods and music downloads are becoming mainstream. Radio can be listened to via the internet, mobile phone and satellite television and digital audio broadcasting allows the transmission of data and pictures. The recorded music business has been decimated; record sales fell 20 per cent between 2000 and 2006 as file sharing over the net increased.[25]

Podcasting allows individuals to generate their own content and send it around the world. It is estimated that 27.8 million blogs have been set up since 1999.[26] Most newspapers and magazines have an online version. By 2001, 85 per cent of local newspapers had their own websites while net users could access more than 350 radio stations.[27] Computer use in the UK grew by 17 per cent between 2002 and 2005, one of the largest increases of any country.[28] People in Britain are using the net in ever greater numbers and they are active in growing numbers in creating, sharing and publishing content.

One example of the 'empowerment' of the individual is the growth of social networking. It is estimated that half of the UK's internet users are viewing almost 1.8 billion web pages every month on community sites such as *MySpace, Facebook*, and *Bebo*. These social networking sites emphasize the ability of individuals to communicate directly with one another and generate their own content. They allow people without difficulty to create their own online page or profile and assemble their own online network of contacts.[29] Their popularity is not simply because they are 'fun, addictive, diverting and so on' but that they also 'meet a basic human need . . . to feel part of something'.[30] Young people 'view social networks as another way of hanging out with their friends'.[31] Many of the features associated with social networking today were around at the outset of the internet: creating personal web pages, chat rooms, message boards, web communities and blogs, and so on. Sites combing the functions of today's social networking made their first impact in world-wide terms with the advent of *Friendster* in 2002. In the UK *Friends Reunited* drew public attention to the phenomenon when it was sold to ITV for £120 million in 2005. Since 2003, these sites have grown rapidly.[32] The development of general sites such as *MySpace* (2003), *Bebo* (2005) and *Facebook* (2006) has been accompanied by more niche sites such as *Flickr*, which is based on the sharing of photographs and *Linkedin*, a business and employment network. In 2007, the travel and insurance company Saga launched *Sagazone* aimed at the over-50s. The growth of social network sites has been assisted by several factors. Increased domestic penetration of the internet encourages their use; public bodies such as libraries have often denied access to such sites. Confidence in basic computing skills has increased and the setting up of blogs or webpages now demands less computer programming knowledge. The versatility of social network sites has been developed with the ability of users to post and share photos, video and music as well as the usual messaging, communicating and displaying functions.

Social networking is particularly fashionable in Britain. London is *Facebook*'s most popular city with an estimated 31 per cent of Britain's capital city's 7.5 million population registered as *Facebook* users; and more than one in four users of *Bebo* are British.[33] Social networking is particular popular among younger people. The sites are not a matter of sharing interests and information or task-based but a means of maintaining contact and building friendships, often with pre-existing groups of people. Communication is the most popular form of activity on social network sites and 69 per cent of those users surveyed by Ofcom used the sites to talk with friends and family whom they saw regularly.[34] The most recent site to grab the attention of internet users is *YouTube* which is a portal for amateur videos. It is at present the world's fastest growing site, attracting 65,000 new video clips daily and claiming that 60 million clips are watched every day.[35] One highly popular video is 'The Easter Bunny Hates You' which shows a man dressed in a bunny outfit harassing people in the street – it is estimated that this video was viewed 3 million times in two weeks.[36]

These sites are seen as examples of how the internet empowers people and threatens the established media industries. For many commentators, developments on the net question the continued existence of the old media industries. It is believed that the newspaper will soon outlive its usefulness as a vehicle for the communication of news, information and entertainment: the *Economist* magazine believes the newspaper is an 'endangered species'.[37] As video has become easier to put online, television is also under threat; 'with shocking speed, new technology has left the industry like a man beheaded: dead and realising it'.[38] The 'channel, the TV schedule and the programme controller are all increasingly pointless' according to the most enthusiastic embracers of the new world of media technology. The future is bleak if what is happening to the record industry is anything to go by. Musicians and music consumers can use the web to by-pass the traditional music labels. *MySpace* enabled five blokes from Sheffield to launch themselves as the Artic Monkeys and achieve worldwide success. In spite of marketing campaigns, litigation and the establishment of legal downloading sites such as *iTunes*, *Rhapsody* and *Napster*, illegal downloading of music is increasing. Illegal downloads grew by 24 per cent in 2006 and it is estimated that one billion tracks are traded illegally every month.[39] *MySpace* and *YouTube* have been the recipients of law suits to curb their users file sharing music; in November 2006, the Universal Music group sued *MySpace* for copyright infringement. In March 2007, the media giant Viacom launched a $1 billion against *YouTube* after requesting them to take down 100,000 clips they claimed were illegally posted.[40] With money haemorrhaging from the industry, and royalty sales declining, the record companies are seeking some accommodation with the social network sites and other net services that exacerbate illegal downloading; they are also considering releasing music onto the net without any restrictions on copying.[41] Without some form of digital rights agreement, the viability of the recorded music industry is threatened. Companies such as Sony are already looking for alternative revenue lines, ironically returning to live events and tours as well as tie-ups with television shows to provide music and promote artists as sources of income.

Other established media industries have responded to the potential threat of the internet. ITV, Channel 4 and the BBC have all sought to make available some of their content on the net. ITV's website offers video-on-demand and Channel 4 has offered clips of some of its shows for mobile phones.[42] The biggest venture into cyberspace by an established broadcaster has been from the BBC. BBC online is Britain's leading content-based website, accessed by millions around the world. Launched with approval from the government in 1998, the site reached 45 per cent of the 23 million net users in the UK by 2004.[43] Commercial net publishers argued that the use of the licence fee to support this development represented unfair competition. Responding to the concerns of the private sector, the government established a review of the BBC's online provision. Chaired by former Trinity-Mirror chief executive, Philip Graf, the review did not find evidence to substantiate claims that BBC Online reduced competition or had an adverse impact on commercial internet publishing. The BBC in the wake of the review closed several sites that were recognized as having some impact on the market and reduced the spend on online development. However, BBC online is an example of the success some of the established media giants have had in responding to the net.

The need for established broadcasters to release content online is highlighted by the ability of UK viewers to access programmes before they are shown on British television. Programmes such as *Lost, Desperate Housewives, 24* and *The Sopranos* can be downloaded before they appear on terrestrial or digital television screens. Similarly fans of *Dr Who* in North America can access new episodes before they arrive on their side of the Atlantic. People are also increasingly happy to buy DVD box sets of their favourite programmes – the success of the *The Wire* which initially reached a small audience on a relatively obscure digital channel in Britain is based on selling a considerable number of DVD box sets. The net offers independent production companies the opportunity to cut out broadcasters and sell content online. Not many have taken up the possibility of launching programmes online. However, developing programmes which can be exploited across a range of platforms and formats has become an established aspect of contemporary television.

As accessing TV content in alternative ways increases, the ability of channels to sell their audiences to advertisers declines. The unravelling of the business model that has underpinned the majority of old media first hit the newspaper industry. The initial expansion of newspapers onto the net was motivated by the need to keep up with the readers' interest in the new technology. Most newspapers began by considering their online version as secondary or separate from their print versions. This was most crudely illustrated by the online site of the *Daily* and *Sunday Express* which simply reproduced a copy of the papers' front pages, urging readers to go out to purchase the papers.[44] The modern-day Luddism of the Express group became atypical as most other newspapers started to develop their two versions to complement and reinforce each other. Guardian Unlimited launched in 1999 became the largest and most widely read newspaper website and in 2006 became the first paper to publish stories first on the web site, thereby ending the pre-eminence of the printed edition.[45] Some newspapers introduced charges for their services – the *Financial Times* requires payments for the majority of its content online. Other newspapers have established a subscription service for particular aspects of their web content, for example, *The Times* charges for its crossword while the *Independent* for articles and analysis by its internationally renowned Middle East correspondent, Robert Fisk.[46] The ability of newspapers to make a profit from their online editions remains doubtful. The three possible business models identified – subscription, advertising and 'ad hoc' sales – have their own problems and limitations[47] and for most newspapers their online edition is a 'financial drain'.[48]

The threat posed to newspaper advertising revenue by the internet is a major consideration in the online presence of the press. The upward momentum of net advertising corresponds to the growing amount of time consumers spend shopping on the net. Regional newspaper advertising fell for the first time in more than a decade in 2004–5 and in response to the threat posed by web-based classified sites such as *Craigslist* and online auction sites such as *eBay*, as well as public bodies advertising posts on their own websites, local newspapers established their own online advertising activity.[49] In 2006, four main regional newspaper groups established a searchable data base, *Fish4*, to provide readers with access to job, real estate and car advertisements. As local newspapers struggle with the efforts to maintain their advertising revenue, broadcasters are now feeling the same pressures.

The total UK advertising market in 2007 stood at £14.9 billion, of which the internet accounts for £2.8 billion. Newspaper advertising still accounts for the largest share of the market but in 2007 internet advertising spend for the first time exceeded that of the combined total of ITV, Channel 4, S4C and Channel 5 (£2.4 billion).[50] Britain has a higher percentage spend on net advertising than other major western countries, including the USA, Germany and France. Advertising on the net, as with the niche digital channels, gives companies the opportunity to target more specifically the audience they want to reach. Prime-time television viewing peaks in the mid-evening when audiences and advertising are at their highest. For advertisers this is being challenged by the array of 'peak times' created by digital media. There is a late morning and early afternoon surge in email traffic, between 11 and 11.30 a.m. and between 1.30 and 2 p.m.; Web browsing peaks at 11a.m. and 8 p.m. while mobile phone traffic, texting, video viewing and calls, is at its height in late afternoon, between 4 and 6 p.m.[51] Many people access video on their mobiles in order to watch something on their way home from work. Changing patterns of media usage brought about by digital media pose questions as to how and when is best to reach audiences. The internet is the only medium that for most of the working day can be used to reach consumers. Ascertaining the right amount of exposure on search engines at key time of the day is crucial and the rise of *YouTube* and video sharing sites poses further difficulties to what is already a highly competitive affair. More money is required to be spent refining advertising in the new media, particularly on the internet. As people migrate from terrestrial television to viewing digital channels and using the internet, advertisers have to follow. This, however, does not mean the end of television as some are predicting.

Television advertising in the new media landscape

The increasing number of television channels, the new ways in which companies can use the medium to reach consumers – from sponsorship to advertiser-funded programming to longer version of ads that can be viewed online – and the opportunity of reaching people through interactive television have made advertising on television a more complex and uncertain business. The guarantee of reaching a particular kind and size of audience through spots in shows like *Coronation Street* no longer exists in the multi-channel, multi-platform world we inhabit today. The capacity to reach more specialized audiences through a variety of outlets has made targeting audiences more difficult and increasingly risky, compounded by the ability of viewers to skip ads. Spot advertising has been regarded as less effective with the arrival of the video recorder. Research has found that viewers with systems such as Sky Plus watch 30 per cent fewer ads than those with conventional digital television. A blurring of the boundaries between advertising and content is taking place. Product placement, PR stunts and programme and event sponsorship have become more common. Some companies have used broadband to cut out the middle man and launch their own channel to reach their target audience. Audi, for example, launched its own channel on Sky in 2005 dedicated to the benefits of buying their cars. Programmes such as ITV's *Beat* and *Dog Rescue* came from ideas generated respectively by the Home Office and the dog food manufacturer Pedigree. Supermarket chain Waitrose co-funded the production of *Market Kitchen* on UKTV. However, linear scheduled TV channels are increasingly considered less effective than non-linear web channels. More money is spent on the net, with growing attempts to tap in to younger users via social networking cites, blogs, advertising-funded programming and viral advertisements. Much of this is collapsing advertising and content together. *YouTube* is increasingly used by advertisers to promote their brands to younger audiences; to the extent that one commentator describes the site as 'a long commercial break dressed up as democratised media'.

Source: Whitehead, J. (2008) 'Innovation rules in the new media landscape', and Fitzsimmons, C. (2008) 'Advertiser-funded masterstroke proves hard to beat', *Guardian*, 3 March; Gibson, O. (2006) 'The ad revolution will not be televised', *Guardian*, 20 March.

Television remains the main source of news and information for most people in the UK. Around 70 per cent still identify television as their prime medium; and 55 per cent of those surveyed by Ofcom state it is the medium they would most miss if taken away.[52] Programme from terrestrial television account for the bulk of viewing of television in digital homes and on the net. Many of the clips posted on video sharing sites are versions, adaptations or extracts from programmes and adverts generated by terrestrial television. The success of terrestrial programmes such as *The X Factor* and *Strictly Come Dancing*, which in the second week of December 2008 attracted more than 10 million viewers to become Britain's most watched TV show, indicates that audiences still have a yearning to come together to view. Watching the same programming at the same time – now dubbed 'water-cooler' TV – allows people to talk about television. Sharing interests and making connections is part of the viewing experience and the desire to be part of a broad community helps to retain people's loyalty to terrestrial television.[53] Technological change is not necessarily accompanied by changes in human behaviour. The desire for interactive TV is limited by the established routines of everyday life. Patrick Barwise, who conducted an independent review of BBC digital services, concluded that 'in general people don't use the TV to interact.[54] Generally they get home from work, and they just want to sit there and watch whatever is on.' Some simply want to be couch-potatoes! Commitment to established television is also a matter of trust.

Fakery, fraud and forgery

The world of the internet is not necessarily what it seems. Behind the vast amount of material, information and images that is pumped out everyday on the net, there are doubts about the quality of user-generated content and the identity of the users. Much of the content of the net is posted anonymously or under an assumed name. Wikipedia, the largest reservoir of knowledge on the net, is compiled and edited by unknown and nameless citizen editors. They are constantly updating, re-editing and redefining what appears on the pages of Wikipedia, sometimes hundreds of times a day.[55] Anyone can involve themselves in drawing up Wikipedia entries regardless of their expertise, knowledge, learning, education, experience, reputation, qualifications or even awareness. With untutored and unreliable content, Wikipedia is the seventeenth most-trafficked site on the net with entries in over 200 languages.[56] The limited capacity users have to substantiate, check and verify what appears on sites such as Wikipedia has implications for the nature of knowledge and truth in the digital world. Wikipedia's policy is that all facts must be verifiable by someone else and their sources cited; but without sanctions to enforce this and with no capacity for users to check who has posted and changed entries, then it is open to abuse. And, according to one individual, there are a lot of 'volunteer vandals with poison-pen intellects' out there willing to compromise the integrity of such sites.[57] Exposés of the anonymous cyber-vandals who 'abuse rivals, spread gossip and cause widespread confusion' have found that many of those changing the free online encyclopaedia are staff at major companies, councils and government departments'.[58]

The huge amateur library garnered by *YouTube* may not all be what it seems. Without any filters, ethical rules, transparency, accountability or penalties for posting doctored material, there is no means by which we can assess the authenticity of what we see on *YouTube* and similar sites. Videos attacking candidates and campaigns with misleading and out-of-context clips have been posted anonymously by opponents as part of electoral strategies. The influence of political blogging appears to be greater in the US than Britain; its 'candidate-centred nature . . . has made it much more open to being reconfigured by the Internet'.[59] Blogs emerged during the 2005 General Election but appeared to supply idiosyncratic takes on politics, marginal to the campaign.[60] Only 8 per cent of those surveyed claimed to have paid attention to politics online.[61] Blogs in fact are rarely used as sources of news and information; only 5 per cent of those who claim to use the internet for news cite blogs as a source.[62] Many blogs are 'faked, hidden or hacked' becoming the tools of corporations, propagandists and identity thieves.[63] It is estimated that nearly 56 per cent of active blogs are splogs, faked blogs designed to trick advertisers and search engines. There are also 'flogs' which are in the pay of a sponsor while claiming to be independent. In 2006, research found that 14 per cent of advertisements sold by search engines were fake clicks, generating payment without a real ad. Click fraud is estimated that year to have added up to a minimum of $3 billion. Web blogs are 'the ultimate vehicle for brand-bashing, personal attacks, political extremism and smear campaigns' according to a senior editor of the American business magazine, *Forbes*.[64] Such attacks often neglect the vulnerability of mainstream, offline media to political and corporate manipulation, as well as the less than efficient way in which such outlets have told the truth in an ever increasing commercial world. But it is possible to see the libertarian world of the net more susceptible to the dissemination of distortion and misinformation, as spam emails, hate mail and corporate and political propaganda hurtle across the web.

This is manifested in public perceptions of the medium. Research has found that public trust in the net as a source of news is much lower than that accorded to most of the mainstream media. Since 2002 trust in the net has risen slightly but analysis in 2006 found that only 29 per cent of those surveyed trusted the net to tell them the truth about the news. Contrast this with BBC, Channel 4 and ITV in which levels of public trust reach 80 per cent or above.[65] Much of the concern about the quality and reliability of information on the net focuses on the provision of news.

Transforming news

Technology has expanded and changed the nature of news provision. Lightweight cameras, satellite relay equipment and video telephones have transformed news gathering. More news can be transmitted more quickly and from the most remote corner of the world. This has encouraged greater emphasis on the immediacy and instantaneous coverage of the news. Live transmission of breaking events and two-way interviews with the man or woman on the spot not only appear to add to the veracity of what is reported but also add to the drama and excitement of the story.[66] Since the 1980s there has been a proliferation of news channels. CNN, the first 24-hour rolling news channel, was joined by Sky in 1989 and BBC News 24 in 1997 as well as foreign channels such as Fox News, MSNBC, France 24, CNBC, Euronews, Bloomberg TV and non-western operations such as Al-Jazeera. ITV's News Channel was closed after only five years of operation. Rolling news around the clock has established itself as part of the UK media environment in which 'people expect to be able to get the news they want, whenever and however they want it'.[67] News on demand is furthered by the growth of news outlets on the net. With national and regional newspapers and news magazines publishing video and audio in addition to printed news on the web, as well as developing means by which to deliver news through other platforms such as mobile telephones, the outlets for news are thriving. New news providers have appeared in the form of Yahoo, Current Events, Google News and Wikinews. Large corporate news providers have been joined by smaller, more personal websites that have broken major news stories. One example is the Drudge Report which broke the story of Clinton's alleged sexual shenanigans in the White House. Websites of non-governmental and non-official sources, newsgroups and individual web blogs also add to the rich vein of news available. Never before has there been so much news, on hand when and where it is wanted.

The proliferation of news outlets has been accompanied by a change in the nature of news. The new technology is calling for a re-evaluation of some of the core values of news journalism such as objectivity, impartiality, accountability, balance and fairness.[68] At the most basic level the arrival of search engines and the establishment of newsblogs threaten the role of the journalist. Research shows a growing number of people are using the net as a source of news.[69] Many young people rely on online sites, friends and social networks for their news.[70] There has been a growth in the possibilities for ordinary citizens 'playing an active role in the process of collecting, reporting, analysing and disseminating news'.[71] The public are able to provide pictures and video of breaking news events they have captured on their mobile phones. News organization encourage people to send in material as well as comment online on what is reported. Citizens' reports are increasingly incorporated into coverage of the issues of the day such as the 2004 tsunami in Asia and Hurricane Katrina in 2005. Citizen journalism thrives in the provision of eyewitness accounts of major disasters. However, the citizen's voice is increasingly heard as part of the routine, daily news agenda as blogs generate a variety of news stories and comment. With mainstream broadcasters finding it more difficult to attract viewers, blogs of all kinds are more used by the public, in particular, the young. However, their influence may be due less to their impact on public opinion and more on the effect they have as sources of information and interpretation for journalists in the mainstream media.

The way in which news is changing in light of these developments is a matter of conjecture. Pessimists point to the increasing banality of what is posted as news on the web and the untrustworthiness and unreliability of news bloggers. Webloggers differ from traditional journalists in that they are 'more opinionated, niche focussed and partisan'; many are more interested in commenting or providing 'riffs' on what journalists write rather than producing news and information about what is happening.[72] Newsblogs are seen as offering first person news which while vivid and voluminous lacks shape, structure and ultimately meaning; 'it is one thing to read hundreds of people's stories; it is another to try and work out what the story actually is'.[73] Without the professional journalist, information overload and confusion can result. Optimists emphasize, in the words of Matt Drudge, that the net brings about 'an era vibrating with the din of small voices'.[74] It allows every citizen to be a reporter and have his or her voice equated with that of the rich and powerful. The news net is widened and is no longer the domain of the rich and powerful – although many of the major sites on the net cannot afford to gather their own news, preferring to buy it from established providers such as the news agencies, Associated Press (AP) and Reuters. Those who feel under-served by the mainstream mass media such as the young and ethnic minorities have taken advantage of online sources of news.[75] Some argue the quality of news reporting has improved; it is more accessible and attractive, appealing to a broader number of people.[76] The net allows people to talk back to the news and through links and connections widen access to reports of what is happening in the world. People have 'more control over content, access to a wider range of opinions' and they have 'their own voice, unedited and unfiltered'.[77] The internet has both 'the potential to challenge the privileges of the rich and powerful' as well as the capacity to swamp information, knowledge and alternative opinions in a deluge of crime, drugs, pornography, trivia, the personal and rock'n'roll, among other kinds of material.[78] Ultimately it depends how people decide to use it, and that is determined by a number of political, economic and social factors.

Regulating the new media

As with all previous new media technologies there are those who warn against the dangers that the internet poses to society and, in particular, vulnerable individuals. Policing the net is more difficult than controlling previous media. Every medium of mass communication has developed under the control of the government, to undergo a process of liberalization. From the beginning, the internet has not followed this model. The transnational nature of the internet's infrastructure and the sheer weight of the material that is processed every day make it impossible for national governments to regulate the new medium.[79] Attempts have been made. Matters of taste, decency and obscenity have exercised policy-makers, moral entrepreneurs and individuals. The spread of offensive material, including child pornography, has been a pressing issue. Sexual predators in cyberspace are seen as a particular problem – stories abound in the press about paedophiles grooming young children through their use of chat rooms. Many methods have been suggested or adopted to control access to the net, including the use of security systems such as passwords to block access to that deemed most unsuitable. Access is barred to some sites and more recently the government has suggested that a classification system be developed such as used in the film industry. However, it is only with the cooperation of the service providers that governments in certain parts of the world have had some success in controlling internet communication.

Britain has a highly controlled media system. In 1992, 251 statutory instruments restricting the media's ability to report government business were listed – this is in addition to the 50 pieces of legislation such as the Obscene Publications Act, the Contempt of Court Act and the Police and Criminal Evidence Act which place limitations on media freedom.[80] In this context the internet provides an opportunity to break free from the restrictions on what we can see, hear and read. While the British public has potential to access more information than ever before, what appears on the net is influenced by economic considerations. The market can create boundaries to cyberspace. Large media conglomerates are buying up innovative and popular sites; Murdoch bought *MySpace* in 2005 and AOL purchased *Bebo* in 2008. Concentration of ownership is an issue confronting the net; between 1999 and 2001 the companies that controlled 60 of all minutes spent online shrunk from 110 to 14.[81] Prior to the advent of blogging, the extent of corporate control of the internet was beginning to resemble that of other media. Ofcom's emphasis on the market in determining the operation of the media industries is assisting this development. Public service and socially responsible media are further threatened by the desire of large corporations, including the new giants in the field such as Yahoo! and Google, to make money. Blogging may prove an antidote to the search to make money from the net but without public service media, the content of the net as well as digital television may narrow and what we see, hear and read could be reduced.

Notes

Readers, rioters and rick burners: an introduction to the history of mass communication in Britain

1 Quoted in Pearson, G. (1984) 'Falling Standards: A Short, Sharp History of Moral Decline', in Barker, M. (ed.) *Video Nasties*. London: Pluto Press, p. 93.
2 Quoted in Root, J. (1986) *Open the Box*. London: Comedia, p. 19.
3 Quoted in Carr, E. H. (1971) *What Is History?* Harmondsworth: Penguin, p. 50.
4 Sorlin, P. (1994) *The Mass Media*. London: Routledge, p. 2.
5 Sreberny-Mohammadi, A. (1995) 'Forms of Media as Ways of Knowing', in Downing, J. *et al.* (eds) *Questioning the Media*, 2nd edn. London: Sage.
6 Ibid., p. 37.
7 See Curran, J. (1982) 'Communications, Power and Social Order', in Gurevitch, M., Bennett, T., Curran, J. and Woollacott, J. (eds) *Culture, Society and the Media*. London: Methuen.
8 McLuhan, M. ([1964] 1987) *Understanding Media: The Extensions of Man*. London: Ark Paperbacks, pp. 170–9.
9 For an outline of the traditional view of the development of the press, see Curran, J. and Seaton, J. (1991) *Power Without Responsibility*. London: Routledge, Chapter 1; Curran, J. (1977a) 'Capitalism and the Control of the Press, 1800–1975', in Curran, J., Gurevitch, M. and Woollacott, J. (eds) *Mass Communications and Society*. London: Edward Arnold.
10 Curran, J. (1977a).
11 Quoted in Pronay, N. and Spring, D. (1982) *Propaganda, Politics and Film, 1918–45*. London: Macmillan, p. 13.
12 Quoted in Curran, J. (1977a), p. 212.
13 Hannah More, quoted in Donald, J. (1981) 'Language, Literacy and Schooling', in *Popular Culture*. Open University Course Block 7, Unit 29, Milton Keynes: Open University Press, p. 51.
14 Quoted in Whitaker, B. (1981) *News Ltd: Why You Can't Read All About It*. London: Comedia.
15 Scannell, P. (1988) 'Public Service Broadcasting and Modern Public Life', *Media, Culture and Society*, 11(2).
16 For a discussion of the development of editorial freedom in the British press, see Tunstall, J. (1977) '"Editorial Sovereignty" in the British Press: Its Past

and Present', in Royal Commission on the Press *Studies on the Press*. London: HMSO.

17 Quoted in Baistow, T. (1985) *Fourth Rate Estate: An Anatomy of Fleet Street*. London: Comedia, p. 51.

18 Golding, P. (1974) *The Mass Media*. London: Longman, p. 14.

19 See Winston, B. (1995) 'How Media Are Born', in Downing, J. *et al.* (eds), pp. 54–73.

20 McLuhan, M. (1962) *The Gutenberg Galaxy*. London: Routledge and Kegan Paul, p. 125.

21 Golding, P. (1974), p. 18.

22 See Clarke, J. and Critcher, C. (1985) *The Devil Makes Work: Leisure in Capitalist Britain*. London: Macmillan.

23 Moores, S. (1988) 'Box on the Dresser: Memories of Early Radio and EverydayLife', *Media, Culture and Society*, 10(1): 25.

1 The 'naughty and lewd word': the birth of mass communication in Britain

1 For a discussion of the impact of the printing press, see McLuhan, M. (1962); Eisenstein, E. (1980) 'The Emergence of Print Culture in the West', *Journal of Communication*, Winter; Febvre, L. and Martin, H-J. (1976) *The Coming of the Book: The Impact of Printing, 1450–1800*. London: New Left Books; Curran, J. (1977b) 'Mass Communication as a Social Force in History', *Mass Communication and Society*. Open University Course Unit 2. Milton Keynes: Open University Press.

2 Quoted in Curran, J. (1977b), p. 27.

3 Quoted in Sreberny-Mohammadi, A. (1995), p. 50.

4 Quoted in Hartley, J., Goulden, H. and O'Sullivan, T. (1985) 'The Development of Printing', Block Two, Unit Three 'Media Institutions', in *Making Sense of the Media*. London: Comedia, p. 5.

5 Quoted in Curran, J. (1977b), p. 28.

6 Quoted in Hartley, J. *et al.* (1985), p. 7.

7 Cranfield, G (1978) *The Press and Society*. London: Longman, p. 1.

8 Sreberny-Mohammadi, A. (1995), p. 51.

9 Cranfield, G. (1978), p. 2.

10 Williams, R. (1980) *The Long Revolution*, 2nd edn. Harmondsworth: Pelican, p. 181.

11 Feather, J. (1988) *A History of Publishing*. London: Routledge, p. 31.

12 Hartley, J. *et al.* (1985), p. 6.

13 Curran, J. (1977b), p. 29.

14 Altick, R. (1957) *The English Common Reader: A Social History of the Mass Reading Public*. Chicago: University of Chicago Press, p. 26.

15 Quoted in Hartley, J. *et al.* (1985), p. 7.

16 Williams, R. (1980), p. 178.

17 Price, S. (1993) *Media Studies*. London: Pitman, p. 364.
18 Feather, J. (1988), pp. 23–5; Hartley, J. *et al*. (1985), p. 6.
19 Hartley, J. *et al*. (1985), p. 8.
20 Altick, R. (1957), p. 10; Davies, J. (1990) *A History of Wales*. London: Penguin, pp. 248, 289.
21 Hartley, J. *et al*. (1985), p. 8.
22 See Laqueur, T. (1976) *Religion and Respectability: Sunday Schools and Working Class Structure, 1870–1950*. New Haven, CT: Yale University Press.
23 Curran, J. (1977b), p. 31.
24 Cranfield, G. (1978), p. 2.
25 Bruce, B. (1992) *Images of Power*. London: Kogan Page, p. 10.
26 Siebert, F. (1965) *Freedom of the Press in England 1476–1976: The Rise and Decline of Government Control*. Urbana, IL: University of Illinois Press, pp. 69–70.
27 Hartley, J. *et al*. (1985), p. 7.
28 Siebert, F. (1965), p. 70.
29 Hartley, J. *et al*. (1985), p. 7.
30 Clyde, W. (1934) *The Struggle for the Freedom of the Press from Caxton to Cromwell*. Oxford: Oxford University Press, p. 20.
31 Quoted in Clyde, W. (1934), p. 21.
32 Curran, J. (1977b), p. 30.
33 Cranfield, G. (1978), pp. 3–4.
34 Steed, W. (1938) *The Press*. London: Penguin, p. 110.
35 Frank, J. (1961) *The Beginning of the English Newspaper, 1620–1660*. Cambridge, MA: Harvard University Press, p. 4.
36 Gerard, D. (1982) 'The Impact of the First Newsmen on Jacobean London', *Journalism Studies Review*, 7(July).
37 Harris, M. (1977) 'The Structure, Ownership and Control of the Press 1620–1780', in Boyce, D. G., Curran, J. and Wingate, P. (eds) *Newspaper History From 17th Century to present day*. London: Constable, p. 83.
38 Feather, J. (1988), p. 46; see also Curran, J. (1977b), p. 36.
39 Davies, J. (1993), p. 289.
40 Cited in Curran, J. (1977b), p. 36.
41 Steed, W. (1938), pp. 110–11.
42 See Frank, J. (1961).
43 Siebert, F. (1965), p. 197.
44 Ibid., p. 201.
45 Cranfield, G. (1978), p. 19.
46 Quoted in ibid., p. 20.
47 Harris, M. (1977), p. 84; see also Black, J. (1987) *The English Press in the Eighteenth Century*. London: Croom Helm, p. 14.
48 Bennett-England, R. (1967) *Inside Journalism*. London: Peter Owen.

49 The statistics used in this paragraph are drawn from the following sources: Curran, J. (1977b); Black, J. (1987), p. 12. For a discussion of the press in Scotland and Wales, see respectively Craig, M. (1931) *The Scottish Periodical Press, 1750–89*. Edinburgh: Oliver & Boyd and Jones, A. (1990) *Press, Politics and Society: A History of journalism in Wales*. Cardiff: University of Wales Press.

50 Manvell, R. (1966) *This Age of Communication*. London: Blackie, p. 11.

51 Quoted in Williams, F. (1959) *Dangerous Estate: The Anatomy of New Papers*. London: Arrow Books, p. 53; for a discussion of the development of women's press, see Braithwaite, B. (1995) *Women's Magazines*. London: Peter Owen; White, C. (1970) *Women's Magazines, 1693–1968*. London: Michael Joseph; Winship, J. (1987) *Inside Women's Magazines*. London Pandora (especially Chapter 2).

52 For a discussion of the growth of provincial papers in the eighteenth century, see Cranfield, G. (1962) *The Development of the Provincial Newspaper, 1700–1760*. London: Clarendon Press.

53 Quoted in Black, J. (1987), p. 17.

54 Quoted in Smith, A. (1977) 'The Long Road to Objectivity and Back Again: The Kinds of Truth We Get in Journalism', in Boyce, D. G. *et al*., p. 157.

55 Cranfield, G. (1978), p. 32.

56 Williams, R. (1980), p. 204.

57 Cranfield, G. (1978), p. 56.

58 Quoted in Curran, J. (1977b), p. 38.

59 Quoted in Whitaker, B. (1981), p. 62.

60 Quoted in Harris, M. (1977), p. 84.

61 Cranfield, G. (1978), pp. 72–5.

62 Harris, M. (1977), p. 85.

63 Smith, A. (1977), p. 158.

64 Curran, J. (1977b), p. 41.

65 Harrison, S. (1974) *Poor Men's Guardians: A Survey of the Struggles for a Democratic Newspaper Press, 1763–1973*. London: Lawrence & Wishart, p. 17.

2 Right against might: the rise and fall of the radical press

1 Curran, J. (1977b), p. 9. For a discussion of the development of the relationship between the press, politics and class formation in the eighteenth and mid-nineteenth centuries, see Barker, H. (2001) *Newspaper, Politics and English Society, 1695–1855*. London: Longman.

2 See O'Malley, P. (1981) 'Capital Accumulation and Press Freedom, 1800–50', *Media, Culture and Society*, 3: 71–83.

3 Harrison, S. (1974), p. 20.

4 Quoted in Manvell, R. (1966), p. 17.

5 Statistics cited in Curran, J. (1977b), p. 47.

6 Williams, R. (1980), p. 184.

7 Donald, J. (1981), p. 50.

8 See Thompson, E. (1968) *The Making of the English Working Class*. Harmondsworth: Penguin.
9 See Mountjoy, P. (1977) 'The Working-class Press and Working-class Conservatism', in Boyce, D. G., *et al.*, p. 271.
10 Quoted in Harrison, S. (1974), p. 101.
11 Quoted in Donald, J. (1981), p. 51.
12 Mountjoy, P. (1977), p. 268.
13 Quoted in Hartley, J. *et al.* (1985).
14 Quoted in Curran, J. (1977b), p. 45.
15 Cranfield, G. (1978), p. 152.
16 Ibid., p. 159.
17 Harrison, S. (1974), p. 38.
18 Ibid., p. 43.
19 Quoted in ibid., p. 42.
20 Williams, F. (1959), p. 65.
21 Ibid., p. 65.
22 Cranfield, G. (1978), p. 94.
23 Ibid., p. 96.
24 Harrison, S. (1974), p. 47.
25 Cranfield, G. (1978), p. 98.
26 Ibid., p. 107.
27 Quoted in Herd, H. (1952) *The March of Journalism*. London: Allen & Unwin, p. 122.
28 See Curran, J. and Seaton, J. (1991), pp. 22–3.
29 Quoted in Hartley, J. *et al.* (1985), p. 10.
30 Quoted in Harrison, S. (1974), p. 103.
31 Ibid., p. 80.
32 See Hollis, P. (1974) *The Pauper Press*. Oxford: Oxford University Press.
33 Quoted in Asquith, I. (1977) 'The Structure, Ownership and Control of the Press, 1620–1780', in Boyce, D. G. *et al.*, p. 107.
34 Berridge, V. (1977) 'Popular Sunday Newspapers and Mid Victorian Society', in Boyce, D. G. *et al.*, p. 247.
35 Anderson, P. (1994) *The Printed Image and the Transformation of Popular Culture, 1790–1860*. Oxford: Clarendon Press, p. 25.
36 Bennett-England, R. (1967), p. 30.
37 Asquith, I. (1977), p. 100; Williams, F. (1959), p. 92.
38 Williams, F. (1959), p. 93.
39 See Thompson, D. (1984) *The Chartists*. London: Morris Temple Smith; Allen, J. and Ashton, O. (2005) *Papers for the People: A Study of the Chartist Press*. London: Merlin Press.
40 *The Charter, 1839* quoted in Harrison, S. (1974), p. 116.
41 Hartley, J. *et al.* (1985), p. 11. See also Harrison, S. (1984), Chapter 6; Curran, J. (1977a), pp. 203–4.

42 Quoted in Curran, J. (1977a), p. 203.

43 Quoted in ibid., p. 204.

44 See ibid.

45 See Epstein, J. A. (1974) 'Feargus O'Connor and the *Northern Star*', *International Review of Social History*, 22(1) for a discussion of the newspaper.

46 Curran, J. (1977a), p. 207.

47 Ibid., p. 207

48 Ibid., p. 210.

49 Ibid., p. 210.

50 Asquith, I. (1977), p. 112.

51 Curran, J. (1977c), 'The Press as an Agency of Social Control', in Boyce, D. G. *et al*.

52 Ibid., p. 55.

53 Quoted in Curran, J. and Seaton, J. (1991), p. 29.

54 Curran, J. (1977a), p. 211.

55 Mountjoy, P. (1977), p. 280.

56 Quoted in ibid., p. 274.

57 Mackenzie, J. (1984) *Propaganda and Empire: The Manipulation of British Public Opinion, 1880–1960*. Manchester: Manchester University Press, p. 254.

58 *Miner and Workman's Advocate*, 1865, quoted in Harrison, S. (1974), p. 158.

59 Curran, J. (1977a), p. 215.

60 Quoted in ibid., p. 221.

61 Curran, J. and Seaton, J. (1991), p. 108.

62 Quoted in Curran, J. (1977a), p. 218.

63 Ibid., p. 221.

3 Get me a murder a day: the Northcliffe Revolution and the rise of the popular press

1 For a discussion of the notion of 'popular' in relation to the development of the press, see Williams, R. (1977) 'The Press and Popular Culture: an Historical Perspective', in Boyce, D. G. *et al*., pp. 41–50.

2 Ibid., p. 49.

3 Ibid., p. 48.

4 Murdock, G. and Golding, P. (1977) 'The Structure, Ownership and Control of the Press, 1914–76', in Boyce, D. G. *et al*., p. 130.

5 Lee; A. (1977) 'The Structure, Ownership and Control of the Press, 1855–1914', in Boyce, D. G. *et al*., p. 122.

6 See Ward, K. (1989) *Mass Communications and the Modern World*. London: Macmillan, p. 42.

7 Weiner, J. (ed.) (1988) *Papers for the Millions: The New Journalism in Britain, 1850s to 1914*. Westport, CT: Westview Press, p. xii.

8 Quoted in Carey, J. (1992) *Intellectuals and the Masses*. London: Penguin, p. 7.
9 Quoted in Weiner, J. (1988), p. 48.
10 Williams, F. (1959), p. 68.
11 Quoted in ibid., p. 15.
12 Berridge, V. (1977), p. 250.
13 Ibid., p. 257.
14 Ibid., p. 257.
15 Williams, R. (1980), p. 219.
16 Quoted in ibid., p. 217.
17 Snoddy, R. (1993) *The Good, the Bad and the Unacceptable: The Hard News about the British Press*. London: Faber and Faber, pp. 46–9.
18 Curran, J. and Seaton, J. (1991), p. 39.
19 Brendon, P. (1982) *The Life and Times of the Press Barons*. London: Secker and Warburg, pp. 78–9.
20 See Anderson, P. (1994).
21 Williams, K. (1977) *The English Newspaper: An Illustrated History to 1900*. London: Springwood Books, p. 79.
22 Elliott, P. (1977) 'Professional Ideology and Organisational Change: The Journalist since 1800', in Boyce, D. G. *et al*.
23 Smith, A. (1977), p. 163.
24 Elliott, P. (1977), pp. 183–4.
25 Quoted in ibid., p. 181.
26 See Brendon, P. (1982), p. 112.
27 Ibid., p. 113; also see Bourne, R. (1990) *The Lords of Fleet Street: The Harmsworth Dynasty*. London: Unwin-Hyman.
28 See Dangerfield, S. (1961) *The Strange Death of Liberal England*. Re-printed London: Serif.
29 See Jeffrey, T. and McClelland, K. (1987) 'A World Fit to Live In: The *Daily Mirror* and the Middle Classes 1918–39', in Curran, J., Smith, A. and Wingate, P. (eds) *Impacts and Influences*. London: Macmillan, pp. 9–27.
30 Curran, J. and Seaton, J. (1991), p. 35.
31 Ibid., p. 56.
32 Lee, A. (1977), p. 119.
33 Murdock, G. and Golding, P. (1977), p. 131.
34 Curran, J. (1980) 'Advertising as a Patronage System', in Christian, H. (ed.) *The Sociology of Journalism and the Press*. Keele: University of Keele Sociological Review Monograph 29, p. 78.
35 Curran, J. (1980), p. 79.
36 Curran, J. and Seaton, J. (1991), p. 43.
37 Curran, J. (1980), p. 72.
38 Ibid., p. 101.
39 Curran, J. (1980), p. 102.

40 Murdock, G. and Golding, P. (1977), p. 131.
41 Ibid., p. 132.
42 Curran, J. and Seaton, J. (1991), p. 51.
43 Ibid.
44 Jenkins, S. (1979) *Newspapers, the Power and the Money*. London: Faber & Faber, p. 27.
45 Williams, F. (1959), pp. 161–77.
46 Murdock, G. and Golding, P. (1977), p. 131.
47 Ibid., p. 135.
48 For details of the press barons, see, for example, Ferris, P. (1971) *The House of Northcliffe: The Harmsworths of Fleet Street*. London: Weidenfeld and Nicholson; Bourne, R. (1990); Brendon, P. (1982); Taylor, A. J. P. (1972) *Beaverbrook*. Harmondsworth: Penguin; Chisholm, A. and Davie, M. (1993) *Lord Beaverbrook: A Life*. New York: Alfred Knopf. The legacy of Northcliffe is examined in a series of essays in Catterall, P., Seymour-Ure, C. and Smith, A. (2000) *Northcliffe's Legacy: Aspects of the British Popular Press, 1896–1996*. London: Macmillan.
49 Quoted in Boyce, D. G. (1987), 'Crusaders without Chains: Power and the Press Barons, 1896–1951', in Curran, J. *et al.*, p. 100.
50 Murdock, G. and Golding, P. (1977), p. 142.
51 Quoted in Boyce, D. G. (1987), p. 101.
52 Angell, N. (1922) *The Press and the Organisation of Society*, London: Labour Publishing Company, p. 16.
53 Quoted in Boyce, D. G. (1987), p. 99.
54 Quoted in Brendon, P. (1982), p. 161.
55 Curran, J. and Seaton, J. (1991), p. 61.
56 Angell, N. (1922), p. 26.

4 Rescued by Rover: British cinema before the Second World War

1 Quoted in Walvin, J. (1978) *Leisure and Society, 1780–1950*. London: Longman, p. 65.
2 Walvin, J. (1978), p. 135.
3 Perry, G. (1985) *The Great British Picture Show*. 2nd edn. London: Michael Joseph, p. 22.
4 Low, R. (1949) *The History of British Film, 1906–14*. London: Allen & Unwin, p. 13.
5 See Medhurst, A. (1986) 'Music Hall and British Cinema', in Barr, C. (ed.) *All Our Yesterdays: 90 Years of British cinema*. London: British Film Institute.
6 Perry, G. (1985), p. 23.
7 Berry, D. (1994) *Wales and the Cinema*. Cardiff: University of Wales Press, pp. 42, 57.
8 See Chanan, M. (1980) *The Dream that Kicks*. London: Routledge and Kegan Paul; Perry, G. (1985), pp. 19–28.

9 Chanan, M. (1980), p. 42.

10 Berry, D. (1994), p. 59.

11 See Dewe Matthews, T. (1994) *Censored – What They Didn't Allow You to See and Why: The Story of Film Censorship in Britain*. London: Chatto & Windus, pp. 9–13.

12 Dewe Matthews, T. (1994), p. 14.

13 Quoted in Low, R. (1949), p. 15.

14 Corrigan, P. (1983) 'Film Entertainment as Ideology and Pleasure: Towards a History of Audiences', in Curran, J. and Porter, V. (eds) *British Cinema History*. New York: Barnes and Noble, p. 27.

15 Corrigan, P. (1983), p. 30.

16 Ward, K. (1989), p. 50.

17 Ibid., p. 51.

18 Low, R. (1949), p. 145.

19 Corrigan, P. (1983), p. 26.

20 Aldgate, A. (1979) *Cinema and History: British Newsreels and the Spanish Civil War*. London: Scolar, p. 19; see also McKernan, L. (1992) *Topical Budget*. London: British Film Institute.

21 Dewe Matthews, T. (1994), p. 15.

22 See Robertson, J. (1985) *The British Board of Film Censors: Film Censorship in Britain 1896–1950*. London: Croom Helm; Robertson, J. (1989) *The Hidden Cinema: British Film Censorship in Action, 1913–75*. London: Routledge; Dewe Matthews, T. (1994); and Kuhn, A. (1988) *Cinema, Censorship and Sexuality, 1909–25*. London: Routledge (especially Chapter 2).

23 Robertson, J. (1985), p. 6.

24 Dewe Matthews, T. (1994), p. 24.

25 Robertson, J. (1985), p. 7.

26 See Pearson, G. (1984).

27 Dewe Matthews, T. (1994), p. 28.

28 Quoted in McNab, G. (1994) *J. Arthur Rank and the British Film Industry*. London: Routledge, p. 21.

29 Quoted in Chanan, M. (1983) 'The Emergence of an Industry', in Curran, J. and Porter, V., p. 50.

30 Ibid., p. 49.

31 Perry, G. (1985), p. 30.

32 Ibid., p. 41.

33 Golding, P. (1974), p. 30.

34 Perry, G. (1985), p. 32.

35 Landy, M. (1991) *British Genres: Cinema and Society, 1930–60*. Princeton, NJ: Princeton University Press, p. 23.

36 Perry, G. (1983), p. 32.

37 Chanan, M. (1983), p. 28.

38 Figures from Dickinson, M. and Street, S. (1985) *Cinema and State: The Film Industry and the British Government, 1927–84*. London: British Film Institute, p. 5.
39 Strinati, D. (1992) 'The Taste of America: Americanization and Popular Culture in Britain', in Strinati, D. and Wragg, S. (eds) *Come on Down? Popular Media Culture*. London: Routledge, p. 69.
40 Quoted in Strinati, D. (1992), p. 67.
41 Quoted in Stead, P. (1982) 'The People and the Pictures: The British Working Class and Film in the 1930s', in Pronay, N. and Spring, D., p. 82.
42 Stead, P. (1989) *Film and the Working Class*. London: Routledge, p. 100.
43 Quoted in Hartog, S. (1983) 'State Protection of a Beleaguered Industry', in Curran, J. and Porter, V., p. 60.
44 Ibid., p. 64.
45 Murphy, R. (1986) 'Under the Shadow of Hollywood', in Barr, C. (ed.), p. 53.
46 Jones, S. (1987) *The British Labour Movement and Film, 1918–39*. London: Routledge and Kegan Paul, p. 15.
47 Ibid., p. 14.
48 Richards, J. (1984) *The Age of the Dream Palace: Cinema and Society, 1930–39*. London: Routledge, p. 21.
49 Ibid., p. 34.
50 Quoted in ibid., p. 11.
51 Statistics from Corrigan, P. (1983), p. 30; Stead, P. (1982), p. 77.
52 Quoted in Aldgate, A. (1983) 'Comedy, Class and Containment: British Domestic Cinema of the 1930s', in Curran, J. and Porter, V., p. 258.
53 Quoted in Richards, J. (1983) 'The Cinema and Cinema-going in Birmingham in the 1930s', in Walvin, J. (ed.) *Leisure in Britain, 1780–1939*. Manchester: Manchester University Press, p. 11.
54 Statistics from Richards, J. (1984), p. 12; Aldgate, A. (1981a) 'British Cinema in the 1930s', in *Popular Culture*. Open University Course Block 2, Unit 7. Milton Keynes: Open University Press, p. 6.
55 Richards, J. (1984), p. 15.
56 Cited in ibid., p. 13.
57 Jones, S. (1987), p. 10.
58 Aldgate, A. (1981a), p. 7.
59 Dickinson, M. and Street, S. (1985), p. 82.
60 Richards, J. (1984), p. 187.
61 Dickinson, M. and Street, S. (1985), p. 76.
62 Ibid., p. 100.
63 Quoted in Armes, R. (1978) *A Critical History of British Cinema*. London: Secker and Warburg, p. 119.
64 Quoted in Dickinson, M. and Street, S. (1985), p. 79.

65 McNab, G. (1994), p. 18.
66 Ibid., p. 1.
67 Armes, R. (1978), p. 162.

5 The golden age of the wireless: the early years of the British Broadcasting Corporation (BBC)

1 Quoted in Kumar, K. (1986) 'Public Service Broadcasting and the Public Interest', in MacCabe, C. and Stewart, O. (eds) *The BBC and Public Service Broadcasting*. Manchester: Manchester University Press, p. 47.
2 ibid., p. 51.
3 Quoted in Briggs, A. (1961) *The History of Broadcasting in the United Kingdom*, Vol. 1, *The Birth of Broadcasting*. Oxford: Oxford University Press, p. 35.
4 Burns, T. (1977a) *BBC: Public Institution and Private World*. London: Macmillan, p. 4.
5 Davies, J. (1994) *Broadcasting and the BBC in Wales*. Cardiff: University of Wales Press, p. 2.
6 Curran, J. and Seaton, J. (1991), p. 132.
7 See Dangerfield, S. (1961).
8 Quoted in Hartley, J. *et al.*, p. 18.
9 Quoted in Pronay, N. and Spring, D. (1982), p. 13.
10 Murdock, G. (1992a) 'Citizens, Consumers and Public Culture', in Skovmand, M. and Schroder, K. (eds) *Media Cultures: Re-appraising Transnational Media*. London: Routledge, p. 26.
11 McIntyre, I. (1994) *The Expense of Glory: A Life of John Reith*. London: HarperCollins.
12 Quoted in Davies, J. (1994), p. 6.
13 Burns, T. (1977a), p. 62.
14 Quoted in Windelsham, Lord (1980) *Broadcasting in a Free Society*. London: Basil Blackwell, p. 17.
15 Quoted in Scannell, P. and Cardiff, D. (1977) 'The Social Foundations of British Broadcasting', Supplementary Material, Units 1–6. Open University Mass Communications and Society Course. Milton Keynes: Open University Press, p. 18.
16 Quoted in Windlesham, Lord (1980), p. 20.
17 Quoted in Scannell, P. and Cardiff, D. (1977), p. 18.
18 Quoted in Sayles, R. (1986) 'An Introduction to Broadcasting History', in Punter, D. (ed.) *An Introduction to Contemporary Cultural Studies*. London: Longman, p. 49.
19 Scannell, P. and Cardiff, D. (1991) *A Social History of British Broadcasting, 1921–39*. Oxford: Blackwell, p. 4.
20 Ibid., p. 7.
21 Golding, P. (1974), pp. 34–5.
22 Scannell, P. and Cardiff, D. (1991), p. 5.

23 Quoted in Scannell, P. (1990) 'Public Service Broadcasting: The History of a Concept', in Goodwin, A. and Whannel, G. (eds) *Understanding Television*. London: Routledge, p. 12.
24 Curran, J. and Seaton, J. (1991), p. 134.
25 McIntyre, I. (1994), p. 122.
26 Quoted in Scannell, P. and Cardiff, D. (1991), p. 24.
27 Joynson-Hicks, W., in Tracey, M. (1977) *The Production of Political Television*. London: Routledge and Kegan Paul, p. 143.
28 Quoted in Scannell, P. and Cardiff, D. (1991), p. 23.
29 Quoted in Lewis, P. and Booth, J. (1989) *The Invisible Medium: Public, Commercial and Community Radio*. London: Macmillan, p. 67.
30 Symons, J. (1987) *The General Strike*, 2nd edn. London: Cresset Library. p. 177.
31 Quoted in Tracey, M. (1977), p. 146.
32 Symons, J. (1987), p. 179.
33 Tracey, M. (1977), p. 152.
34 Quoted in Burns, T. (1977a), p. 16.
35 Quoted in Tracey, M. (1977), p. 151.
36 Quoted in ibid., p. 155.
37 *Radio Times*, 21 May 1926.
38 Briggs, A. (1961), p. 384.
39 Madge, T. (1989) *Beyond the BBC*. London: Macmillan, p. 20.
40 Scannell, P. and Cardiff, D. (1991), p. 358.
41 Pegg, M. (1983) *Broadcasting and Society, 1918–39*. London: Croom Helm, p. 48.
42 *Radio Year Book*, 1925, quoted in Walvin, J. (1978), p. 137.
43 Crisell, A. (1994) *Understanding Radio*, 2nd edn. London: Routledge, p. 19.
44 Quoted in Pegg, M. (1983), p. 58.
45 Quoted in Scannell, P. and Cardiff, D. (1991), p. 362.
46 Moores, S. (1988), pp. 23–40.
47 Ibid.
48 Quoted in Lewis, P. and Booth, J. (1989), p. 67.
49 Quoted in Scannell, P. and Cardiff, D. (1991), p. 370. The BBC went on to point out that 'If you listen with half an ear, you haven't a quarter of a right to criticise.'
50 Quoted in Scannell, P. and Cardiff, D. (1991), p. 107.
51 Ibid., p. 118.
52 Quoted in ibid., p. 160.
53 Scannell, P. and Cardiff, D. (1977), p. 21.
54 Quoted in Scannell, P. and Cardiff, D. (1991), p. 224.
55 Ibid., p. 226.
56 Quoted in ibid., p. 230.
57 See ibid., Chapter 12.

58 See ibid., pp. 268–9, 344–9.
59 Quoted in Scannell, P. and Cardiff, D. (1977), p. 24.
60 Scannell, P. and Cardiff, D. (1991), p. 225.
61 Ibid., p. 304.
62 Davies, J. (1994), p. 44. For a discussion of the evolution of local broadcasting during the inter-war years, see ibid., Chapter 14.
63 Ibid., p. 319.
64 Ibid., p. 317.
65 Quoted in Davies, J. (1994), p. 42.
66 Quoted in Lucas, R. (1981) *The Voice of a Nation? A Concise Account of BBC Wales, 1923–73*, Llandysul: Gomer Press, p. 52.
67 Quoted in Davies, J. (1994), p. 65.
68 Pegg, M. (1983), p. 31.
69 Bourke, J. (1994) *Working Class Cultures in Britain, 1890–1960*, London: Routledge, p. 189.

6 Sing as we go: representing British society in the 1930s

1 Stevenson, J. and Cook, C. (1977) *The Slump*. London: Quartet Books. For a discussion of the popular memory, media representation and the 1930s, see Baxendale, J. and Pawling, C. (1996) *Narrating the Thirties*. London: Macmillan; also Aldgate, A. (1981b) 'Ideological Consensus in British Feature Films 1935–47', in Short, K.R.M. (ed.) *Feature Films as History*. London: Croom Helm.
2 Quoted in Stevenson, J. and Cook, C. (1977), p. 3.
3 Graves, R. and Hodge, A. (1995) *The Long Weekend*. London: Abacus, p. 328.
4 For a discussion of the history of the New Left Book Club, see Lewis, J. (1970) *The New Left Book Club: A Historical Record*. London: Gollancz.
5 Spender, S. (1978) *The Thirties and After: Poetry, Politics and People, 1933–75*. London: Collins, p. 18. For a discussion of the role of writers and the media in the 1930s, see Williams, K. (1996) *British Writers and the Media, 1930–45*. London: Macmillan.
6 Burns, T. (1977b) 'The Organisation of Public Opinion', in Curran, J., Gurevitch, M. and Woollacott, J. (eds), pp. 63–4.
7 Hennessy, P., Cockerell, M. and Walker, D. (1984) *Sources Close to the Prime Minister*. London: Macmillan.
8 Whitaker, B. (1981), p. 68.
9 Cohen, Y. (1988) 'News Media and the News Department of the Foreign and Commonwealth Office', *Review of International Studies*, 14: 118. See also Tulloch, J. (1993) 'Policing the Public Sphere – the British Machinery of News Management', *Media, Culture and Society*, 15: 371–4; Wilson, K. (1983) 'The Foreign Office and the "Education" of Public Opinion during the First World War', *The Historical Journal*, 26(2): 403–11.

10 Middlemas, K. (1979) *Politics in Industrial Society: The Experience of the British System since 1911*. London: Andre Deutsch, p. 337.

11 See Knightley, P. (1982) *The First Casualty: The War Correspondent as Hero, Propagandist and Mythmaker*. London: Quartet Books.

12 Constantine, S. (1986) 'Bringing the Empire Alive: The Empire Marketing Board and Imperial Propaganda', in MacKenzie, J. (ed.) *Imperialism and Popular Culture*. Manchester: Manchester University Press, p. 202.

13 Ibid., p. 196.

14 Ibid., p. 200.

15 Ibid., p. 204.

16 Ibid., pp. 205, 207.

17 Ibid., p. 207.

18 Ibid., p. 208.

19 Armes, R. (1978), p. 132.

20 Jones, S. (1987), p. 18.

21 See Hollins, T. (1981) 'The Conservative Party and Film Propaganda between the Wars', *English Historical Review*, 96: 359–69.

22 Jones, S. (1987), p. 19.

23 Ryan, T. (1983) '"The New Road to Progress": The Use and Production of Films by the Labour Movement 1929–39', in Curran, J. and Porter, V., p. 122.

24 Jones, S. (1987), p. 146.

25 Ibid., p. 43.

26 For a discussion of being a photographer with Mass Observation, see Spender, H. (1978) 'Humphrey Spender: M.O. Photographer', *Camerawork*, 11.

27 Graves, R. and Hodge, A. (1995), p. 423; for a discussion of *Picture Post*, see Hall, S. (1972) 'The Social Eye of *Picture Post*', *Working Papers in Cultural Studies*, 2. Birmingham: CCCS; Hopkinson, T. (1970) *Picture Post, 1938–50*. Harmondsworth: Penguin.

28 Calder, A. and Sheridan, D. (eds) (1985) *Speak for Yourself: A Mass Observation Anthology, 1937–49*. Oxford: Oxford University Press.

29 Swann, P. (1983) 'John Grierson and the G.P.O. Film Unit, 1933–39', *Historical Journal of Film, Radio and Television*, 3(1): 19–34.

30 Quoted in Bond, R. (1979) 'Cinema in the 1930s: Documentary Film and the Labour Movement', in Clark, J., Heinemann, M., Margolis, D. and Snee, C. (eds) *Culture and Crisis in Britain in the Thirties*. London: Lawrence & Wishart, p. 250.

31 Hood, S. (1983) 'John Grierson and the Documentary Film Movement', in Curran, J. and Porter, V., p. 107.

32 See Higson, A. (1986) 'Britain's Outstanding Contribution to Film: The Documentary-realist Tradition', in Barr, C.; Armes, R. (1978); Hood, S. (1983).

33 See Scannell, P. (1979) 'The Social Eye of Television, 1946–55', *Media Culture and Society*, 1: 97–106; Higson, A. (1986).

34 Quoted in Hood, S. (1983), p. 107.

35 See ibid., p. 108.

36 Bond, R. (1979), p. 250.

37 Hood, S. (1983), p. 108.

38 Ibid., p. 102.

39 Quoted in Armes, R. (1978), p. 133.

40 Quoted in Hood, S. (1983), p. 101.

41 Swann, P. (1983), p. 27.

42 Aldgate, A. (1981b), p. 100.

43 See Lunn, K. (1996) 'Reconsidering "Britishness": The Construction and Significance of National Identity in Twentieth-Century Britain', in Jenkins, B. and Sofos, S. (eds) *Nation and Identity in Contemporary Europe*. London: Routledge, p. 91.

44 Aldgate, A. (1981b), p. 105.

45 See Richards, J. (1984), Chapter 10; Aldgate, A. (1981a).

46 Marwick, A. (1982) 'Press, Pictures and Sound: The Second World War and the British Experience', *Daedalus*, Fall, 138.

47 Quoted in Richards, J. (1984), p. 120.

48 Quoted in ibid., p. 119.

49 Ibid., pp. 121–2.

50 Quoted in Dickinson, M. and Street, S. (1985), p. 8.

51 Aldgate, A. (1987) 'The Newsreels, Public Order and the Projection of Britain', in Curran, J., Smith, A. and Wingate, P., p. 147.

52 Pronay, N. (1987) 'Rearmament and the British Public: Policy and Propaganda', in Curran, J., Smith, A. and Wingate, P., p. 74.

53 Aldgate, A. (1987), p. 149.

54 Ibid., p. 147.

55 Quoted in Scannell, P. and Cardiff, D. (1991), p. 57.

56 Quoted in Scannell, P. and Cardiff, D. (1977), p. 23.

57 Quoted in Cockett, R. (1989) *Twilight of Truth: Chamberlain, Appeasement and the Manipulation of the Press*. London: Weidenfeld and Nicholson, p. 27.

58 Adamthwaite, A. (1983) 'The British Government and the Media, 1937–38', *Journal of Contemporary History*, 18: 289.

59 Quoted in Whitaker, B. (1981), p. 62.

60 Adamthwaite, A. (1983), p. 288.

61 Quoted in Richards, J. (1984), p. 125.

62 Ibid., p. 127.

63 Adamthwaite, A. (1983), p. 282,

64 Scannell, P. and Cardiff, D. (1991), pp. 76–7.

65 Quoted in ibid., p. 88.

66 Lunn, K. (1996), p. 94.

67 Cockett, R. (1989), p. 4.
68 Ibid., p. 105.
69 Quoted in ibid., p. 63.
70 Williams, K. (1996), p. 45.
71 Quoted in Aldgate, A. (1987), p. 145.
72 Quoted in ibid., p. 151.
73 Aldgate, A. (1981a), p. 9.
74 Quoted in ibid., p. 11.
75 Marwick, A. (1982), p. 138.
76 See Higson, A. (1986), p. 77 on the documentary movement.
77 Hood, S. (1983), p. 108.
78 Quoted in Lunn, K. (1996), pp. 94–5. For more details of Baldwin and the media, see Ramsden, J. (1982) 'Baldwin and Film', in Pronay, N. and Spring, D. (eds).

7 Their finest hour: the Second World War and the British way of censorship

1 Quoted in Marwick, A. (1990) *Class: Image and Reality*. London: Macmillan, p. 213.
2 Ibid., p. 216.
3 Quoted in Dawson, G. and West, B. (1984) 'Our Finest Hour? The Popular Memory of World War II and the Struggle over National Identity', in Hurd, G. (ed. *National Fictions: World War Two and British Film and Television*. London: British Film Institute, p. 8.
4 Addison, P. (1994) *The Road to 1945: British Politics and the Second World War*. London: Pimlico.
5 Quoted in Aldgate, A. and Richard, J. (1994) *Britain Can Take It: The British Cinema in the Second World War*. Edinburgh: Edinburgh University Press, p. 14.
6 For a discussion of the morale during the war, and the role of the Ministry of Information in its maintenance, see McLaine, I. (1979) *The Ministry of Morale*. London: Allen and Unwin.
7 *Time*, 18 September 1939, quoted in Larson, C. (1941) 'The British Ministry of Information', *Public Opinion Quarterly*, Fall: 412–31.
8 Quoted in Yass, M. (1983) *This is Your War: Home Front Propaganda in the Second World War*. London: HMSO, p. 13.
9 Ibid., p. 6.
10 Ibid.
11 Ibid.
12 Quoted in ibid., p. 12.
13 Calder, A. (1971) *The People's War: Britain 1939–45*. London: Granada, p. 75.
14 Ibid., p. 542.

15 Ibid., p. 441.
16 Yass, M. (1983), p. 57.
17 Quoted in ibid., p. 28.
18 Quoted in ibid., p. 58.
19 Quoted in Calder, A. (1971), p. 612.
20 Ibid., p. 609.
21 Cardiff, D. and Scannell, P. (1986) '"Good Luck Workers!" Class, Politics and Entertainment in Wartime Broadcasting', in Bennett, T., Mercer, C. and Woollacott, J. (eds) *Popular Culture and Social Relations*. Milton Keynes: Open University Press, p. 107.
22 Pronay, N. (1982) 'The News Media at War', in Pronay, N. and Spring, D., p. 174.
23 Quoted in Pronay, N. (1982), p. 178. Italics in original.
24 Marwick, A. (1982), p. 141.
25 Aldgate, A. and Richards, J. (1994), p. 3.
26 Richards, J. and Aldgate, A. (1983) *The Best of British Cinema and Society, 1930–70*. London: Basil Blackwell, p. 43.
27 Harrisson, T. (1982) 'Films and the Home Front – the Evaluation of their Effectiveness by Mass Observation', in Pronay, N. and Spring, D., p. 273.
28 Cited in Aldgate, A. and Richards, J. (1994), p. 7.
29 Lant, A. (1991) *Blackout: Reinventing Women for Wartime British Cinema*. Princeton, NJ: Princeton University Press, p. 21.
30 Lant, A. (1991), p. 34.
31 Aldgate, A. and Richards, J. (1994), p. 12.
32 Quoted in Stead, P. (1988) 'The People as Stars', in Taylor, P. (ed.) *Britain and the Cinema in the Second World War*. London: Macmillan, p. 72.
33 Quoted in Curran, J. and Seaton, J. (1991), p. 71.
34 Quoted in ibid., p. 74.
35 Quoted in Marwick, A. (1982), p. 144.
36 Curran, J. and Seaton, J. (1991), p. 75.
37 Smith, A. C. H. (1975) *Paper Voices: The Popular Press and Social Change, 1935–65*. London: Chatto and Windus, p. 83.
38 Marwick, A. (1982), p. 142.
39 Curran, J. and Seaton, J. (1991), p. 76.
40 Hickman, T. (1995) *What Did You Do in the War, Auntie?: The BBC at War, 1939–45*. London: BBC Books, p. 15.
41 Ibid.
42 Curran, J. and Seaton, J. (1991), p. 154.
43 Cardiff, D. and Scannell, P. (1986), pp. 109–10.
44 Quoted in ibid., p. 109.
45 Quoted in Marwick, A. (1982), p. 149.
46 *Radio Times*, September 1939, quoted in O'Sullivan, T. (1995) 'Listening Through: The Wireless and World War Two', in Kirkham, P. and Thomas, D.

(eds) *War Culture: Social Change and Changing Experience in World War Two*. London: Lawrence & Wishart, p. 177.

47 Cardiff, D. and Scannell, P. (1981), p. 35.

48 Quoted in Cardiff, D. and Scannell, P. (1986), p. 102.

49 Quoted in Curran, J. and Seaton, J. (1991), p. 160.

50 Addison, P. (1994), p. 118.

51 Quoted in Cardiff, D. and Scannell, P. (1986), p. 105.

52 Ibid., p. 106.

53 Ibid., p. 108.

8 The cosy duopoly: the development of television

1 See Currie, T. (1995) 'Back for Good This Time', *The Journal of the Royal Television Society*, May, 22–5, for an outline of the programmes and politics of BBC television in the late 1940s. Statistics cited in opening paragraphs are drawn from Briggs, A. (1979) *The History of Broadcasting in the United Kingdom*, Vol. 4, *Sound and Vision*, Oxford: Oxford University Press.

2 Scannell, P. (1979), p. 100.

3 O'Sullivan, T. (1991) 'Television Memories and Cultures of Viewing, 1950–65', in Corner, J. (ed.) *Popular TV in Britain*. London: British Film Institute, p. 193.

4 Lewis, P. (1989) *The Fifties: Portrait of a Period*. London: The Herbert Press, reprint, p. 30.

5 Cain, J. (1992) *The BBC: 70 Years of Broadcasting*. London: BBC, p. 69.

6 See Selwyn Lloyd (1949) *Minority Report, Report of the Broadcasting Committee* (the Beveridge Report). London: HMSO.

7 Curran, J. and Seaton, J. (1991), p. 190.

8 Bourke, J. (1994), p. 188.

9 Marwick, A. (1990) *British Society since 1945*. Harmondsworth: Penguin, p. 114.

10 Quoted in Hood, S. (1987) *On Television*, 3rd edn. London: Pluto Press, p. 65.

11 Wilson, H. H. (1961) *Pressure Group*. London: Secker and Warburg.

12 Hood, S. (1987), pp. 64–5.

13 Ibid.

14 Paulu, B. (1961) *British Broadcasting in Transition*. London: Macmillan, p. 70.

15 Accounts of the impact of ITV on political reporting can be found in Goldie, G. W. (1977) *Facing the Nation: Television and Politics 1936–76*. London: Bodley Head; Day, R. (1975) *Day to Day*. London: Kimber.

16 Paulu, B. (1961), p. 62.

17 Hood, S. (1987), p. 71.

18 Quoted in Harbord, J. and Wright, J. (1992) *40 Years of British Television*. London: Boxtree, p. 14.

19 Davies, J. (1994), p. 231.

20 See Sendall, B. (1983) *Independent Television in Britain*, Vol. 2, *Expansion and Change, 1958–68*. London: Macmillan, Chapter 8, for the story of WWN. See also Medhurst, J. (2005) 'Mammon's Television? ITV in Wales, 1959–63', in Johnson, C. and Turnock, R. (eds) *ITV Cultures: Independent Television over Fifty Years*. Milton Keynes: Open University Press.

21 Murdock, G. (1992b) 'Embedded Persuasions: The Fall and Rise of Integrated Advertising', in Strinati, D. and Wagg, S., p. 211.

22 Davies, J. (1994), p. 214.

23 Quoted in Whannel, G. (1992) 'The Price Is Right but the Moments Are Sticky', in Strinati, D. and Wagg, S., p. 183.

24 Davies, J. (1994), p. 231.

25 See Hebdige, D. (1981) 'Towards a Cartography of Taste', *Block*, 4.

26 Cardiff, D. and Scannell, P. (1981) 'Radio in World War II', Unit 8, *The Historical Development of Popular Culture in Britain* 2. Open University Popular Culture Course U203. Milton Keynes: Open University Press.

27 Quoted in Root, J. (1986) *Open the Box*. London: Comedia, p. 59.

28 Hoggart, R. (1958) *The Uses of Literacy*. Harmondsworth: Penguin.

29 See Harbord, J. and Wright, J. (1992).

30 See Sendall, B. (1983), p. 374.

31 *Report of the Committee on Broadcasting* (1962) London: HMSO, p. 68.

32 Ibid.. See Chapter VII for the appraisal of the service provided by ITV and Chapter VIII for the assessment of advertising on television.

33 Hood, S. (1987), p. 76.

34 Quoted in Corner, J. (1991) 'Television and British Society in the 1950s', in Corner, J. (ed.), p. 9.

35 For an overview of the career of Hugh Greene, see Tracey, M. (1983) *A Variety of Lives*. London: Bodley Head; Greene, H. (1969) *The Third Floor Front*. London: Bodley Head.

36 Quoted in Lennon, P. (1986) 'A Legendary Director-General', *The Listener*, 30 October.

37 Quoted in Cain, J. (1992), p. 88. For an overview of the career of Mary Whitehouse, see Tracey, M. and Morrison, D. (1979) *Whitehouse*. London: Macmillan.

38 Quoted in Lennon, P. (1986).

39 Quoted in Davies, J. (1994), p. 279.

40 See Tracey, M. (1982) 'Censored: The War Game Story', in Aubrey, C. (ed.) *Nukespeak: The Media and the Bomb*. London: Comedia.

41 Quoted in Cockerell, M. (1988) *Live from Number 10: The Inside Story of Prime Ministers and Television*. London: Faber & Faber, p. 134.

9 Crisis? What crisis? The demise of British broadcasting in the 1980s and 1990s

1 Burns, T. (1977a).
2 Leapman, M. (1986) *The Last Days of the Beeb*. London: Allen & Unwin.
3 O'Malley, T. (1994) *Closedown? The BBC and Government Broadcasting Policy 1979–92*. London: Pluto Press, p. 4.
4 Negrine, R. (1994) *Politics and the Mass Media*, 2nd edn. London: Routledge, p. 92.
5 Abercrombie, N. (1996) *Television and Society*. Cambridge: Polity Press, p. 80.
6 Murdock, G. (1995) 'Television and Citizenship: In Defence of Public Service Broadcasting', in Tomlinson, A. (ed.) *Consumption, Identity and Style*. London: Comedia, p. 79; Abercrombie, N. (1996).
7 Abercrombie, N. (1996), p. 81.
8 Quoted in Harvey, S. (1994) 'Channel 4 Television: From Annan to Grade', in *Behind the Scenes: The Structure of British Television in the Nineties*. London: Lawrence & Wishart, p. 112.
9 Ingham, quoted in O'Malley, T. (1994), p. 66.
10 O'Malley, T. (1994), p. 67.
11 For an outline of the dispute between the government and media during the conflict, see Harris, R. (1983) *Gotcha! The Media, the Government and the Falklands Conflict*. London: Faber & Faber.
12 Quoted in Barnett, S. and Curry, A. (1994) *The Battle for the BBC: A British Broadcasting Conspiracy*. London: Aurum, p. 17.
13 Quoted in ibid., p. 19.
14 Ibid., p. 25.
15 Quoted in O'Malley, T. (1994), p. 18.
16 Quoted in ibid., p. 117.
17 Ibid.
18 Quoted in Franklin, B. (1994) *Packaging Politics: Political Communications in Britain's Media Democracy*. London: Edward Arnold, p. 62.
19 Franklin, B. (1994), p. 66.
20 See Murdock, G. (1994) 'Corporate Dynamics and Broadcasting Futures', in Aldridge, M. and Hewitt, N. (eds) *Controlling Broadcasting: Access Policy and Practice in North America and Europe*. Manchester: Manchester University Press, p. 15.
21 *Guardian*, 31 January 1994.
22 Quoted in the *Guardian*, 27 November 1993.
23 Independent Television Commission (ITC) (1996) *Annual Performance Review – Wales and the West of England: HTV*. 24 April.
24 McNair, B. (1994) *News and Journalism in the U.K.* London: Routledge, p. 92.
25 Franklin, B. (1994), p. 69.
26 Ibid.

27 *Independent on Sunday*, 9 February 1992.
28 Snoddy, R. (1996) *Greenfinger: The Rise of Michael Green and Carlton Communications*. London: Faber & Faber, p. 238.
29 Quoted in McNair, B. (1994), p. 84.
30 O'Malley, T. (1994), p. 165.
31 Franklin, B. (1994), p. 70.
32 *Guardian*, 14 August 1993.
33 *Independent*, 11 July 1993; *Guardian*, 14 July 1993.
34 See the *Guardian*, 29 August 1992, for Grade's remarks and the *Guardian*, 28 August 1993, for those of Dennis Potter.
35 For a round-up of the press comment on Birt's performance in the renewal of the charter, see Barnett, S. and Curry, A. (1994), p. 231.
36 Henry, G., *Guardian*, 4 December 1995.
37 Ibid.
38 Franklin, B. (1994), p. 65.
39 Quoted in the *Guardian*, 4 December 1995.
40 For a discussion of TV criticism, see Poole, M. (1994) 'Lowering the Box', *Guardian*, 4 April.
41 *Broadcast*, 12 January 1996.
42 Snoddy, R. (1996), p. 290.
43 Williams, G. (1993) 'Murdochvision', *Free Press Journal of the Campaign for Press and Broadcasting Freedom* ,September/October.

10 Carrying on – the British film industry since 1945

1 Dickinson, M. (1983) 'The State and the Consolidation of Monopoly', in Curran, J. and Porter, V., p. 74.
2 Corrigan, P. (1983), p. 30.
3 Ibid., p. 24.
4 McNab, G. (1993) *J. Arthur Rank and the British Film Industry*. London: routledge, p. 174.
5 Ibid., p. 182.
6 Dickinson, M. and Street, S. (1985), p. 192.
7 McNab, G. (1993), p. 41.
8 See Murphy, R. (1989) *Realism and Tinsel: Cinema and Society in Britain, 1939–49*. London: Routledge, pp. 35–42.
9 See Barr, C. (1977) *Ealing Studios*. London: Cameron & Tayleur Books; Green, I. 'Ealing: in the Comedy Frame', in Curran, J. and Porter, V. (1986).
10 Tunstall, J. (1983) *The Media in Britain*. London: Constable, p. 60.
11 Hill, J. (1986) *Sex, Class and Realism: British Cinema, 1956–63*. London: BFI Books; and Tunstall, J. (1983), Chapter 6.
12 Hill, J. (1986), p. 37.
13 Golding, P. (1974), p. 31.
14 Quoted in Hill, J. (1986), p. 35.

15 Tunstall, J. (1983).
16 Hill, J. (1986), p. 35.
17 Tunstall, J. (1983), p. 59.
18 Ibid., p. 67.
19 Murphy, R. (1983) 'Rank's Attempt on the American Market, 1944–9', in Curran, J. and Porter, V., (1986), p. 166.
20 Quoted in Armes, R. (1978), p. 162.
21 Quoted in Macnab, G. (1993), p. 49.
22 Murphy, R. (1983), p. 170.
23 Macnab, G. (1993), p. 43.
24 Perry, G. (1985), p. 120.
25 Macnab, G. (1993), p. 101.
26 Perry, G. (1985), p. 124.
27 Murphy, R. (1983), p. 176.
28 Perry, G. (1985), p. 140.
29 Hill, J. (1986), pp. 38–9.
30 Quoted in Macnab, G. (1993), p. 183.
31 Perry, G. (1985), p. 115.
32 See Murphy, R. (1983), p. 172.
33 Petley, J. (1986) 'Cinema and State', in Barr, C. (1986), p. 37.
34 Macnab, G. (1993), pp. 162–3.
35 Armes, R. (1978), p. 171.
36 Macnab, G. (1993), p. 190.
37 Perry, G. (1985), p. 138.
38 Macnab, G. (1993), p. 191.
39 See Armes, R. (1978), pp. 228–33.
40 Murphy, R. (1992) *British Sixties Cinema*. London: British Film Institute, p. 10.
41 Medhurst, A. (1984) '1950s War Films', in Hurd, G. (ed.).
43 Macnab, G. (1993), pp. 219–20.
44 Porter, V. (1983) 'Creativity at Ealing Studies and Hammer Films', in Curran, J. and Porter, V., pp. 193–207; Landy, M. (1991), pp. 405–22; Pirie, D. (1973) *A Heritage of Horror: The English Gothic Cinema, 1946–72*. London: Gordon Fraser.
45 Medhurst, A. (1986) in Barr, C. (1986).
46 Jordan, M. (1983) 'Carry On . . . Follow the Stereotype', in Curran, J. and Porter, V. (1986). For an appreciation of the work of Donald McGill, see Orwell, G., 'The Art of Donald McGill', in Orwell, S. and Angus, I. (eds) (1970) *The Collected Essays, Journalism and Letters of George Orwell*, Vol. II, Harmondsworth: Penguin, pp. 183–95.
47 Jordan, M. (1983), p. 323.
48 Quoted in Murphy, R. (1992), p. 10.
49 Hill, J. (1986), p. 128.

50 Ibid., p. 150. The discussion of these films is also drawn from Armes, R. (1978) and Perry, G. (1985).
51 Hill, J. (1986), p. 127.
52 Armes, R. (1978), p. 277.
53 Ibid., p. 264.
54 Hill, J. (1986), p. 174.
55 Ibid., p. 41.
56 Ibid., p. 42.
57 Perry, G. (1985), p. 215.
58 Tunstall, J. (1983), p. 63.
59 See Stead, P. (1989), p. 191.
60 Hill, J. (1993) 'Government Policy and the British Film Industry', *European Journal of Communication*, 8: 207.
61 Murphy, R. (1986) 'Under the Shadow of Hollywood', in Barr, C. (ed.) (1986), p. 67.
62 Quoted in Hill, J. (1993), p. 205.
63 Ibid., p. 209.
64 Ibid., p. 216.
65 Quoted in ibid., p. 214.
66 Ibid., p. 210.
67 Quoted in Giles, P. (1993) 'History with Holes: Channel Four Television Films of the 1980s', in Friedman, L. (ed.) *British Cinema and Thatcherism*. London: UCL Press, p. 70.
68 Quoted in UK Film Industry mimeo.
69 Hill, J. (1996) 'British Film Policy', in Moran, A. (ed.) *Film Policy: International, National and Regional Perspectives*. London: Routledge, p. 105.
70 All these figures from Hill, J. (1996), p. 106.
71 Petrie, D. (1992) *New Questions of British Cinema*. London: British Film Institute, p. 4.
72 Giles, P. (1993), p. 75.
73 Ibid., p. 77.
74 Quoted in ibid., p. 77.
75 See Quart, L. (1993) 'The Religion of the Market: Thatcherite Politics and the British Film of the 1980s', in Friedman, L. (ed.) (1993).
76 Williams, C. (1996) 'The Social Art of Cinema: A Moment in the History of British Film and Television Culture', in Williams, C. (ed.) *Cinema: The Beginnings and the Future*. London: University of Westminster Press, p. 198.
77 See Hill, J. (1996).
78 UK Film Industry mimeo.
79 The statistics cited in this section are drawn from the UK Film Council Statistical Yearbook, 2008.

80 Redfern, N. (2005) 'Defining British Cinema: Transnational and Territorial Film Policy in the United Kingdom', *Journal of British Cinema and Television*, 4: 150–64.

81 British Film Council (2003) *Response to Culture, Media and Sport Committee Inquiry 'Is There a British Film Industry?'*, 3 March; UK Film Council press release, 15 January 2007.

82 'Boost for British Film Industry as Movies Rake in £1.65bn', *The Independent*, 22 July 2008.

83 'Britain Loves Film and the World Loves Our Films', UK Film Council, www.ukfilmcouncil.org.uk/10308

84 A discussion of Channel Four and film is found in Brown, M. (2007) *A Licence to be Different: The Story of Channel 4*. London: BFI.

85 Jury, L. (2002) 'Film Four Exits the Big League', *The Independent*, 10 July.

86 Macnab, G. (2008) 'The Big Exodus: Is the British Film Industry in Crisis?', *Guardian*, 5 June.

11 Goodbye to Fleet Street: the slow decline of the British press since the Second World War

1 Tunstall, J. (1983) *The Mass Media in Britain*. London: Constable, p. 80.

2 Murdock, G. and Golding, P. (1977), p. 133.

3 Tunstall, J. (1983), p. 80.

4 Seymour-Ure, C. (1996) *The British Press and Broadcasting since 1945*, 2nd edn. Oxford: Blackwell, p. 16.

5 Franklin, B. (1994), p. 29; Seymour-Ure, C. (1996), p. 17.

6 Franklin, B. (1994), p. 30.

7 Seymour-Ure, C. (1996), p. 45.

8 Tunstall, J. (1983), p. 82.

9 Jenkins, S. (1979), p. 33.

10 Ibid., p. 32.

11 See discussion on readership in Royal Commission on the Press (1977) *Report*. London: HMSO.

12 For a discussion of some of these problems, see Cleverley, G. (1976) *The Fleet Street Disaster: British National Newspapers as a Case Study in Mismanagement*. London: Constable; Sisson, K. (1975) *Industrial Relations in Fleet Street*. London: Hutchinson; The Royal Commission on the Press (1961/2) *Report*. London: HMSO.

13 Murdock, G. and Golding, P. (1977), p. 134.

14 Ibid.

15 Franklin, B. (1994), p. 42.

16 Curran, J. (1980), p. 89.

17 Baistow, T. (1985), p. 33.

18 Quoted in Curran, J. and Seaton, J. (1991), p. 107.

19 Curran, J. (1980), p. 91.

20 Quoted in Curran, J. (1978), p. 245.
21 Ibid., p. 235.
22 Franklin, B. and Murphy, D. (1991) *What News? The Market, Politics and the Local Press*. London: Routledge, p. 85.
23 Ibid., p. 78.
24 Ibid., p. 88.
25 McNair, B. (1994), p. 173.
26 Franklin, B. and Murphy, D. (1991), p. 10.
27 Ibid., p. 11.
28 Baistow, T. (1985), p. 11.
29 See Chippindale, P. and Horrie, C. (1992) *Stick It Up Your Punter!: The Rise and Fall of the Sun*. London: Mandarin Press; Lamb, L. (1989) *Sunrise: The Remarkable Rise and Rise of the Best-Selling Soaraway Sun*. London: Macmillan; Grose, R (1989) *The Sun-sation: Behind the Scenes at Britain's Bestselling Daily Newspaper*. London: Angus & Robertson; Pursehouse, M. (1991) 'Looking at 'the *Sun*': Into the Nineties with a Tabloid and its Readers', in *Cultural Studies*, Birmingham: CCCS.
30 Baistow, T. (1985), p. 42.
31 Jenkins, S. (1986) *The Market for Glory: Fleet Street Ownership in the 20th Century*. London: Faber & Faber, p. 40, and Baistow, T. (1985), p. 42.
32 Jenkins, S. (1986), p. 41.
33 Quoted in Baistow, T. (1985), p. 43.
34 Quoted in Jenkins, S. (1986), p. 46.
35 Quoted in McNair, B. (1994), p. 147.
36 Ibid., p. 149.
37 See Snoddy, R. (1993).
38 Curran, J. and Seaton, J. (1991), p. 117.
39 Pilger, J. (1991) 'A Betrayal of Purpose', *New Statesman and Society*, 13 December.
40 See Benton. S. (1987) 'The Remarkably Rapid Death of Hope, Idealism & £6.5 m.', *New Statesman*, 26 June; Chippindale, P and Horrie, C (1988) *Disaster: The Story of News on Sunday*. London: Sphere Books; Paul Foot emphasizes the importance of the economic structure of the British newspaper industry in accounting for the failure of *NoS* when he states that it was 'because of insurmountable difficulties of advertising, promoting and circulating a new popular paper without any real wealth behind it' (quoted in McNair, B. (1994), p. 140).
41 Murdock, G. and Golding, P. (1977), p. 135.
42 Curran, J. and Seaton, J. (1991), p. 91.
43 Ibid., p. 92.
44 Williams, G. (1996) *Britain's Media: How They Are Related*, 2nd edn. London: Campaign for Press and Broadcasting Freedom, p. 55.

45 Curran, J. and Seaton, J. (1991), p. 92; Franklin, B. and Murphy, D. (1991), p. 12.
46 Murdock, G. and Golding, P. (1977), p. 145.
47 Ibid.
48 Williams, G. (1996), p. 6.
49 Quoted in Seymour-Ure, C. (1991), p. 111.
50 See Curran, J. and Seaton, J. (1991), pp. 91–102.
51 Tunstall, J. (1983), p. 180.
52 For a more detailed and elaborate discussion, see Murdock, G. (1982) 'Large Corporations and the Control of the Communications Industries', in Gurevitch, M., Bennett, T., Curran, J. and Woollacott, J.
53 *Guardian*, 5 March 1990.
54 Quoted in Baistow, T. (1985).
55 Quoted in Williams, G. (1996), p. 44.
56 Quoted in Murdock, G. and Golding, P. (1977), p. 142.
57 Quoted in Curran, J. and Seaton, J. (1991), p. 112.
58 Quoted in ibid., p. 85.
59 See Tunstall, J. (1996) *Newspaper Power: The New National Press in Britain*. Oxford: Claredon Press, Chapters 5–8.
60 Seymour-Ure, C. (1991), p. 23.
61 See Wintour, P. and Goodhart, D. (1986) *Eddy Shah and the Newspaper Revolution*. London: Coronet Books.
62 *Independent*, 22 June 1994.
63 McNair, B. (1994), p. 144.
64 Snoddy, R. (1993), p. 11.
65 Tunstall, J. (1996), p. 398.
66 Ibid., p. 401.
67 Seymour-Ure, C. (1996), p. 260.
68 Tench, D. (2008) 'Max Mosley: The Media Feels the Whip', *Guardian.co.uk*, 24 July; http://www.guardian.co.uk/media/2008/jul/24/mosley.newsoftheworld
69 For a wide-ranging discussion of the case and its implications for press freedom and individual privacy, see *Guardian*, 'Privacy & the Media: Max Mosley Case'; http://www.guardian.co.uk/media/privacy
70 Horrie, C. (2008) 'A Canny Kiss and Tell', *Guardian*, 28 July.
71 The figures in this paragraph are taken from the tables in the Introduction to Franklin, B. (2008) *Pulling Newspapers Apart*. London: Routledge.
72 Herbert, J. and Thurman, N. (2007) 'Paid Content Strategies for News Websites', *Journalism Practice*, 1(2): 208–226
73 Quoted in Wintour, P. (2007) 'Blair: Media is Feral Beast Obsessed with Impact', *Guardian*, 13 June.
74 Toynbee, P. (2007) 'We Need a Rebellion against a Press that's Damaging Our National Psyche', *Guardian*, 15 June.

75 Marsh, K. (2004) 'Power, but Scant Responsibility', *British Journalism Review*, 15(4): 17.

76 Lloyd, J. (2004) *What the Media Are Doing to Our Politics*. London: Constable.

77 Curran, J. and Seaton, J. (2003), p. 103.

78 Greenslade, R. (2003) *Press Gang: How Newspapers Make Profits from Propaganda*. London: Macmillan, p. 565.

79 Greenslade, R. (2004) 'Have the Regional Takeovers Run out of Steam?', *Guardian*, 16 May; also see Aldridge, M. (2007) *Understanding the Local Media*. Milton Keynes: Open University Press, p. 38.

80 *The Economist* (2006) 'Who Killed the newspaper?' 24 August. www .economist.com/opinion/cfm?story_id=7830218

81 Franklin, B. (2008), p. 13.

12 Dumbing down? Declining standards and structural change in the contemporary media

1 Aldridge, M. (2007), pp. 10–12.

2 See Marr, A. (2004) *My Trade: A Short History of British Journalism*. London: Macmillan; Lloyd, J. (2004) *What Are the Media Doing to Our Politics?* London: Constable & Robinson; Schlesinger, P. (2006) 'Is There a Crisis in British Journalism?', *Media, Culture & Society*, 28(2): 299–307.

3 Cited in Beers, R. and Egglestone, P. (2007) 'UK Television News', in Anderson, P. and Ward, G. (eds) *The Future of Journalism in the Advanced Democracies*. Aldershot: Ashgate, p. 143.

4 Quoted in Hoggart, R. (2004) *Mass Media in a Mass Society*. London: Continuum, p. 130.

5 Ward, G. (2007) 'UK National Newspapers', in Anderson, P. and Ward, G., p. 74.

6 Williams, G. (2006) 'Profits before Product? Ownership and Economics of the Local Press', in Franklin, B. (ed.) *Local Journalism and Local Media: Making the Local News*. London: Routledge, p. 86.

7 Ibid., p. 85.

8 Corbett, B. (1996) 'Go Directly to Jail . . . Do Not Pass "Go"', NUJ mimeo.

9 Bourne, C. (1996) 'Reshaping Regional Newspapers', *Free Press: Journal of Campaign for Press & Broadcasting Freedom*, 94. Sept/October.

10 Williams, G.(2006), p. 89.

11 McDonald, P. (1999) 'The Music Industry', in Stokes, J. and Reading, A. (eds) *The Media in Britain; Current Debates and Developments*. London: Palgrave, p. 94.

12 Meech, P. (1999) 'Advertising', in Stokes, J. and Reading, A., p 26.

13 Cornford, J and Robins, K (1999) 'New Media', in Stokes, Jane and Reading, A., p. 118.

14 Freedman, Des (2008) *The Politics of Media Policy*. London: Polity, p. 103.

15 Ibid., p. 6.
16 Tunstall, J. (2007) *The Media Were American*. Oxford: Oxford University Press, p. 259.
17 Quoted in Abercrombie, N. (1996), p. 106.
18 Quoted in Dunkley, C. (1985) *Television Today and Tomorrow: Wall-To-Wall Dallas?* Harmondsworth: Penguin, p. 101.
19 Weymouth, A. (1996) 'The Media in Britain', in Weymouth, A. and Lamizet, B. (eds) *Markets and Myths: Forces for Change in European Media*. London: Longman, p. 49.
20 Freedman, D. (2008), p. 114.
21 Quoted in Williams, G. (1996), p. 5.
22 Houses of Parliament (2003) *The Communications Act, 2003*. Norwich: HMSO, Clause 264, 4 (d).
23 Kuhn, R. (2007) *Politcs and the Media in Britain*. London: Palgrave, p. 116.
24 Douglas, T. (2008) 'Ofcom's Damning Verdict on ITV', *BBC News* http://news.bbc.co.uk/go/pr/fr/-/1/hi/entertainment/7390779.stm
25 Freedman, D. (2008), p. 149.
26 Harvey, S. (2006) 'Ofcom's First Year and Neoliberalism's Blind Spot', *Screen*, 47(1), Spring.
27 Kuhn, R. (2007), p. 127.
28 Crisell, A. (1994), p. 30.
29 Ibid., p. 34.
30 Seymour-Ure, C. (1996), pp. 73–88.
31 Weymouth, A. (1996), p. 58; Seymour-Ure, C. (1996), p. 80.
32 Quoted in Williams, G. (1996), p. 54.
33 Franklin, B. (1994), p. 56.
34 Davis, J. (1994) 'BBC Regional Policy: Network Television and the Regions', in Harvey, S. and Robins, K. (eds) *The Regions, the Nations and the BBC*. London: British Film Institute.
35 Robins, K. and Cornford, J. (1994) 'Local and Regional Broadcasting in the New Media Order', in Amin, A. and Thrift, N. (eds) *Globalisation, Institutions and Regional Development in Europe*. Oxford: Oxford University Press, pp. 217–39. See also Robins, K. and Cornford, J. (1993) 'Not the London Broadcasting Corporation: The BBC and the New Regionalism', in Harvey, S. and Robins, K. (1994).
36 Tusa, J. (1996) 'A Mission to Destroy', *Guardian*, 10 June.
37 Thompson, M. (2008) Keynote address at Television from the Nations and Regions conference, Salford Quays, 22 January. www.bbc.co.uk/pressoffice/speeches/stories/thompson_salford.shtml
38 See Dyke, G. (2004) *Inside Story*, London: HarperCollins, pp. 196–7.
39 BBC Trust Impartiality Report: BBC Network News and Current Affairs Coverage of the Four UK nations: http://www.bbc.co.uk/bbctrust/assets/files/pdf/review_report_research/impartiality/uk_nations_impartiality.pdf

40 Quoted in Robins, K. and Cornford, J. (1994), p. 230.

41 Ibid.

42 Sparks, C. (1991) 'The Popular Press and Political Democracy', in Scannell, P., Schlesinger, P. and Sparks, C. (eds) *Culture and Power*. London: Sage, p. 58; Baistow, T. (1985), p. 95.

43 Curran, J. and Seaton, J. (1991), p. 105.

44 Sampson, A. (1996) 'The Crisis at the Heart of Our Media', *British Journalism Review*, 7(3): 45.

45 Graef, R. (1996) 'Why TV Now Asks the Real Questions', *Evening Standard*, 26 June.

46 Woolwich, P. (1992) 'Against the Current', *Guardian*, 18 May; and Franklin, P. (1990) 'Crying All the Way to the Bank', *TV Producer*, November.

47 Quoted in Barnett, S. (1992) 'Ducking the Issues', *Impact*, August.

48 Woffinden, B. (1996) 'Fast and Loose: Why Is Scandal-Busting Journalism Losing its Edge in Television and the Press?', *Guardian*, 12 August. See also early concerns expressed by Pilger, J. (1993) 'True Mirror to Events: The Values of Current Affairs Must Be Upheld', *New Statesman and Society*, 15.

49 Cited in Hilmes, M. (2003) *The Television History Book*. London: British Film Institute, p. 104.

50 Franklin, B. (1997) *Newszak & News Media*. London: Arnold, p. 4.

51 Franklin, B. (2008), p. 15.

52 Quoted in Harrisson, J. (2006) *News*. London: Routledge, p. 19.

53 Hargreaves, I. and Thomas, J. (2002) *New News, Old News*. London: ITC and BSC, pp. 6–7.

54 Quoted in Hilmes, M. (2006), p. 104.

55 Creeber, G. (2001) *The Television Genre Book*. London: British Film Institute, pp. 134–6.

56 Temple, M. (2008) *The British Press*. London: McGraw-Hill, p. 152.

57 This discussion is drawn from Cockerell, M. (1988).

58 Cockerell, M. (1988), p. 74.

59 Scammell, M. (1995) *Designer Politics: How Elections Are Won*. London: Macmillan, p. 51.

60 Franklin, B. (1994), p. 141.

61 Cockerell, M., Hennessy, P. and Walker, D. (1984), p. 191.

62 Ibid., p. 192.

63 Quoted in McNair, B. (1995), p. 100.

64 Franklin, B. (2001) 'The Hand of History: New Labour, News Management and Governance', in Ludlam, S. and Smith, M. (eds) *New Labour in Government*. London: Macmillan.

65 Quoted in Scammell, M. (1995), p. 167.

66 Franklin, B. (1994), p. 103.

67 Ibid., p. 86.

68 Scammell, M. (1995), p. 178.

69 Harris, R. (1990) *Good and Faithful Servant*. London: Faber & Faber.

70 Jones, N. (1999) *Sultans of Spin: the Media, and the New Labour Government*. London: Orion, p. 67.

71 Franklin, B. (2004) *Packaging Politics; Political Communications in Britain's Media Democracy*. London: Hodder, pp. 66–7.

72 Temple, M. (2008), p. 157.

73 Franklin, B. (2004), p. 58.

74 Ibid., p. 72.

75 Wring, D. (2005) 'Politics and the Media: the Hutton Inquiry, the Public Relations State, and Crisis at the BBC', *Parliamentary Affairs*, 58(2): 386.

76 Hobsbawm, J. (2006) *Where the Truth Lies: Trust and Morality in PR and Journalism*. London: Atlantic Books, p. 3.

77 Davies, N. (2008) *Flat Earth News*. London: Chatto & Windus.

78 Lewis, J., Williams, A. and Franklin, B. (2008) 'A Compromised Fourth Estate: UK News Journalism, Public Relations and News Sources', *Journalism Studies*, 9(1): 1–20.

79 Lloyd, J., quoted in Lewis, J. *et al*. (2008), p. 2.

80 Miller, D. and Dinan, W. (2000) 'The Rise of the PR Industry in Britain, 1979–98', *European Journal of Communication*, 15(1): 5–35. See also Miller, D. and Dinan, W. (2008) *A Century of Spin: How Public Relations Became the Cutting Edge of Corporate Power*. London: Pluto Press; Miller, D. and Dinan, W. (2007) *Thinker, Faker, Spinner, Spy: Corporate PR and the Assault on Democracy*. London: Pluto Press.

13 Living in a digital world: experiencing mass communication in the twenty-first century

1 Mackay, H. (1995) 'Patterns of Ownership of IT Devices in the Home', in Heap, N., Thomas, R., Einon, G., Mason, R. and MacKay, H. (eds) *Information Technology and Society: A Reader*. London: Sage, pp. 310–40.

2 Collins, R. and Murroni, C. (1996) *New Media, New Policies*. Cambridge: Polity Press, p. 42.

3 Quoted in Williams, G. (1996), p. 10.

4 Garfield, S. (2008) 'Cable, Digital, Satellite. . .or Strictly Come Dancing?', *Guardian*, 29 November.

5 Armstrong, S. (2008) 'Everyone's a Winner', *Guardian*, 3 March.

6 Reevell, P. (2007) 'Top 100 of 2006', *Broadcast*, 12 January. It should be noted that in prime time when most people are watching, the share of BBC1 and ITV 1 rises to just under 50 per cent of the available audience.

7 Ofcom (2008a) *Communications Market Report*, August, www.ofcom.org.uk/research/cm/cmr08/cmr08_1.pdf.

8 Cited in Gomery, D. and Hockley, L. (2006) *The Television Industries*. London: BFI Publishing, p. 4.

9 Sarikakis, K. (2004) *British Media in a Global Era*. London: Hodder, p. 109.
10 British Audience Research Bureau (2008) Annual Report.
11 Drawn from schedules for Thursday, 18 December 2008.
12 Freedman, D. (2008) *The Politics of Media Policy*. London: Polity, p. 183.
13 Beers, R. and Egglestone, P. (2007), p. 139.
14 Kuhn, R. (2007) *Politics and the Media in Britain*. London: Palgrave, p. 16.
15 Harrison, J. (2006) *News*. London: Routledge, p. 235.
16 Curran, J. and Seaton, J. (2003) *Power Without Responsibility*, 6th edn. London: Routledge, p. 278.
17 See Hewlett, S. (2005) 'In Danger of a Backlash', *Guardian*, 12 October.
18 Freedman, D. (2008), p. 177.
19 Ibid., p. 171.
20 Ibid., p. 182.
21 Ibid.
22 Freedman, D. (2008), p. 183.
23 Naughton, J. (2006) 'Consumers Show Gatekeepers the Door', *Guardian*, 20 March.
24 Freedman, D. (2006) 'Internet Transformations: "Old" Media Resilience in the "New Media" Revolution', in Curran, J. and Morley, D. (eds) *Media and Cultural Theory*. London: Routledge, p. 278.
25 Keen, A. (2008) *The Cult of the Amateur: How blogs, MySpace, You Tube and the Rest of Today's User-Generated Media Ate Killing Our Culture and Economy*. London; Nicholas Brealey Publishing, p. 8.
26 François, N., Ward, M. and Rawlinson, A. (2007) 'Online Journalism', in Anderson, P. and Ward, G. (eds) *The Future of Journalism in the Advanced Democracies*. Aldershot, Ashgate, p. 126.
27 Ibid. p. 124.
28 Ibid., p. 122.
29 Ofcom (2008b) *Social Networking: A Quantitative and Qualitative Research Report into Attitudes, Behaviour and Use*. Research Document, 2 April. www.ofcom.org.uk
30 Quoted in Beckett, C. (2008) *SuperMedia*. London: Blackwell Publishing, p. 52.
31 Whitehead, J. (2008) 'Can TV Hold its Own?', *Guardian*, 3 March.
32 History of social networking is drawn from Ofcom (2008b), section 3.
33 Johnson, B. (2008) 'All American', *Guardian*, 17 March.
34 Ofcom (2008b).
35 Keen, A. (2008), p. 5.
36 Ibid.
37 *The Economist* (2006).
38 Hammersley, B. (2006) 'Get with the Programme', *Guardian*, 20 March.
39 Freedman, D. (2008), p. 193.
40 Keen, A. (2008), pp. 198–9.

41 Freedman, D. (2008), p. 194.
42 Smith, D. and O'Keeffe, A. (2006) 'TV – So How Will You Watch It?', *The Observer*, 12 March.
43 Dean, P. (2006) 'BBC Online', in Gomery, D. and Hockley, L. (eds), p. 20.
44 Harrison, J. (2006), p. 77.
45 Ibid.
46 Herbert, J. and Thurman, N. (2007).
47 Ibid.
48 Crosbie, V. (2004) 'What Newspapers and their Websites Must do to Survive', Online *Journalism Review*, 4 March, cited in Franklin, B. 'The Future of Newspapers', *Journalism Studies*, 9(5): 636.
49 Williams, A. and Franklin, B. (2007) *Turning the Tanker Around: Implementing Trinity-Mirror's Online Strategy*. Cardiff: Cardiff University Press, p. 14.
50 Ofcom (2008a).
51 Grande, C. (2006) 'Digital Media's Challenge to Advertisers', *Financial Times*, 30 October.
52 Ofcom (2008a).
53 Garfield (2008).
54 Quoted in Smith, D. and O'Keeffe, A. (2006).
55 Keen, A. (2008), p. 20.
56 Ibid., p. 44; Allan, S. (2006) *Online News*. Milton Keynes: Open University Press, p. 136.
57 Quoted in Allan, S. (2006), p. 137.
58 McLeod, M. (2007) 'Wikipedia Saboteurs are Traced and Unmasked', *Scotland on Sunday*, 26 August. The newspaper reports that employees of the Ministry of Defence in the UK were responsible for 4600 anonymous edits in the previous four years.
59 Chadwick, A. (2006) *Internet Politics*. Oxford: Oxford University Press, p. 151.
60 Bartle, J. (2005) 'The Press, Television and the Internet', *Parliamentary Affairs*. 58(4): 699–711.
61 Cited in Kuhn, R. (2007), p. 240.
62 Ofcom (2007) *Annexes to New News, Future News: Research and Evidence Base*, 26 June.
63 Keen, A. (2008), pp. 84–5. Rest of figures cited in this paragraph drawn from this source.
64 Quoted in Allan, S. (2006), p. 174.
65 Figures drawn from Ofcom (2007), p. 40.
66 Harrison, J. (2006), p. 78.
67 Richard Sambrook, former Director of BBC News, quoted in Beers, R. and Egglestone, P. (2007), p. 140.
68 Hall, J. (2001) *Online Journalism*. London: Pluto Press, p. 3.
69 Ofcom (2007).

70 Beckett , C. (2008), p. 21.
71 Quoted in Francois, N. *et al.* (2007), p. 125.
72 Quoted in Beckett, C. (2008) p. 15.
73 Quoted in Francois, N. *et al.* (2007), p. 129.
74 Quoted in Hargreaves, I. (2003), p. 132.
75 Hargreaves, I. and Thomas, J. (2002), p. 46.
76 Stuart Purvis, ex-editor of ITN, quoted in Beckett, C. (2008), p. 32.
77 Quoted in McNair, B. (2007) *Cultural Chaos: Journalism, News and Power in a Globalised World.* London: Routledge, pp. 153, 154.
78 Cited in Beckett, C. (2008), p. 101.
79 Kuhn, R. (2007), p. 141.
80 Petley, J. (1999) 'The Regulation of Media Content', in Stokes, J and Reading, A. (eds), p. 143.
81 Jupiter Media Metrix (2001) 'Rapid Media Consolidation Dramatically Narrows Number of Companies Controlling Time Online', 4 June; http://www.jup.com/company/press relase.jsp?doc=pr010604. See also Arup Shah, http://www.globalissues.org/article/159/media-conglomerates-mergers-concentration-of-ownership.

Bibliography

Abercrombie, N. (1996) *Television and Society*. Cambridge: Polity Press.

Adamthwaite, A. (1983) 'The British Government and the Media 1937–38', *Journal of Contemporary History*, 18: 281–97.

Addison, P. (1994) *The Road to 1945: British Politics and the Second World War*. London: Pimlico.

Aldgate, A. (1979) *Cinema and History: British Newsreels and the Spanish Civil War*. London: Scolar.

Aldgate, A. (1981a) 'British Cinema in the 1930s', in *Popular Culture*. Open University Course Block 2, Unit 7. Milton Keynes: Open University Press.

Aldgate, A. (1981b) 'Ideological Consensus in British Feature Films 1935–47', in Short, K.R.M. (ed.) *Feature Films as History*. London: Croom Helm.

Aldgate, A. (1983) 'Comedy, Class and Containment: British Domestic Cinema of the 1930s', in Curran, J. and Porter, V. (eds) *British Cinema History*. New York: Barnes and Noble.

Aldgate, A. (1987) 'The Newsreels, Public Order and the Projection of Britain', in Curran, J., Smith, A. and Wingate, P. (eds) *Impacts and Influences*. London: Methuen.

Aldgate, A. and Richards, J. (1994) *Britain Can Take It: The British Cinema in the Second World War*. Edinburgh: Edinburgh University Press.

Aldridge, M. (2007) *Understanding the Local Media*. Milton Keynes: Open University Press.

Allan, S. (2006) *Online News*. Milton Keynes: Open University Press.

Allen, J. and Ashton, O. (2005) *Papers for the People: A Study of the Chartist Press*. London: Merlin Press.

Altick, R. (1957) *The English Common Reader: A Social History of the Mass Reading Public*. Chicago: University of Chicago Press.

Anderson, P. (1994) *The Printed Image and the Transformation of Popular Culture 1790–1860*. Oxford: Clarendon Press.

Anderson, P. and Ward, K. (eds) *The Future of Journalism in the Advanced Democracies*. Aldershot: Ashgate.

Angell, N. (1922) *The Press and the Organisation of Society*. London: Labour Publishing Company.

Armes, R. (1978) *A Critical History of British Cinema*. London: Secker and Warburg.

Armstrong, S. (2008) 'Everyone's a Winner', *Guardian*, 3 March.

Ascherson, N. (1988) *Games with Shadows*. London: Radius.

Asquith, I. (1977) 'The Structure, Ownership and Control of the Press 1620–1780', in Boyce, D. G., Curran, J. and Wingate, P. (eds) *British Newspaper History*. London: Constable.

Bailey, M. (2008) *Narrating Media History*. London: Routledge.

Baistow, T. (1985) *Fourth Rate Estate: An Anatomy of Fleet Street*. London: Comedia.

Barker, H. (2001) *Newspapers, Politics and English Society 1695–1855*. London: Longman.

Barnett, S. (1992) 'Ducking the Issues', *Impact*, August.

Barnett, S. (2005) Opportunity or Threat: The BBC, Investigative Journalism and the Hutton Report', in Allan, S. (ed.) *Journalism: Critical Issues*. Maidenhead: Open University Press.

Barnett, S. and Curry, A. (1994) *The Battle for the BBC: A British Broadcasting Conspiracy*. London: Aurum.

Barr, C. (1977) *Ealing Studios*. London: Cameron & Tayleur Books.

Barr, C. (1986) *All Our Yesterdays: 90 Years of British Cinema*. London: British Film Institute.

Bartle, J. (2005) 'The Press, Television and the Internet', *Parliamentary Affairs*, 58(4): 699–711.

Baxendale, J. and Pawling, C. (1996) *Narrating the Thirties*. London: Macmillan.

Beckett, C. (2008) *SuperMedia*. Oxford: Blackwell Publishing.

Benn, T. (ed.) (1984) *Writings on the Wall*. London: Faber & Faber.

Bennett-England, R. (1967) *Inside Journalism*. London: Peter Owen.

Benton. S. (1987) 'The Remarkably Rapid Death of Hope, Idealism & £6.5 m', *New Statesman*, 26 June.

Berridge, V. (1977) 'Popular Sunday Newspapers and Mid Victorian Society', in Boyce, D. G., Curran, J. and Wingate, P. (eds) *British Newspaper History*. London: Constable.

Berry, D. (1994) *Wales and the Cinema*. Cardiff: University of Wales Press.

Black, J. (1987) *The English Press in the Eighteenth Century*. London: Croom Helm.

Black, J. (2001) *The English Press 1621–1861*. Stroud: Sutton Publishing.

Blain, N. and Hutchinson, D. (2008) *The Media in Scotland*. Edinburgh: Edinburgh University Press.

Bond, R. (1979) 'Cinema in the 1930s: Documentary Film and the Labour Movement', in Clark, J., Heinemann, M., Margolis, D. and Snee, C. (eds) *Culture and Crisis in Britain in the Thirties*. London: Lawrence & Wishart.

Bourke, J. (1994) *Working Class Cultures in Britain 1890–1960*. London: Routledge.

Bourne, R. (1990) *The Lords of Fleet Street: The Harmsworth Dynasty*. London: Unwin-Hyman.

Boyce, D. G. (1987) 'Crusaders without Chains: power and the Press Barons 1896–1951', in Curran, J., Smith, A. and Wingate, P. (eds) *Impacts and Influences*. London: Methuen.

Boyce, D. G., Curran, J. and Wingate, P. (1977) *Newspaper history: from the 17th century to the present day*. London: Constable.

Braithwaite, B. (1995) *Women's Magazines*. London: Peter Owen.

Brendon, P. (1982) *The Life and Times of the Press Barons*. London: Secker and Warburg.

Brewer, J. (1997) *The Pleasures of the Imagination: English Culture in the Eighteenth Century*. London: HarperCollins.

Briggs, A. (1961) *The History of Broadcasting in the United Kingdom*, Vol. 1, *The Birth of Broadcasting*. Oxford: Oxford University Press.

Briggs, A. (1979) *The History of Broadcasting in the United Kingdom*, Vol. 4, *Sound and Vision*. Oxford: Oxford University Press.

Briggs, A. and Burke, P. (2005) *A Social History of the Media: From Gutenberg to the Internet*. London: Polity.

Bromley, M. (1999) 'Was it the Mirror Wot Won it? The Development of the Tabloid Press during the Second World War', in Hayes, N. and Hill, J. (eds) *Millions Like Us: British Culture in the Second World War*. Liverpool: Liverpool University Press.

Bruce, B. (1992) *Images of Power*. London: Kogan Page.

Burke, P. (2000) *The Social History of Knowledge*. London: Polity Press.

Burns, T. (1977a) *BBC: Public Institution and Private World*. London: Macmillan.

Burns, T. (1977b) 'The Organisation of Public Opinion', in Curran, J., Gurevitch, M. and Woollacott, J. (eds) *Mass Communications and Society*. London: Edward Arnold.

Cain, J. (1992) *The BBC: 70 Years of Broadcasting*. London: BBC.

Calder, A. (1971) *The People's War: Britain 1939–45*. London: Granada.

Calder, A. and Sheridan, D. (1985) *Speak for Yourself: A Mass Observation Anthology 1937–49*. Oxford: Oxford University Press.

Cardiff, D. and Scannell, P. (1981) 'Radio in World War II', Unit 8, *The Historical Development of Popular Culture in Britain 2*. Open University Popular Culture course U203. Milton Keynes: Open University Press.

Cardiff, D. and Scannell, P. (1986) '"Good Luck Workers!" Class, Politics and Entertainment in Wartime Broadcasting', in Bennett, T., Mercer, C. and Woollacott, J. (eds) *Popular Culture and Social Relations*. Milton Keynes: Open University Press.

Carey, J. (1992) *Intellectuals and the Masses: Pride and Prejudice among the Literary Intelligentsia, 1880–1939*. London: Faber & Faber.

Catterall, P., Seymour-Ure, C. and Smith, A. (2000) *Northcliffe's Legacy: Aspects of the British Popular Press, 1896–1996*. London: Macmillan.

Cavallo, G. and Chartier, R. (1999) *A History of Reading in the West*. London: Polity Press.

Chadwick, A. (2006) *Internet Politics*. Oxford: Oxford University Press.

Chanan, M. (1980) *The Dream that Kicks*. London: Routledge and Kegan Paul.

Chanan, M. (1983) 'The Emergence of an Industry', in Curran, J. and Porter, V. (eds) *British Cinema History*. New York: Barnes and Noble.

Chippindale, P. and Horrie, C. (1988) *Disaster: The Story of News on Sunday*. London: Sphere Books.

Chippindale, P. and Horrie, C. (1992) *Stick It Up Your Punter!: The Rise and Fall of the Sun*. London: Mandarin Press.

Chisholm, A. and Davie, M. (1993) *Lord Beaverbrook: A Life*. New York: Alfred Knopf.

Clarke, J. and Critcher, C. (1985) *The Devil Makes Work: Leisure in Capitalist Britain*. London: Macmillan.

Cleverley, G. (1976) *The Fleet Street Disaster: British National Newspapers as a Case Study in Mismanagement*. London: Constable.

Clyde, W (1934) *The Struggle for the Freedom of the Press from Caxton to Cromwell*. New York: Burt Franklin.

Cockerell, M. (1988) *Live from Number 10: The Inside Story of Prime Ministers and Television*. London: Faber & Faber.

Cockerell, M., Hennessy, P. and Walker, D. (1984) *Sources Close to the Prime Minister*. London: Macmillan.

Cockett, R. (1989) *Twilight of Truth: Chamberlain, Appeasement and the Manipulation of the Press*. London: Weidenfeld and Nicholson.

Cohen, Y. (1988) 'News Media and the News Department of the Foreign and Commonwealth Office'. *Review of International Studies*, 14: 108–22.

Collins, R. and Murroni, C. (1996) *New Media, New Policies*. Cambridge: Polity Press.

Conboy, M. (2003) *The Press and Popular Culture*. London: Sage.

Conboy, M. (2004) *Journalism: A Critical History*. London: Sage.

Constantine, S. (1986) 'Bringing the Empire Alive: The Empire Marketing Board and Imperial Propaganda', in MacKenzie, J. (ed.) *Imperialism and Popular Culture*. Manchester: Manchester University Press.

Corbett, B. (1996) 'Go Directly to Jail . . . Do Not Pass "Go"', NUJ mimeo.

Corner, J. (1991a) 'Television and British Society in the 1950s', in Corner, J. (ed.) *Popular Television in Britain*. London: British Film Institute.

Corner, J. (ed.) (1991b) *Popular Television in Britain*. London: British Film Institute.

Corrigan, P. (1983) 'Film Entertainment as Ideology and Pleasure: Towards a History of Audiences', in Curran, J. and Porter, V. (eds) *British Cinema History*. New York: Barnes and Noble.

Cox, G. (1995) *Pioneering Television News*. London: John Libbey.

Craig, M. (1931) *The Scottish Periodical Press 1750–89*. Edinburgh: Oliver & Boyd.

Cranfield, G. (1962) *The Development of the Provincial Newspaper, 1700–1760*. London: Clarendon Press.

Cranfield, G. (1978) *The Press and Society*. London: Longman.

Creeber, G. (2001) *The Television Genre Book*. London: British Film Institute.

Crisell, A. (1994) *Understanding Radio*, 2nd edn. London: Routledge.

Crisell, A. (2006) *A Study of Modern Television: Thinking Inside the Box*. London: Palgrave.

Crosbie, V. (2004) 'What Newspapers and their Websites Must Do to Survive', Online *Journalism Review*, 4 March, cited in Franklin, B 'The Future of Newspapers', *Journalism Studies*, 9: 5.

Curran, J. (1977a) 'Capitalism and the Control of the Press, 1800–1975', in Curran, J., Gurevitch, M. and Woollacott, J. (eds) *Mass Communications and Society*. London: Edward Arnold.

Curran, J. (1977b) 'Mass Communication as a Social Force in History', in *Mass Communication and Society*. Open University Course Unit 2. Milton Keynes: Open University Press.

Curran, J. (1977c) 'The Press as an Agency of Social Control', in Boyce, D.G., Curran, J. and Wingate, P. (eds) *British Newspaper History*. London: Constable.

Curran, J. (1980) 'Advertising as a Patronage System', in Christian, H. (ed.) *The Sociology of Journalism and the Press*. Keele: University of Keele Sociological Review Monograph.

Curran, J. (1982) 'Communications, Power and Social Order', in Gurevitch, M., Bennett, T., Curran, J. and Woollacott, J. (eds) *Culture, Society and the Media*. London: Methuen.

Curran, J. (2002) 'Media and the Making of British Society c1700–2000', *Media History*, 8(2): 135–54.

Curran, J. and Porter, V. (1986) *British Cinema History*. New York: Barnes and Noble.

Curran, J. and Seaton, J. (1991) *Power without Responsibility*, 3rd edn. London: Routledge.

Curran, J. and Seaton, J. (2003) *Power without Responsibility*, 6th edn. London: Routledge.

Dahl, H. (1994) 'The Pursuit of Media History', *Media, Culture and Society*, 16: 551–63.

Dangerfield, S. (1961) *The Strange Death of Liberal England*. Re-printed London: Serif.

Davies, J. (1994) *Broadcasting and the BBC in Wales*. Cardiff: University of Wales Press.

Davies, N. (2008) *Flat Earth News*. London: Chatto & Windus.

Day, R. (1975) *Day to Day*. London: Kimber.

Dewe Matthews, T. (1994) *Censored – What They Didn't Allow You to See and Why: The Story of Film Censorship in Britain*. London: Chatto & Windus.

Dickinson, M. and Street, S. (1985) *Cinema and State: The Film Industry and the British Government 1927–84*. London: British Film Institute.

Donald, J. (1981) 'Language, Literacy and Schooling', in *Popular Culture*. Open University Course Block 7, Unit 29. Milton Keynes: Open University Press.

Douglas, T. (2008) 'Ofcom's Damning Verdict on ITV', *BBC News*. http://news.bbc.co.uk/go/pr/fr/-/1/hi/entertainment/7390779.stm

Dunkley, C. (1985) *Television Today and Tomorrow: Wall-To-Wall Dallas?* Harmondsworth: Penguin.

Dyke, G. (2004) *Inside Story*. London: HarperCollins.

Eisenstein, E. (1983) *The Printing Revolution in Early Modern Europe*. Cambridge: Cambridge University Press.

Elliott, P. (1977) 'Professional Ideology and Organisational Change: The Journalist since 1800', in Boyce, D.G., Curran, J. and Wingate, P. (eds) *British Newspaper History*. London: Constable.

Ellison, M. (1994) 'But for TV Support, Industry Would be Gone with the Wind', *Guardian*, 19 February.

Epstein, J.A. (1974) 'Feargus O'Connor and the *Northern Star*', *International Review of Social History*, 22(1).

Feather, J. (1988) *A History of Publishing*. London: Routledge.

Febvre, L. and Martin, H-J. (1976) *The Coming of the Book: The Impact of Printing 1450–1800*. London: New Left Books.

Ferris, P. (1971) *The House of Northcliffe: The Harmsworths of Fleet Street*. London: Weidenfeld and Nicholson.

François, N., Ward, M. and Rawlinson, A. (2007) 'Online Journalism', in Anderson, P. and Ward, G. (eds) *The Future of Journalism in the Advanced Democracies*. Aldershot: Ashgate.

Frank, J. (1961) *The Beginning of the English Newspaper 1620–1660*. Cambridge, MA: Harvard University Press.

Franklin, B. (1994) *Packaging Politics: Political Communications in Britain's Media Democracy*. London: Edward Arnold.

Franklin, B. (1997) *Newszak and the News Media*. London: Arnold.

Franklin, B. (2001) 'The Hand of History: New Labour, News Management and Governance', in Ludlam, S. and Smith, M. (eds) *New Labour in Government*. London: Macmillan.

Franklin, B. (2004) *Packaging Politics: Political Communications in Britain's Media Democracy*. London: Hodder.

Franklin, B. (2006) *Local Journalism and Local Media: Making the Local News*. London: Routledge.

Franklin, B. (2008) *Pulling Newspapers Apart*. London: Routledge.

Franklin, B. and Murphy, D. (1991) *What News? The Market, Politics and the Local Press*. London: Routledge.

Franklin, B. and Murphy, D. (1998) *Making the Local News: Local Journalism in Context*. London: Routledge.

Franklin, P. (1990) 'Crying all the Way to the Bank', *TV Producer*, November.

Freedman, D. (2006) 'Internet Transformations: "Old" Media Resilience in the "New Media" Revolution', in Curran, J. and Morley, D. (eds) *Media and Cultural Theory*. London: Routledge.

Freedman, D. (2008) *The Politics of Media Policy*. London: Polity.

Friedman, L. (1993) *British Cinema and Thatcherism*. London: UCL Press.

Garfield, S. (2008) 'Cable, Digital, Satellite. . .or Strictly Come Dancing?' *Guardian*, 29 November.

Garnham, N. (2000) *Emancipation, the Media and Modernity*. Oxford: Oxford University Press.

Gerard, D. (1982) 'The Impact of the First Newsmen on Jacobean London', *Journalism Studies Review*, (7) July.

Giles, P. (1993) 'History with Holes: Channel Four Television Films of the 1980s', in Friedman, L. (ed.) *British Cinema and Thatcherism*. London: UCL Press.

Glover, S. (ed.) (1999) *Secrets of the Press*. London: Allen Lane.

Goldie, G. W. (1977) *Facing the Nation: Television and Politics 1936–76*. London: Bodley Head.

Golding, P. (1974) *The Mass Media*. London: Longman.

Gomery, D. and Hockley, L. (2006) *The Television Industries*. London: BFI Publishing.

Goodwin, P. (1998) *Television under the Tories: Broadcasting Policy 1979–1997*. London: British Film Institute.

Gorham, M. (1948) *Sound and Fury*. London: Marshall

Graef, R. (1996) 'Why TV Now Asks the Real Questions', *Evening Standard*, 26 June.

Grande, C. (2006) 'Digital Media's Challenge to Advertisers', *Financial Times* 30 October.

Grant, M. (1994) *Propaganda and the Role of the State in Inter-War Britain*. Oxford: Oxford University Press.

Graves, R. and Hodge, A. (1995) *The Long Weekend*. London: Abacus.

Green, I. (1986) 'Ealing: in the Comedy Frame', in Curran, J. and Porter, V. (eds) *British Cinema History*., New York: Barnes & Noble.

Greene, H. (1969) *The Third Floor Front*. London: Bodley Head.

Greenslade, R. (2003) *Press Gang: How Newspapers Make Profits from Propaganda*. London: Macmillan.

Greenslade, R. (2004) 'Have the Regional Takeovers Run out of Steam?', *Guardian*, 16 May.

Grose, R. (1989) *The Sun-sation: Behind the Scenes at Britain's Bestselling Daily Newspaper*. London: Angus & Robertson.

Gurevitch, M., Bennett, T., Curran, J. and Woollacott, J. (eds) (1982) *Culture, Society and the Media*. London: Methuen.

Hall, J. (2001) *Online Journalism*. London: Pluto Press.

Hall, S (1972) 'The Social Eye of *Picture Post*', in *Working Papers in Cultural Studies* 2. Birmingham: CCCS.

Halsey, A. (1986) *Change in British Society*. Oxford: Oxford University Press.

Hammersley, B. (2006) 'Get with the Programme', *Guardian*, 20 March.

Hampton, M. (2004) *Visions of the Press in Britain, 1850–1950*. Urbana, IL: University of Illinois Press.

Harbord, J. and Wright, J. (1992) *40 Years of British Television*. London: Boxtree.

Hargreaves, I. (2003) *Journalism: Truth or Dare*. Oxford: Oxford University Press.

Hargreaves, I. and Thomas, J. (2002) *New News, Old News*. London: ITC and BSC.

Harris, M. (1977) 'The Structure, Ownership and Control of the Press 1620–1780', in Boyce, D.G., Curran, J. and Wingate, P. (eds) *British Newspaper History*. London: Constable.

Harris, R. (1983) *Gotcha! The Media, the Government and the Falklands Conflict*. London: Faber & Faber.

Harris, R. (1990) *Good and Faithful Servant*. London: Faber & Faber.

Harrison, J. (2006) *News*. London: Routledge.

Harrison, S. (1974) *Poor Men's Guardians: A Survey of the Struggles for Democratic Newspaper Press 1763–1973*. London: Lawrence & Wishart.

Harrisson, T. (1982) 'Films and the Home Front: The Evaluation of their Effectiveness by Mass Observation', in Pronay, N. and Spring, D. (eds) *Propaganda, Politics and Film 1918–45*. London: Macmillan.

Hartley, J., Goulden, H. and O'Sullivan, T. (1985) 'The Development of Printing'. Block Two, Unit Three 'Media Institutions', in *Making Sense of the Media*. London: Comedia.

Hartog, S. (1983) 'State Protection of a Beleaguered Industry', in Curran, J. and Porter, V. (eds) *British Cinema History*. New York: Barnes and Noble.

Harvey, S. (1994) 'Channel 4 Television: From Annan to Grade', in *Behind the Scenes: The Structure of British Television in the Nineties*. London: Lawrence & Wishart.

Harvey, S. and Robins, K. (1994) *The Regions, the Nations and the BBC*. London: British Film Institute.

Hastings, M. (2002) *Editor: An Inside Story of Newspapers*. London: Pan Books.

Herbert, J. and Thurman, N. (2007) 'Paid Content Strategies for News Websites', *Journalism Practice*, 1(2): 208–26.

Herd, H. (1952) *The March of Journalism*. London: Allen & Unwin.

Hewlett, S. (2005) 'In Danger of a Backlash', *Guardian* 12 October.

Hickman, T. (1995) *What Did you Do in the War; Auntie?: The BBC at War 1939–45*. London: BBC Books.

Higson, A. (1986) 'Britain's Outstanding Contribution to Film: The Documentary-Realist Tradition', in Barr, C. (ed.) *All Our Yesterdays: 90 Years of British Cinema*. London: British Film Institute.

Hill, J. (1986) *Sex, Class and Realism: British Cinema 1956–63*. London: BFI Books.

Hill, J. (1993) 'Government Policy and the British Film Industry', *European Journal of Communication*, 8: 203–24.

Hill, J. (1996) 'British Film Policy', in Moran, A. (ed.) *Film Policy: International, National and Regional Perspectives*. London: Routledge.

Hilmes, M. (2003) *The Television History Book*. London: British Film Institute.

Hobsbawm, J. (2006) *Where the Truth Lies: Trust and Morality in PR and Journalism*. London: Atlantic Books.

Hoggart, R. (1958) *The Uses of Literacy*. Harmondsworth: Penguin.

Hoggart, R. (2004) *Mass Media in a Mass Society*. London: Continuum.

Hollins, T. (1981) 'The Conservative Party and Film Propaganda between the Wars', *English Historical Review*, 96: 359–69.

Hollis, P. (1974) *The Pauper Press*. Oxford: Oxford University Press.

Hood, S. (1983) 'John Grierson and the Documentary Film Movement', in Curran, J. and Porter, V. (eds) *British Cinema History*. New York: Barnes & Noble.

Hood, S. (1987) *On Television*, 3rd edn. London: Pluto Press.

Hooper, D. (1987) *Official Secrets: The Use and Abuse of the Act*. London: Martin, Secker & Warburg.

Hopkinson, T. (1970) *Picture Post 1938–50*. Harmondsworth: Penguin.

Horrie, C. (2003) *Tabloid Nation: From the Birth of the Daily Mirror to the Death of the Tabloid*. London: Andre Deutsch.

Horrie, C. (2008) 'A Canny Kiss and Tell', *Guardian*, 28 July.

Hoyer, S. and Pottker, H. (eds) (2005) *Diffusion of the News Paradigm 1850–2000*. Gothenburg: Nordicom.

Hurd, G. (1984) *National Fictions: World War Two and British Film and Television*. London: British Film Institute.

James, L. (1978) *Print and the People 1819–1851*. London: Peregrine.

Jeffrey, T. and McClelland, K. (1987) 'A World Fit to Live In: the *Daily Mirror* and the Middle Classes 1918–39', in Curran, J., Smith, A. and Wingate, P. (eds) *Impacts and Influences*. London: Macmillan.

Jenkins, S. (1979) *Newspapers, the Power and the Money*. London: Faber & Faber.

Jenkins, S. (1986) *The Market for Glory: Fleet Street Ownership in the 20th Century*. London: Faber & Faber.

Johnson, B. (2008) 'All American', *Guardian*, 17 March.

Jones, A. (1990) *Press, Politics and Society: A History of Journalism in Wales*. Cardiff: University of Wales Press.

Jones, A. (1996) *Powers of the Press: Newspapers, Power and the Public in Nineteenth-Century England*. Aldershot: Scolar Press.

Jones, N. (1996) *Soundbites and Spin Doctors*. London: Cassell.

Jones, N. (1999) *Sultans of Spin: The Media, and the New Labour Government*. London: Orion.

Jones, S. (1987) *The British Labour Movement and Film 1918–39*. London: Routledge and Kegan Paul.

Jordan, M. (1983) 'Carry On . . . Follow the Stereotype', in Curran, J. and Porter, V. (eds) *British Cinema History*. New York: Barnes and Noble.

Keen, A. (2008) *The Cult of the Amateur: How Blogs, MySpace, You Tube and the Rest of Today's User-generated Media Are Killing Our Culture and Economy*. London: Nicholas Brealey Publishing.

Kirkham, P. and Thoms, D. (1995) *War Culture: Social Change and Changing Experience in World War Two*. London: Lawrence & Wishart.

Knightley, P. (1982) *The First Casualty: The War Correspondent as Hero, Propagandist and Mythmaker*. London: Quartet Books.

Koss, S. (1990) *The Rise and Fall of the Political Press in Britain*. London: Fontana.

Kuhn, A. (1988) *Cinema, Censorship and Sexuality 1909–25*. London: Routledge.

Kuhn, R. (2007) *Politics and the Media in Britain*. London: Palgrave.

Kumar, K. (1986) 'Public Service Broadcasting and the Public Interest', in MacCabe, C. and Stewart, O. (eds) *The BBC and Public Service Broadcasting*. Manchester: Manchester University Press.

Lamb, L. (1989) *Sunrise: The Remarkable Rise and Rise of the Best-selling Soaraway Sun*. London: Macmillan.

Landy, M. (1991) *British Genres: Cinema and Society 1930–60*. Princeton, NJ: Princeton University Press.

Lant, A. (1991) *Blackout: Reinventing Women for Wartime British Cinema*. Princeton, NJ: Princeton University Press.

Laqueur, T. (1976) *Religion and Respectability: Sunday Schools and Working Class Structure 1870–1950*. New Haven, CT: Yale University Press.

Larson, C. (1941) 'The British Ministry of Information', *Public Opinion Quarterly*, Fall: 412–31.

Leapman, M. (1986) *The Last Days of the Beeb*. London: Allen & Unwin.

Lee, A. (1976) *The Origins of the Popular Press, 1855–1914*. London: Croom Helm.

Lee, A. (1978) 'The Structure, Ownership and Control of the Press 1855–1914', in Boyce, D.G., Curran, J. and Wingate, P. (eds) *Newspaper History: from the 17th Century to the Present Day*. London: Constable.

Leigh, D. (1980) *The Frontiers of Secrecy*. London: Junction Books.

Lennon, P. (1986) 'A Legendary Director-General', *The Listener*, 30 October.

L'Etang, J. (2004) *Public Relations in Britain: A History of Professional Practice in the Twentieth Century*. New Jersey: Lawrence Erlbaum Associates.

Lewis, J. (1970) *The New Left Book Club: A Historical Record*. London: Gollancz.

Lewis, J., Williams, A. and Franklin, B. (2008) 'A Compromised Fourth Estate: UK News Journalism, Public Relations and News Sources', *Journalism Studies*, 9(1): 1–20.

Lewis, P. (1989) *The Fifties: Portrait of a Period*. London: The Herbert Press.

Lewis, P. and Booth, J. (1989) *The Invisible Medium: Public, Commercial and Community Radio*. London: Macmillan.

Lloyd, J. (2004) *What the Media are Doing to Our Politics*. London: Constable.

Low, R. (1949) *The History of British Film 1906–14*. London: Allen & Unwin.

Lucas, R. (1981) *The Voice of a Nation? A Concise Account of BBC Wales 1923–73*. Llandysul: Gomer Press.

Lunn, K. (1996) 'Reconsidering "Britishness": The Construction and Significance of National Identity in Twentieth-Century Britain', in Jenkins, B. and Sofos, S. (eds) *Nation and Identity in Contemporary Europe*. London: Routledge.

MacCabe, C. and Stewart, O. (1986) *The BBC and Public Service Broadcasting*. Manchester: Manchester University Press.

Mackay, H. (1995) 'Patterns of Ownership of IT Devices in the Home', in Heap, N., Thomas, R., Einon, G., Mason, R. and MacKay, H. (eds) *Information Technology and Society: A Reader*. London: Sage.

Mackenzie, J. (1984) *Propaganda and Empire: The Manipulation of British Public Opinion 1880–1960*. Manchester: Manchester University Press.

Macnab, G. (1993) *J. Arthur Rank and the British Film Industry*. London: Routledge.

Macnab, G. (2008) 'The Big Exodus: Is the British Film Industry in Crisis?', *Guardian*, 5 June.

Madge, T. (1989) *Beyond the BBC*. London: Macmillan.

Manvell, R. (1966) *This Age of Communication*. London: Blackie.

Margach, J. (1978) *The Abuse of Power: The War between Downing Street and the Media from Lloyd George to Callaghan*. London: W.H. Allen.

Marr, A. (2004) *My Trade: A Short History of British Journalism*. London: Macmillan.

Marsh, K. (2004) 'Power, but Scant Responsibility', *British Journalism Review*, 15(4).

Marwick, A. (1982) 'Press, Pictures and Sound: The Second World War and the British Experience', *Daedalus*, Fall: 138.

Marwick, A. (1990) *Class: Image and Reality*. London: Macmillan.

McDonald, P. (1999) 'The Music Industry', in Stokes, J. and Reading, A. (eds) *The Media in Britain: Current Debates and Developments*. London: Palgrave

McIntyre, I. (1994) *The Expense of Glory: A Life of John Reith*. London: HarperCollins.

McKernan, L. (1992) *Topical Budget*. London: British Film Institute.

McLaine, I. (1979) *The Ministry of Morale*. London: Allen and Unwin.

McLeod, M. (2007) 'Wikipedia Saboteurs Are Traced and Unmasked', *Scotland on Sunday*, 26 August.

McLuhan, M. (1962) *The Gutenberg Galaxy*. London: Routledge and Kegan Paul.

McLuhan, M. (1987) *Understanding Media: The Extensions of Man*. London: Ark Paperbacks (1st edition, 1964).

McNair, B. (1994) *News and Journalism in the U.K.* London: Routledge.

McNair, B. (2004) 'PR Must Die: Spin, Anti-spin and Political Public Relations in the UK, 1997–2004', *Journalism Studies*, 5(3): 325–38.

McNair, B. (2007) *Cultural Chaos: Journalism, News and Power in a Globalised World*. London: Routledge.

Medhurst, A. (1984) '1950s War Films', in Hurd, G. (ed.) *National Fictions: World War Two and British Film and Television*. London: British Film Institute.

Medhurst, A. (1986) 'Music Hall and British Cinema', in Barr, C. (ed.) *All Our Yesterdays: 90 Years of British Cinema*. London: British Film Institute.

Medhurst, J. (2005) 'Mammon's Television? ITV in Wales, 1959–63', in Johnson, C. and Turnock, R. (eds) *ITV Cultures: Independent Television over Fifty Years*. Milton Keynes: Open University Press.

Michie, D. (1998) *The Invisible Persuaders*. London: Bantam.

Middlemas, K. (1979) *Politics in Industrial Society: The Experience of the British System since 1911*. London: Andre Deutsch.

Miller, D. and Dinan, W. (2000) 'The Rise of the PR Industry in Britain, 1979–98', *European Journal of Communication*, 15(1): 5–35.

Miller, D. and Dinan, W. (2007) *Thinker, Faker, Spinner, Spy: Corporate PR and the Assault on Democracy*. London: Pluto Press.

Miller, D. and Dinan, W. (2008) *A Century of Spin: How Public Relations Became the Cutting Edge of Corporate Power.* London: Pluto Press.

Moore, M. (2006) *The Origins of Modern Spin: Democratic Government and the Media in Britain, 1945–51*. London: Palgrave.

Moores, S. (1988) 'Box on the Dresser: Memories of Early Radio and Everyday Life', *Media, Culture and Society*, 10(1): 23–40.

Moran, A. (ed.) (1996) *Film Policy: International, National and Regional Perspectives*. London: Routledge.

Mountjoy, P. (1977) 'The Working-class Press and Working-class Conservatism', in Boyce, D.G., Curran, J. and Wingate, P. (eds) *British Newspaper History*. London: Constable.

Murdock, G. (1992a) 'Citizens, Consumers and Public Culture', in Skovmand, M. and Schroder, K. (eds) *Media Cultures: Re appraising Transnational Media*. London: Routledge.

Murdock, G. (1992b) 'Embedded Persuasions: The Fall and Rise of Integrated Advertising', in Strinati, D. and Wagg, S. (eds) *Come on Down? Popular Media Culture*. London: Routledge.

Murdock, G. (1994) 'Corporate Dynamics and Broadcasting Futures', in Aldridge, M. and Hewitt, N. (eds) *Controlling Broadcasting: Access Policy and Practice in North America and Europe*. Manchester: Manchester University Press.

Murdock, G. (1995) 'Television and Citizenship: In Defence of Public Service Broadcasting', in Tomlinson, A. (ed.) *Consumption, Identity and Style*. London: Comedia.

Murdock, G. and Golding, P. (1977) 'The Structure, Ownership and Control of the Press, 1914–76', in Boyce, D. G., Curran, J. and Wingate, P. (eds) *British Newspaper History*. London: Constable.

Murphy, R. (1983) 'Rank's Attempt on the American Market 1944–9', in Curran, J. and Porter, V. (eds) *British Cinema History*. New York: Barnes & Noble.

Murphy, R. (1986) 'Under the Shadow of Hollywood', in Barr, C. (ed.) *All Our Yesterdays: 90 Years of British Cinema*. London: British Film Institute.

Murphy, R. (1989) *Realism and Tinsel: Cinema and Society in Britain 1939–49*. London: Routledge.

Murphy, R. (1992) *British Sixties Cinema*. London: British Film Institute.

Naughton, J. (2006) 'Consumers Show Gatekeepers the Door', *Guardian*, 20 March.

Negrine, R. (1994) *Politics and the Mass Media*, 2nd edn. London: Routledge.

Ofcom (2007) *Annexes to New News, Future News: Research and Evidence Base*, 26 June.

Ofcom (Office of Communications) (2008a) *Communications Market Report*. August. London: TSO.

Ofcom (Office of Communications) (2008b) *Social Networking: A Quantitative and Qualitative Research Report into Attitudes, Behaviour and Use*, Research Document, April.

O'Malley, P. (1981) 'Capital Accumulation and Press Freedom 1800–50', *Media, Culture and Society*, 3: 71–83.

O'Malley, T. (1994) *Closedown? The BBC and Government Broadcasting Policy 1979–92*. London: Pluto Press.

O'Malley, T. (2002) 'Media History and Media Studies: Aspects of the Development of the Study of Media History in the UK 1945–2000', *Media History*, 8(2): 155–73.

Orwell, G. (1970) 'The Art of Donald McGill', in Orwell, S. and Angus, I. (eds) *The Collected Essays, Journalism and Letters of George Orwell*, Vol. II. Harmondsworth: Penguin, pp. 183–95.

O'Sullivan, T. (1991) 'Television Memories and Cultures of Viewing 1950–65', in Corner, J. (ed.) *Popular Television in Britain*. London: British Film Institute.

O'Sullivan, T. (1995) 'Listening Through: The Wireless and World War Two', in Kirkham, P. and Thomas, D. (eds) *War Culture: Social Change and Changing Experience in World War Two*. London: Lawrence & Wishart.

Paulu, B. (1961) *British Broadcasting in Transition*. London: Macmillan.

Paulu, B. (1981) *Television and Radio in the United Kingdom*. London: Macmillan.

Pearson, G. (1984) 'Falling Standards: A Short, Sharp History of Moral Decline', in Barker, M. (ed.) *Video Nasties*. London: Pluto Press.

Pegg, M. (1983) *Broadcasting and Society 1918–39*. London: Croom Helm.

Perry, G. (1985) *The Great British Picture Show*. 2nd edn. London: Michael Joseph.

Petley, J. (1986) 'Cinema and State', in Barr, C. (ed.) *All Our Yesterdays: 90 Years of British Cinema*. London: British Film Institute.

Petley, J. (1999) 'The Regulation of Media Content', in Stokes, J and Reading, A. (eds), *The Media in Britain: Current Debates and Developments*. London: Palgrave.

Petrie, D. (1992) *New Questions of British Cinema*. London: British Film Institute.

Phillis, B. (2004) *An Independent Review of Government Communications*. London: Cabinet Office.

Pilger, J. (1993) 'True Mirror to Events: The Values of Current Affairs Must Be Upheld', *New Statesman and Society*, 15 January.

Pirie, D. (1973) *A Heritage of Horror: The English Gothic Cinema 1946–72*. London: Gordon Fraser.

Porter, V. (1983) 'Creativity at Ealing Studies and Hammer Films', in Curran, J. and Porter, V. (eds) *British Cinema History*. New York: Barnes & Noble.

Pronay, N. (1987) 'Rearmament and the British Public: Policy and Propaganda', in Curran, J., Smith, A. and Wingate, P. (eds) *Impacts and Influences*. London: Methuen.

Pronay, N. and Spring, D. (1982) *Propaganda, Politics and Film 1918–45*. London: Macmillan.

Pursehouse, M. (1991) 'Looking at 'the *Sun*': Into the Nineties with a Tabloid and its Readers', in Biressi, A. and Nunn, H. (2007) *The Tabloid Culture Reader*. Milton Keynes: Open University Press.

Quart, L. (1993) 'The Religion of the Market: Thatcherite Politics and the British Film of the 1980s', in Friedman, L. (ed.) *British Cinema and Thatcherism*. London: UCL Press.

Ramsden, J. (1982) 'Baldwin and Film', in Pronay, N. and Spring, D. (eds) *Propaganda, Politics and Film 1918–45*. London: Macmillan.

Redfern, N. (2005) 'Defining British Cinema: Transnational and Territorial Film Policy in the United Kingdom', *Journal of British Cinema and Television*, 4: 150–64.

Richards, J. (1983) 'The Cinema and Cinema-going in Birmingham in the 1930s', in Walvin, J. (ed.) *Leisure in Britain 1780–1939*. Manchester: Manchester University Press.

Richards, J. (1984) *The Age of the Dream Palace: Cinema and Society 1930–39*. London: Routledge.

Richards, J. and Aldgate, A. (1983) *The Best of British: British Cinema and Society 1930–70*. Oxford: Blackwell.

Robertson, J. (1985) *The British Board of Film Censors: Film Censorship in Britain 1896–1950*. London: Croom Helm.

Robertson, J. (1989) *The Hidden Cinema: British Film Censorship in Action 1913–75*. London: Routledge.

Robins, K. and Cornford, J. (1993) 'Not the London Broadcasting Corporation: The BBC and the New Regionalism', in Harvey, S. and Robins, K. (eds) *The Regions, the Nations and the BBC*. London: British Film Institute.

Robins, K. and Cornford, J. (1994) 'Local and Regional Broadcasting in the New Media Order', in Amin, A. and Thrift, N. (eds) *Globalisation, Institutions and Regional Development in Europe*. Oxford: Oxford University Press.

Root, J. (1986) *Open the Box*. London: Comedia.

Royal Commission on the Press (1961/2) *Report*. London: HMSO.

Royal Commission on the Press (1977) *Report*. London: HMSO.

Ryan, T. (1983) '"The New Road to Progress": The Use and Production of Films by the Labour Movement 1929–39', in Curran, J. and Porter, V. (eds) *British Cinema History*. New York: Barnes & Noble.

Sampson, A. (1996) 'The Crisis at the Heart of Our Media', *British Journalism Review*, 7(3): 45–53.

Sarikakis, K. (2004) *British Media in a Global Era*. London: Hodder.

Sayles, R. (1986) 'An Introduction to Broadcasting History', in Punter, D. (ed.) *An Introduction to Contemporary Cultural Studies*. London: Longman.

Scammell, M. (1995) *Designer Politics: How Elections are Won*. London: Macmillan.

Scannell, P. (1979) 'The Social Eye of Television 1946–55', *Media Culture and Society*, 1: 97–106.

Scannell, P. (1989) 'Public Service Broadcasting and Modern Public Life', *Media, Culture and Society*, 11(2): 136–55.

Scannell, P. (1990) 'Public Service Broadcasting: The History of a Concept', in Goodwin, A. and Whannel, G. (eds) *Understanding Television*. London: Routledge.

Scannell, P. and Cardiff, D. (1977) 'The Social Foundations of British Broadcasting', Supplementary Material, Units 1–6. Open University Mass Communications and Society Course. Milton Keynes: Open University Press.

Scannell, P. and Cardiff, D. (1991) *A Social History of British Broadcasting 1921–39*, London: Blackwell.

Schlesinger, P. (2006) 'Is There a Crisis in British Journalism?', *Media, Culture and Society*, 28(2): 299–307.

Sendall, B. (1982) *Independent Television in Britain*, Vol. 1, *Origin and Foundation 1946–28*. London: Macmillan.

Sendall, B. (1983) *Independent Television in Britain*, Vol. 2, *Expansion and Change 1958–68*. London: Macmillan.

Seymour-Ure, C. (1996) *The British Press and Broadcasting since 1945*, 2nd edn. London: Blackwell.

Short, K.R.M. (1983) *Feature Films as History*. London: Croom Helm.

Siebert, F. (1965) *Freedom of the Press in England 1476–1976: The Rise and Decline of Government Control*. Urbana, IL: University of Illinois Press.

Sisson, K. (1975) *Industrial Relations in Fleet Street*. London: Hutchinson.

Smith, A. (1977) 'The Long Road to Objectivity and Back Again: The Kinds of Truth We Get in Journalism', in Boyce, D.G., Curran, J. and Wingate, P. (eds) *British Newspaper History*. London: Constable.

Smith, A.C.H. (1975) *Paper Voices: The Popular Press and Social Change 1935–65*. London: Chatto and Windus.

Smith, D. and O'Keeffe, A. (2006) 'TV – So How Will You Watch It?', *The Observer*, 12 March.

Smith, M. (1994) *Paper Lions: The Scottish Press and National Identity*. Edinburgh: Polygon.

Snoddy, R. (1993) *The Good, the Bad and the Unacceptable: The Hard News about the British Press*. London: Faber & Faber.

Snoddy, R. (1996) *Greenfinger: The Rise of Michael Green and Carlton Communications*. London: Faber & Faber.

Sorlin, Pierre (1994) *The Mass Media*. London: Routledge.

Sparks, C. (1991a) 'The Popular Press and Political Democracy', in Scannell, P., Schlesinger, P. and Sparks, C. (eds) *Culture and Power*. London: Sage.

Sparks, C. (1991b) 'Goodbye, Hildy Johnson: The Vanishing "Serious" Press', in Dahlgren, P. and Sparks, C. (eds) *Communication and Citizenship: Journalism and the Public Sphere*. London: Routledge.

Sparks, C. and Tulloch, J. (1999) *Tabloid Tales: Global Debates over Media Standards*. Lanham, MD: Rowman & Littlefield.

Sparrow, A. (2003) *Obscure Scribblers: A History of Parliamentary Journalism*. London: Politico's.

Spender, S. (1978) *The Thirties and After: Poetry, Politics and People 1933–75*. London: Collins.

Sreberny-Mohammadi, A. (1995) 'Forms of Media as Ways of Knowing', in Downing, J. *et al.* (eds) *Questioning the Media*, 2nd edn. London: Sage.

Stead, P. (1988) 'Wales and film', in Herbert, T. and Elwyn Jones, G., *Wales between the Wars*. Cardiff: University of Wales Press.

Steed, W (1938) *The Press*. London: Penguin.

Stephenson, H. and Bromley, M. (1999) *Sex, Lies and Democracy: The Press and the Public*. London: Longman.

Stevenson, J. and Cook, C. (1977) *The Slump*. London: Quartet Books.

Stokes, J. and Reading, A. (1999) *The Media in Britain: Current Debates and Developments*. London: Palgrave.

Strinati, D. (1992) 'The Taste of America: Americanization and Popular Culture in Britain', in Strinatı, D. and Wragg, S. (eds) *Come on Down? Popular Media Culture*. London: Routledge.

Swann, P. (1983) 'John Grierson and the G.P.O. Film Unit 1933–39', *Historical Journal of Film, Radio and Television*, 3(1): 19–34.

Swingewood, A. (1977) *The Myth of Mass Culture*. London: Macmillan.

Symons, J. (1987) *The General Strike*, 2nd edn. London: Cresset.

Taylor, A.J.P. (1972) *Beaverbrook*. Harmondsworth: Penguin.

Taylor, A.J.P. (1975) *English History 1914–45*. Harmondsworth: Penguin.

Taylor, P. (ed.) (1988) *Britain and the Cinema in the Second World War*. London: Macmillan.

Taylor, P. (1995) *Munitions of the Mind*. Manchester: Manchester University Press.

Taylor, P. (1999) *British Propaganda in the Twentieth Century: Selling Democracy*. Edinburgh: Edinburgh University Press.

Temple, M. (2008) *The British Press*. Maidenhead: McGraw-Hill.

Thompson, D. (1984) *The Chartists*. London: Morris Temple Smith.

Thompson, E.P. (1968) *The Making of the English Working Class*. London: Pelican.

Toynbee, P. (2007) 'We Need a Rebellion Against a Press That's Damaging Our National Psyche', *Guardian*, 15 June.

Tracey, M. (1977) *The Production of Political Television*. London: Routledge and Kegan Paul.

Tracey, M. (1982) 'Censored: the War Game Story', in Aubrey, C. (ed.) *Nukespeak: The Media and the Bomb*. London: Comedia.

Tracey, M. (1983) *A Variety of Lives*. London: Bodley Head.

Tracey, M. and Morrison, D. (1979) *Whitehouse*. London: Macmillan.

Tulloch, J. (1993) 'Policing the Public Sphere – the British Machinery of News Management', *Media, Culture and Society*, 15: 371–84.

Tunstall, J. (1977) '"Editorial Sovereignty" in the British Press: Its Past and Present', in Royal Commission on the Press, *Studies on the Press*. London: HMSO.

Tunstall, J. (1983) *The Media in Britain*. London: Constable.

Tunstall, J. (1996) *Newspaper Power: The New National Press in Britain*. Oxford: Clarendon Press.

Tunstall, J. (2007) *The Media Were American*. Oxford: Oxford University Press.

Vincent, D. (1989) *Literacy and Popular Culture 1790–1840*. Cambridge: Cambridge University Press.

Walvin, J. (1978) *Leisure and Society 1780–1950*. London: Longman.

Ward, K. (1989) *Mass Communications and the Modern World*. London: Macmillan.

Weiner, J. (ed.) (1988) *Papers for the Millions: The New Journalism in Britain 1850s to 1914*. Westport, CT: Westview Press.

Weymouth, A. (1996) 'The Media in Britain', in Weymouth, A. and Lamizet, B. (eds) *Markets and Myths: Forces for Change in European Media*. London: Longman.

Whannel, G. (1992) 'The Price Is Right but the Moments Are Sticky', in Strinati, D. and Wagg, S. (eds) *Come on Down? Popular Media Culture*. London: Routledge.

Whitaker, B. (1981) *News Ltd: Why You Can't Read All About It*. London: Comedia.

White, C. (1970) *Women's Magazines, 1693–1968*, London: Michael Joseph.

Whitehead, J. (2008) 'Can TV Hold its Own?', *Guardian*, 3 March.

Williams, A. and Franklin, B. (2007) *Turning the Tanker Around: Implementing Trinity-Mirror's Online Strategy*. Cardiff: Cardiff University.

Williams, C. (1996a) 'The Social Art of Cinema: A Moment in the History of British Film and Television Culture', in Williams, C. (ed.) *Cinema: The Beginnings and the Future*. London: University of Westminster Press.

Williams, C. (ed.) (1996b) *Cinema: The Beginnings and the Future*. London: University of Westminster Press.

Williams, F. (1959) *Dangerous Estate: The Anatomy of New Papers*. London: Arrow Books.

Williams, F. (1969) *The Right to Know*. London: Longman.

Williams, G. (1993) 'Murdochvision', *Free Press Journal of the Campaign for Press and Broadcasting Freedom*, September/October.

Williams, G. (1996) *Britain's Media: How They Are Related*, 2nd edn. London: Campaign for Press and Broadcasting Freedom.

Williams, G. (2006) 'Profits before Product? Ownership and Economics of the Local Press', in Franklin, B. (ed.) *Local Journalism and Local Media: Making the Local News*. London: Routledge.

Williams, K. (1977) *The English Newspaper: An Illustrated History to 1900*. London: Springwood Books.

Williams, K. (1996) *British Writers and the Media 1930–45*. London: Macmillan.

Williams, R. (1980) *The Long Revolution*, 2nd edn. Harmondsworth: Pelican.

Wilson, H.H. (1961) *Pressure Group*. London: Secker and Warburg.

Wilson, K. (1983) 'The Foreign Office and the "Education" of Public Opinion during the First World War', *The Historical Journal*, 26(2): 403–11.

Windelsham, Lord (1980) *Broadcasting in a Free Society*. London: Basil Blackwell.

Winship, J. (1987) *Inside Women's Magazines*. London: Pandora.

Winston, B. (1995) 'How Media Are Born', in Downing, J. *et al.* (eds) *Questioning the Media*, 2nd edn. London: Sage.

Wintour, P. (2007) 'Blair: Media Is Feral Beast Obsessed with Impact', *Guardian*, 13 June.

Wintour, P. and Goodhart, D. (1986) *Eddy Shah and the Newspaper Revolution*. London: Coronet Books.

Woffinden, B (1996) 'Fast and Loose: Why Is Scandal-Busting Journalism Losing its Edge in Television and the Press?', *Guardian*, 12 August.

Woolwich, P. (1992) 'Against the Current', *Guardian*, 18 May.

Wring, D. (2005) 'Politics and the Media: the Hutton Inquiry, the Public Relations State, and Crisis at the BBC', *Parliamentary Affairs*, 58(2).

Yass, M. (1983) *This Is Your War: Home Front Propaganda in the Second World War*. London: HMSO.

Index

NOTE: Titles in italics are press titles unless otherwise indicated.

Lightning Source UK Ltd.
Milton Keynes UK
UKOW01f1600240816

281375UK00006B/192/P